VHS

D0190478

BRAT PACK AMERICA

A LOVE LETTER TO '80S TEEN MOVIES

KEVIN SMOKLER

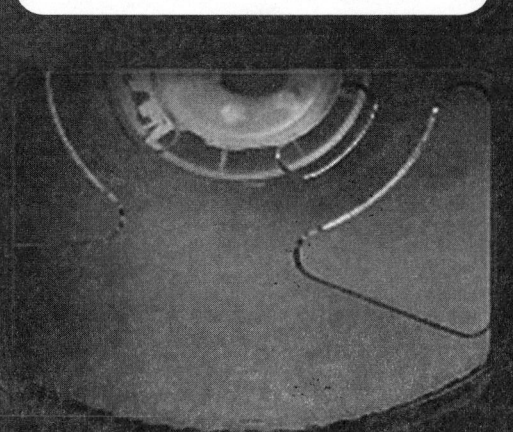

A GENUINE VIREO BOOK
RARE BIRD BOOKS
LOS ANGELES, CALIF.

BRAT
PACK
AMERICA

Kevin Smokler

This is a Genuine Vireo Book

A Vireo Book | Rare Bird Books
453 South Spring Street, Suite 302
Los Angeles, CA 90013
rarebirdbooks.com

FIRST TRADE PAPERBACK ORIGINAL EDITION

Set in Minion
Printed in the United States

Book design by STARLING

10 9 8 7 6 5 4 3 2 1

Publisher's Cataloging-in-Publication data

Names: Smokler, Kevin, author.
Title: Brat Pack America : a love letter to '80s teen movies / Kevin Smokler.
Description: Includes bibliographical references. | First Trade Paperback
Original Edition | A Vireo Book | New York, NY; Los Angeles, CA: Rare Bird
Books, 2016.
Identifiers: ISBN 978-1-942600-67-1
Subjects: LCSH Teenagers in motion pictures. | Teen films—United States—
History and criticism. | Motion pictures—United States. | Nineteen eighties. |
Popular culture—History—20th century. | Motion pictures and youth. | BISAC
PERFORMING ARTS / Film & Video / History & Criticism
Classification: LCC PN1995.9.Y6 .S66 2016| DDC 791.43/652055—dc23

To teenagers now, who love these movies as we did, but also have Ferris Buellers and Breakfast Clubs of their own.
Room in the DeLorean for all.

CONTENTS

1 • Back in Time with the Power of Love

11 • Chapter 1: Before

43 • Chapter 2: A Shermer, Illinois, of the Mind

71 • *Brat Pack America* talks to...Actor Gedde Watanabe (a.k.a. Long Duk Dong of *Sixteen Candles*)

77 • Chapter 3: Valley Girls, Karate Kids, Repo Men

115 • *Brat Pack America* talks to...Writer/Director Amy Heckerling

121 • Chapter 4: Beat Streets and House Parties

147 • Chapter 5: Back (and Forth) to the Future

175 • Chapter 6: The Sweetest Victory

197 • *Brat Pack America* Talks to...Writer/Director Savage Steve Holland

201 • Chapter 7: "We Can't Rewind, We've Gone Too Far"

227 • *Brat Pack America* Talks to...Director Martha Coolidge

233 • Chapter 8: "Now That You're Dead, What Are You Gonna Do with the Rest of Your Life?"

263 • *Brat Pack America* Talks to...Writer Daniel Waters

269 • Chapter 9: After the Movies Came to Town

307 • Chapter 10: "Where We're Going, We Don't Need Roads"

327 • Selected Bibliography

BACK IN TIME WITH THE POWER OF LOVE

I
T BROKE MY HEART that I couldn't visit Hill Valley. It seemed like such a nice town to grow up in, even if it'd had a run of bad luck since 1955. Still, I was pretty sure that if I stood near the clock tower right as the high school let out, I'd see Marty McFly rolling by on his skateboard. I'd yell, "Hey, McFly," but in a nice way, and thank him for being a weird kid from a weird family with a pretty girlfriend and a band and a mad scientist for a best friend. If I could visit Hill Valley, California, which I guessed was somewhere around the bend in the state's elbow, I could tell Marty McFly, "When I'm seventeen, I want to be just like you."

I was only twelve in the summer of 1985 when Marty, via a DeLorean filled with plutonium, traveled back in time. By December, I'd seen *Back to the Future* fourteen times and learned that Hill Valley, seemingly the most realistic part of a movie overflowing with imagination, was just as made up as the flux capacitor. My family had taken a trip to Southern California to escape the Michigan winter, and, on a Universal Studios tour, we stopped at the Hill Valley clock tower wedged in between the shark from *Jaws* and a black glass office building with employees leaving for lunch.

"Where's the real Hill Valley?" I asked our tour guide. I'd seen enough entertainment news segments on TV to know that movies were made in giant empty rooms with smooth cement floors called sound stages, or the outdoor version of that called a studio lot. You wheel in flat pieces of wood resembling gazebos or doctors' offices and you've got yourself something called a set. Since there's no way they could fit an entire town inside one sound stage or on one studio lot, the *Back to the Future* set pieces we were looking at now must be based on the *real* Hill Valley. And this guy leading our tour would know where it was.

"They made the movie right here, all of it. This is Hill Valley," our tour guide gushed.

I wanted to push him off the tram. Hill Valley wasn't anything but planks and paint and movie make-believe. It wasn't even based on a real place, because I asked that, too, and our tour guide smiled at me the way a bully does before stealing your Halloween candy.

Apparently, twelve-year-old me couldn't "visit" Hill Valley because I just had.

Still thinking that growing up sucked, I was dropped off by my parents the next day in Pasadena to visit a friend from summer camp. "Wanna see Doc Brown's house?" he asked me, right after I arrived. While I tried to explain to him that Doc Brown's house was probably a pile of lumber being giggled at by a stupid tour guide named Trent in khaki shorts this very minute, my friend dug two bicycles out of his garage. Soon he had us racing north through his neighborhood, around a golf course and under an overpass to 4 Westmoreland Place in the center of town. There, near the junction of the 134 and 210 freeways, stood the Gamble House, a historic landmark designed in 1908 and open to the public.

It's also the exact spot where Doctor Emmett Brown marches furiously downhill, arms filled with blueprints, and bellows, "So tell me, future boy, who's president in 1985?" And Marty McFly answers, "Ronald Reagan," which Doc thinks as crazy as the idea of Jerry Lewis being Vice President.

We acted out the whole scene right there. I even got to be Marty. That winter afternoon on the gentle slope of the Gamble House lawn marked the first time I'd ever stood in the precise spot where both a favorite movie scene happened and, by extension, where the actors, director, and crew had brought it to life. If I were a Civil War buff, this would have been visiting Antietam, Gettysburg, and Appomattox Court House, all on one historic patch of grass in Central Pasadena.

Except when visiting a Civil War battlefield, you stand where important events happened long before you were born. Being in that spot, where the narrative of history changed, collapses time, shrinking in our minds the distance between then and now. On the other hand, when we return to our elementary school playground or the site of our first kiss, we're dropping in on our own history years later. Visiting those same places in the present not only collapses time, but also memory.

A pilgrimage to where a beloved movie moment was filmed does all of that and more. It not only races us back to the first time we saw that movie, but enables us to enter the movie itself. A fan can play Marty McFly on a hill in Pasadena, or insult a pretend llama named Tina at Napoleon Dynamite's house in Preston, Idaho, or fake an orgasm at Katz's Deli on the Lower East Side of Manhattan like Meg Ryan in *When Harry Met Sally*. There's actually a sign in Katz's Delicatessen above the very table where that faked orgasm happened.

These hills, houses, and delis are not built movie sets like the Hill Valley clock tower, but places where ordinary people live, work, eat, and pass through every day. They are also the exact spots where moments of our shared cinematic consciousness became real. When we visit these movie places, it collapses not just time and memory, but the distance between reality and imagination, between familiarity and the dreams of directors, screenwriters, actors, and crew. If we care enough about the movie to visit those places, it's likely the dreams of that movie have become ours, too.

This is a book about movie places. Specifically, a movie like *Back to the Future* and a place like Hill Valley—the teen movies of the 1980s and the places, real and imagined, where they happened.

A lot of time has passed and a lot of movies made since Marty McFly and the Breakfast Club, Ferris Bueller and the Heathers came to theaters and changed the way pop culture portrayed teenagers.

More than a few books have been written both singing their praises and asking with irritation why, thirty years later, anyone still cares, other than the nostalgic fans who were teenagers back then.

Fair enough. Here in 2016, it can seem like every other week another beloved eighties movie is getting remade for its twenty-fifth, thirtieth, or thirty-fifth anniversary. A lot of that is media and movie studios thinking there are easy profits in the memories of the middle-aged—everyone who saw *Ghostbusters* or *Top Gun* or *Pretty in Pink* as a teenager and are now probably the parents of teenagers themselves. But I can still imagine that a bunch of attention and hype directed at a movie from the Reagan Era would seem pretty boring to anyone who a) doesn't love or remember these movies, b) thinks nostalgia is for the birds, or c) prefers to focus on the pop culture of now. Let's not forget, many favorite eighties teen movies have not aged well both in superficial detail (skinny ties, shoulder pads) and deeply ugly tendencies (casual racism and homophobia played off as jokes).

But eighties teen movies endure not just because their original fans miss them, and not even because *Back to the Future*, *The Goonies*, and *Stand by Me* remain great movies to this day. Between 1978 and 1989, right after *Star Wars* and *Animal House* and right up to *Heathers*, American film, for the first time in its century of existence, consistently portrayed teenagers as human beings. Adolescence, in the hands of filmmakers like John Hughes, Amy Heckerling, Martha Coolidge, and Savage Steve Holland, becomes a time in life with the same trials—friendship, love, independence, a desire to fit in—as childhood or adulthood, not a hormonal psychodrama to be suffered through then picked over by adults. The pop culture ecosystem we live in now—*The Hunger Games* and *Divergent* movie franchises, the mystery boyfriend songs of Taylor Swift, the novels of John Green, and the media empire of Tavi Gevinson—would not exist without the seismic shift in the way we view teenagers brought about by the teen movies of the Reagan years.

Seven teen movies from the 1980s, including *Fast Times at Ridgemont High*, *Ferris Bueller's Day Off*, and *Back to the Future*, are in the Library of Congress's National Film Registry alongside *Gone with the Wind*, *It's a Wonderful Life*, and *Lawrence of Arabia*. The National Film Registry's mission is to "preserve works of enduring importance to American culture." No other decade in the history of American cinema has more than two teen movies represented.

The eighties teen movie—side ponytails, Jordache Jeans, oblivious homophobia and all—didn't invent the teen movie genre and wasn't always the best example of it, but it did show what the genre, at its best, could be. The group of films represented by *Fast Times at Ridgemont High* and *Some Kind of Wonderful*, by *Weird Science* and *Real Genius* weren't Bach, but Mozart; not pioneering like Little Richard, but barrier-shattering like The Beatles.

But what about eighties teen movie places? Why do John Hughes's films take place in a barely mentioned, fictional Chicago suburb named Shermer, and why is Shermer inseparable from the Hughes canon? Is it a coincidence that so many eighties teen movies set in Los Angeles—*Valley Girl*, *The Karate Kid*, *Repo Man*, *Suburbia*—are also about class and money and feature poor kids trying to climb invisible, slippery walls of wealth and privilege?

Why do a disproportionate number of eighties teen sports movies take place in a dying industrial town the main character tries to play their way out of? What do we make of how proud the earliest hip-hop movies from this period—*Wild Style*, *Beat Street*—are of their connection to New York City? Why do so many eighties teen movies take place in small towns in the 1950s? And, in the real world, why does the population of Astoria, Oregon, double every five years in celebration of "*Goonies* Weekend," even though Astoria is only onscreen for about fifteen minutes of *The Goonies*?

The eighties teen movie showed teenagers as they had never been shown onscreen before. Why did the places where these movies happened, the America of the 1980s, seem so important, too? Why did the background of eighties teen movies seem to affect so much of the foreground?

The eighties teen movie arrived at a particular moment in American film history. The decade before had been dominated by the first generation of directors to attend university film schools, which were almost entirely located in New York and Southern California. These filmmakers made movies both about young people (*American Graffiti, Saturday Night Fever, Mean Streets*) and not (*The Godfather, All the President's Men, The French Connection*), which seem to reflect that geographic bias and happen in the Northeast, California, and pretty much nowhere else.

On the other side of the decade, by the early 1990s, Hollywood had given up on the teen movie, only to have their interest rekindled by the box-office success of *Clueless* in the summer of 1995. Great teen nineties movies like *Rushmore, Election,* and *Ten Things I Hate About You* followed, and while each of those is a more interesting movie for taking place in Houston, Omaha, and Seattle, respectively, it'd be hard to argue those backgrounds are essential to the drama that happens in front of them.

Here in the twenty-first century, teen movies also seem to regard location and setting as a benefit, but not an essential one. *Paper Towns* (2015), *The Fault in Our Stars* (2014), and *The Perks of Being a Wallflower* (2012) are all better films thanks their skillful use of neighborhoods in Orlando, Indianapolis, and Pittsburgh, but wouldn't be fundamentally different without them. Now, can you imagine *Breaking Away* without Bloomington, Indiana; *Ferris Bueller's Day Off* without downtown Chicago; or *The Lost Boys* without the Santa Cruz Beach Boardwalk?

The teen movies of today and the teenagers watching them have never known life without the Internet and smartphones, both of which complicate the very idea of location and place. *Clueless* came along at the dawn of both the Internet and mobile phones, and has a great, early joke where the main character Cher (Alicia Silverstone) and her best friend Dionne (Stacey Dash) have a cell phone conversation while standing about four feet away from each other—hilarious in 1995, and prescient, too. By that time, the very idea of teenagers seeing place and geography as a fixed part of their lives, and therefore essential to a movie attempting to portray adolescence truthfully, had already begun to fade.

Today, any teenager with a smartphone can summon images, sounds, and conversations from all over the world. The 1980s were the last decade before this change, and therefore the last decade when teenagers used physical locations as signifiers of who they were. As a result, where you worked, hung out, fell in love, and got your heart broken had a much stronger effect on how you saw yourself as a teenager of the eighties and how you thought others saw you. Where teenagers interacted with and consumed pop culture, and how pop culture reflected their experience back to them, ended up being just as linked to place and location.

This happened due to several trends that crash-landed in the 1980s seemingly all at once.

- Summer Blockbusters: Record-shattering movies from the decade before like *Jaws* and *Star Wars*, both of which were seen repeatedly in theaters by young people, had dragged the median age of moviegoers downward. One study estimated that by the early 1980s, 86 percent of movie tickets were bought by someone under the age of thirty, making movie theaters and movie-going the domain of the young and reorienting how pop culture was marketed and sold to the behavioral patterns of teenagers.

- Jobs: The 1980s had the highest participation of teenagers in the American workforce since the Department of Labor began tracking in 1948. The result: teenagers with disposable income shopping at record stores, arcades, movie theaters, and clothing stores, largely staffed by other teenagers, who then spent that money at the same kinds of places where they worked.

- Suburbanization: In retrospect, the 1980s were the low point for the American city—a feudal shell of its old self, occupied by the very poor and the very rich. Which meant that an average teenage life in the 1980s probably equaled (and was shown onscreen as) a suburban home, getting around by car, and shopping in malls. Cities were viewed as sexy but dangerous field trips where a high schooler could go for adventure and fun, but sprint back to the suburbs before dark.

- The Mall: Around since the 1950s, the shopping mall peaked in cultural relevancy in the 1980s. Which meant shopping in America at this time generally looked like a giant enclosed building filled with stores, movie theaters, and food courts geared toward, staffed, and patronized by teenagers.

- MTV: In 1980, the average age of an artist with a number-one song on Billboard's pop charts was thirty-four, a time in music *AV Club* referred to as the age of "Divorce Rock." Arriving the following summer in August of 1981, MTV favored telegenic younger musicians and their fans. That—in tandem with the boom in Top 40 radio, the corporate consolidation of record store chains, and, later, the coming of the CD—meant the eighties equaled a reawakening of pop music as a teenage commodity, and all the record-store shopping, concert-ticket buying, and style imitating that went with it.

- Personal Technology: Cable television, the VCR, video games, and the personal computer all came into the lives of teenagers at this time. This meant a blurring of boundaries between home and school, between work and fun, and between consuming pop culture elsewhere and in the privacy of one's basement or bedroom.

Take these factors in pairs or all together, and we get a picture of teenage life in 1980s America anchored by places. Reflecting this, teen movies from this moment in history give a special role to their settings and locations, sometimes as crucial to their success as a great performance, a killer sound, or unforgettable lines of dialogue.

Combined, these places show, via the drama and wish fulfillment of the movies, what it meant to be young in America three decades ago. I've called these places, and this love letter to them, Brat Pack America.

The term "Brat Pack" came from a 1985 *New York Magazine* article with the subhead: "The young movie stars you can't quite keep straight... They're who kids want to see and what kids want to be." This was a flawed premise from the start: only some of the actors writer David Blum lumped into the "Pack" were friends or even knew each other. A few key members had made their reputations in movies that were about adults or families, not young people. Others who did work together, like Judd Nelson and Molly Ringwald, were nearly ten years apart in age, which made it a stretch to call them members of the same generation.

I accept that the term Brat Pack is full of holes. I've used it because it gets right at the time and films we'll be looking at. The "America" in Brat Pack America gives us some geographic parameters.

A few more: I've defined a teen movie as one where the main character is between the ages of thirteen and nineteen. This meant ruling out some great movies where the characters are too young (what I would have given to make room for, say, *Monster Squad* or *The Explorers*) or where the protagonist is an adult in a movie about high school students (say *Stand and Deliver*—letting go of that one hurt). I've set the boundaries of "the 1980s" as 1978–1989 to make room for proto-eighties teen movies like *Animal House* and *Grease*. I've also focused only on movies filmed and set in the United States and had to regretfully leave out some films that simply couldn't find a place in the story I am telling (apologizing to fans of *Red Dawn* right now). When using the word *location*, I mean where a movie scene was filmed in the real world (e.g. the Gamble House in Pasadena). When I say *setting*, I mean the name of that same place in the movie (e.g. Doc Brown's house in Hill Valley).

Movie locations are found and secured by skilled professionals who must balance the artistic visions of the filmmakers and the real cost of a film crew taking over that location. Those costs, between getting the actors and crew onsite, permits from local government, rerouting traffic, making a street look sunny when it is raining or like 1943 when it's not 1943, often win out over exactly what the director or screenwriter had in mind.

This is the simplest explanation why movies claiming to take place in Rome or Tokyo can just as easily look like back lots and soundstages, or why, say, the neighborhoods of "Hill Valley, California" or *Halloween*'s "Haddonfield, Illinois" look suspiciously like rows of houses in South Pasadena. Movies can keep to their budgets with these shortcuts.

Knowing this, movie places still resonate with us movie lovers, despite the often boring and ordinary reasons why important scenes were filmed there. Therefore, I won't be spending much time on what filmmakers intended or meant by the choice of a location. I'll instead assume the movie, now out in the world, belongs to those of us in the audience and we get to have our own feelings about and responses to it.

Thanks to social media, it's now painfully easy to find out where your favorite movie was filmed. There's an entire digital cottage industry of movie fans capturing themselves visiting Forks, Washington, on a self-created *Twilight* tour or placing a prank phone call from the atrium of the Sherway Gardens mall in Toronto, just like Regina George does at the beginning of *Mean Girls*. Air New Zealand named itself "The Official Airline of Middle Earth" to take advantage of tourists keen to visit the hotspots of *The Lord of the Rings* trilogy. "Location Vacations" and town-wide celebrations of a beloved movie filmed there are now established pieces of the travel and tourism industry.

Movie locations can now be big businesses long after the movie has come and gone. Yet the desire to visit them is as basic as my own seventh-grade delusion that Hill Valley was real: to hold your favorite movie even closer to your heart by entering it for only a moment, to let its spell overtake you in the physical world, to make its dreams yours.

The eighties teen movie captured a special time for this kind of dreaming. I invite you into the DeLorean with me, to go back in time for a different kind of visit to some old favorites—a visit across the map of a Brat Pack America.

Thank you for riding along.

CHAPTER 1: BEFORE

Where the '80s Teen Movie Came From

Movies Discussed: *Star Wars, Jaws, American Graffiti, Grease, Breaking Away, My Bodyguard, Animal House, Fame, The Warriors*

WHERE DID THE EIGHTIES teen movie and its interest in places come from? How did teenagers onscreen go from being studied or romanticized from the point of view of adults to being real people at the center of their own stories? How did those same teenagers go from being filmed against nondescript or overused backgrounds in New York and California to being characters with their own neighborhoods, schools, workplaces, and hangouts, in locations all over America? And why was the 1980s the moment when this all happened?

Our first stop on this trip across Brat Pack America is to the years right before. The Hollywood (and America) of the 1970s drew the first lines on our map that a half-dozen teen movies from that time would then bring into view. Without these six movies, the table wouldn't have been set for *Sixteen Candles, The Karate Kid*, or *Dirty Dancing* a few years later. Without these six movies, it would hard to see how location and setting were one of the quiet yet big factors that made the teen movies of the 1980s so special.

Let's program the DeLorean for the middle and late years of the 1970s. American moviemaking is in the midst of a seismic change, while America itself seems to be in free fall. Concurrently, teen movies seem at cross-purposes, *about* teenagers yet *for* adults nostalgic for their youth. And then a group of movies about teenage bicyclists, street gangs, bodyguards, and dancers come along and change everything.

The Adolescence of the American Teen Movie

BY THE 1970S, THE teen movie genre was around twenty years old, its earliest examples coming from the middle years of the Eisenhower Administration. Those first teen movies looked at adolescence as a social problem in need of solving, like homelessness or drug addiction. Consequently, settings and locations in these movies were either partly to blame for the new social disease of teenagers (see the unforgiving west Manhattan neighborhoods of 1953's *Blackboard Jungle* and later 1961's *West Side Story*) or the victims of it (the small California towns terrorized by outlaw bikers in 1953's *The Wild One*). The most famous teen movies of this first generation, 1955's *Rebel Without a Cause* (the name came from a book on psychopathology), was shot in Los Angeles because its studio, Warner Brothers, considered a story about teenagers a low-priority, quickie project and wanted to save money filming nearby. *Rebel Without a Cause* isn't an "LA Movie" the way, say, *Chinatown* or *Repo Man* are inseparable from the city where they happen, but *Rebel Without a Cause* did have the accidental and enduring benefit of transforming the city's Griffith Park Observatory from a local attraction into an international emblem of Los Angeles. *Rebel's* famous fight scene involving the observatory's gently twisting staircases, outdoor telescopes, and James Dean pursued by thugs has been commemorated by a white stone monument and bust of the star. It sits on the west side of the building's lawn to this day.

By the late 1960s, the beach teen films (think Gidget, Frankie, and Annette) earlier in the decade had been overtaken by rock and roll and the Vietnam War. The result was movies that felt like news reports from the front lines of the counterculture: *Riot on Sunset Strip* (1967) was an eighty-seven-minute retelling of an actual riot on the Sunset Strip that had happened the year before. *Wild in the Streets* (1968) took a made-up news event (America elects a twenty-four-year-old president) and stretched it into a wacked-out political satire (young president amends Constitution and imprisons anyone over thirty-five). The ripped-from-the-headlines nature of these teen movies meant plot dictated setting. Locations had to serve as backdrop for the actual events that happened in front of them, even as the movies reworked those events as fiction.

But by the 1970s, the twenty-year-old American teen movie was in the middle of a post-adolescent regression. On the one hand, Hollywood had been saved from financial oblivion and cultural irrelevance by a generation of young filmmakers nicknamed the "Movie Brats," who weren't that far past adolescence themselves. On the other hand, these filmmakers were largely interested in making movies either for or about people like them: college graduates living in big cities on the coasts. Likewise, their few movies about teenagers were almost always set in the past and meant to stir the nostalgic hearts and memories of the adults they and their peers had just become.

By the 1970s, the teen movie, barely into its twenties, already longed for its lost youth.

It would take two members of the Movie Brat generation, making two of the biggest blockbusters ever, to smooth out our map and ready it for the dots and lines of Brat Pack America. Those blockbusters wouldn't be called teen movies, even though one of them had a late-teenage protagonist and teenagers saw both in droves. Instead, their creators had deliberately positioned them as rousing entertainment from an earlier age of movie-going, when kids and adults could enjoy the same movies and not glower across the generational divide at one another.

The eighties teen movie arrives, then, through these fractured circumstances: from seventies teen movies really made for adults, and two giant blockbusters made with every moviegoer on the planet in mind, but which ended up largely being watched by teenagers.

Pre–Brat Pack America

BY THE TIME OF those two giant blockbusters, in the second half of the 1970s, America's efforts to shake the hangover of the Vietnam War and Watergate were not going well. The nation's biggest, baddest metropolis, New York City, went bankrupt in 1975 then had a citywide blackout in the summer of 1977, where arson and looting led to nearly 4,000 arrests and $1 billion in damages. So many fires consumed the city during the decade that an HBO documentary about the NYFD simply referred to this time as "the war years."

War in the Middle East caused oil shortages in 1973 and again in 1979, leading to hour-long waits at gas stations. Factories in factory towns, humming nonstop for generations, suddenly went dark, the labor shipped overseas. And Jimmy Carter's presidency (1976–1980) introduced the terms "stagflation" and "malaise" into the public conversation about the nation's economy. Production fell, inflation rose, and it started to look a whole lot like America was an old horse headed for the glue factory. For the first time in the twentieth century, economists predicted the generation of children growing up in the 1970s, would be worse off than their parents.

Things sucked. America had been on a three-decade winning streak since the end of World War II as the world's richest and most powerful country. Now the party was over, and it looked like America would be cleaning beer bottles and vomit off its carpet for who knew how long.

But for popular culture, bad times often lead to great things. The 1970s were also the first years of punk, hip-hop, Philadelphia soul, and disco. In literature, the decade gave us the ascendency of John Updike and Joyce Carol Oates, Toni Morrison and E. L. Doctorow. The visual arts leapt from museum and gallery walls to three-dimensional installations and public streets via the work of Jean-Michel Basquiat and Keith Haring. The founding of Atari in 1972 and Apple in 1977 led to twin revolutions in video games and personal computing. And in movies, the 1970s were a time of the Movie Brats, a generation of filmmakers whose best movies are still considered classics over four decades later.

Pre–Brat Pack America Hollywood

THE ERA OF THE Movie Brats, also called the New Hollywood (roughly 1967 to, at the latest, 1980), happened because, by the middle years of the Vietnam War, Hollywood was in a world of trouble and knew why: the American moviegoer was getting younger, smarter, and no longer cared about its product. The counterculture was in full swing, and movies from Europe and Asia had been unexpected hits in the US, while the studios' normal fare of musicals and historical epics landed like lead balloons. Between 1969 and 1971, American movie attendance would slip, fall, then bottom out at about one-sixth of what it had been in the 1940s. "The once-proud studio system," wrote Peter Biskind in his 1998 book *Easy Riders, Raging Bulls: How the Sex-Drugs-and-Rock 'N' Roll Generation Saved Hollywood*, "already a leaky vessel, was now listing badly."

Out of desperation, studios let the first generation of recent film school graduates (Martin Scorsese, Francis Ford Coppola, George Lucas, and Steven Spielberg) not only direct big projects but also have unparalleled creative control over them. With their heads filled with French, Japanese, and German movies from their university campuses and local repertory movie theaters, these young directors decided to take American film business in a very different direction. Hollywood wanted this new, younger audience. The young directors represented it, and the listing, leaky film studios were running out of ways to bail water.

Beginning in 1967 with *The Graduate* and *Bonnie and Clyde*, the signature movies from the New Hollywood—*Mean Streets, The Godfather, Five Easy Pieces, Chinatown*, and *Harold and Maude*—have complicated heroes, rare happy endings, and a screw-you attitude toward authority. Also, with few exceptions, the movies of this era are overwhelmingly set and filmed in New York and California, echoing either where the filmmakers grew up, went to school, or had their first jobs in the movie business. When their movies did happen somewhere else, they would either say so very loudly (*Nashville* in 1975), have somewhere else be integral to the story (road movies set in multiple places like *Easy Rider* or *Alice Doesn't Live Here Anymore*), or happened in a place that no longer exists, a mythic American past like *Bonnie and Clyde*'s Depression-era South or *The Wild Bunch*'s end-of-the-frontier West.

The American New Wavers saw themselves as widening the definition of American movies and widening the minds of American moviegoers. The best of the movies they made, which hit the grand slam of winning awards, critical acclaim, making money, and enduring through time, are proof positive that they succeeded. But these guys weren't called the Movie Brats just because they were young and suddenly rich and powerful. They also thought the old Hollywood way of trying to make movies "for everybody" was for squares. Make them for yourself and your friends, they figured. Everyone else will catch up.

Where Were You...In '62?

EVEN THOUGH THE MOVIE Brats were largely young men in their mid-to-late twenties, youth as a cinematic subject wasn't very interesting to them. When it did show up in their movies, it tended to present in one of two ways and was usually held at arm's length: the most famous movies from the period with young protagonists—*Easy Rider* (1969), *Bonnie and Clyde*, *The Graduate*, *M*A*S*H* (all 1970), *Badlands* (1973), *Harold & Maude* (1971), and *Saturday Night Fever* (1975)—look at youth as metaphor for either the rebellious power or hopeless confusion of a generation. The other approach was movies set in a "simpler" past that looked at being young though the eyes of adult nostalgia—*Summer of '42* (1971), *Cooley High* (1975), *Next Stop, Greenwich Village* (1978), *Same Time, Next Year* (1978). In both cases, the lives of young people were rarely worthy subjects on their own, but instead had to represent or remind the audience of something else.

The most important teen movie from this time did equal shares of both.

American Graffiti (1973), George Lucas's second film, is the story of a group of high school seniors killing time on the last night of summer. The year is 1962; the location, California's Central Valley. (Lucas's childhood home of Modesto was the inspiration, but filming actually took place in the city of Petaluma, 120 miles to the northwest.) The kids talk about moving away, going to college, leaving friends and childhood behind. Since the movie was released in the immediate aftermath of the Vietnam War and during Watergate, but was about being young a decade before all of that, *American Graffiti* felt not just like a funeral for the characters' adolescence but for the youth of an entire generation—the parents of the children of Brat Pack America who remembered cruising and sock hops and make-out spots called Inspiration Point. The movie's tagline: "Where Were You...In '62?" was nostalgia and metaphor at the same time.

American Graffiti made an astounding $140 million on a budget of $777,000 and gave Lucas the money and clout to make *Star Wars* three years later. It also set off a wave of late-fifties/early-sixties nostalgia in popular culture—the TV show *Happy Days,* which debuted the following year, the movie version of the Broadway musical *Grease* (1978)—that lasted well into the 1980s with movies like *Hairspray*, *Peggy Sue Got Married*, and *Dirty Dancing* (we'll look at those movies in Chapter 5).

Most importantly, *American Graffiti* changed the way Hollywood packaged movies about teenagers. The New Hollywood directors and their audience were now in their mid-to-late twenties, settling into careers and families. Their adolescence had been shaken by war, the Civil Rights Movement, the assassinations of Martin Luther King Jr., Medgar Evers, and two Kennedys. *American Graffiti* unleashed a thirst for memories of a simpler time.

American Graffiti and *Grease*, five years later, are the greatest evidence that the teen movie of the 1970s didn't want to be contemporary, but rather remain nostalgic, viewing adolescence either at symbolic distance or as a memory from adulthood. Teen movies didn't have the self-awareness or regard—not yet, anyway—to see being a teenager as interesting on its own.

The eighties teen movie also picked up a tailwind during this period from an unexpected source: two giant blockbusters, neither of which was about teenagers but got teenagers buying tickets in record numbers. These two blockbusters traded in the cynical reality of their contemporaries for straightforward entertainment. Their settings were as unforgettable as their characters, their special effects, or their now-classic lines of dialogue. But those unforgettable settings were also the background of stories powered by giant, archetypal emotions with a capital "E"—the unique in service of the universal we'd see as fundamental to the movies of Brat Pack America several years later.

The Shark and the Force

THE BEGINNING OF THE end of this golden age of American movies in the 1970s often gets unfairly laid at the feet of Steven Spielberg and George Lucas. Spielberg's third film, *Jaws*, came out in June of 1975, a summer release that made more money than its studio Universal Pictures (or anyone, really) ever thought possible and set the template for the modern summer blockbuster (easy to explain, lots of chills and thrills, massive advertising campaign, and showing every five minutes on every movie screen all at once). George Lucas's third film, *Star Wars* (May 1977), beat *Jaws* for the crown of most successful movie of all time only two summers after the record had been set.

Suddenly there was more cheddar in movies than anyone could have dreamed, and the way to get it seemed to be not mobsters killing each other or the stink of police corruption but bigger and simpler movies that worked first as entertainment for everybody, not a poke in the eye of those too uncool to get it. And though "everybody" meant young and middle-aged and old alike, it was really kids and teenagers who showed up to *Jaws* and *Star Wars*, bought the T-shirts and lunchboxes, then came back to the theater multiple times with their friends.

The American movie audience was changing. By the mid-1960s, the majority of ticket buyers were under thirty. By the mid-1970s, the majority were under twenty.

It seems pretty easy, then, to draw a line from *Star Wars* and *Jaws* to the most glaring flaws of summer movie season now—loud, over-marketed comic books designed to thrill sixth-graders and live just as much in action figures, video games, and Halloween costumes as great moviemaking. But that wouldn't be fair or even true. For starters, *The Godfather* had already broken box office records three years before *Jaws*, proving moviegoers could fall just as in love with a bloody family tragedy as they could with a mechanical shark named Bruce and a droid named R2-D2. Second, both Spielberg and Lucas had begun their careers with the same kinds of bleak adult-facing movies their contemporaries made, and which Spielberg would return to in middle age with *Saving Private Ryan* (1997), *Minority Report* (2002), and *Munich* (2005). And though both Spielberg and Lucas identified with filmmakers of their generation (Coppola had mentored both, but they also buddied around with Brian De Palma, John Milius, and Martin Scorsese), both had grown up on fairy tales and the reliable genres of classic Hollywood (westerns, war films, pirate movies, and historical romances) and wanted to make versions of them for their own time. Third, by most accounts, New Hollywood's influence didn't get squashed by *Jaws* and *Star Wars* but hung around at least until 1980 (Scorsese's *Raging Bull* and Hal Ashby's *Coming Home*, both released that year, feel a decade older) and was as much done in, according to Peter Biskind in *Easy Riders, Raging Bulls*, by changes in studio ownership, terminated executive and producer contracts, and the "hard white snow falling on Hollywood" in the form of cocaine addiction that tripped up the career of Martin Scorsese and so many gifted filmmakers like him.

More likely, *Star Wars* and *Jaws*, George Lucas and Steven Spielberg, lead us out of the Movie Brat era and into the 1980s by performing the neat trick of being both rebellious and middle-of-the-road at the same time. Both *Jaws* and *Star Wars* have the classically teenage values of being suspicious of authority and on the side of iconoclasts and doubters. Both also do so in movies where you can avoid thinking about those values and just focus on being entertained by shark attacks and TIE fighter battles.

It's a formulation John Hughes—whose movies were always on the side of the outcast but in service of old-fashioned entertainment and emotional payoff that outcast, bully, and parent all could relate to—would use a little bit later. And both *Jaws* and *Star Wars* apply that same micro/macro calculation to setting and location. The places *Jaws* and *Star Wars* happen are completely unique, but they work in service of a kind of storytelling and toward a set of emotions that are deliberately universal.

In Peter Benchley's novel *Jaws*, the source material for Spielberg's movie published in 1974, the fictional town of Amity is a resort community off the coast of New York's Long Island. Spielberg and his team filmed *Jaws* in the fishing village of Menemsha on Martha's Vineyard off the coast of Massachusetts. Menemsha was chosen because it looked scruffy enough that a loss in summer tourism due to shark attacks would be cataclysmic—a picture-postcard seaside town like Mystic, Connecticut, would look prosperous enough to make its July Fourth profit some other way. The corrupt Amity officials who want to ignore the shark attacks are even more evil if Amity looks down on its luck—and the ocean water off the beach was shallow enough to set up camera equipment safely. Spielberg also made sure to cast respected actors but not giant movie stars (*Jaws*'s studio, Universal, suggested Charlton Heston and *Starsky and Hutch* heartthrob Jan-Michael Vincent), as he wanted *Jaws* to be about fear everyone could relate to, not an action movie about matinee idols beating the crap out of a deadly fish.

"My goal was to find someone who'd never been on the cover of *Rolling Stone*," Spielberg said, "so you would believe this was happening to people like you and me."

It worked. The heroes of *Jaws* are middle-aged men with dad bods, but teenagers saw it in droves, hung posters of it in suburban bedrooms, and then scared each other by making shark fin hands and uttering *duh-duh-duh-duh* at the community swimming pool. Spielberg chose to zoom *Jaws* in on one town's very specific shark problem during a single holiday weekend, while also crafting the film to resonate on the universal level of fearing what you can't see and don't understand, a terror as common as the wolf in *Little Red Riding Hood* or the monster under the bed. No wonder *Jaws* made people scared even to take a bath.

George Lucas and his crew filmed *Star Wars* in Tunisia (which served as the planet Tatooine), Guatemala (the Rebel base on the planet Yavin), and on soundstages in the United Kingdom. Several desert scenes were also shot in Southern California's Death Valley, but we weren't supposed to know that. George Lucas conceived *Star Wars*, as he's said about eighteen thousand times, for a generation of children who did not have their own fairy tales. He wanted to give them their own set of myths inspired by his childhood love of Buck Rogers, Flash Gordon, and a "kind of basic morality," saying, "Everybody's forgetting to tell the kids, 'Hey, this is right and this is wrong.'" None of it was meant to resemble the beaten, exhausted America of the 1970s they lived in, but the mythic absolutes of good and evil that ruled a long, long time ago in a galaxy far, far away.

Star Wars also featured a protagonist with a classic teenage set of problems. Luke Skywalker wants to leave home to go to the academy (a.k.a. college? The army? The circus?). His family needs him at home to work on the farm. Luke's probably a late teenager (maybe nineteen or twenty, though I'm sure eighty-five super fans just raised their hand with a correction). He also joins up with something called the Rebel Alliance to take down the Empire, which we later find out is lead by his dad. "*Star Wars* was a generation gap drama that sided with the kids," wrote Peter

Biskind in an essay for the 1990 anthology *Seeing Through Movies*. He argued that Lucas had meant the faltering empire desperately grabbing for power and crushing rebellion to stand in for post-Vietnam America. (Lucas has said as much since, even suggesting the Emperor as a stand-in for Richard Nixon.) The Ewok sequence in *Return of the Jedi* (1983), wrote Biskind, was a hippie dream of "an empire brought down by a children's crusade—of teenagers and teddy bears."

Anti-establishment in values, yet fun for all in execution, *Jaws* and *Star Wars* seemed both of the New Hollywood and the exit door out of it. Those hard, cynical movies by the friends and colleagues of Lucas and Spielberg aimed big in terms of political and social commentary, narrative strategy, and filmmaking chops. But they also had a certain nearsightedness in terms of how who they were for was reflected in where they happened: for movies aimed at changing the way we see movies and America itself, the "America" where their films happened was almost entirely missing.

Spielberg and Lucas were building a big tent. The relatability Spielberg fought to have in *Jaws* served the same archetypes and universal emotions of Lucas's fairytales—man vs. nature, fear of the unknown, courage in the face of doubt—rather than the specifics of setting and plot. Both movies have a sense of place that is entirely theirs—*Star Wars* is fictional and interplanetary, but forty years later, its fans can describe Tatooine better than the next town over, and parts of Martha's Vineyard remain iconic enough to be spots on a *Jaws* tour—but aim for the audience to shriek, sigh, or gasp as one. John Hughes would do the same, using a subjective notion of place (in his case, the north suburbs of Chicago where he was raising his own family) as the stage for universal stories and emotions, big themes seen through a very small keyhole.

It's not hard to see how this can go wrong. No movie speaks to everyone, no matter how much its creators try. And if movies' big ideas don't speak to you (if, say, man vs. shark or the power of a mythical energy field called the Force leaves you cold), it's easy to zoom in on how its specifics don't either ("That shark looked unrealistic," "I've never liked sci-fi movies").

Paradoxically, a movie aiming to please everybody can still feel like it has a specific moviegoer in mind. Which may explain why there seem to be way more *Star Wars* fans who work as software engineers than social workers, and why John Hughes devotees seem disproportionately to have grown up in suburbs and small towns rather than dense urban centers.

Jaws and *Star Wars* weren't specifically about teenagers but felt like they were made for them. The teen movies from the 1970s were really for adults who missed being teenagers. The six movies from this time that were the older siblings of eighties teen movies were a little of both—nostalgic yet contemporary, iconic in story while specific in detail. Their tales of bicyclists and bodyguards, of dancers and Deltas, of Thunderbirds and Warriors, did something else without quite meaning to: through a few smart choices in setting and location, they point the way toward the big themes of the eighties teen movie and bring the map of the entire country of Brat Pack America into view.

The Six Movies of Pre–Brat Pack America

Breaking Away (1979)

BREAKING AWAY CAME OUT in July of 1979 and won that year's Oscar for Best Original Screenplay and a Golden Globe for Best Picture. It marked the cinematic coming-out party for actors Dennis Quaid and Daniel Stern, and Paul Dooley's best dad role until he topped it as Molly Ringwald's father in *Sixteen Candles* (1984). *Breaking Away* is also in the top ten of the American Film Institute's list of "Most Inspiring Movies" and "Best Sport Movies." As of this writing, it has a 94 percent fresh rating on Rotten Tomatoes.

For my money, it also holds the title of being the very first eighties teen movie.

Along with *My Bodyguard*, which came out the following year, *Breaking Away* concerns itself with friendship, loyalty, and the uncertainty of growing up. But unlike teen movies from the decade before, both also seem to have no other motive than to listen to their characters talk and watch them be themselves. *Breaking Away* and *My Bodyguard* have nothing profound to say about youth culture or society at large, and their target audience isn't an adult who misses being a teenager. Instead, these are movies about being teenagers told by characters experiencing it.

Breaking Away takes place in summertime, one year after the high school graduation of its four main characters. These are working-class kids, sons of laborers and service employees, natives of Bloomington, Indiana, unsure of what to do next. The protagonist Dave (Dennis Christopher) distracts himself with bicycle racing, his passion. Mike (Dennis Quaid) is an ex-football star, resentful that his accomplishments on the field mean nothing now that high school is over. Their friend Cyril (Daniel Stern), the Ringo Starr of the group, seems content not to worry about the future. Moocher (Jackie Earle Haley) has plans to marry his high school girlfriend.

The quartet's parents worked in the state's rock quarries, cutting the limestone used in the buildings at nearby Indiana University, but those jobs are disappearing and Bloomington is increasingly resembling a college town instead of an industrial community: more Cambridge than Dorchester, more Ann Arbor than Detroit. The painful transition from one Bloomington to another gets played out in scraps and bar fights between the four friends and Indiana University students who sneer and call them "cutters." Predicting early eighties fashion, the villainous IU boys always appear in pressed khakis, fraternity sweaters, and haircuts parted severely to the right.

The movie's climax is the Little 500 bicycle race, an actual bicycle race held the third week of April at Indiana University since 1951. The four friends form a team called the Cutters and end up in the final laps competing for victory against the same bullies who menaced them earlier. I won't tell you who wins, but the feeling you leave *Breaking Away* with is a fifty-fifty split of "Hooray!" and "Okay, now what?"

What makes *Breaking Away* both magical and important for our purposes is Bloomington. Screenwriter Steve Tesich based the film's Oscar-winning script on his own experience as both an IU student and an avid cyclist. But Bloomington isn't just an autobiographical detail, it's all these four protagonists have ever known.

"My dad says Jesus never lived more than fifty miles from home," says Cyril in the movie's opening scene. "Look what happened to him," retorts Mike.

Bloomington is changing and leaving these four young men behind. *Breaking Away* doesn't see this as social commentary but a reminder of the inevitability of time and the need to do something before time rolls over you.

Move *Breaking Away* to a big city that's always on the move or a small town where nothing ever changes and all the beauty and pain of this moment in the four friends' lives is lost. The movie needs someplace like Bloomington, in transition but with a bright future (university towns are, on the whole, places of economic stability, even in states down on their luck), or else the four guys have nothing to head toward and the title *Breaking Away* is just a cruel joke. (Break away? TO WHAT?)

Breaking Away made way for the eighties teen movie in three ways: 1) It's a movie about growing up that observed rather than editorialized or commented on its teenage characters doing it; 2) it showed young people worried about a future in a declining American industrial economy, a plot device for a whole ecosystem of eighties teen movies including *All the Right Moves* and *Vision Quest*; and 3) with Bloomington as a major character, it began to rearrange the map of the American teen movies. The movies of the 1970s said important things happen on America's coasts. *Breaking Away* made a strong case for the American Midwest, not as a foreign land within US borders (the way, say, *Deliverance* the decade before had portrayed rural Georgia) but as a place both unique and archetypal. It may have looked different from New York or California, but the characters had the same struggles, difficulties, and hopes as people anywhere else.

It would take John Hughes and his enormous influence to make the Midwest the capital region of Brat Pack America, but *Breaking Away* began that process 250 miles southeast of Hughes country in Bloomington, a town unique and crucial to its story that also staged an archetypal story of time, change, and the uncertainty and confusion of growing up.

My Bodyguard (1980)

A SIMPLER, LESS AMBITIOUS movie than *Breaking Away*, *My Bodyguard* is often cited as a lead-in to many of the best known eighties teen movies. It not only has teenagers as both the narrators and main characters of their own story, but also positions the city of Chicago as the theater for the dramas of adolescence. *My Bodyguard* will be the first of many films in this story that symbolically viewed the home of the Sears Tower and the elevated train as what the late critic Roger Ebert called "a teenage Hollywood."

My Bodyguard has a premise so simple that the movie's beauty lies almost entirely in its execution, not what it's doing but how it's doing it. Clifford (Chris Makepeace) is a curly-haired, thin-armed adolescent. Following his parents' divorce, his father (Martin Mull) takes a new job managing the Ambassador Hotel, moving Clifford and Clifford's grandmother (the immortal Ruth Gordon, Maude in *Harold and Maude*) from the Chicago's South Side to the hotel in the city's Gold Coast neighborhood. This makes Clifford the new kid at a new school, and when he runs afoul of bully Melvin Moody (Matt Dillon, in his second film role), he gets the idea to hire the class weirdo Ricky (Adam Baldwin, in his film debut), the only kid in school Moody doesn't mess with, as his bodyguard.

My Bodyguard is a movie about friendship: Ricky and Clifford get to know one other and Clifford learns why Ricky has avoided letting anyone in. It ends in a climactic (and needless) fight scene with Adam Baldwin, Matt Dillon, and Chris Makepeace all punching the snot out of each other. That fight happens right by a pond in Lincoln Park next to Chicago's Lincoln Park Zoo. The pond plays a key role in the events leading up to the fight.

Watching over the entire scene in the background is the solemn black triangle of the John Hancock Center, probably the city's most famous building after the Sears Tower.

My Bodyguard loves Chicago and its landmarks. The movie opens with an aerial shot of Clifford bicycling down Lake Shore Drive, an unmistakable view that may as well be scored to Frank Sinatra singing, "Chicago, That Toddlin' Town." Clifford's family lives at the Ambassador Hotel (now called Public Chicago) at 1301 N. State Street, probably the city's most historic hotel after the Drake. (Trivia: The Ambassador contains the Pump Room restaurant, where, after being denied a table because he wasn't wearing a suit, Phil Collins decided to call his third solo album *No Jacket Required*. Pump Room management later mailed Collins a sport coat and told him to come back any time he liked). The film's beautiful we-are-becoming-friends montage of Ricky and Clifford riding Ricky's newly refashioned motorcycle is a two-wheeled tour of Windy City icons: Sears Tower, under the L tracks on Wacker Drive, around the giant red Alexander Calder *Flamingo* sculpture on South Dearborn Street, where Cameron would later yell, "You're crazy!" to his best friend Ferris Bueller right before Ferris sang "Twist and Shout."

Clifford is a city kid, a rare thing in the eighties teen movies that followed *My Bodyguard*. He doesn't visit friends who have driveways and front lawns. There's no mention of his dad commuting from the south suburbs, nor any warning about how "dangerous" the city is for a scrawny teenager riding around on a motorbike. Shot and released a few years before John Hughes began directing, *My Bodyguard* stays entirely within Chicago city limits and does not acknowledge Hughes's home base in the northern suburbs at all. Chicago is Clifford's whole world. *My Bodyguard* never leaves it.

But director Tony Bill and screenwriter Alan Ormsby go a step further and also use negative spaces, what Chicago is not as well as what it is, to tell us more about *My Bodyguard*'s characters. Before they become friends, Clifford follows Ricky home from school to see where his mysterious bodyguard lives. Ricky comes to an intersection, turns down an alley and arrives at a modest ranch house with its address numbers falling off. Clifford doesn't know where this is, underlining that Ricky is still a remote and mysterious presence ("Where the hell am I and how do I get out of here?" he asks after Ricky catches him spying). But if you knew Chicago in the early 1980s, you'd know that this part of town is Little Italy on the city's West Side (street signs for both Thirteenth Street and W. Maxwell Street help, too). Culturally self-contained and removed from downtown despite its nearness to it, the area contained activist Jane Addams's Hull House in the nineteenth century. Today, the neighborhood has been gentrified thanks to its proximity to downtown and, in the early 2000s, the tearing down of nearby public housing projects and developing by the University of Illinois at Chicago nearby. A real estate agent these days might call it "University Village."

Why the filmmakers chose this for Ricky's neighborhood probably has everything to do with cost, convenience, and local color. But the choice is also a wink to anyone who knows Chicago's neighborhoods and geography: we know almost nothing of Ricky's background that would explain how he ended up living in this part of the city. But it makes sense that *My Bodyguard*'s most remote, least knowable character lives in a part of Chicago that most residents not from there wouldn't know either.

The location, if you recognize it, underlines Clifford's (lack of) understanding of Ricky and points to where their friendship at the movie's center begins. It's also bonus points and an inside joke for anyone who loves Chicago as much as this movie does.

Now, look at Matt Dillon as the villain: slicked hair, a lolloping walk, and jutting chin. His accent could be Italian or Irish (Moody is an Irish name and Matt Dillon is Irish-American), but lacks the long vowels and flat consonants of a Chicago-born teenager. When we first see him, he's wearing a satin navy-blue baseball starter jacket with white trim, the color scheme not of the Cubs or the White Sox but of the New York Yankees.

Moody may rule Clifford's school, but the filmmakers have cast and dressed the character as seemingly not from Chicago, or at least not loyal to it. (What teenager would wear a Yankees jacket to a North Side high school and not get beaten to death by Cubs fans? The school bully who can beat back.)

It may actually be saying nothing that *My Bodyguard*, a movie Chicago-born and proud, has a villain that seems like an import from the Bronx and gets his ass kicked in the movie's last scene, but I like to think that, as in *Breaking Away*, we are seeing the slight shift of the American teen movie away from just New York and California and toward a more diverse map of teenage lives onscreen.

I may be making something of nothing, but read on and see where it happens again.

National Lampoon's Animal House (1978)

IF YOU'VE SEEN A movie recently about a bunch of male friends chasing girls and having disgusting but hilarious adventures along the way, you owe *National Lampoon's Animal House* a dollar—two dollars if you own a sweatshirt with simply the word "college" printed across the front, have ever chanted "toga, toga" when wrapped in a bed sheet, or danced to the song "Shout" at a wedding.

Animal House is the reason for all of these now-immoveable mountains of American popular culture. Made for $3 million, grossing $140 million, it's widely considered one of the funniest movies of all time. As of this writing, it has a 91 percent fresh rating on Rotten Tomatoes and has been a member of the Library of Congress's National Film Registry since 2001.

Yes, *Animal House* is a movie about college (Faber College, circa 1962; motto: learning is good) and therefore should be out of bounds for our look at eighties teen movies. But *Animal House* influenced so many latter-day teen movies (from *Porky's* to *American Pie* to *Superbad* and *The Hangover* films) that we'd be remiss in leaving it out of this discussion of the older brothers and sisters of Brat Pack America. *Animal House* also perfected the plot of a gang of losers and outcasts sticking it to the bullies and brownnosers in the halls of power, an idea we see repeated often in

Brat Pack America movies like *The Goonies* and *Real Genius*, and in the twin comedies of Savage Steve Holland: *Better Off Dead* and *One Crazy Summer*.

Animal House doesn't specify where Faber College is. A logical answer might be Hanover, New Hampshire, as coscreenwriter Chris Miller based the wild Delta fraternity at the movie's center on his own Alpha Delta fraternity at Dartmouth College. Another screenwriter, Harold Ramis, had gone Greek at Washington University, but *Animal House* looks too rural to have been filmed in the Central West End of St. Louis. A good fallback answer for this question is always "somewhere around Los Angeles," but *Animal House* had too many cast members wearing winter coats and scarves while barfing and too many campus quads bordered by trees in glorious fall colors to be Southern California.

Animal House was filmed in and around Eugene, Oregon, home of the University of Oregon. In the mid 1960s, William Beaty Boyd had been an administrator at the University of California at Berkeley when *The Graduate* asked to shoot there. Boyd said no and *The Graduate* went on to make cinematic history, with the majority of its "Berkeley" scenes filmed at the University of Southern California in Los Angeles instead. By the late 1970s, Boyd was president of the University of Oregon, and determined not to make the same mistake twice.

"We knew that we wanted to shoot on the grounds of a real university," wrote producer Matty Simmons in his 2012 book *Fat, Drunk, and Stupid: The Inside Story Behind the Making of Animal House*. "Getting not only college buildings and classrooms as exteriors but also the students as extras." But most universities took one look at the drugs, booze, and nudity in *Animal House* and passed. Boyd, on the other hand, flung open the campus gates after the filmmakers promised to tone down the raunchy stuff (sure). He even let his own office double as the evil Dean Wormer's office, where a dead horse is, shall we say, disposed of with a chain saw.

Many of the *Animal House* locations are still around today. The main campus cafeteria called the Fishbowl, host of the most famous food fight scene in movie history, looks pretty much as it did in 1978. The Dexter Lake Club (at 39128 Dexter Road in nearby Dexter, Oregon), where the fraternity brothers recruit the band that plays "Shout," is still in business as the Rattlesnake BBQ. The building used for the Delta House was torn down, but a plaque commemorating the movie is on site. The interiors of the Delta House belong to the University's Sigma Nu fraternity, which is still active on campus.

But does Eugene, Oregon, or the University of Oregon change the influence of *Animal House*? Does it mean anything for our story of eighties teen movies and the places where they happened?

In the late seventies, when *Animal House* was filmed, fraternities on American college campuses were in bad shape. The counterculture of the 1960s had made them seem like bastions of privilege where "the man" got his early training in oppressing others. By the 1970s, fraternities "moldered, all but forgotten. Membership fell sharply, fraternity houses slid into increasing states of disrepair, and hundreds of chapters closed," wrote journalist Caitlin Flanagan in her 2014 *Atlantic* article "The Dark Power of Fraternities." And whether demographics actually bore this out, in the public mind, fraternities were the remnants of a dying Northeastern WASP establishment.

Animal House changed all of that. Suddenly fraternities were cool again, not just for the privileged few but also for the weird and rejected, the handsome and homely, the fat, drunk, and stupid. Fraternities were now places you went not just to party but to stick it to the man by partying. Partying now had a weird moral imperative, and pledging skyrocketed.

Animal House looks like a movie filmed on the East Coast, its preppy autumnal costumes, early sixties date stamp, and, well, focus on fraternities. That it looks Northeastern but was actually Pacific Northwest did not put the region on pop culture's radar (we'd have to wait for Gus Van Sant, Nike, Starbucks, and Riot Grrrls to do that a decade later). Instead the fake Faber College from the real University of Oregon sent a faint signal into the next decade: young people are having a great time here among the pine trees and mountain roads of Eugene and sticking it, using cleverness, mischief, and fun, to a whole town's worth of adult losers in the process.

It may not have altered the geography of the teen movies to come as much as *Breaking Away* and *My Bodyguard*, but it changed completely how, at the movies, we viewed young people and success. College immediately after *Animal House* becomes a battleground between students with win-at-all-costs ambition (these students almost always looked as white and Northeastern as the Princeton crew team) and misfits eager to succeed on their own terms through silliness, loyalty, and common decency. If you look at the success stories that came out of Pacific Northwest colleges around this time (Nike shoes), shortly after (Matt Groening, Steve Jobs), and then a generation later (Sleater-Kinney), they look a lot more like Deltas than silver-spooned Omegas, bands of outsiders first inspiring each other and then having their creativity produce silly, beautiful things.

Animal House may have made fraternities cool again. It's a longer but no less pronounced line from *Animal House* to *Real Genius* to Burning Man camps, hackathons, Etsy, and Maker Faires.

Fame (1980)

AN EARLY SETTLER OF Brat Pack America, *Fame* deals most directly with the conflict joked about in *Animal House*: between ambition and fun, loyalty and winning, success and what success actually means and can do to you. That makes *Fame* one of the starting points for a whole series of eighties teen movies about the price of being really good at something (the thing was usually sports, but science, academia, and building stuff figure in here, too) and the ways in which adolescence appears to arbitrarily and unfairly separate the successful from the less so according to its own harsh definitions. These ideas may be baked into the plot of a movie like *Fame*, which is about being a teenager and wanting to make it as an artist, but the movie's most famous scene brings home that message not through plot or dialogue or character but a very savvy bit of location scouting.

An ensemble movie about eight students at New York City's High School of Performing Arts, *Fame* begins with its characters showing up for first-year orientation and ends with their graduation recital. In the four years between, director Alan Parker (a Brit who would later make *Pink Floyd: The Wall* (1982), *The Commitments* (1991), and *Evita* (1996)) and screenwriter Christopher Gore throw plenty of obstacles at these young people: conflicts with teachers, misunderstanding parents, failed love affairs with each other, and a world of professional performance just outside the school door, tempting them before they are ready for it.

Fame was an immediate hit upon its release in May of 1980 and received six Academy Award nominations, winning for Best Original Score and Best Original Song. Nominated for his screenplay, Christopher Gore also wrote several episodes of the TV show *Fame*, which ran from 1982–87. *Fame* was adapted as a stage musical in 1995 and has had seven runs in London's West End. A remake of the movie came to theaters in 2009. The original ranks number forty-two on *Entertainment Weekly*'s list of the Fifty Best High School Movies.

Parker wanted to shoot *Fame* at the actual High School of Performing Arts (the inspiration for Gore's screenplay), which at the time was located at 120 W. Forty-Sixth Street, just a block from both Times Square and the Broadway theater district. "Filmmakers of my generation shot in the streets and in real places. You can smell a real place," Parker remarked in his director's commentary. "The idea of using a soundstage never came up." But the New York City School Board didn't like that the high school kids in *Fame* were shown having sex and said no. According to Parker, one school board member told him, "I can't risk you doing for New York high schools what you did for Turkish prisons in [Parker's previous film] *Midnight Express*."

Instead, the filmmakers shot the movie's interiors in three different high schools around Manhattan and Brooklyn. But when it came to filming what became *Fame*'s iconic moment, they not only got the last laugh on the school board killjoys, but used the

High School of Performing Arts anyway to bring home the power of *Fame* and the eighties movies it would later inspire.

If you know nothing about *Fame*, you still know the iconic moment I'm talking about. Bruno Martelli (Lee Curreri), one of the eight students profiled, is a poor kid from the outer boroughs and a musical prodigy. His father is a New York City taxi driver. One morning, while school is in session, Mr. Martelli drives his cab to the school's front door and stops in the middle of the street, blocking traffic. The loudspeaker on top of his cab starts blaring music (it happens to be movie's theme song) his son composed. "That's my music," Bruno yells from a piano practice room in the school building. His classmates hear it, rush out into the streets, and begin dancing on gridlocked cars, swinging around lampposts, and leaping over trashcans. "That's my son's music!" declares the proud father while traffic honks and yells at him. "Today, Forty-Sixth Street. Tomorrow, Madison Square Garden!"

The scene actually *was* filmed on Forty-Sixth Street, between Sixth and Seventh Avenues, directly in front of the actual High School for Performing Arts. Parker got permission to use an abandoned church across the street to stand in for the school's front door. The school that hadn't let Parker in their front door to tell its own story instead had to watch it being filmed sixty feet away, tying up traffic all over midtown Manhattan.

Though it was an expensive pain in the ass, filmmakers were committed to the location anyway. More than once, recalled Parker, his crew asked why they weren't just recreating the damn thing on a Hollywood soundstage and saving themselves the headache of rerouting traffic near the world's busiest intersection while keeping forty-five dancers on point (the entire "spontaneous" dance sequence is choreographed). More than once, Parker circles back to the film's locations being not only authentic but true to *Fame*'s message: the school sat within eyeshot of both Broadway and Times Square, which in 1979 was a skid row of addicts, drug dealers, and porno theaters. "Its unique geography represented that fine balance between success and disaster," Parker said. From its front stoop, students training to be performers could see physical representations of how much they could succeed and how far they could fall, the rewards and risks of fame.

Fame's most famous scene couldn't have taken place anywhere else. Through one uncompromising location choice, a silly dance sequence becomes a lot more, demonstrating not only what the movie's teenagers had at stake but that winning and success would be a crucial and cruel part of the eighties teen movies that would follow.

The 1980s were a decade obsessed with victory. Wall Street traders called themselves Masters of the Universe. Tom Cruise became the era's cinematic action hero by always being the best at what he did (flying planes, racing cars, bartending). The teen movies of the time often linked success in sports (*Hoosiers*, *Vision Quest*) or school (*Risky Business*, *How I Got into College*) to happiness and fulfillment.

Fame offers up this idea and at the same time questions it. The school itself sits right between representations of success and failure. The closing number, "I Sing the Body Electric," grabs its opening lines from Walt Whitman, America's greatest poet who never saw financial success in his lifetime. The song, riffing on perhaps Whitman's most famous sentences, goes like this:

I sing the body electric

I celebrate the me yet to come

I toast to my own reunion, when I become one with the sun

And I'll look back on Venus, I'll look back on Mars

And I'll burn with the fire of ten million stars

And in time, and in time, we will all be stars

Fame doesn't even pretend that will be true. Some of the eight main characters get solos and lead dance parts in the finale. Some are in the chorus. Some we don't see at all. "For a moment, everyone matters. Everyone can be great," says Parker of the closing number in his director's commentary. But only for a moment. Not all of the issues the kids wrestled with earlier have been resolved. We don't find out what happens to them in little text epilogues, like we do in *American Graffiti*, *Animal House*, or *Fast Times at Ridgemont High*. The movie's closing shot is of the conductor, not the kids.

It's a glorious number that feels like winning something huge and wouldn't be out of place at the end of *Rocky*. But it deliberately leaves a lot out, telling us both what 120 W. Forty-Sixth Street told us and what many places on the map of Brat Pack America would build on: it's always better to win, but winning will cost something.

The Warriors (1979)

Principal photography on *Fame* began in the summer of 1979, and by that time, New York was showing up less and less as a setting for movies about young people. The city had been in terrible shape—bankruptcy, blackouts, riots, serial killers—for most of the 1970s. By decade's end, movies shot in New York smelled of hopelessness and featured adult characters spiraling downward, at war with themselves and a crumbling, indifferent metropolis—*Serpico*, *Cruising*, *Dressed to Kill*, *Escape from New York*, *Prince of the City*. The rare exception came from comedies featuring the young trying to "make it" in early eighties New York. These movies would start to turn things around. Beginning with *Arthur* (1981), then *Annie* (1982), *Tootsie* (1982), and *Desperately Seeking Susan* (1984), New York had begun—a laugh at a time—to look like a place onscreen where a young person could imagine their dreams coming to life.

Right in the middle of this transition came *The Warriors*, released in February of 1979 and shot all over New York the summer before. *The Warriors* is undoubtedly a movie set in a grimy, crumbling war zone. It's also a movie where just about every character (and there are hundreds) is a person in their late teens and early twenties, a rare sight in New York movies of the grimy, crumbling 1970s.

The Warriors used setting as the engine of its plot instead of a backdrop for it, and in doing so built a bridge from the nihilistic urban movies of the Hollywood New Wave (*Mean Streets*, *Klute*,

Taxi Driver) to the nihilistic teen movies of the 1980s (*Over the Edge, River's Edge, Heathers*). Though there would be many steps in between, *The Warriors* is how movies got from adult Robert De Niro in an army jacket trying to shoot a presidential candidate to Winona Ryder stopping Christian Slater from blowing up Westerburg High School and killing everyone inside.

The time is the near future; the place, New York City. Gangs from all over the region arrive at a citywide meeting in the Bronx convened by Cyrus, leader of the Gramercy Riffs from the Gramercy neighborhood in Manhattan. At the summit, Cyrus unveils his master plan: There are far more gang members in New York than there are police officers. If the gangs stopped fighting with one another over turf and worked together, the entire city could be their turf. New York would be ruled by nineteen- and twenty-year-old men with no one to stop them.

Before Cyrus can finish, shots ring out and the leader of the Riffs falls over dead. The assassin, throwing the scent off his trail, convinces the crowd that the Warriors, a gang from Coney Island, committed the murder. Now the Warriors must make it the thirty miles from the Bronx back to their home turf in the middle of the night. "We'll only be safe when we can see the ocean," one of the Warriors says. But Coney Island is a long way away, and every gang in the city wants them dead for supposedly killing Cyrus.

The Warriors is ninety-three minutes of chase and pursuit, and it makes location a kind of destiny for the characters. As you'd expect in a movie about street gangs, the Warriors and their enemies are defined by the neighborhoods they come from, and many—the Turnbull ACs, Van Cortlandt Rangers, Gramercy Riffs—even work their turf into their name. And since the subway is New York's circulatory system and the quickest way for a large group to travel in the middle of the night, director Walter Hill continually returns to subway maps and signs as a visual motif, reminding us not only where the Warriors are but how close they are to making it home to Coney Island and surviving.

Hill based *The Warriors* on an ancient Greek legend of a maritime army surrounded by enemies, which had to reach the ocean in order to sail home. In the film's DVD commentary, producer Frank Marshall said the filmmakers agreed the movie had to be cast entirely with New York actors and shot on location. Only a single set piece—a subway restroom where the Warriors take on an overall-wearing gang called the Punks—was built for the movie. Marshall also worked with the NYPD to find real-life locations safe for filming locations with the least amount of actual nighttime gang activity.

The Warriors was a surprise hit upon release in the winter of 1979, and in an ironic twist, its studio, Paramount, yanked the film from theaters after reports of young people showing up at screenings, trashing the places, and getting into fights with each other. It's now considered a cult classic, a regular at midnight movies and festivals, and spawned an Xbox game in 2005 and a comic book series. It's most famous lines of dialogue ("Warriors. Come out to playyyyyy!") have been referenced in about 9,000 hit hip-hop songs including 2Pac & Dr. Dre's duet "California Love," Craig Mack's "Flava in Ya Ear," and Wu-Tang Clan's "Shame on a Nigga." And for a movie that feels every inch a low-budget comic book, it maintains, as of this writing, an 89 percent fresh rating on Rotten Tomatoes.

The Warriors is one of the most New York movies ever made, but this isn't the same New York as *Taxi Driver* (an ordinary metropolis by day, a teeming sludge bucket by night) or *Dog Day Afternoon* (a sunburnt village of the desperate and damned), made just a few years before. *The Warriors'* New York is dank and scary but also empty of civilians and adults. Other than a few policemen and merchants, the movie contains essentially no one over the age of thirty. And other than a few innocent bystanders, every young person out on the streets is wearing gang colors. For "the city that never sleeps," New York in *The Warriors* seems as lonely and desolate as the surface of the moon. The only New Yorkers in this most New York of movies are teenage hoodlums.

The Warriors, without meaning to, predicted this kind of fear and paranoia of a world out of control and overrun by teenagers, which Hollywood would exploit in the teen films of the 1980s. If the movies of John Hughes—about good kids from good homes and neighborhoods trying to do the right thing—were like pop music, then the younger siblings of *The Warriors* were like punk rock—apocalyptic, caustic, darkly comic in service of a larger political point.

Beginning with *Rosemary's Baby* in 1968, a recurring theme in horror movies from the 1970s was "child gets possessed by evil and goes crazy"—see *The Exorcist* (1973) and *The Omen* (1976). Scholars of the horror genre have written repeatedly that the popularity of this theme reflected a Baby Boomer generation terrified about growing up and the responsibility of having children. *The Warriors* predicted this fear essentially repeating itself in the 1980s, except now the Baby Boomers had teenagers instead of young kids. The darker teen movies of the eighties played into this paranoia but also criticized it. Hinted at first in *The Warriors* but really finding its footing in later movies like *Over the Edge* (1980), *The Legend of Billie Jean* (1984), and *Heathers* (1988), these movies seemed to be saying two things at odds with one other: "Wasn't it a scary, stupid move giving teenagers power in the sixties, and do we want to make that mistake again?" While also saying, "If the eighties was supposed to be America recovering from the seventies, why do American teenagers still feel like fugitives in their own country?"

Grease (1978)

By the time *Grease* arrived in movie theaters on June 16, 1978, it had already been a ridiculously successful Broadway musical. On stage, it had also originally been a very different version of a high school love affair between a greaser boy and a clean-cut girl than the one we see onscreen.

Inspired by *Hair*, which had arrived on Broadway only a few years earlier, *Grease* the musical played raunchy offhanded, and natural, aiming for how actual teenagers rather than actors playing teenagers sounded. To get it that way, writers Jim Jacobs and Warren Casey rehearsed the cast for only three and a half weeks before opening to keep *Grease* from seeming too polished.

They based the fictional Rydell High School on their own William Howard Taft High School in a working-class neighborhood on Chicago's east side.

In the introduction to the musical's 1972 published script, critic Michael Feingold wrote: "The people of *Grease* are a special class of aliens, self-appointed cynics in a work-oriented, upwardly mobile world." We know from the prologue that history has played its dirty trick on them before they even appear. They are not at the reunion; they will not be found among the prosperous Mrs. Honeywells and the go-getting vice presidents of Straight-Shooters, Unlimited. Nor, on the other hand, did they actively drop out; that was left to their younger siblings and cousins. (Memory of a line too explicit, and cut from the script early on: "Course I like life. Whaddaya think I am, a beatnik?") They were the group who thought they had, or chose to have, nowhere to go.

This probably sounds absolutely nothing like the John Travolta/Olivia Newton-John *Grease* you know. Other than a few zingers from Stockard Channing's Rizzo (*What do you punks think this is, a gangbang?*), the language is pretty tame. Each of the principal actors in *Grease* the movie were several years removed from high school and didn't look anything like teenagers. The movie's producer, Allan Carr, had made his name creating marketing campaigns and glittering premieres for the movies *Tommy* (1975) and *Saturday Night Fever* (1977) and had a boundless appetite for large, showy set pieces. Shaggy, unpolished, with minimal rehearsal was not his way. And standing in for Chicago's scruffy East Side, Rydell High was the gleaming white Art Deco structure of Venice High School at 13000 Venice Boulevard on the west side of Los Angeles. Though *Grease* the movie never says where it takes place, the palm trees, drag race through the concrete canyons of the Los Angeles River, and the school carnival finale with Griffith Park Observatory seen in the background makes it pretty obvious.

If *American Graffiti* launched a pre-Beatles nostalgia craze at American movie theaters in 1973, it reached some kind of crazy stratospheric zenith with *Grease* in 1978. The movie grossed nearly $200 million during its initial theatrical run, an ungodly amount in the late seventies, and as of this writing, remains the most successful movie musical of all time. Nominated for five Golden Globes, *Grease* is number twenty on the American Film Institute's list of the Greatest Movie Musicals. Its soundtrack produced two number-one singles—"You're the One That I Want" and the title song, in a weird-cross generational pairing, sung by Frankie Valli but written by the Bee Gees' Barry Gibb.

"One of the reasons people have loved this movie for so long is it reflects a more innocent time in America. Before everything fell apart," said *Grease* choreographer Patricia Birch in the DVD commentary. As if this idea couldn't get any bigger than it had already, *Grease* would lead to a whole series of teen movies in the 1980s from this same "more innocent time in America." Some were modest hits (*The Outsiders, Peggy Sue Got Married*), others bigger (*Stand by Me*). The biggest, *Back to the Future* (1985), was as big as *Grease* had been seven years before and was a favorite movie of President Ronald Reagan.

Movies about young people set in the late 1950s were huge in the 1980s, not only because *Grease* had set precedent and not just because of the dependable cycles of nostalgia. America wanted to feel good about itself again, actor Rob Lowe said in his narration of the 2013 National Geographic Series *The '80s: The Decade That Made Us*, and looked for help in movies "from a simpler time. Before the sixties wrecked everything."

The innocence of *Grease*, combined with its sun-dappled California setting (it never rains or even gets cloudy in this movie; no one wears a coat that doesn't have their gang affiliation emblazoned on the back), would also be ahead of its time while looking back. The idea of Southern California as sun, fun, and pretty girls in convertibles might have been in fashion in 1959 (the year *Grease* takes place) but was already a museum piece by 1978. Southern California had lived through the Riots on the Sunset Strip, the Manson murders, and recessions in aerospace and moviemaking, the region's major industries. When he inducted Jackson Browne, who made his name as the troubadour of a post-1960s Los Angeles, into the Rock and Roll Hall of Fame in 2004,

Bruce Springsteen said, "If The Beach Boys had been California as paradise, then Warren Zevon and Jackson Browne were California as paradise lost."

But the sun-and-fun optimism of long ago came roaring back in the 1980s. Think Sweet Valley High novels, the Ocean Pacific fashion label, and the Moon Unit Zappa song "Valley Girl." In the eighties teen movies that came on the heels of *Grease*, we see Southern California as a place in the midst of an identity crisis, not quite sure which previous version of itself it wants to be. The Los Angeles of pretty young people heading into a sunlit future now resides in the San Fernando Valley (see *The Karate Kid* and *Fast Times at Ridgemont High*). The city of Los Angeles itself in the eighties teen movie becomes a place of the neglected and forgotten, as we see in *Repo Man* and *Suburbia*.

Grease took the handoff of pre-sixties California nostalgia from *American Graffiti*. Yet it would become bigger and more complicated in the eighties teen movies coming right up behind it.

Breaking Away, My Bodyguard, Animal House, Fame, The Warriors, and *Grease*. Six movies that landed right before the 1980s that begin to lay out and color the map of what was to come: Teen movies that would focus less on New York and Los Angeles and more on towns and cities all over America. Teen movies that, when they did end up in California, complicated our simpleminded ideas of what "California" meant to whom. Movies that turned adults' fear of teenagers against themselves. Movies that would recall the 1950s fondly but also indict the willful blindness that comes with nostalgia. Movies that used the geography of America to make movies about being a teenager in America deeper, more authentic, and better than they had ever been made before.

Our first stop on this visit to our favorite eighties teen movies and the places they happened, on this trip through Brat Pack America, is a made-up town north of Chicago called Shermer, Illinois.

CHAPTER 2: A SHERMER, ILLINOIS, OF THE MIND

The John Hughes Movies

Movies Discussed: *Sixteen Candles, Ferris Bueller's Day Off, The Breakfast Club, Lucas, About Last Night*

"They are so bloody real
It is as if they really still existed
And they do
Only the landscape has changed."
—"A Coney Island of the Mind" by Lawrence Ferlinghetti

"John Hughes? You know that guy, too? That fucking guy... See, all his movies take place in this small town called Shermer, in Illi-noise. Where all the honeys are top-shelf and the dudes are whiny pussies... But best of all, there was no one dealing, man. Then it hits me: we could live like fat rats if we were the blunt connection in Shermer, Illi-noise. So we collected some money we were owed and caught a bus.

"But you know what the fuck we found out when we got there? There is no Shermer in Illi-noise.

"Movies are fuckin' bullshit."
—Jay of *Jay and Silent Bob* in Kevin Smith's *Dogma* (1999).

SHERMER. IN ILLI-NOISE. WHERE Molly Ringwald's family forgot her sixteenth birthday. Where two nerds built a dream girl with a home computer and weird science. Where an Athlete, a Brain, a Princess, a Basket Case, and a Criminal came into Saturday detention as strangers and left as the Breakfast Club. Where Ferris Bueller departed from and returned to for his day off. Where apparently no one had the hookup for decent weed.

It's a made-up town somewhere in the northern suburbs of Chicago and only gets mentioned once onscreen. But Shermer, Illinois, was so completely realized in the mind of its creator, John Hughes, that when the movies he wrote and directed became icons of a genre and a generation, their setting did, too.

Say the words "eighties teen movie" and most people will assume you're talking about the work of writer/director John Hughes. When he died of a heart attack in 2009, an NPR tribute called him "the philosopher of puberty, the auteur of adolescent angst." I'm okay calling him the greatest maker of teen cinema that ever lived. The teen movie as we know it now would not exist without him, any more than horror movies would without Alfred Hitchcock or comedies without Charlie Chaplin.

If anyone can claim it, John Hughes is the cartographer of Brat Pack America. Thanks to his imagination, Shermer, Illinois, became its capital city. If you're talking about eighties teen movies and their iconic places, you have to begin here.

John Hughes did not invent the teen movie, which had been a recognized film category since at least his own childhood in the 1950s. Instead, in a half-dozen examples—*Sixteen Candles, Weird Science, The Breakfast Club, Pretty in Pink, Ferris Bueller's Day Off,* and *Some Kind of Wonderful*—John Hughes changed teen movies forever by both making them his own and showing what they could be. Samantha Baker, Cameron Frye, John Bender, Andie Walsh, Duckie Dale, and Ferris Bueller were not vehicles of adult nostalgia the way the characters in *Grease* and *American Graffiti* had been the decade before. They weren't there to titillate or be murdered by a madman, even though, at the time, movies like *Porky's* and

Friday the 13th were making mountains of money doing both of those things. Nor were Hughes's characters moral lessons wrapped in acid-washed jeans, even though television shows of the same era—*The Cosby Show, Family Ties, Growing Pains,* and *The Wonder Years*—had been all about teenagers learning something by the end of the episode while wearing acid-washed jeans (*Seinfeld,* a nineties show created in deliberate opposition to this, had a standing rule: "No hugging and no learning").

John Hughes took what *Breaking Away* and *My Bodyguard* had done for the teen movie a few years before he started directing and raised it to the level of myth. Like *Breaking Away* and *My Bodyguard,* his teenage characters occupied the center of a story told from their point of view. But unlike *Breaking Away* and *My Bodyguard,* which stayed grounded to the specifics of plot and character, a John Hughes movie reaches for big themes with capital letters—Class, Acceptance, Growing Up, True Love—and anchors those themes to big, obvious movie moments designed to squeeze at your heart. John Hughes's teenagers live in fables of, not documentaries about, being young in America in the 1980s.

A Shermer, Illinois, of the Mind

THE IDEAS IN A John Hughes movie were as big as his talent and output, even though the worldview that inspired them was not. Hughes wrote thirty-two produced screenplays, many under a pseudonym after he stopped directing film in 1991. After his death in 2009, Hughes's sons found hundreds of notebooks and digital files of screenplays not made, novels and short stories never published. Shermer, the fictional town he created for the movies he did make, also found its way into many unmade, unpublished stories. The citizens of these works connected to those of Ferris Bueller, Principal Vernon, Jake Ryan, and other characters that did show up in Hughes's fictional world onscreen.

"John told me he knew everyone in Shermer, not just the people in his movies. He knew where they lived and what they did for a living," wrote P. J. O'Rourke in a 2015 tribute to the director in *The Daily Beast*. "He could tell you about the amities, enmities, passing acquaintanceships, extramarital relations, and distant cousinhoods of Assistant Principal Vernon, the Benders, the Standishes, the fellow *Breakfast Club* families of Reynoldses, Clarks, and Johnsons, plus the ever-vacationing Griswolds, the always-losing-a-kid McCallisters, and Uncle Buck's bookie." The director's 2015 biography, *John Hughes: A Life in Film*, felt it necessary to devote a sidebar to whether Shermer, Illinois, really exists.

"John never wrote anything he hadn't personally done, seen, or been a part of," wrote biographer Kirk Honeycutt. Hughes's big break, the screenplay for *National Lampoon's Vacation* (1983), came from his childhood road trips with his parents, the scripts for *Mr. Mom* (1983) and *She's Having a Baby* (1988) inspired by becoming a father in his mid-twenties. He and his girlfriend (later his wife) and best friend were an inseparable trio in high school, and the inspiration for Ferris Bueller, Cameron Frye, and Sloane Peterson. *The Breakfast Club*'s title arrived via the son of one of Hughes's friends, who told him the name kids gave Saturday morning detention at nearby New Trier High School.

Nearly all of his movies circled back to the north suburbs of Chicago, where Hughes moved as a teenager and then settled with his own family as an adult. He'd seen plenty before then, countless blocks and boulevards of Detroit near where he grew up, then endless hours going to concerts and record stores and museums in Chicago as a teenager. He'd traveled to major cities in the US, where he worked first in advertising, then for *National Lampoon*, visited Europe in the late 1970s, and was flown to New Zealand as a screenwriter in the early 1980s. Hughes also admired and read Joseph Mitchell, the great chronicler of mid-century Manhattan, and loved London and the writers and humorists who poked fun at its aristocratic traditions and the aristocrats who abided by them.

And yet the fictional suburb of Shermer, Illinois, which Hughes built from the same streets and school districts where he lived as a teenager and then raised his children, got the majority share of his creativity. All the movies he directed and most of the screenplays he wrote as *the* creator of the eighties teen film happened there. Shermer, then, feels enormous in its depth and detail but tiny in scope. John Hughes, who had been far and seen much by the time he started making movies his early thirties, only drew from this one very specific place when giving settings to those movies. The place he had lived the longest also seemed to be the only place he wanted to make movies about.

You can't really talk about a John Hughes movie without talking about Shermer, Illinois. If his best-known films deal in archetypal experiences—first kisses, breakups, fights with parents and best friends, wanting to be cool—every teenager has, Shermer became the archetypal Anytown, USA where those moments happen.

"I was a normal kid, at a normal school, trying to meet a nice girlfriend, and my parents sat down for dinner every night at a big oak table with us kids and the family dog just cute as a button begging for scraps as we laughed and talked about our day," wrote journalist Jason Diamond in a 2014 *BuzzFeed* article called "I Grew Up in a John Hughes Movie." "It always felt like that's what families in Shermer were supposed to do, because despite some kinks here and there, Shermer looked as close to normal as I could imagine."

The Shermer you see in *Sixteen Candles*, *Weird Science*, and *Ferris Bueller's Day Off* was actually a composite of normalcies from different North Shore communities like Evanston (Molly Ringwald's house, where Long Duk Dong passed out on the front lawn, is at 3022 Payne Street), Highland Park (Gary and Wyatt bring their dream girl to life via computer at 1200 Linden Avenue), and Des Plaines (*The Breakfast Club*'s "Shermer High School" is now a police station at 9511 Harrison Street). Teenage John Hughes had grown up in the village of Northbrook (the "Save Ferris" water tower is near Northbrook's public library at 1201 Cedar Lane). Northbrook was originally called "Shermerville" (after Frederick Schermer, who had donated the land for the village's train station). John Hughes came up with the name "Shermer" as an inside joke for his friends and neighbors.

Hughes, wrote Jason Diamond, "Made the suburbs seem, if not cool, at least honest. His landscapes were skillful facsimiles, noticeable to anybody who actually grew up in the type of town where the houses look the same, the lawns are kept nice and trim by some local kid getting paid $20 a job."

But it's those same landscapes that also show what we don't like to admit about our creative heroes: their work comes in equal parts from talent and limitations. John Hughes was a filmmaker of big ideas too often shoved into little boxes, an artist who wanted to let teenagers tell their own stories and have his movies take their feelings seriously, who drew from a very shallow pool of experiences to do so. His movies embody that contradiction and make where they happen the Grover's Corners, the Wittenberg, Ohio, the archetypal anywhere of the eighties teen movie. But Shermer—tree-lined, quiet, upper middle class, and white—also meant that a John Hughes movie aimed for the universals of being a teenager but didn't look very universal at all.

It's an old rule of good writing that you get to big ideas through a needle's eye of specifics. (*Moby Dick* is a novel with big ideas like man vs. nature, blinding obsession, and the deadly trap of pride that gets there via a ton of detail about whale blubber.) But as seen in Brat Pack America forerunners like *Star Wars* and *Jaws*, movies that aim to be "for everybody" never really are. Instead they are most loved by exactly who they think their biggest fans will be, who then stand in for "everybody." The fans that don't see themselves in a movie's characters will often latch onto something less central—a setting, a feeling, or a detail—and love a movie because of that. I read somewhere about a group of male *Dirty Dancing* fans who love that movie's generous use of early sixties cars.

Star Wars has a faithful following of all shapes, sizes, colors, and backgrounds, but a *Star Wars* fan convention will likely not have a bunch of former prom kings in attendance. And were someone to throw Hughestock or Shermercon, its fair to say that the bulk of attendees would be over forty and Caucasian.

"I was not a child of the North Shore [a.k.a. Shermer] by any stretch of the imagination," Chicago journalist Scott Smith, who grew up on the other side of the metro area in the south suburb of Lansing, Illinois, told me over the phone. "But if you were a white kid growing up in the suburbs at that time, his movies were incredibly relatable. Plot and characters…acted as ciphers for your own experience. The setting was generic enough that you could lay your own town right on top of it."

"I knew what I was seeing wasn't an exact replica of my high school experience," Oakland-based journalist George Kelly wrote me in an email. "I attended Benjamin Banneker Model Academic Senior High School in Washington, DC, not some suburban Illinois celluloid fantasy. We were more than 90 percent black, with strong volunteer requirements for graduation and stellar college admission rates. I was aware of the systems that weren't getting displayed, the things that were outside the frame, and I was weighing how to feel about it. Even as I remember thinking what it would have been like to see a black kid like me in *The Breakfast Club*."

"No, nobody looked like me in *Sixteen Candles*," said Denise Richards, an author and public speaker based in Miami. "There weren't even a lot of tall, athletic black girls where I grew up in Yellow Springs, Ohio. But that meant I was also a girl who never registered with a guy like Michael Schoeffling (Molly Ringwald's love interest Jake Ryan) but who had lots of friends like Anthony Michael Hall ('Farmer' Ted) back then. So I still related to it."

How did John Hughes create something so influential from a point of view so subjective and small? If John Hughes invented the modern-day archetype of the teen movie, it can't be overlooked that he did it by using one fictional town, taken from one metropolitan area, where only white teenagers seem to live, as source material.

Did John Hughes do something dishonest by claiming to make movies for all teenagers that clearly didn't include anything close to that? Or did he simply make movies from what he knew and inspired him, and their longevity speaks to how much bigger his fans saw Hughes's cinematic universe than he did?

Shermer, Illinois, the capital city of Brat Pack America, is where those contradictions collide.

"Chicago, the Teenage Hollywood"

IN THE SPRING OF 1984, the late film critic Roger Ebert visited John Hughes during principle photography of *The Breakfast Club*. Cast, crew, and director were staked out at a former high school in the north Chicago suburb of Des Plaines about twenty miles northeast of the *Chicago Sun-Times* building downtown where Ebert worked as film critic. Hughes, thirty-four and directing his second film, was not yet a superstar but on his way.

"Consider these two titles, *Sixteen Candles* and *The Breakfast Club*," Ebert wrote in the column he filed later. "They are both about fairly typical American teenagers, kids you like even when you can't always stand them. Kids who are vulnerable and serious… Both movies are set near Chicago—which…is becoming the teenage Hollywood."

Ebert had grown up in Urbana in central Illinois, 150 miles to the south, and had moved to Chicago in his early twenties to attend graduate school. He became a film critic at the *Chicago Sun-Times* at age twenty-five and lived and worked in Chicago for the next forty-six years, until his death in 2013. Hughes had grown up in the Detroit suburb of Grosse Pointe. He was a middle-class kid living in a rich neighborhood acutely aware of feeling inferior because of the size of his family's house or the street on which it sat. (He'd remember those feelings well and make them central to the screenplays for *Pretty in Pink* and *Some Kind of Wonderful*.) He had moved to Northbrook in Chicago's north suburbs at age twelve and fell deeply in love with the city, spending long weekend hours as a teenager at the Art Institute of Chicago (later used in the "museum montage" in *Ferris Bueller*).

Neither Ebert nor John Hughes were originally from Chicago, but both arrived there as young men and embraced the city like religious converts. In Hughes, Ebert saw a filmmaker doing great work in a film genre that seemed inspired by and flowering in the city they both loved.

John Hughes had a very different life trajectory in Chicago than Ebert's, which made his relationship to the city different, too.

Ebert had come to Chicago as a working person in his twenties and remained a single, childless man, going to screenings and festivals and drinking at his favorite taverns until well into his forties. Although eight years younger, John Hughes was married by age twenty, a father by twenty-six, a non-drinker who preferred to stay home and work. As an adult, he settled his family not far from where he had lived as a teenager, first in Glencoe and then the nearby suburb of Northfield. His first screenplays were written on the commuter train to his job downtown at the Leo Burnett advertising agency.

"My dad was a great urban explorer," James Hughes, thirty-seven, the director's younger son, told me over email. "When we'd visit a city as a family, he'd get up way before everyone else and just walk for a few hours. But he was also completely aware of himself as a suburbanite."

In 1979, *National Lampoon*, which had just hired Hughes as a staff writer, asked him to relocate his young family to the magazine's headquarters in New York. Hughes dismissed the request, calling New York "a great city if you cleaned it up and moved everything back ten feet." In 1984, Paramount Pictures, the studio behind *The Breakfast Club*, threatened to take the final cut of the film away from Hughes unless he relocated to Los Angeles to supervise the movie's editing and post-production. The Hughes family lived on the west side of Los Angeles from 1984–1988, at the height of the director's fame, but kept their home back in Northfield and returned to it the moment they could. Hughes didn't feel at home in Los Angeles, and made *Ferris Bueller's Day Off* during this time. ("Chicago is a working city, where people go to their jobs and raise their kids and live their lives. In Hollywood, I'd be hanging around with a lot of people who don't have to pay when they go to the movies.") In hindsight, *Ferris Bueller* seems like his "homesick for Chicago" movie. *Planes, Trains and Automobiles,* made the year after, his son told me, can be seen as his "welcome back to Chicago" movie.

Roger Ebert came to Chicago as a young adult and saw it as the place where everything happened. John Hughes came to the greater Chicago area as a teenager and saw its northern suburbs as the place where everything happened. Ebert loved Chicago as a place to work, play, and live. Hughes loved Chicago, too, but more as a point of interest than a home. In his movies, the city is off in the distance, a place of dreams and excitement. His teenage characters visit, enjoy themselves, and make mischief in Chicago. They don't live there or typically stick around after dark.

Ignore the hairstyles and acid-washed jeans, and this is where John Hughes's movies seem most dated. Here in the twenty-first century, when was the last time you saw a movie about teenagers visiting the big dangerous city and running back to the safe suburbs before nightfall? But the eighties teen movie coincided with the low point for the American metropolis. Starbucks, yoga studios, and loft apartments wouldn't make their presence felt in city neighborhoods until the 1990s, when John Hughes had quit directing altogether. Maybe before then, his movies both reflected the reality of life in Chicago and its northern suburbs and the uniformity of those suburbs he drew such inspiration from.

John Hughes didn't fear cities. He'd spent plenty of time exploring them both before and after becoming famous, and encouraged his children to, as well. "When I was going to concerts in Chicago as a kid, I thought I was building a good track record," James Hughes wrote to me. "Then my dad would quietly unspool the list of concerts he saw in Chicago in the sixties and seventies, which defied belief. The more he opened up about his adolescent days, and his years as a copywriter and creative director in the city in his twenties, I realized he'd logged more hours experiencing meaningful culture in the city than I'd previously known." As James Hughes also reminded me, both *Ferris Bueller's Day Off* and *Planes, Trains and Automobiles* are legitimate love letters to Chicago: its skyscrapers, lakefronts, and elevated trains.

"My father was drawn to fish-out-of-water scenarios, and he mined those situations for comedic effect," James Hughes continued. "I don't interpret his depictions of suburban kids in cities as judgments of urbanites or cautionary tales about being out after dark. It was simply a chance to see characters out of their element. Likewise, characters played by John Candy in *Uncle*

Buck (1989) or Alec Baldwin in *She's Having a Baby* (1988) were urbanites who were mystified by suburban rituals."

Both of these films happened later in Hughes's directing career, after he had moved on from movies about teenagers to movies about kids and families. As those interests shifted, the geography of his movies got bigger, too. *Ferris Bueller*, the fourth film he directed, happens in the north suburbs of Chicago, but mostly the city itself. His three teen movies that came before—*Sixteen Candles*, *Weird Science*, and *The Breakfast Club*—happen entirely in Shermer and never make it to Chicago. After *Ferris*, the majority of Hughes-directed movies have characters traveling (*Planes, Trains and Automobiles*) or relocating to chase opportunity (*She's Having a Baby, Curly Sue*). They often end up in Chicago's north suburbs but have considerable stretches of time filmed elsewhere.

It would seem that despite how completely John Hughes saw Shermer, Illinois, in his imagination, he relied on it less and less the further he got from making movies about teenagers. Let's visit Shermer and see if it provides some answers why.

The "Hughes-iverse"

OF THE HALF-DOZEN MOVIES about teenagers John Hughes wrote or directed, four take place in Shermer, Illinois. The two that don't—*Pretty in Pink* and *Some Kind of Wonderful*—were written by Hughes but directed by Howard Deutch, a music video director who went on to direct nearly a dozen other movies you've heard of (*The Great Outdoors, Article 99*). Deutch filmed both *Pink* and *Wonderful* in Los Angeles, which we'll discuss in the next chapter.

Shermer, as Hughes's movies showed it, consisted of wide green lawns, Tudor-style downtowns ringed with trees and diagonal parking, and high schools that looked either like the summer castles of English nobility or battleships make of brick. Practically speaking, the image of Shermer comes from an assortment of locations and scenes Hughes and his team filmed in separate movies over a four-year span.

John Hughes worked fast. He pitched *Weird Science* to Anthony Michael Hall during the filming of *The Breakfast Club*, a few months before *Sixteen Candles* landed in theaters. *Weird Science* and *The Breakfast Club* were then released within six months of each other in 1985. Between their release dates, he completed the screenplay for *Ferris Bueller's Day Off*, which he wrote in a week.

Hughes's first three movies as director were made practically at the same time. And since he never wanted his work to disrupt family life ("When he had three movies in production, he must have spent an incredible amount of time away from home," said James Hughes. "But I never sensed his absence."), he filmed them all not far from home and not far from each other. Shermer, which is mentioned most directly in *The Breakfast Club* and only in the background of *Weird Science* and *Sixteen Candles*, came to life onscreen as much out of efficiency as its creator's imagination.

"John understood the subtleties of the different towns and villages around here," Billy Higgins, location manager of *Sixteen Candles* and most of the other films Hughes directed, told me over the phone. "I'd start with a basic marching list and refine from there. He would know that, say, Molly Ringwald's family in *Sixteen Candles* might live in Evanston, but not on a street of Old World mansions in Evanston where a famous Northwestern University professor would live, or that a church in Glencoe might be one her family would hold a wedding at more than a church in Winnetka."

In those years before digital photography, Higgins told me he'd spend the morning shooting nearly a hundred rolls of film of prospective locations, drop them off at a photo lab in the afternoon, then spend the evening pinning up pictures of the best finds to boards. Higgins and Hughes would then meet at the director's home or the Northfield Diner the next morning to go over what he found.

"John knew what he wanted, how Skokie would work better for this scene than Kenilworth," said Higgins. "But he also let me bring in my own ideas." Something practically everyone who worked with Hughes would also say. "Originally, the scene of the Ferrari crashing in *Ferris Bueller* was written very differently, until

I found the house with the glass garage and suggested we could use that instead."

That house where that Ferrari meets its untimely end sits at 370 N. Beech Street in Highland Park, walking distance from Wyatt's house in *Weird Science* at 280 Cedar Avenue, where outlaw bikers and missiles growing out of the floor raid the party our heroes throw. About four blocks away stands Jake Ryan's house at 1407 Waverly Road, site of the giant party in *Sixteen Candles*. The kiss that ends *Sixteen Candles*—dining-room table, birthday cake, and all—was filmed on the actual dining-room table of the house. One scene earlier, Samantha Baker got in Jake's Ryan's Porsche in front of Glencoe Union Church at 263 Park Avenue in the town of Glencoe, four miles due south. Ferris Bueller and friends go to Glenbrook North High School at 2300 Shermer Road, which Hughes himself graduated from in 1968, five miles to the west. Only five miles south from there sits the town of Des Plaines, where John Bender raises his fist at the end of detention in *The Breakfast Club,* walking across the Maine North High School football field at 9511 Harrison Street.

Plot each of these on a map and you can visit them all in an afternoon. Drive a little above the speed limit and you can visit most of John Hughes's cinematic universe and still be home by dark.

That's also how John Hughes saw Shermer in his imagination. The kids from *Sixteen Candles* probably knew Ferris Bueller, or at least the myth of him, from school. Roughneck Charlie Sheen from *Ferris* probably lived in the same scruffier part of Shermer as "criminal" Judd Nelson from *The Breakfast Club*. Even later, when he wrote and directed movies less about teenagers than families and kids, he imagined Uncle Buck and Del Griffith from *Planes, Trains and Automobiles* (both played by John Candy) were probably in the same bowling league or that the McCallisters (Macaulay Culkin's family in *Home Alone*) probably sat on the PTA with Samantha Baker's mom from *Sixteen Candles*.

Many in the generation of filmmakers who cite Hughes as an influence have adopted a version of Shermer to stage their own movies. Kevin Smith, who I believe gets credit for the term "Hughes-iverse," modeled his own interlocking movies about the Northern New Jersey suburbs—*Clerks, Mallrats, Chasing Amy*—on Hughes's Shermer, Illinois. Judd Apatow, who cites Hughes as an influence and often gets named as his successor, likes to set his movies in Los Angeles, featuring characters living three to a studio apartment, as Apatow did before success kicked in. Apatow doesn't use a lot of repeat locations or characters, but his tendency to cycle the same actors through his films at different levels—a lead in one Apatow production might have been a supporting player in the movie before and make a cameo in the movie after—gives the impression that the Apatow universe, even in a major city like Los Angeles, is small enough that the residents probably know one another. Jason Reitman, who on the 25th Anniversary "Buller... Bueller...Edition" DVD called *Ferris Bueller* "the perfect movie" and has organized staged readings of *Ferris* and *The Breakfast Club*, works the Hughes-iverse idea in reverse: Reitman's movies—*Juno, Up in the Air, Young Adult*—feel placeless on purpose. The action in the foreground—snappy, memorable dialogue, young people tugging at their leashes, characters that seem both aware of yet fall for their own melodrama—feels very John Hughes. But Reitman's characters also feel like they've got a foot out the door, heading somewhere other than where the movie has them now, perhaps fitting a filmmaker who grew up on movie sets (Jason Reitman is the son of director Ivan Reitman) and a twenty-first-century sensibility of "place" as a more vague and complicated idea.

The Homesickness of *Ferris Bueller's Day Off*

IN 1984, RIGHT AFTER filming *The Breakfast Club*, John Hughes had to relocate his family to Los Angeles, where they would stay until 1988 and then move back to Chicago's north suburbs. But even living across the country did not stop Hughes from continuing to build out the map of Shermer and its relationship to the city nearby. In a now out-of-print director's commentary of *Ferris Bueller's Day Off*, the only director's commentary Hughes ever did, his first line of narration is effectively how annoyed he was that the Bueller house was in Long Beach, California (at 4160 Country Club Drive, if you'd like to see it) because they couldn't find the right house near Chicago. Most of the rest of the movie is luxuriously, resplendently Chicago, and Hughes didn't leave many of his favorite places out: Lake Shore Drive, the giant red Alexander Calder sculpture *Flamingo* downtown (Cameron and Sloane are standing in front of it when Ferris hijacks the parade), and the Art Institute of Chicago, Hughes's old teenage hangout where, as an adult, he became the first filmmaker allowed to shoot there.

"I wanted lots of shots of Chicago," he tells his DVD audience during the gorgeous aerial footage of the city skyline when Ferris and friends first drive in and the song "Beat City" pounds away on the soundtrack. "It was my city and I wanted to show it at its best." Other than a few scenes filmed in Los Angeles—the pizza parlor where Principal Rooney threatens an imaginary Ferris who turns out to be a girl, the restaurant where Ferris pretends to be Abe Froman, "the sausage king of Chicago"—*Ferris Bueller's Day Off* is all Chicago, maybe the best the city has ever looked in a movie set there.

And yet if you plot where Ferris, Cameron, and Sloane went in Chicago on their day off, their stops would be close enough together to make Chicago look about the size of Shermer. Other than the Cubs game at Wrigley Field (and to be fair, Hughes was a White Sox fan who wanted to shoot at their stadium on Chicago's south side—it wasn't available), all of the events of *Ferris Bueller's Day Off* happen in the downtown loop or the city's near north side, about where you'd go if you were in from Cody, Wyoming, visiting Chicago for the first time, not a local from a couple of train stops away.

"Anyone who grew up nearby knows that Ferris and Cameron and Sloane do only the most touristy and familiar things to do in Chicago, if you've ever been there before," Scott Smith told me. "These kids live right up north, and yet the movie doesn't give you a full sense of the city, only the safe aspects of the city. "

"It's not like *Blues Brothers*, which took you to gritty, out-of-the-way places most people outside Chicago—and even some who lived here—had never seen. Even *Blues Brothers*, which had a lot of fantastical elements, still feels more real than the theme-park Chicago version of *Ferris Bueller*."

"Chicago at the time was a super divided place, Harold Washington as the first black mayor, the race wars that came out of that election," said Erin Shea Smith, an SVP at Weber Shandwick PR in Chicago. "My dad commuted from working-class Joliet south of the city to downtown, and what crime looked like downtown was appreciably different. The garage where Ferris parks the Ferrari, areas in the loop like that were very gritty… The West loop, before Oprah put her studio there, was desolate and crime-ridden."

A gritty downtown dotted with a few touristy high points might have been 100 percent accurate to John Hughes and kids from up north, who got a sanitized look at a day playing hooky in Chicago from this movie. It still leaves us in the present with a few of the more troubling moments of *Ferris Bueller's Day Off*, where the movie seems uncomfortably narrated from a position of suburban privilege. There's Ferris asking a swarthy garage attendant (Richard Edson) if he speaks English. (The attendant replies, "What country do you think this is?" then proceeds to steal Cameron's dad's Ferrari with his African-American colleague.) There's the all African-American group of dancers popping and locking in sync during the "Twist & Shout" parade scene. Hughes explains during his DVD commentary that the garage-attendant-joyriding-the-Ferrari plot exists to give Cameron a reason to stand up to his dad and to grab an amazing shot of the city's skyline as the Ferrari hurls into the distance. He also says that the dancers were a local troupe hired specifically for the parade scene, an actual German Day parade, where Hughes and crew grabbed many ordinary people downtown just plain having fun (the construction worker dancing on scaffolding and a baby dancing in a stroller were unplanned), and to see Dearborn Street in downtown Chicago on a beautiful fall Saturday. All of which are perfectly reasonable explanations. But at times it can also feel like the local color Ferris and friends experience in Chicago seems to arrive in the form of people of color.

And there's Ferris's practically drooling at the chance to drive a luxury car, over his best friend Cameron's objections. "It is true that while his heroes, most notably Ferris Bueller…are in conflict with authority, they are also stubborn in their individualism and often unapologetically materialistic," said *New York Times* film critic A. O. Scott of the director in an appraisal. We also know there won't be any real consequences for Ferris and friends. The worst-case scenario comes in the form of evil Principal Rooney (Jeffrey Jones) making good on his threat to hold Ferris back another year. But were they to end up in the hospital or in jail, there'd be money and parents to bail them out.

"Essentially, anyone who sees Ferris as a hero ignores the fact that he's manipulative and self-centered," writer Will Stegemann told me. "Cameron is the only one who risks anything of real value and faces any consequences in that movie. I think that teenagers love Ferris because they feel powerless, but mature adults understand consequences and can identify with Cameron."

Hughes keeps most of his *Ferris Bueller's Day Off* commentary to how the movie celebrates the city of his childhood memories, of beautiful skylines and boulevards and favorite places in the most visited areas of town. It also pays tribute to his high school best friend, who served as the model for Cameron, and a certain kind of teenage disposition that fascinated him and he imbued in Ferris Bueller, when you feel a power that comes in part from not knowing whom you may hurt with it. "Ferris Bueller is generous, but not virtuous," Hughes says. He doesn't speak of the movie's economic or cultural point of view, but he doesn't say we should be emulating Ferris Bueller's approach to or outlook on life either.

"Being a working-class, Latina kid in the suburbs, I saw this kind of fake rebellion all the time," said Veronica Arreola, the assistant director of the University of Illinois at Chicago's Center for Research on Women and Gender. "I went to middle and high school with rich kids having their Ferris Bueller moments and thinking they were badasses for it but always having a safety net to fall into… Today, a John Hughes movie might look narrow-minded, limiting. But back then, there were in fact only a few African-American kids at my school. I was one of only a few Latinas in my honors and AP classes."

"Artists write what they know, and their worldview is incomplete," Arreola continued. "That's the problem with deeming anything the universal experience. Lena Dunham's experience looks nothing like most of the young women of her generation."

Arreola, who grew up in the northwest suburbs of Chicago, now lives with her family in the Rogers Park neighborhood on the city's North Side.

"I graduated from high school in June and was in my Chicago apartment by July," she told me. "Whatever message was in *Ferris Bueller* about Chicago being a place you visited then left was completely lost on me. I couldn't wait to get there and stay."

The Shermer of *Ferris Bueller* is largely there as a contrast to Chicago and is never mentioned by name. In fact, only one John Hughes movie does, and another comes close. The town in *Weird Science* has an ugly green neon sign screaming, "Welcome to Shermer, Illinois!" that flickers when the boys (who go to Shermer High School, their gym uniforms tell us) throw the power on their girlfriend-making personal computer. The bedroom that contains that computer is thick with Sears Tower posters and Cubs memorabilia, and so when Lisa, the robot girlfriend (Kelly Le Brock), offers to take them "into town," it's unlikely she's talking about Milwaukee. But it's *The Breakfast Club* that gave us the name Shermer, and also shows the least of the town itself, the movie with exactly one location (indoors) that makes incredibly wise use of the very idea of location.

Saturday, March 24, 1984

THE BREAKFAST CLUB OPENS by namedropping its own birthday. After the onscreen quote from David Bowie's "Changes" (suggested to Hughes by cast member Ally Sheedy) shatters like a brick thrown through a window, we get a low wide shot on the front door of a high school. A familiar, frightened voice whispers:

Saturday, March 24, 1984. Shermer High School, Shermer, Illinois, 60062 (a.k.a. Hughes's own zip code).

The line is part inside joke (the movie began principal photography the week of March 24, 1984), part date stamp for reasons that only become clear by the last scene. Anthony Michael Hall's character Brian opens a letter to the evil Principal Vernon with this line. His letter frames the movie. But we don't know that when *The Breakfast Club* starts, so the date only tells us where we are and when: it's probably after spring break, but still cold outside (the cast is all wearing multiple layers and winter coats). The area around the school, best we can tell, is large(r) houses with neat lawns, probably upper middle class. We'll see in a second that the school seems well-funded enough to have an enormous central library containing a fifteen-foot-high work of modern art and a radio station control room. But it looks like only two of the kids in detention come from that level of privilege: Molly Ringwald and Ally Sheedy's characters arrive in fancy cars (a BMW and a Cadillac) driven by their parents. Emilio Estevez and Anthony Michael Hall arrive in far more modest vehicles. Judd Nelson's John Bender walks.

That's about all we can tell about Shermer, Illinois, from *The Breakfast Club*, the only one of John Hughes's teen movies to mention the town by name. What can we tell about these five kids from Shermer High School who must spend an entire Saturday together in detention?

First off, it's not exactly clear how old these teenagers are. In real life, Judd Nelson was twenty-four, Estevez twenty-two, Ally Sheedy twenty, and Molly Ringwald and Anthony Michael Hall both sixteen. We sense that Anthony Michael Hall's character Brian is younger than the rest of them and Molly Ringwald's character has to be old enough to be elected prom queen. But other than that, we get Carl the janitor's (John Kapelos) remark about "following shitheads like you around with the broom for the last eight years," and not much else. Does that mean Shermer

High School is sixth through twelfth grade, or that Carl's been on the job for eight years? It's never explained. Also, though Andrew (Estevez) has the opportunity for a college athletic scholarship and Brian mentions needing to maintain his GPA, presumably to get into a good school, the characters rarely discuss the future or their plans for it. Other than a generalized dread of becoming the kind of adults their parents are, there seems almost nothing happening in the world of *The Breakfast Club* outside of here and now.

The Breakfast Club is a movie resolutely in the present. We learn about the characters in the same way and at the same pace that they learn about each other. It feels to me like an adolescent *Iceman Cometh*, a chorus of characters imprisoned and waiting for something to happen who realize they are the only something that will.

John Hughes shot *The Breakfast Club* at Maine North High School in Des Plaines, Illinois. The school had recently been shut down due to consolidation, and the hallways where the cast flees Principal Vernon were used a year later in *Ferris Bueller's Day Off*, where students try to collect money for Ferris's "illness" only to be met with "Go piss up a flagpole" by his doubting younger sister. The library where all-day detention happens was built in the school's gymnasium. The actors dressed in nearby classrooms and bunked down at a glamour-free hotel near O'Hare Airport. Hughes didn't want his cast thinking about being young actors with careers on the rise, the allure of Chicago down the freeway, or having the spell of an immersive story like this one broken.

"We rehearsed it like a play…just sitting together and we just read through the script every day…like a family praying together," Anthony Michael Hall remembered for the 2010 book *You Couldn't Ignore Me If You Tried: The Brat Pack, John Hughes, and Their Impact on a Generation.*

The shoot lasted just over a month, but Hughes and his team had to make it look like one day. Harder still, the entire movie took place in a single setting (the crew joked it should have been called *Long Day's Journey into Detention*), and the movie's plot, mission, and eventual tagline was, "Five strangers with nothing in common, except each other." That meant the built library that housed the entire film had to begin as a place of isolation and anger and turn, over ninety minutes, into a place of warmth and togetherness.

Watching *The Breakfast Club* for perhaps the fiftieth time, it is still remarkable how everyone working on the movie made this happen. Costume designer Marilyn Vance dressed the actors in layers that come off as the intimacy between them grows. Cinematographer Thomas Del Ruth shoots the opening scenes with cold industrial lighting in brutal, static colors (the orange of the school lockers looks like the color of prison jumpsuits), but as the day goes on, the library becomes airier, almost hazy. Hughes's screenplay deliberately removes the adults for the last third of the movie, quietly guiding the story from being about the unfairness of detention to what is happening to the students serving it. And the final moments, where the characters sit on the floor and understand that, somehow, without any of them knowing how or trying to, they have become friends, are blocked with the cast facing away from the entire library set, their former prison in soft focus behind them.

Those last scenes comprised thirty-five pages of script, took three days of filming, and came near the end of the shoot. The movie was originally over two hours long, Hughes was behind schedule, and the studio was angry and frustrated with him. One of those three days was the day Roger Ebert visited, and on that day, both Anthony Michael Hall and Ally Sheedy had to break down and cry, their dialogue explaining that Hall's character had considered suicide and Sheedy's saying the now immortal line, "When you grow up, your heart dies." According to Hughes, the whole set, including Ebert, was crying with them. I like to think it was the moment they saw the theme of the movie come to life: we are more alike than we realize.

The Breakfast Club was John Hughes's most personal film, the vessel for his highest ideals: that difference does not equal destiny, that trying to be good usually results in being good, and that struggles that seem so basic to an adult can feel like life or death to a teenager, and we should take that seriously because teenagers do.

Not coincidentally, *The Breakfast Club* is also the Hughes movie that identifies itself as coming from Shermer, the place where the filmmaker saw all his movies happening—the cinematic landscape of his mind and imagination. *The Breakfast Club* was his second movie as a director but intended to be his first. No surprise that it's also the one to declare the existence of the town that was Hughes's creation but also his muse.

It's clear that the environment and personal experience Hughes drew from to create Shermer had limitations. The kids do talk about class and money, about how some of them, as John Bender said, "have everything and I don't have shit." The movie has a certain bravery and prescience around gender issues, too. (The slut/prude trap for teenage girls the characters discuss shows up in other eighties teen movies. None of them get into how the unfairness of this either/or hurts everyone involved the way *The Breakfast Club* does.) But that they are all white kids shows us that the dream Hughes put into *The Breakfast Club*, of teenagers seeing past their differences, only went so far.

"So much of John Hughes was like a handbook for me, negotiating being a working-class kid at a middle and high school in the suburbs with rich kids," Veronica Arreola told me. "Even though none of those kids were Mexican-American like me."

The Breakfast Club was Hughes's first box-office success as a director, eventually grossing nearly fifty times its budget when it was released in February of 1985. The theme song "Don't You Forget About Me" by the Scottish band Simple Minds became a number-one song in America. In 2012, *Entertainment Weekly* called *The Breakfast Club* the greatest high school movie of all time.

The film's last scene has the cast leaving detention at the end of the day and Principal Vernon reading the letter Brian has written: "What we found out is that each of us is a brain and an athlete and a basket case and a princess and a criminal." The music gets louder, and in the distance Judd Nelson walks alone across the school's athletic field. When he gets close enough to fill the center of the frame, he throws a fist in the air. Freeze frame. Roll credits.

Filmmaker Kevin Smith called it "truth concentrate in every way. It helped shaped an entire generation."

What to make of that moment? Has John Bender given a victory salute because he got to kiss the prom queen? Because he and his new friends have stuck it to their shithead principal? Because he made friends he thought he'd never have? Or maybe he felt, at the end of this very hard day, that his world had opened up. And as the sun comes down on Shermer, Illinois, in the movie that named it, in a place whose chief value seems a lack of surprises—in a remembrance of Hughes, *New York Times* film critic A. O. Scott called Shermer "a pastoral city on a hill where everyone is comfortable and everyone's the same"—maybe the moment says that even here, in a single day, everything can be different.

The "Shermer" of today looks different, too. Nearly 20 percent of Des Plaines residents are Latino. The northernmost neighborhoods of Chicago, 90 percent white in 1980, have no majority ethnic group as of 2010. A demographic map of the Chicago metropolitan area published in the Spring 2010 issue of *Perspecta*, the journal of the Yale School of Architecture, shows large patches of the city's northern suburbs with significant African-American and Asian-American populations.

That wasn't the world John Hughes drew from. But it's what Shermer, Illinois looks like now.

The final shot of the *The Breakfast Club* was filmed on the last day of shooting. According to a 1999 oral history article called "Teen Days that Shook the World," the cast and crew knew something very special was coming to an end. Hughes had also received the order from Paramount, the movie's studio, that he would have to relocate his family to Los Angeles to keep *The Breakfast Club* from falling into someone else's hands. "I was heartbroken," he said. Once they had the right take of John Bender and his raised fist, Hughes yelled, "Cut. We got it." Nelson just kept walking until he was out of sight. Hughes, too sad for ceremony and too angry at having to move away from the place he loved and that loved his art back, said nothing, got in his car, and drove away.

The Chicago that John Hughes Built

In 1980, *My Bodyguard* had begun pulling teen movies of the period toward the city of Chicago. John Hughes gave them the great yank while defining "Chicago" very differently. His love for the city and its suburbs looms large in the history of Chicago filmmaking. In the 1970s, an average of three movies a year were filmed in Chicago. In the 1980s, that number jumps to twelve. Thanks to movies like *My Bodyguard* and *The Blues Brothers* (1980) prying open the door to Chicago as a movie location, and then to John Hughes kicking that door down, production in the city still comes in regular waves rather than occasional spurts. According to the Chicago Film Office, the 1990s saw an average of twenty movies a year filmed in the Chicago area; the 2000s, twenty-five.

But John Hughes also influenced how Chicago appeared onscreen while still directing movies there. *Lucas* (1986), another great movie from this time with astute, sensitive treatment of teenagers, was shot in the western suburb of Glen Ellyn. A few scattered scenes were filmed in Chicago itself, but the city, along with wherever *Lucas* takes place, is never mentioned. *Lucas*, writer/director David Seltzer's directorial debut, is light on plot, but has thoughtful, deep focus on characters and friendship. It's possible that seltzer, who grew up in the north suburb of Highland Park, wanted to make his first movie close to home. It's possible that he considered it autobiographical. But I also think that for a movie so much about its characters and the wonder of growing up (*Lucas*'s central metaphor is the locust, an insect helpless in its own body until it can fully fly), a setting that called attention to itself would have seemed distracting. By 1986, John Hughes had made Chicago's northern suburbs the everyplace, all-purpose background where teen movies occured. *Lucas* succeeds at being a great teenage character study in part by the setting for great teenage character studies John Hughes created.

That same summer, *About Last Night*, the story of a young couple in their twenties (Rob Lowe and Demi Moore) getting together and breaking up while being supported and criticized by their more interesting best friends (Elizabeth Perkins and Jim Belushi) became a box-office hit. The directorial debut of Chicago native Ed Zwick, *About Last Night* is not only based on a play by Chicago-based David Mamet, but also entirely set against the backdrop of iconic Chicago places—Grant Park, Wrigley Field, the Michigan Avenue Bridge. Much like *My Bodyguard* six years earlier, *About Last Night* does not contain a single scene outside the city limits.

Rob Lowe and Demi Moore would next make *St. Elmo's Fire*, the movie that would group them, along with John Hughes's favorite actors, under the heading "The Brat Pack." This makes *About Last Night* look something like a movie about what happens to John Hughes's characters when they grow up, get jobs, and move out of suburbs like Shermer and into the city. These characters are following Roger Ebert's path instead of Hughes's.

Whose Hughes?

As PART OF A tribute to John Hughes during the 2010 Academy Awards, Molly Ringwald said, "John's genius was taking the pain of growing up and relating it to everyone." This nails what is both magical and difficult about him and his movies: a John Hughes film says what it wants to more through feelings than plot. Every teenager has had the same emotional highs and crushing lows of his characters. Very few teenagers have served all-day detention, roomed with a caricature named Long Duk Dong, or taken over a German Day Parade.

Emotional realism paired with plots that lean toward exaggeration and fantasy give a Hughes movie a mythical air. Some of that also comes from the debt they owe to reality-free Hollywood movies from an earlier era. John Hughes loved old movies and wolfed them down as a teenager. *Ferris Bueller's Day Off* is essentially *On the Town* (1949) told with high school students instead of sailors on leave. *Sixteen Candles*' girl-boy-girl's-weird-friend setup makes it a niece of Doris Day/Rock Hudson movies from the early 1960s.

But Hughes was also a good long way from being a teenager when he started making movies about them. By that time, he was a married father of two, living in the same Chicago suburbs where he had once been the age of his characters. Part of his genius, then, must come from this return to the place of his own adolescence: by raising his own kids where he'd been a teenager, he could see being a teenager from both up close and afar.

Because of where they happen and what kinds of citizens John Hughes's cinematic universe does and doesn't include, his movies are all-encompassing and archetypal, yet specific and a bit suffocating all at once. Their genius was to understand that the drama of being a teenager may not have really been as consequential as it felt, but that didn't make the feelings any less real. Or any less important for adults, particularly those tasked with telling the story of teenagers, to take seriously.

But is a John Hughes movie trying to tell the story of all teenagers, or just those teenage lives he heard about, or once experienced himself? Is it fair to criticize his work for seeming a little stodgy with its casting, a little too unaware of the position of privilege it spoke from? Or do we only have these criticisms *because* so many fans of so many different backgrounds found something of their own teenage selves in the movies of John Hughes? Do we only think he failed at the former after succeeding so monumentally at the latter?

As far as John Hughes's less-than-progressive moments, I'll say this: I think Long Duk Dong in *Sixteen Candles* is a dumb, juvenile stereotype, elevated to a force-of-nature comedic performance by Gedde Watanabe, as great as John Belushi in *Animal House*. The saloon of ill repute in *Weird Science* that mysteriously contains only black patrons and the immigrant parking attendants who joyride Cameron's Ferrari in *Ferris Bueller* are lazy, obvious caricatures, beneath the talents of a writer as gifted as Hughes. But for a guy who cut his teeth at *National Lampoon* and wrote jokes for Rodney Dangerfield in his early twenties, dumb, juvenile, and obvious were in his comic DNA. When it came to comedy, Hughes didn't discriminate by color or ethnicity. The three movies I just named are filled with many other varieties of stupid, childish stereotypes—fussy grandparents, moronic sons-in-law, snotty restaurant maître d's. If Hughes hated anyone, as all his movies make clear, it was the petty tyrant, the bully, and the resentful adult who hates kids. That said, there was nothing keeping him from casting non-white actors (post *Fast Times at Ridgemont High*, Forest Whitaker would have made a great Athlete in *The Breakfast Club*), other than maybe a lack of imagination and that he probably didn't see too many of them running around the north suburbs of Chicago, his well of inspiration.

When John Hughes died, on August 6, 2009, a predictable rush to claim his work as belonging to this or that camp followed. Kevin Smith, speaking for filmmakers his age, called Hughes "Our J. D. Salinger." Courtney Love weighed in, calling *The Breakfast Club* "the defining moment for the alternative generation." Conservative publications like *The American Spectator* hurried to label Hughes one of filmmaking's few out and proud Republicans, an artist whose characters believe in self-sufficiency, loyalty, and hard work, a guy who hung out with Ben Stein (deliverer of the immortal line "Bueller, Bueller" before becoming a game show host and Fox News talking head) and P. J. O'Rourke. I would argue that these same conservatives who claim Hughes as their own probably get some charge out of his movies seeming to place extraordinary value on the experiences of ordinary but exclusively white teenagers.

What makes John Hughes's movies both great and a great starting point for our story is they, and he, were never that simple. They give dignity to teenagers while showing how hard it can be for teenagers to give dignity to themselves. They revolutionized adolescent cinema in kaleidoscopic fashion by painting with a limited palette of adolescent types, places, and experiences. They embodied the 1980s by drawing from influences both of that time and many decades before it. And they created something called Brat Pack America, an eighties teen cinema all about place, by happening in a very limited number of places.

John Hughes's work would be the pop music of the eighties teen movie genre, the mainstream by which both imitators and revisers would measure themselves. Maybe, then, Hughes's real achievement can be seen not just in his movies, but in how rich and varied the category he personified would become around him.

The rest of our journey is how that happened.

BRAT PACK AMERICA TALKS TO...ACTOR GEDDE WATANABE (A.K.A. LONG DUK DONG OF SIXTEEN CANDLES)

ASK SOMEONE TO QUOTE a line from *Sixteen Candles* and there's a good chance it was uttered by Gedde Watanabe. Thanks to "What's happenin', hot stuff?" "Ohhh, sexy girlfriend!" and (my favorite) "Auto-Moovil?" his character, Long Duk Dong, lives on in ringtones, comedic folklore, and a debate about whether he's an offensive stereotype or just a caricature, like nearly every other supporting role in the movie.

Long Duk Dong was Gedde Watanabe's film debut. In the years since, he has appeared more than two dozen movies (*Gung Ho, UHF, Parental Guidance*), played Nurse Yosh on *ER*, and done voice work for *Disney* and *The Simpsons*.

Kevin Smokler: You're now part of the adolescence of two generations.

Gedde Watanabe: Actually, it's quite incredible. I'm still sideswiped by it all. I did an autograph show in New Jersey and a screening in California with Debbie Pollack, who played Long Duk Dong's girlfriend Marlene. Maybe because it's been so many years since the movie, and even several years since I've seen it, I expected, like, two people to show up. And when so many did, and brought their kids and talked about how much the movie meant to them, I don't know—I'm humbled and I'm grateful. It also says so much about John Hughes, his movies, their resilience, and his brilliance. Bless his heart, because we don't have him anymore.

KS: How did you get the part of Long Duk Dong?

GW: I was living in New York and had been in the original cast of [Stephen Sondheim's] *Pacific Overtures* and done work with the Public Theater and Joe Papp. My agent at the time sent me the script. It said the character of Long Duk Dong was a foreign exchange student and from Asia, but that was about it.

To set myself apart, I asked a friend of mine who had a thick Korean accent if I could hang out with him and learn. I then went to the audition in character using my friend's accent, which wasn't a very smart idea because I was basically lying and would have to tell them at some point that I only spoke English and was one of the few Japanese-American kids from my hometown of Ogden, Utah.

The casting director, Jackie Burch, kept talking to me like I was from another country. Finally, I had to admit I was lying. She wanted me for the role and said, "Don't tell John [Hughes]." So we kept it a secret until the table read in Chicago, when I took him aside and said, "John, I have to tell you something." He said, "Where's your accent?" I was just so nervous telling him that I was afraid I'd get fired. But John just had a big chuckle as if to say, "Boy was I duped."

KS: What was working with John Hughes like?

GW: John made a movie shoot a situation where you want to join in, jump in the hot tub, and try things. Oh, let's try this, you want to try this? Sure, let's try this. It was always, "Let's go play."

Like in the scene where I'm lying on the lawn the next morning after the big party. We did so many takes that my voice got hoarse and I couldn't laugh anymore. The way we got that take is John found a feather and started tickling my feet. Then I couldn't stop laughing, but the crew couldn't either!

The scene on the exercise bike was another one of those "let's try this" moments. I found an exercise bike upstairs where we were shooting that day and told about John about it. I figured the character had seen one before and knew what to do with it, but there was something funny in him riding it with his dream girl. So that scene worked its way into the script. I'm kind of hit or miss with improv, but that scene stayed.

I've worked with directors where you hesitated. With John, you wanted to make sure he got what he wanted, but never felt censored as an actor and didn't hesitate to try anything. I guess the right word for that is safe.

You just don't want a shooting experience like that to end. You wish they could all be like that. And because it was my first movie, I thought all the movies were going to be like that.

KS: *Sixteen Candles* was filmed in the northern Chicago suburbs of Skokie, Glencoe, and Evanston in the summer of 1983. I'm guessing at that time there weren't a lot of other Japanese-Americans running around. What was that experience like?

GW: I gotta say, with John, you felt so protected. I never felt out of place or like I didn't belong. Everyone on set was just so much fun. I actually felt sorry for Molly [Ringwald] and Anthony [Michael Hall], who were fifteen at the time and had their parents on set with them. I was twenty-eight, so I could drive, take trips to Chicago, go out on my own. I didn't feel stuck anywhere.

But I was so new to movies I didn't think much about where I was. I was mostly worried about hitting my marks and stuff like that.

KS: Where did the character of Long Duk Dong come from?

GW: My training and my teachers had taught me that getting a character is about going for the intention. The Donger loved everything about America—the fun, the girls, the cars. So I didn't so much go for the jokes, but played to his excitement and enthusiasm.

On one of the DVD extras, I think I said something about the movie being about "the innocence of Molly wanting to find the right guy and me wanting to find the right America." There's also a few deleted scenes out there, one of the Donger and Marlene having a smoke in bed and one of him rapping. I really hope Universal puts those on a future DVD release.

KS: You've heard a thousand times that Long Duk Dong is an offensive stereotype of a young Asian man who just arrived in this country.

GW: Yes, and all I'll say about that is that, because there weren't enough Asians on screen, comedy was kind of looked down upon. I was not in the film business. I was studying theater in New York. It was my first movie, and I had no idea what I was stepping into.

I know that periphery is loosening. But because there were so few Asian actors on screen at that time, people were looking for Kurosawa in a comedy and *Sixteen Candles* wasn't that kind of movie.

KS: And to single out your character to me misses the point. *Sixteen Candles* is filled with stereotypes—from blonde queen bees to uptight grandparents and bratty little brothers—which makes Molly Ringwald's very normal desire for a great sixteenth birthday and a handsome boyfriend seem that much funnier.

GW: Yes, the movie isn't mean to the character and doesn't single him out. A lot of people complained when the grandmother kicked me. Why does the Asian kid need to get kicked?

KS: But the grandmother kicks Long Duk Dong because he's been out partying and not being the nice studious Asian boy she thought she was getting when she agreed to a foreign exchange student from China.

GW: Exactly. Maybe indirectly, John thought he was breaking a stereotype.

KS: Have you ever gotten as wasted as Long Duk Dong did?

GW: Of course I have. Are you kidding? Especially when I was living in New York in the 1970s. And I did a lot of singing in piano bars that closed at 4:00 a.m. So flat on my back after falling out of a cab? Oh please, yes.

KS: If Long Duk Dong, Takahara from *Gung Ho*, and Nurse Yosh from *ER* all met, would they recognize that they all came from the same man?

GW: No, not at all. I like to put on the mask. I do better with somebody other than myself. I love putting on the costume just like when I was a little kid in theater. *ER* was less interesting as an actor, as the character was closer to who I actually am as a person.

When I get cast, I never feel like I fit the part. I need to find someone who does fit it so I can.

KS: What is forty-seven-year-old Long Duk Dong doing now?

GW: He's lost some of his hair. He has eight or nine kids, I would imagine. They are all not in the arts. By choice! [Laughs] Probably lots of grandchildren. It's a mixed marriage. Probably married someone blonde, so his kids are mixed race. Actually, he's probably been married a few times. And for someone who fell so in love with America, he's probably changed his name.

Some of his kids are in the arts, one in a rock band probably, some are teachers, a few doctors.

I think he owns restaurants. They're kinda famous. And he's kinda well known for it. And he's about to make a bid for the LA Clippers.

KS: I would see that movie.

GW: I have a friend writing something about the Donger. You just might.

CHAPTER 3: VALLEY GIRLS, KARATE KIDS, REPO MEN

The Los Angeles Teen Movie

Movies Discussed: *Valley Girl, The Karate Kid, Suburbia, Pretty in Pink, Some Kind of Wonderful, Bill & Ted's Excellent Adventure, Fast Times at Ridgemont High, The Sure Thing*

OUR NEXT STOP IN Los Angeles seems too obvious to be worth it. Why spend time on movies set in Los Angeles, when so many movies seem set there by default? Back in the 1980s, before American movie studios had found greener (and cheaper) pastures filming in places like Atlanta, Toronto, and Vancouver, you could pretty much assume a movie, unless it explicitly said differently, had been filmed within driving distance of the studio that paid for it. John Hughes may have insisted on only shooting his movies in and around Chicago. He was an exception that largely proved this rule.

What the heck, then? Should we just name this chapter: "Omelets: The ones made of eggs?"

Not quite. There was something special about the eighties teen movies that weren't just filmed in Los Angeles but were also *about* Los Angeles. In the 1980s, LA had its first African-American mayor, Tom Bradley, who would hold the office through the entire decade until 1992. Bradley had grown up in town, attended UCLA, and served two decades as an officer in the LAPD before getting into politics. He'd been a teenager in 1932 when Los Angeles first played host to the Summer Olympics. The future mayor remembered watching the games through a hole in the fence surrounding Los Angeles Memorial Coliseum in the city's Exposition Park neighborhood.

Tom Bradley would tell this story often when, in the middle of his tenure as mayor and in the dead center of the 1980s, the Olympics would not only come back to Los Angeles but also try to rebrand the city as the unified, peaceful metropolis of the future. Bizarrely, the Los Angeles teen movies of this era would tell a more truthful story about the palce they came from than Mayor Bradley, the 1984 Olympics or even Los Angeles itself was willing to accept.

"The Apex of Human Possibility" meets "Operation Hammer"

THE EIGHTIES TEEN MOVIES with Los Angeles as their setting—comedies like *Valley Girl* and *Fast Times at Ridgemont High*, coming-of-age tales like *The Karate Kid*, and darker teen movies like *Suburbia* and *Repo Man*—come from a decade defined by the city's hosting of the 1984 Summer Olympics. Taken together, they do something teen movies don't do very often: reflect reality better than reality sees itself. One of the biggest goals of the 1984 Summer Olympics was to change the world's image of Los Angeles from an inhuman tangle of freeways under a sky of smog to what *Grantland* in 2014 called a "perpetually sunny, free-market wonderland...the apex of human possibility." Without quite meaning to, the Los Angeles shown in the teen movies of that same time managed to more accurately reflect how life actually was for whole neighborhoods of teenagers living there during the Olympics.

Los Angeles had already been readying itself for the Olympics—refurbishing venues, lining up sponsors, and designing a visual identity for the games—when director Amy Heckerling shot *Fast Times at Ridgemont High* in Hollywood and the San Fernando Valley in late 1981, and when Nicolas Cage and Deborah Foreman played Hollywood and San Fernando Valley teenagers who fell in love in *Valley Girl* the following year. Runners were carrying the Olympic Torch across America toward the opening ceremony in the Los Angeles Memorial Coliseum when *The Karate Kid* came to movie theaters in June of 1984. *Pretty in Pink* and *Some Kind of Wonderful*, both released after the games, were LA teen movies about money and class divides that pointed to the city's deep cultural and economic inequalities the Olympics tried so hard to make invisible.

Somehow, Brat Pack America movies that are *about* Los Angeles also managed to be a more truthful picture *of* Los Angeles than the unified, peaceful whole perpetuated by the Olympics—an intention *Los Angeles Magazine* had characterized in a 2014 assessment as, "to knit together what had been seen as merely sprawl."

Never mind that "knitting together" often came, as we will see, via handcuffs and the business end of a nightstick.

The work of several urban theorists, including MacArthur Genius Grant-winner Mike Davis, draws a direct line from policing methods implemented during the 1984 Olympics to the climate of fear and distrust between citizens and law enforcement that lead to the 1992 Los Angeles riots. LAPD chief Daryl Gates had visited Sarajevo, host of the 1984 Winter Olympics to see how the Yugoslavian capitol handled security during the games. Writing about it in his 1992 autobiography, *Chief*, Gates admits to taking Sarajevo's policy of arresting and jailing anyone during the Olympics who even remotely looked like a troublemaker and reframing it so it wouldn't be thrown out as unconstitutional in an American court. That meant planting stories in local newspapers that the city's street gangs were planning on disrupting the games with violence (giving the LAPD an excuse to arrest them all en masse as domestic terrorists), partnering with the US Military to build wide perimeter fences around the Olympic Villages that bordered poor neighborhoods, and then swarming those neighborhoods with hundreds of officers and police vehicles to keep residents and gang members alike good and scared. These

"Olympic Gang Sweeps,"—arresting and detaining anyone young, male, and not white on suspicion of wrongdoing, implementing selective curfews for poorer neighborhoods in South and East Los Angeles, preemptively seizing and destroying the personal property of suspects—went from being special circumstances law enforcement used during the Olympics, to explicit departmental policy afterward. Gates named the program Operation Hammer, which went into effect in April of 1987 and governed much of how LAPD officers acted toward suspected gang members and drug dealers.

Five officers trained in Operation Hammer tactics arrived at the scene in the early morning of March 3, 1991, when a car of three men was stopped for speeding at the intersection of the 210 Freeway and Osbourne Street about twenty-five miles northwest of Downtown Los Angeles. The three men in that car were Bryant Allen, Freddie Helms, and Rodney King.

LA movies about teenagers in the years around the Rodney King beating and the riots that followed a year later—*Colors* (1988), *Boyz n the Hood* (1991), *Menace II Society* (1993)—often focused on those likely to find themselves in the LAPD's crosshairs: poor, marginally employed, young African-American and Latino men. It was these teenagers, children, and junior high school students in 1984 whose families, friends, and neighbors lived in areas of the city the LAPD occupied like a conquering army during the Olympic Games.

The 1990s were a particularly awful time in Los Angeles—the riots in April of 1992, the 1994 Northridge earthquake, the OJ Simpson trial, and the decade's twin spikes in gang-related violence and findings of widespread police department corruption. Former state librarian Kevin Starr called his book on the period *Coast of Dreams: California on the Edge, 1990-2003.* "As someone attuned primarily to the imaginative dimension of social experience and to the moral drama of California as an American experiment, I became increasingly disturbed by the grim realities around me," he wrote. "Was California an aberration, a sideshow, or worse, a case study in how things could go wrong for the United States?"

Los Angeles teen movies of the 1990s seemed to reflect Professor Starr's worry: the violent desperation of growing up poor and black in *Boyz n the Hood* and *Set it Off* (1996), the snare of gangs as substitute families in *Mi Vida Loca* (1993) and *Blood In Blood Out* (1993). Even a polar opposite sunny comedy like *Clueless* (1995) got a bunch of its laughs from how little its Beverly Hills heroine Cher understood the Los Angeles around her (when she misses curfew, her dad asks her, "Where are you, Kuwait?" and she asks, "Is that in the Valley?"), and therefore how sprawling and alien Los Angeles feels even to those who live there in wealth and comfort. (Remember that great scene where Cher and her friends argue about the best way to drive home from a party in the Valley, who lives where, and who would have to get off the freeway to drop off someone else? And these are all kids who go to the same school.)

The LA teen movies of the 1980s had just as much to say about the tearing social fabric of their home city. They said it through stories of class, money, brutal conformity, and misunderstanding, even in harmless, sweet packages like *Valley Girl*. They also happened to be talking about class and inequality when Los Angeles was selling itself to the world as a unified city where things like class and inequality didn't matter so much.

The Games that Saved the Games

Los Angeles hosted the Games of the XXIII Olympiad because no one else wanted them. The 1968 Summer Olympics in Mexico City and the '72 games in Munich had been stained by state-sponsored violence and acts of international terrorism. Montreal ended the 1976 Summer Olympics $1.5 billion in debt, red ink that did not fade away until 2006. The US had boycotted the 1980 games in Moscow, so Russia and East Germany turned around and did the same for the 1984 Olympics in Los Angeles.

By the time of Brat Pack America, hosting an Olympics looked like a stupid choice for anyone—a dangerous, expensive political garbage fire waiting to happen. The International Olympic

Committee worried the games were living on borrowed time if no city could risk having them. Other than Los Angeles, only Tehran put in a bid to host the 1984 Summer Games, which the Iranian capital later had to withdraw due to political unrest within its own borders. Los Angeles got the Games of the XXIII Olympiad by forfeit.

The combined minds of Mayor Tom Bradley, appointed Olympic organizer Peter Ueberroth (a California businessman, who would soon after be named the commissioner of Major League Baseball), and the Ueberroth-selected 150-member Olympic committee, chose to use the natural strengths of the city to solve the problems of the previous games. At great cost savings, only two new venues were built for the Olympics, while most events were held at venues the city already had, such as stadiums that hosted LA's professional sports teams, as well as pools and tracks at universities throughout Southern California. Ueberroth also created tiered levels of corporate sponsorship and pre-sold television rights, practices that weren't done at the time and then became standard for every Olympics to follow. This meant the games avoided debt and abandoned ruins on its landscape (rotting venues from past Olympics to this day scar Sarajevo, Athens, and Beijing) and hit profitability almost from the moment the Olympic torch arrived at the opening ceremony. That Opening Ceremony drew the largest television audience in history for an Olympic Games.

The 1984 Olympics ended with a surplus of $232 million, and remains to this day the most profitable games ever. More Americans watched it than any televised event since Neil Armstrong landed on the moon. Ronald Reagan became the first US president to preside over an Olympic opening ceremony and urged America's athletes to not just win but to remember, as journalist Michael Weinreb wrote, "that the American ideal was actually about going as far as you can go." Team USA did, collecting eighty-three medals. No other country won more than twenty. *TIME* magazine named Peter Ueberroth their 1984 Man of the Year.

Since 1972, the first time the Olympics had been televised globally, hosting the Olympics has meant giving your city a new image in the eyes of the world: the 1972 Summer Games were Munich's chance chance to pull Germany out from the long shadow of Nazism, and the 1988 Summer Games in Seoul gets a large of chunk of credit for making South Korea a player on the international stage. Ditto the 2008 Summer Games in Beijing, a display of China's new might as a world economic power. In the early 1980s, Los Angeles saw the same opportunity. LA's rebranding would be in the name of civic and cultural unity. The world would see America's second-largest city not as a mess of traffic jams and air pollution, but a visually unified celebration of the best parts of America—big cities with small-town pride, winning and success as emblems of social good. The legendary Southern California design firms of Jerde Partnership and Sussman/Prejza called the look they created for the 1984 Olympics "Frontier Federalism," implying both triumph and togetherness.

More than any other moving part of the 1984 Olympics, the visual elements had to do more with less. Given only a budget of $10 million, the designers had to create signage, logos, bus stops, walkways, exit and entrance gates that not only got everyone around three hundred square miles safely, but that worked on television as well as in the flesh. The color palette—bright, high-contrast, graphic—took its inspiration from shades and tones of the American West and the Pacific Rim. The materials had to be cheap and easily repurposed. Unlike most Olympic structures, expensively built and designed to last forever whether anybody wanted them to or not, the Los Angeles Olympics used design elements like stage props, hung up for the show, packed away after closing night.

Sadly, that metaphor fit a little too well. The face of unity and oneness the 1984 Olympics wanted Los Angeles to show would fade after the games were over, some reasons for which happened after the fact. Crack cocaine arrived in South Los Angeles that fall (a city district already suffering a 45 percent unemployment rate), and brought with it terrible spikes in addiction, gang warfare, and territorial homicides. Cold War military buildup ended in 1985, spelling disaster for the city's aerospace businesses and workforce. The years 1984–1989 saw a 33 percent increase in citizen complaints of police brutality against the LAPD, a trend that coincides with the implementation of LAPD Chief Daryl Gates' Olympics containment and neighborhood occupation strategies. Gates' dedicated gang units and police-staffed SWAT teams are now considered law enforcement innovations, but also examples of how tragically he misread thuggish over-policing as the needed strategy for calm and peace during the Olympics, which then became accepted police tactics thereafter. In the aftermath of the riots brought on by the acquittal of the officers responsible for the beating of Rodney King (an incident which cost Daryl Gates his job), Mayor Bradley hired a familiar face to head up Rebuild Los Angeles, the city's official healing and reunification effort: Peter Ueberroth.

That Los Angeles felt it had to resort to putting whole neighborhoods of its own citizens under martial law in order to present an image of unity to the world uncomfortably shows how little faith organizers actually had in that notion. The dark side of that lack of faith—a city divided against itself by suspicion and misunderstanding—would take root in Los Angeles's creative firmament. It'd show up in the films of Penelope Spheeris and John Singleton, in the albums of punk bands like the Circle Jerks and hip-hop artists like Ice-T and N.W.A. Even the Los Angeles movies of Brat Pack America, innocent and huggable as they may be, nearly all deal in discord and division, in kids on opposite sides torn by class, money, and neighborhood. The eighties LA teen movie managed to stand in truthful opposition to the comforting lie Los Angeles had used the Olympics to tell about itself.

Valley Girls and All-Valley Karate Tournaments

VALLEY GIRL (1983), A "Romeo and Juliet story about a girl from the Valley and a boy from Hollywood," in the words of its director Martha Coolidge, is probably the most obvious example of a Brat Pack America movie that used a divided Los Angeles as a major plot point. A graduate of the Rhode Island School of Design and a mentee of Francis Ford Coppola, Coolidge had been researching the city's music scene for a different project when *Valley Girl* became her directorial debut. Coolidge's later movies would be split fairly evenly between stories about adults—*Lost in Yonkers* (1993), *Angie* (1994), *Introducing Dorothy Dandridge* (1999)—and films about young people—*Real Genius* (1985), *Rambling Rose* (1991), *The Prince and Me* (2004). Nearly all her work features a protagonist overcoming misunderstandings and prejudices of class, age, and circumstance.

"Really the whole movie is about conformity and peer pressure," said Coolidge of *Valley Girl* in her director's commentary. "Understanding your own feelings and choices and being yourself." It's a theme Coolidge would return to often in her work, but only in *Valley Girl* would the obstacles facing her characters be represented by the terrain of Los Angeles itself.

Valley Girl opens with an aerial shot, a look down from a helicopter at the Hollywood Sign, panning right over Mt. Lee and into the San Fernando Valley on the other side. (Look carefully and you can see the helicopter wobble. The movie's budget was a tiny $350,000 and a cheapo helicopter was all they could afford.) The radio station we've been hearing on the audio track playing "Hollywood's Best Rock!" now goes to static, then comes back in playing a sugary new wave pop tune. Roll credits. We're in the Valley now. The typeface is in bright pink.

Over the sugary pop tune, we meet Julie Richman (Deborah Foreman), a pretty, popular teenager shopping with her friends at the Sherman Oaks Galleria mall. She's got an equally popular jock boyfriend (Michael Bowen, who you might recognize as white supremacist Jack Welker from *Breaking Bad*). He doesn't treat her very well, and in the first scene she breaks up with him. Later that day she meets Randy (Nicolas Cage, in the role that made him a star), a kid from Hollywood High School, at the beach. Randy overhears that Julie and her friends are headed to a party that night so he decides to crash. There he convinces Julie to take a drive with him. They wind up at a favorite spot, a nightclub he calls "his home away from home." (The nightclub used was an earlier incarnation of the Viper Room, owned in the 1990s by Johnny Depp. Actor River Phoenix went into cardiac arrest in front of the venue on Halloween night 1993 and died early the next morning.) Randy and Julie have their first kiss at the club, and thus begins a love affair that will end at the prom, but first has to run the obstacle course laid down in the movie's tagline: "She's cool. He's hot. She's from the Valley. He's not." Julie's friends have a big problem with this though not quite as big as Julie thinks they do.

The script for *Valley Girl*, written by producers Andy Lane and Wayne Crawford, tried to grab the tail of a cultural meme. In 1982, musician Frank Zappa woke his fourteen-year-old daughter, Moon Unit Zappa, in the middle of the night to record her repeating phrases he'd heard her say to her friends at the dinner table and on the telephone. He then laid a corrosive guitar and staccato backing vocals underneath and came up with the song "Valley Girl," a minor hit for father and daughter but actually the most commercially successful of Zappa's thirty-year music career. The Zappas meant the whole thing as a joke—there's a line where the fourteen-year-old narrator gets asked if she practices S&M—and the family didn't even live in the Valley. But pretty soon teenagers all over America were repeating lines from the song like, "Gag me with a spoon!" "Barf me out!" and ending every sentence with a question mark whether or not they were asking a question.

The trend came and went, but "valley girl" as shorthand for a femmy, materialistic airhead and "the Valley" as shorthand for a bland dumping ground of shopping malls and people with nothing to say for themselves stuck around. The mean girls in *Heathers* (1989) would never call themselves valley girls, but Winona Ryder calling them "Swatch dogs and Diet Coke heads" effectively meant the same thing. *Clueless* (1995) turns the stereotype inside out, telling the story of a Beverly Hills princess who would never be caught dead in the Valley (of course she gets stranded there after getting mugged coming home from a "Val party") but learns by movie's end to be less of a materialistic airhead and "make over her soul," i.e. become less of the valley girl stereotype. The Kardashian sisters and the undue attention paid to the vocal fry in women's voices (a creak as the voice goes up in register) are all descendants of the Valley girl meme knocking around here in the twenty-first century.

The original idea for *Valley Girl* the movie was a quickie teen romp designed to catch this wave, but Coolidge could tell immediately she had something more. Cage and Foreman had an undeniable chemistry, but it was also unforced and quirky, intrigue as much as puppy lust. The director also knew that the she's-from-the-valley-he's-from-Hollywood device would work best if not only a) Julie and Randy learned ultimately it didn't matter, but b) if the movie seemed to know that a little before they did. The movie isn't a story of kids in love who can't be together, but kids being honest with their own feelings. The geographic divide between Julie and Randy ultimately represents less where they live and much more the real difficulty of being a teenager and being yourself.

Everywhere you look, *Valley Girl* reminds the audience that these divides are more imaginary than real. Coolidge and her cinematographer Frederick Elmes (who would later shoot most of David Lynch and Jim Jarmusch's movies) lit the Valley kids in pastels and the Hollywood kids in saturated red and black. But the further we get into Julie and Randy's love story, even when they have broken up and Julie has taken Tommy back, the more we see them wearing the colors of the other side of the hill or clothes that symbolize neither one (a lot of brown and grey). Randy's parents are unseen but Julie's are not the snotty country clubbers one would expect them to be, like Elisabeth Shue's mom and dad in *The Karate Kid* (another Valley movie, which came out the year after). Instead Julie's parents (Frederic Forrest and Colleen Camp) are ex-hippies who own a health food store. Forrest has a wonderful heart-to-heart with Julie when she tells her dad how hard it is to date someone your friends don't like, and about how Julie's parents went through the same thing: her dad used to wear his hair long and be a peacenik bum, but Julie's mom loved him anyway.

Coolidge also knew from her late nights and early mornings of research for her unfinished music project that the kids dancing alongside her were just as often Julies from the Valley as they were Randys from Hollywood, and that a good bit of the music history of Los Angeles had been a blend of urban and suburban participation. Super-groupie Pamela Des Barres, a fixture of the Sunset Strip in West Hollywood for thirty years, arrived in 1966 as a kid from Reseda in the Valley. The Go-Gos, who had broken nationally just before *Valley Girl*, lived, worked, rehearsed, and recorded in West Hollywood, but their sound was a perfectly crafted hybrid of their neighborhood's punk scene and the chirpy, girly pop all over the *Valley Girl* soundtrack. A generation before, Ritchie Valens had been known as the "Little Richard of the Valley." Los Lobos, the band that had worshipped Valens as teenagers and played his songs for the Valens biopic *La Bamba* (1987), had been city kids, deeply proud of their roots in East Los Angeles. Even the band X, flag-bearers for the Hollywood-and-points-south punk scene of the late 1970s and early 1980s, passed on having their songs featured in *Valley Girl* for fear of seeming like they were making fun of their fans from points north in the Valley.

Julie and Randy's first kiss happens immediately after their first serious conversation. Randy looks around his hangout and tells Julie "this is the real world. It's not fresh and clean like a television show." Julie comes back with, "I always thought the Valley was real enough for me." They argue about the music each of them likes. "You guys think you're so different," Julie says. Randy comes back with, "We are. We're ourselves." They circle around their differences, where they live, what they like to do for fun, until Randy asks when he can see Julie again.

"I'm here with you now, aren't I?" she says, flirting but telling him to have a little patience and respect.

"I know," he says.

"I can't explain it," Julie goes on. "I feel like we're connected, like we're linked." She then laughs as she says she probably sounds like her parents.

The rest of the conversation we can't hear over the music in the club—the song playing, "A Million Miles Away" by The Plimsouls, also turned into a hit thanks to the movie, and speaks perfectly about lovers trying to connect across a chasm. Julie and Randy seem to be saying as best they can that they really like each other. At which point we in the audience realize that a moment ago, neither one of them was right. That the "being yourself" Randy boasts about happens once you *stop* defining yourself by the music you like or where you live. The courage of *Valley Girl* comes from respecting how hard that is when you're only seventeen and your friends' disapproval is the worst thing you can imagine.

Valley Girl begins at the Sherman Oaks Galleria—the Vatican of Valley girl culture at 15301 Ventura Boulevard (Moon Zappa cracked about it being "so bitchin'" in the song)—and ends there symbolically, too, as Julie and Randy drive past it in their prom limo on their way to begin the second chapter of their romance (the movie's last shot is the mall's sign and front driveway). But in an ironic collision of movie plot and moviemaking, the *Valley Girl* crew could only afford to shoot exteriors of the Galleria, not inside the mall itself. The opening scenes of Julie and her friends shopping and the we're-falling-in-love montage of Julie and Randy hanging out in each other's worlds forty minutes later—the song "I Melt with You" by Modern English became famous thanks to this montage—had to be filmed at a way-less-fashionable mall in Torrance, twenty-five miles south on the 405 freeway from the Galleria. Any teenager who logged hours at the Galleria back then would recognize that the movie named for what the mall personified didn't take place there at all. *Valley Girl*, a movie that rests on perceived divisions of wealth, class, and geography, actually couldn't *afford* the location so culturally intertwined with its title. The lesson of the movie—that feelings and honesty mean more than money and neighborhood—mattered here, too.

Valley Girl was a hit both critically (83 percent on Rotten Tomatoes as of this writing) and with fans ($17 million in tickets on a budget of $350,000). It launched the careers of Nicolas Cage and Martha Coolidge and made "I Melt with You" one of the most famous teen movie anthems in history. As of 2012, Paramount and MGM have a musical remake of *Valley Girl* in development.

Valley Girl's about as innocent and sweet as its name would predict, a lovely, unforced movie about being yourself and doing right by people who matter to you. Maybe the best thing about it is its honesty, how little the actors need to try to make scenes work, how the direction gives them the space to, how the story doesn't wring too much out of its simple presence. Yet even with these very modest aims, *Valley Girl* is a movie that acknowledges a divided Los Angeles, even for teenagers, right before Los Angeles would tell the world that the Olympics had erased such divisions.

The Karate Kid arrived in movie theaters on June 22, 1984, a little over a year after *Valley Girl* and just before the opening of the Olympics in Los Angeles. The movie's first scene is Daniel LaRusso (Ralph Macchio), a high school sophomore whose father has recently died, moving with his mom from Newark, New Jersey, to the San Fernando Valley. "California, here we come!" sings his mom (Randee Heller, who later would play dead-too-soon secretary Ida Blankenship on *Mad Men*) as they drive across the country in an overpacked station wagon. In a neat coincidence, if you saw *The Karate Kid* in its first few weeks in theaters, you'd see Daniel and his mom headed across the country toward Los Angeles at the same time the Olympic torch was making its thirty-state journey across America in real life.

In the symbol of the torch, wrote *TIME* magazine in their January 1985 appreciation of Ueberroth and his Olympic achievement, America saw itself:

"...heading west for California, toward the light. Running away from recession, Americans might almost subconsciously have imagined, away from Jimmy Carter's 'malaise,' away from gas shortages and hostage crises and a sense of American impotence and failure and limitation and passivity, away from dishonored presidents and a lost war. Away from what had become an American inferiority complex. Away from descendant history. Running away from the past, into the future."

The torch had a hero's welcome waiting for it in Los Angeles Memorial Coliseum: nearly 100,000 cheering spectators and the world watching on television. Daniel and Lucille LaRusso had a shabby two-story apartment building in working-class Reseda named South Seas (still there at 19223 Saticoy Street, if you'd like to have a look). The pool in the building's courtyard has about three inches of algae-filled water. When it came time to film that scene, the crew had to drain the pool and add the green slime to represent, recalled location manager Richard Davis Jr., the "the shabby California dream that [Daniel] wasn't buying just yet."

No wonder. We quickly see that the dream Daniel's mom believed in, of not just a better life for the two of them but of a kind of glistening paradise where, in Ms. LaRusso's words, "the whole world has gone blonde!" isn't happening like she'd hoped. There may be a nice (blonde) girl named Ali (Elisabeth Shue) Daniel meets at a beach party, but there's also Ali's ex (blond) boyfriend Johnny Lawrence (Billy Zabka), a SoCal-golden-bully who seems like a first cousin of Tommy from *Valley Girl*. Johnny happens to know karate and uses it to wipe the sand with Daniel for talking to his ex.

The Karate Kid screenwriter, Robert Mark Kamen (who had written *Taps* a few years prior), had been a practicing martial artist for many years, and based the script on a local news story about a kid who had moved to the San Fernando Valley and learned karate to keep from getting hounded by bullies at his new school. Director John G. Avildsen didn't want the project at first. He'd directed *Rocky* in 1976, another story about a working-class, overmatched Italian-American with a wise mentor that ends in the ring with a championship bout. "They're going to call me '*The Ka-Rocky Kid*,'" Avildsen remembered of his initial fears in a thirtieth anniversary retrospective of the movie in *LA Weekly*. But as he dug in, Avildsen recalled he soon noticed how different the two movies were: "*Rocky* is a love story, but *The Karate Kid* is about a vulnerable teenager transplanted from New Jersey and his surrogate father." Which is why 99 percent of the time, if you mention *Rocky* to someone, they'll answer you with a yell of "Adrian!" (Rocky's wife), and if you do the same with *The Karate Kid*, they'll say, "Wax on, wax off," and make big circles with their hands like Daniel's teacher and surrogate father Mr. Miyagi (Pat Morita), the maintenance man at his apartment building, who offers to teach him karate after another brutal pounding from Johnny.

The Karate Kid was a giant hit for its studio, Columbia ($90 million on its initial run and it cost a fraction of that), and launched the careers of pretty much everyone who starred in it. It spawned three sequels, a 2010 remake starring Jayden Smith (son of Will Smith) and Jackie Chan, a Saturday morning cartoon, and a pile of licensed toys and video games. Pat Morita received an Oscar nomination for Best Supporting Actor. The movie has a 90 percent fresh rating on Rotten Tomatoes, is number forty on *EW*'s 2010 list of Fifty Greatest High School Movies Ever, and made "wax on, wax off" and its dark twin "sweep the leg" part of our shared vocabulary.

"*The Karate Kid* is an LA movie to its core," wrote Jared Cowan in the *LA Weekly*'s thirtieth anniversary story, which fudges the map a little since the movie's feet are firmly planted in the suburban San Fernando Valley, north of the city. The class conflict between Daniel, a poor transplant living in Reseda, and Ali, a rich kid from Encino, is a conflict between towns *within* the Valley, rather than the suburban Valley and within-city-limits Hollywood as in *Valley Girl*. The movie ends with Daniel beating Johnny and his evil Cobra Kai team in the All-Valley (not All-Southland or All–Los Angeles) Karate Tournament.

It'd be more accurate to call *The Karate Kid* "a Valley movie to its core." The Valley is the only "LA" that matters here.

When *The Karate Kid* concerns itself with class—through what is really a supporting plot connected to Daniel and Ali's courtship, while the Miyagi/Daniel story of mentoring and friendship is front and center—the divisions money creates are specific to the geography of the Valley. "It's not like these kids were from Beverly Hills or Santa Monica. The Valley is a real place," remembered Elisabeth Shue in the *LA Weekly* retrospective. "Where you live becomes who you are." Agreed, but *The Karate Kid* handles it differently than *Valley Girl*, which said, "Hey, this who-lives-where thing? Not so important."

Instead, *The Karate Kid* sees the Valley (oddly, a place Robert Mark Kamen had never been before writing the movie) in almost archeological terms, an arrival hall for several kinds of people at different moments in their lives, at different points in American history. "Just what the prevailing image [of the Valley] is at any given moment has evolved through time," wrote Kevin Roderick in his 2001 book *The San Fernando Valley: America's Suburb*. In the early 1900s, Roderick wrote, the Valley had a reputation as a landing spot for hard-working new immigrants to California (which Daniel and Lucille LaRusso were, but in the mid-1980s). By the 1940s, the Valley had also become a refuge for movie stars, people whose kids were probably friends of Ali's parents and also dined at Encino Oaks Country Club (where Daniel was supposed to meet Ali for a date but ended up crashing into a cart filled with spaghetti plates instead). After WWII, the region got its reputation as a safe yet dull suburb, the kind of place Daniel's mom probably had in mind when she moved there with her teenage son. In the 1980s, the US population of Asian immigrants increased by 70 percent, mostly in West Coast cities and suburbs. Mr Miyagi's key role both as Daniel's mentor and a decorated WWII veteran, points out Cowan in *LA Weekly*, suggests this was a positive trend for the Valley and California as a whole.

In presenting all of these different Valleys in one very specific story of the region in the fall of 1983 (when *The Karate Kid* completed principal photography), Kamen's script and the movie that came from it treated class and economic difference as a sad fact of life, but one that good people will naturally see past and walk through. Daniel gets a new car from Mr. Miyagi for his birthday a few scenes after the rich bullies at school make fun of his mom's old station wagon. Ms. LaRusso gets a promotion at work. Ali's snotty parents might not come around on Daniel being a "Reseda boy," but she doesn't pay them much mind and goes out with Daniel anyway. Her friends never liked Daniel because of his attitude, not because of where he lives. Johnny only seems to hate Daniel for moving in on his ex-girlfriend. At the movie's end, Johnny, the former All-Valley Karate Tournament champion, hands the trophy over to the new champion with a "You're all right, LaRusso." Daniel thanks him.

The Karate Kid shared the cinematic summer of 1984 with *Footloose, Beverly Hills Cop, Indiana Jones and the Temple of Doom,* and *Revenge of the Nerds,* all movies about very American kinds of heroes, underdogs who outwit rather than overrun the bad guys. The villains in each of these movies are locals who rule over their territory like warlords. Daniel LaRusso, Axel Foley, Indiana Jones, and the brothers of Lambda Lambda Lambda are all, in one way or another, new kids in town.

Each of these movies also shared that summer with the 1984 Olympics in Los Angeles. The Olympics told the exact opposite story. Host Team USA won four times as many metals as any other country, with crowds chanting, "U-S-A, U-S-A" nonstop during volleyball matches, track and field meets, and equestrian competitions. "Oh, what we've done to the Olympics," sighed legendary sportswriter Frank Deford in *Sports Illustrated.* "America, so bountiful and strong, with every advantage, including the home court…gracelessly trumpeting its own good fortune while rudely dismissing its guests." The Olympics saw their America's story as Daniel LaRusso's—hard luck then hard work ending in triumph—but acted a whole lot more like Johnny Lawrence.

You can still visit most of the Valley locations in *The Karate Kid* today—the LaRussos' apartment building, the front of the Cobra Kai dojo, the beach where Ali and Daniel met, the athletic facilities at Cal State Northridge, where the All-Valley Karate Tournament was filmed. The only real exception is Mr. Miyagi's house in Canoga Park. The oil drums, train tracks, and industrial equipment (which cause Daniel to remark, "This reminds me of Newark") in Mr. Miyagi's front yard were props, but the house stood until 1989, when it was torn down to make way for development. A series of yards and driveways now sit on the property.

"The Rejected" and Otto Maddox

IN THE SPRING OF 1983, a little movie called *Suburbia* came and went, but is now considered a time capsule of a moment in the history of Los Angeles. *Suburbia* told the story of a group of teenagers who all live together in an abandoned house (they call themselves "T.R." for "The Rejected") next to the freeway. The group drives to punk shows together in Hollywood, looks out for one another, and gets by as best they can. Most of the T.R. kids come from lousy circumstances, getting beat up by step-parents or growing up too poor to have room for bigger dreams. I suppose you could argue they should have finished school and gotten jobs to pay for community college, but *Suburbia* makes the all-too-fair point that this one group of kids isn't bothering anyone and that they seem to be taking care of each other as well as can be expected. The older kids make sure the younger kids get fed and have a place to sleep. They guard each other's backs when fights break out at shows. The movie doesn't glamorize the drugs they do or the stealing to get food and supplies. Instead, writer/director Penelope Spheeris effectively asks in *Suburbia*, "Why do a bunch of teenagers have to go through these lengths to make sure their friends are clothed and fed and safe, when their parents actually have the legal responsibility to do so?"

Trouble comes (it always does) in the form of residents of one of the neighborhoods where the kids carry out their petty burglaries. A few neighbors driving pickup trucks and wearing belts with giant buckles have formed the Citizens Against Crime, and take it upon themselves to get the kids removed from the squat house. The goons enlist a local cop (Donald Allen), who happens to be the stepfather of one of the kids. The cop is a decent guy but doesn't understand that these friends have adopted squatting and stealing because the adults in their life have failed them. The kids probably don't help their case when one of them ODs and at her funeral, they get into a scuffle with her parents. But overall *Suburbia* isn't looking to debate the merits of how this community of young people lives. Instead it asked a pretty uncomplicated question: What harm would it do to just leave the kids alone? *Suburbia* was Penelope Spheeris's second feature film. A New Orleans native who'd broken into filmmaking shooting music videos and producing for Albert Brooks, Spheeris had found her people in the Los Angeles punk scene centered around Hollywood in the late 1970s and early 1980s. Her first feature film, a documentary about her new community called *Decline of Western Civilization, Part I* (1981), had focused on the musicians as planets the scene revolved around (and some it didn't). Detractors of the movie accused Spheeris of leaving out smarter, more thoughtful local bands because they didn't play as well on camera as the scene's violent lunkheads. For her next movie, Spheeris told the *AV Club* in a 1999 interview, she thought to herself, *Okay, I know this subject matter and I've learned a lot. And I love these kids, so I'm going to sit down and write a narrative picture about them.* The audience in the background of *Decline* would become the protagonists in the foreground of *Suburbia*.

Spheeris used kids she knew from the scene (including a twenty-one-year-old Michael "Flea" Barzaly, just before his band the Red Hot Chili Peppers released their first album) instead of professional actors. Spheeris shot in and around an actual group of vacant houses along the 605 freeway in Norwalk, a suburb in the southeast corner of Los Angeles County where at the time punk kids would squat in groups (the houses were torn down in the early 1990s under eminent domain to make room for an extension of the 105 freeway). The "nice" houses the kids steal from were in Downey, one town over from Norwalk. To go see bands like T.S.O.L. and The Vandals, who performed in the movie, the group of friends would have had to drive twenty miles from their squat house up the I-5 into Hollywood.

At first *Suburbia* seems like a dumb joke of a title for a movie about a Los Angeles punk house and its tribe of friends. "Suburbia" brings to mind station wagons, mowed lawns, and polo shirts, not mohawks, safety pin jewelry, and sleeping off a bad trip in the bathtub. But in context, the movie's title seems a lot smarter than just irony for its own sake. The word "suburbia" represents the ideal Citizens Against Crime think they are protecting, but also where the punk kids have fled and where their messed-up families live. Also, by 1983, the year *Suburbia* came out, the LA punk scene was on its last legs—ruined, some of the pioneers would insist, by violent jerks from places like Huntington Beach and Orange County who wanted to use the music and its culture as an excuse to get in fights. These old-timers viewed the destruction of what they had created as an invasion of an urban arts movement by morons from suburbia.

Penelope Spheeris would direct two more *Decline of Western Civilization* movies, each about youth culture in and around Hollywood. *Decline Part II* (1988) was about heavy metal bands coming to prominence along the Sunset Strip and *Part III* (1998) was about homeless punk kids that felt like a decade-later update of the culture she captured in *Suburbia*. Geography and demographics held the three *Decline* movies (released in a commemorative DVD box set in 2015) together. Her subjects were always young people who saw this one particular area of Los Angeles as theirs. Some viewed it as a clubhouse. Others saw it as an audition space for becoming rock stars. A forgotten few ended up there, looking for a place to sleep and other kids in their same crappy predicament.

Geographically speaking, the world of *Suburbia* is tiny, a sliver of outer LA County and a couple of field trips to Hollywood. But by zooming in this tight, the movie's themes of misunderstanding and prejudice feel bigger. The Citizens Against Crime get fed up with the punk kids only after the kids invade *their* neighborhood. They then try and stick it to the Rejected by invading their neighborhood in turn, first calling the police on the squat, then showing up themselves for retribution. The conflict of *Suburbia* isn't just cultural but a pointless turf war, as much about ownership of place as ripped jeans and body piercings versus crew cuts and mustaches.

Released a few months before the 1984 Olympics, *Suburbia* is a diorama-sized look at a city divided and warring with law enforcement, helpless and ineffective. It probably only acted as a metaphor for the deep divisions throughout Los Angeles at the time by accident. But its older brother, a film about suburban punks in a pitiless metropolis of filthy dreams, would bring the message home, if not harder than weirder.

Meet *Repo Man* (March, 1984), the leader of this small, proud band of LA punk movies. Its hero, Otto Maddox (Emilio Estevez), is a proud suburban punk with a dangly earring and lousy attitude who gets a job he loves wearing a tie and repossessing cars from owners who haven't made their payments. The world of his work feels tactile—sweaty, squinting, with dirt under its fingernails and smog in its lungs. But *Repo Man* pairs that realism with brazen leaps of imagination, a subplot about aliens, federal agents, and the holy grail of car repossessions, a 1964 Chevy Malibu with magical, deadly powers. Broadsides at capitalism and consumer culture are everywhere (products in *Repo Man* all have generic white labels with a single word like "Soup"), but the movie's sense of humor sometimes packs jokes three and four deep like a Marx Brothers comedy. (My favorite: a hospital PA announcement to "please be quiet" seconds before a terrifically loud shootout.) And for a movie set in what the video series "Los Angeles, The City in Cinema" called "a Los Angeles by, for, and about the automobile," *Repo Man* doesn't drive very far. Writer/director Alex Cox and his crew filmed almost entirely in the industrial neighborhoods east of downtown and along the LA River—no Hollywood, no Beverly Hills, no Venice Beach. It makes *Repo Man* a movie where everybody is either driving or getting their wheels taken from them but where the characters all seem like fish circling the same, dirty aquarium. "The more you drive, the less intelligent you are," the movie's wisest character says. And yet no one in *Repo Man* gets any smarter or dumber. Just varying degrees of ambition, greed, and want.

Repo Man was Alex Cox's debut film. His next two movies—*Sid and Nancy* (1986) and *Straight to Hell* (1987)—would also go down in history as classics of punk cinema. A former law student, Cox left his hometown of Bristol in England to study film at UCLA on Los Angeles's Westside. The year was 1977, and the first generation of punk had reached its zenith in both New York and the UK but had only just begun in Los Angeles. Cox had gotten across town to Hollywood clubs like the Starwood to attend shows by the city's punk forerunners. The expanse of Los Angeles terrified him—"a vast miasma of smog, buildings, roads, and garbage," he told the *Onion AV Club* in a 2000 interview—but it shrunk in size and grew in familiarity when, for extra money, he started going on rides with his neighbor who worked as a repo man.

Repo Man's LA punk movie siblings viewed the city as either a village of citizens with common interests (the *Decline* documentaries) or as a scattering of territories whose citizens hated each other (*Suburbia*). *Repo Man* viewed Los Angeles as belonging to nobody, and, as Roger Ebert wrote in his review of the film, "a wasteland of human ambitions where a few bucks can be made by the quick, the bitter, and the sly." Los Angeles feels vast, yet barely occupied and strangely repetitive, the Downtown skyline viewed from multiple angles while driving over multiple bridges, chase scenes in the concrete open-tomb of the LA River seen in dozens of other movies. Sets are glaringly lit yet anonymously dull—warehouses, loading docks, parking lots, and beat-up office waiting rooms. Huge and forbidding, but boringly ordinary, *Repo Man's* LA matches the split between grandiosity of the job's sense of purpose (Otto's mentor Bud, played by Harry Dean Stanton, lives by a "Repo Code," like a gunslinger of the Old West) and the shady, penny ante work they do.

The look and feel of *Repo Man*, created brilliantly by Cox and his cinematographer Robby Müller (whose work also includes a good chunk of the films of Wim Wenders), rests on a continuum of arch, cynical visions of Los Angeles as a kind of bus station of the damned. We see it in Nathanael West's portrait of Hollywood bit players in his novel *Day of the Locust* (1939), then soon after in the film noir masterpieces *Double Indemnity* (1944) and *Kiss Me Deadly* (1955). The novel and film *Save the Tiger* (1973) played with this desperation, too, and won Jack Lemmon an Oscar as the owner of a bankrupt clothing warehouse who considers torching it in order to save himself from financial ruin. Steve Erickson's first book *Days Between Stations*, published the year after *Repo Man*, begins his series of novels about a Los Angeles of failed dreams and unexplained encounters under descending clouds of insanity. In the 1990s, Quentin Tarantino, a student and fan of *Repo Man*, built his own universe from its DNA: all-night diners with harsh lighting, questionable ambitions characters seem all too ready to kill for, shot through with a humor that comes from talking faster than you can think.

Released just before the Olympics, but made as Los Angeles geared up for them, *Repo Man* feels less an opposite of the Olympics, like many of the other films we've visited here, than a parallel. Amid the revving, "all in this together" boosterism of the Los Angeles Olympics stood *Repo Man*, a small, tightly wound movie with a lot under the hood. Its vision of the city could be best summed up as "unified by our own basic instincts"—thieves zeroing in on the same big score. The city is a set of bank vault doors that only creak open after dark.

John Hughes in Los Angeles

JOHN HUGHES WROTE AND produced but did not direct both *Pretty in Pink* (1986) and *Some Kind of Wonderful* (1987). Beginning with *Sixteen Candles* (1984) then on through *The Breakfast Club* and *Weird Science*, Hughes had directed three movies in two years and found writing more suited to his creative temperament. Howard Deutch, who had worked with Hughes making the trailers for both *Sixteen Candles* and *The Breakfast Club*, got the job and made his directorial debut on *Pink*, then followed it up admirably with *Wonderful*. (Side note: Deutch met Lea Thompson, who played Amanda Jones, on the set of *Some Kind of Wonderful*. They've been married since 1989). Both movies deal more explicitly with class and money than any of the others in Hughes's body of work. And perhaps it's only coincidence, but both are the only of Hughes's teen movies to be filmed in Los Angeles.

Pretty in Pink is the story of Andie Walsh (Molly Ringwald, whom Hughes had written the part for), a working-class high school senior with an unemployed father and an absent mother who walked out on them both. Andie works at a record store after school with her boss and friend Iona (Annie Potts), who, unlike most adult confidantes in teen movies, actually gets a backstory of her own. Andie's childhood best friend Philip "Duckie" Dale (Jon Cryer) is secretly in love with her but won't say so. Complicating matters, Andie has her eye on a rich kid named Blaine (Andrew McCarthy) who feels the same about her. Blaine's best friend Steph (James Spader) is your basic rich kid asshole who has always had an unrequited thing for Andie. Steph's friends and hangers-on are assholes to Andie and Duckie because they aren't rich. The title "Pretty in Pink" comes from a 1981 song by the English band The Psychedelic Furs. The movie ends at the prom, where Andie wears a pink dress that she made herself.

The question of whether Andie should end up with Blaine or Duckie—"Duckie-gate," as its been called by the movie's most committed fans—still singes the back pages of Brat Pack America all these years later. The story goes something like this: the filmmakers test screened *Pretty in Pink* with an ending where Duckie and Andie are last seen dancing together at the prom and Blaine walks out alone. The audience booed loudly. Whether the change the audience wanted—Andie and Blaine ending up together—should have happened depends on how much the phrase "selling out" means to you. Or, I guess, if you considered yourself a Duckie or a Blaine. Or whom you would rather have as your date to the prom.

I've no objection to *Pretty in Pink*'s final draft. It's pretty clear even to me, a terrible judge of these things, that the movie's real chemistry happens between Ringwald and McCarthy, not Ringwald and Cryer, and the final scene has been rewritten so that the three leads all embody the movie's message about class being less important than who you are inside. That message doesn't really work if Andie ends up turning down the rich guy.

It does, however, feel like *Some Kind of Wonderful*, released just about a year later, tries to correct the *Pretty in Pink* we got, with the protagonist choosing their quirky best friend over their rich, popular crush. I've no evidence that these were Hughes's intentions or anyone else's. But as reported in Susannah Gora's book *You Couldn't Ignore Me If You Tried: The Brat Pack, John Hughes, and Their Impact on a Generation* (2010), even on the set of *Some Kind of Wonderful*, the actors were asking if the movie they'd auditioned for was its own creation or really *Pretty in Pink* 2.0.

The same issues, but framed at different angles, are at work in *Some Kind of Wonderful*. Both protagonist Keith (Eric Stoltz) and best friend Watts (Mary Stuart Masterson) are high school seniors and working class, but here Keith's popular crush, Amanda is, too. The houses Deutch and his crew used for where Keith, Watts, and Amanda lived are all within a few blocks of each other in a town near the Port of Los Angeles called Wilmington, which gives Amanda Jones a few more dimensions than Blaine. Amanda is a young woman who knows what her beauty can get her (a hot, jerky boyfriend and rich yet fair weather friends). Those gains feel both shallow and wrong to Amanda, but also too appealing to resist. That conflict makes why Amanda takes an interest in Keith (after he asks her out and she says yes because she's mad at said hot, jerky boyfriend) believable. Yet, it also adds something more to Watts' unrecognized love for Keith (the easy way out would be to make Amanda a mean girl who delights in using Keith, which then sends him rushing back to Watts).

I'm not sure I entirely buy Watts offering to be the chauffeur for their date (the equivalent of something like Duckie volunteering to drive Blaine and Andie to the prom), which makes up *Some Kind of Wonderful*'s climatic last scenes, or Keith spending his college savings on a gift for Amanda right before realizing he should have really given it to Watts.

I forgive both of these missteps, however, because a few scenes earlier, Watts offers to teach Keith how to kiss in case Amanda expects it at the end of their date. The two practice kissing at Keith's workplace, an auto body garage. (He's wearing coveralls and has grease all over his hands. She sits on an oil drum.) What happens—two best friends making out in the name of one helping the other end up with someone else while the helper is secretly in love with the helpee—is twice as good when you consider what's implied rather than said or done. For my money, it's the best kiss in any eighties teen movie, and most of the teen movies from other decades, too.

Neither *Pretty in Pink* nor *Some Kind of Wonderful* mention where they take place. In keeping, perhaps, with the archetypal themes of both movies—love triumphs over class and standing, what you're looking for might be right next to you—settings are only referred to in the abstract as "our neighborhood" or the homes of "the rich and powerful." You can find Andie's house at 1010 Hope Street next to the Metro Gold Line railroad tracks in South Pasadena, the archetypal middle- and lower-middle-class neighborhood in several Brat Pack America movies, including *Back to the Future.* The same holds true for John Marshall High School at 3939 Tracey Street in the city's Los Feliz neighborhood. It's the campus in *Pretty in Pink,* but also the site of the prom in *Grease.* The homes of rich jerk Steph (site of the party where Andie and Blaine have their first date) and rich jerk Hardy Jenns (Amanda Jones's ex, played by Craig Schaffer; Keith and Amanda's date ends at a party there) are about nine hundred feet from each other, at 366 S. June Avenue and 516 S. Hudson Avenue in the Hancock Park neighborhood in Los Angeles. This means Keith tells Watts "you look good wearing my future"—the last line of the movie and the beginning of their romance—around the corner from where Blaine promises Andie he won't make a move on her on their first date (the beginning of their romance).

By all accounts, *Pretty in Pink* and *Some Kind of Wonderful* were both filmed in LA for practical rather than artistic reasons. John Hughes had been forced to move his young family from suburban Chicago to the West Coast after *The Breakfast Club* completed filming in the late spring of 1984. Deutch was already based in Los Angeles, and with an inexperienced director in the captain's chair, whom Hughes had gone to bat for, it probably made sense to keep production close by to calm nerves. And unlike *Weird Science, The Breakfast Club,* or *Ferris Bueller's Day Off,* none of these movies make much use out of where they happen.

There are two exceptions: The prom in *Pretty in Pink* was filmed at the Biltmore Hotel in downtown Los Angeles, site of hundreds of movies and television shows and familiar to anyone who has set foot in its frescoed lobby. (Trivia: Molly Ringwald had a terrible case of the flu during the prom scenes and had to bunk at the hotel because she was too sick to get herself home.) And on Keith and Amanda's date, they have a heart to heart while sitting on the stage of the instantly recognizable Hollywood Bowl. The Hollywood Bowl played host to the 1984 Olympics opening night gala, and the International Olympic Committee had their headquarters at the Biltmore Hotel during the games. Both of these facts are coincidence. The John Hughes movies about class and race were both filmed in Los Angeles, after the games, when the city was in the midst of waking up to the inequity the games both hid and perpetuated. That's a coincidence, too, but seen with other LA movies of Brat Pack America, it feels less like one.

Fast Times, a Sure Thing, and An Excellent Adventure

LET'S WIND DOWN OUR tour of Los Angeles eighties teen movies with three quick stops: *Fast Times at Ridgemont High* (1982), *The Sure Thing* (1985), and *Bill & Ted's Excellent Adventure* (1988). Only one and a half of these three movies are filmed in Los Angeles, and only *The Sure Thing* says so, but without the *idea* of Southern California as a sun-and-surf paradise of Hawaiian shirts and hot blondes driving convertibles, none of these movies would exist. This is despite the fact that the idea of a hot blonde paradise was already old-fashioned when Jeff Spicoli said memorably at the end *Fast Times*, "All I need are some tasty waves, a cool buzz, and I'm fine."

The 1980s saw a resurgence of Southern California portrayed onscreen as a tanned, sun-bleached Eden. That notion had been most popular two decades before, thanks to movies like *The Endless Summer* (1966), TV shows like *Gidget* (1965), and the songs of The Beach Boys. The Los Angeles singer/songwriters that came immediately after—Jackson Browne, Warren Zevon, Joni Mitchell, and Crosby, Stills & Nash—had come of age creatively during the Vietnam War, Watergate, and a Los Angeles in the aftermath of the Charles Manson murders. To them, embracing Southern California as the home of beach parties and endless summers was a naïveté no one could afford.

The 1980s wanted those endless summers back. A movie star from a long-ago Hollywood sat in the White House. Valley girls repurposed early sixties surfer lingo for use in a decade when fun meant the mall. The *Sweet Valley High* series of young adult novels (about a pair of blonde, perfect twin sisters who live in fictional Sweet Valley, California) debuted in 1983 and played on or reacted to a cultural fascination with blonde, perfect Southern California, depending on when you read them and how much you wanted to be friends with the Wakefield sisters.

Fast Times at Ridgemont High, *The Sure Thing*, and *Bill & Ted's Excellent Adventure* all seem like featherweight goofy comedies. All three also feel smarter about Los Angeles than the city's easy stereotypes of a sunny paradise with its edges, dark corners, and difficulties removed. Each used this abstract idea of Los Angeles in order to subvert it.

Fast Times at Ridgemont High feels like an LA movie right down to the black-and-white checkered Vans shoes on its feet. Director Amy Heckerling, a New Yorker, had graduated from LA's American Film Institute in 1977 and shot the movie in Hollywood and in the Valley as her directorial debut in late 1981. An ensemble film about a half-dozen high school students, *Fast Times* did for the 1980s what *American Graffiti* had done the decade before, and *Dazed and Confused* (1993) would the decade after: serve as a yearbook snapshot of the disproportionate number of up-and-coming young actors featured in a single movie who would go on to bigger things. In *Fast Times*, Sean Penn, Jennifer Jason Leigh, Forest Whitaker, Eric Stoltz, Nicolas Cage, and Anthony Edwards all appeared early in their careers, which makes it as much a portrait of a sector of Los Angeles's creative community at the time as a portrait of the era's Southern California teenagers. In particular, Sean Penn's performance both launched his career and created the most famous surfing stoner in cinematic history (Bill & Ted, Wayne and Garth from *Wayne's World*, and Stifler from *American Pie* are all younger brothers of Jeff Spicoli).

Fast Times is based on a novel by Cameron Crowe, who wrote it at age twenty-two after going undercover at Clairemont High School in San Diego. He'd grown up in San Diego, and at sixteen became the youngest contributor ever to *Rolling Stone* magazine— his 2001 film, *Almost Famous*, came from this experience. Although only a few years had passed between his own time in high school and his undercover reporting on it, Crowe saw immediately that the class of 1981 had a different set of concerns and pressures than his own.

"Everybody had a job," said Crowe on *Fast Times*'s audio commentary. "There was this quest to have money for records, clothes."

Heckerling saw it, too. In her late twenties during filming, she and her team could tell that while they'd ostensibly been hired to make a comedy about teenagers, any teenager watching this movie would know being in high school in the early years of Brat Pack America meant having concerns bigger than passing history class, saving up for a used car, or getting a date to the prom.

"These weren't California kids prancing around in swimming pools," Heckerling said on the movie's commentary. "They had bigger problems that they were too young for. One of the things that made it possible for them to, say, go out to restaurants on dates was that they worked. They were like little grown-ups."

In a now-famous scene, sophomore Stacy Hamilton (Jennifer Jason Leigh) and her classmate Mark Ratner (Brian Backer) go on a first date to a German restaurant. Both work at the nearby mall—Mark as the "assistant to the assistant manager" at the movie theater, Stacey at a pizza joint across the main atrium. At the end of the date, Mark notices he's forgotten his wallet. He calls his friend Mike Damone (Robert Romanus), who brings it to him. The comedy on one level comes from typical first-date jitters and averting the embarrassment of not being able to pay the check. But

Heckerling adds a different kind of fear and pathos to the scene by oversizing the menus, chairs, and tables. Stacy and Mark don't look like teenagers on a first date, Heckerling says, but children pretending to be grown-ups on a first date.

"Fast times. The times are too fast for the people. They have so much drug pressure, sex pressure, career pressure. Even though they are children," said Heckerling. And even though *Fast Times* came out early in the decade (mid-1982), Heckerling was onto something: The explosion in shopping mall construction and chain retail in the early eighties meant a flood of teenagers entering the workforce, and clothes, music, and entertainment on which to spend new paychecks. On television, the workplace drama (*Hill Street Blues*), the big business soap opera (*Dallas*), and the sitcom featuring two-income families (*The Cosby Show, Family Ties*) and kids with jobs (*The Facts of Life*) reigned. The public profile of Wall Street traders Ivan Boesky and Michael Milken (both later convicted of insider trading) made long hours at the office wearing a tie seem sexy and lucrative. In the 1980s, going to work and the benefits that came from having your own spending money became hot.

Much of this was still to come when Amy Heckerling made *Fast Times*. Her strategy to deglamorize and present this pressure for kids to act like adults now seems ahead of its time, too. The movie has plenty of scenes of kids getting stoned, employed Moon Unit Zappa as a "technical consultant" so it could get teenagers right, and contains perhaps the most famous bikini drop in movie history (Phoebe Cates emerging from a swimming pool in slow motion set to The Cars song "Moving in Stereo"). It also has perhaps the least glamorous lose-your-virginity scene in recent film history—Heckerling describes it in her commentary, "Bare lightbulb, harsh shadow... It's the Valley, it's your virginity, there it goes"—and an abortion subplot decades ahead of its time but still photographed without music or effect in the everydayness of a late spring day in high school.

Fast Times ends happily with a surprising amount of sweetness. Stacy, the character who has undergone the largest transformation, tells her friend/mentor Linda (Phoebe Cates), "I don't want sex. Anybody can have sex. I want romance." To which Linda replies, "You want romance? In Ridgemont? We can't even get cable TV in Ridgemont and you want romance." The implication is that this slice of American teenage life happens in some town a little small, a little behind contemporary culture, despite the fact that Stacy's realization sounds mature, even a little urbane for a high school sophomore. "Ridgemont" is recognizably Los Angeles and its suburbs and nowhere else. But "Ridgemont" also seems like a place slightly outside and out of step with America's second-largest city just down the freeway.

Fast Times was only a modest hit upon release in August of 1982. Its real status as a generational classic came thanks to home video and the careers its actors, director (Heckerling would go on to write and direct *Clueless*), and screenwriter (Crowe wrote/directed *Say Anything*, *Singles*, *Almost Famous*, and *Jerry Maguire*, among others) would have afterward. In 2005, the Library of Congress selected *Fast Times* for admission into its National Film Registry.

It's now very hard to say, "Aloha, Mr. Hand," or "What are you, people? On dope?" to any movie fan and have them not know what you mean. And despite his two Oscars and rightful status as one of our greatest living actors, Sean Penn and his career can't be looked at without seeing Jeff Spicoli—shoulder-length hair, Vans shoes, flanked on the movie poster by two blonde clichés of a certain Southern California beauty—as a key chapter of it.

Fast Times uses Jeff Spicoli—board shorts, sunburnt nose, and all—as both a throwback to a simpler Los Angeles (where nothing mattered but tasty waves and a cool buzz) and as a critique of Reagan-era teenage careerism (all the other characters work at the mall or run a hustle there, like Mike Damone, Mark Ratner's best friend, does scalping concert tickets, while Spicoli just hangs out at the mall arcade wasting time). Spicoli's "tasty waves" quote might be the answer to Brad Hamilton (Judge Reinhold, playing Stacy's older brother) asking him why he doesn't have a job, but it could also be why he seems happier than all the characters that do.

"One of, obviously, my favorite characters in *Fast Times* is Jeff Spicoli," Heckerling said in *As If!: The Oral History of Clueless* (2015). "He doesn't mean anything negative about anybody else, and it wouldn't occur to him that they are thinking that about him."

Both Spicoli's dim innocence and surf-and-sun hedonism seem to come from an earlier Los Angeles, as if he arrived in 1980s Ridgemont from 1960s Malibu Beach. The character comfortably sits in both past and present (and, for that matter, with one Vans shoe in the future: His styled sloppiness and distaste for ambition predicted grunge), presenting like the former to both live in and satirize the latter. He's a bleached, stoned civic identity crisis, a representation of an LA of guiltless pleasure surrounded by the labor of others, a contradiction *Fast Times at Ridgemont High* finds funny and a little admirable.

The Sure Thing (1985) is a cross-country road trip movie that ends in Los Angeles, so only a few of its last scenes happen there. The film's title, however, refers to the same Southern California fantasy of blonde, Rose Parade perfection behind the *Sweet Valley High* books and on the *Fast Times at Ridgemont High* poster. The comedy and heart of *The Sure Thing* comes from dismantling the Southern California fantasy the "sure thing" embodies.

On the day of their high school graduation, Walter "Gib" Gibson (John Cusack) laments to his best friend, Lance (Anthony Edwards), that he's had a run of bad luck with girls. Lance sympathizes but then gives Gib a hard time for choosing to go to an East Coast college where the "girls all have bruised knees from playing the cello." Lance, a man with his priorities in the right place, is headed to UCLA, "home of the waves and the babes."

At school, Gib falls in love with Alison Bradbury (Daphne Zuniga), who Lance would probably describe as having bruised knees from playing the cello. Allison is an uptight preppy with a boyfriend named Jason (Boyd Gaines, who went on to be a three-time Tony winner) at (aha!) UCLA. Meanwhile, Lance has extended an invitation to Gib to come visit and score with a girl he has lined up for him: A "sure thing" blonde knockout just out of Catholic school and "in her experimental phase." When he sends

Gib a photo of a lookalike, Lance scrawls on the back of it: "This is the ugliest girl in California."

Come Christmas break, Gib and Allison end up in the same rideshare car on their way to Los Angeles. Mishaps ensue and the two end up stranded by the roadside somewhere in the middle of America. Love develops, but slowly, after many an argument and misunderstanding. Director Rob Reiner has said the initial pitch for *The Sure Thing* was "*It Happened One Night* with teenagers."

Reiner filmed the movie's UCLA scenes—Gib meeting his "sure thing" at Lance's fraternity house and Allison reuniting with Jason—at, well, UCLA. Few other moments in *The Sure Thing* were shot in the same state as where the movie says they happened. Gib and Allison's unnamed "East Coast college" was the University of the Pacific in Stockton, California, eighty miles east of San Francisco. For continuity, Reiner and screenwriters Stephen L. Bloom and Jonathan Roberts (who were actual college roommates) kept a journal of where in the US the rideshare car carrying Gib and Allison would be during any one scene. Except even the scenes that supposedly happened in North Carolina, Georgia, and Texas were filmed in Arizona and California. *The Sure Thing* crew did head east for the few shots that required snow on the ground and picked them up at Cornell University in Upstate New York. "With a $4 million budget, you make adjustments," said Reiner on *The Sure Thing*'s director's commentary. That's all the explanation I need for why *The Sure Thing* gets much of its comedy from East Coast/West Coast stereotypes, but was really only filmed within a day's drive of Los Angeles.

In a theme Reiner would return to in both *When Hally Met Sally* (1989) and *The Story of Us* (1999), the male half of this romantic comedy is loose and fun-loving and the female half-ordered and a bit stiff. But in *The Sure Thing*, Allison's uptightness has a particular New England bent. She dresses in grey sweaters and plaid skirts. Jason and Allison intend to graduate, become lawyers "somewhere in Vermont," and restore an old farmhouse. As if that didn't sound enough like a page out of the J. Peterman catalog, Allison, when discussing the farmhouse, throws in, "We're both crazy about basset hounds."

You're supposed to see Allison as the cultural opposite of Gib's bikinied blonde California dream girl with not a lot in between. The dictates of the story also don't allow for the "sure thing" (Nicollette Sheridan) to be anything but a pretty face, nor for Gib and Allison not to realize there's more to people than we first see, and fall for each other. All that said, *The Sure Thing* still works, even though its screenplay doesn't allow for a lot of surprises. It conflates one idea of Southern California beauty (blonde, carefree, willing) with a limited idea of female sexuality (willing and lacking complication or humanity), then has its characters be too smart for both.

The Sure Thing is a California movie because that's all it could afford to be. But its depth comes from using knee-jerk ideas about what Southern California is and then finding them rather shallow and dumb.

Released in early spring of 1985, *The Sure Thing* earned back nearly five times its budget, and, as of this writing, holds at 87 percent fresh rating on Rotten Tomatoes. I'd match it any day of the week against Cusack's *Better Off Dead* or Zuniga's *Spaceballs*, zanier movies the two stars of the lesser-known, but just as worth it, *The Sure Thing* did around this time.

Finally, we pull in San Dimas, California, for *Bill & Ted's Excellent Adventure* (1989), easily the most famous and only movie I can think of that proudly claims San Dimas, California, as home. San Dimas is a real city, population 33,000, about thirty miles east of Los Angeles, which was complete news to me when I first saw this movie in theaters. I figured "San Dimas" was some fictional beachside hamlet populated by the little brothers of Jeff Spicoli and their hot blonde stepmoms in red convertibles.

The movie concerns a pair of best friends/lovable dimwits (Alex Winter and Keanu Reeves) who have to pass their history final or they won't graduate high school. If they don't graduate, Ted's jerk of a dad will ship him off to military school, separating the best friends perhaps forever. Bill & Ted agree to pull an all-nighter, but being teenage boys of a certain Southern California vintage (they say "excellent" and "bogus" a lot, wear cut-off shirts and board shorts, have a third-rate heavy metal band called Wyld Stallyns, and use air guitar as punctuation) they are pretty convinced that all hope is lost.

Just then, a magical phone booth arrives from the great beyond (Bill & Ted happen to be sitting in a convenience store parking lot when this happens, prompting one of the movie's best lines, "Strange things are afoot at the Circle K") and out jumps Rufus (comedian George Carlin), who tells Bill & Ted the phone booth will take them back to any moment in history. Bill & Ted figure the best way to pass history is to convince great historical figures like Socrates, Napoleon, and Joan of Arc to be part of the presentation of their final history paper. Into the booth they go.

The specific assignment for their history paper is, "What would a famous historical figure think of San Dimas in the present?"— one of many indications that *Bill & Ted's Excellent Adventure* intends for San Dimas to be not just location but also supporting character. The two attend San Dimas High (most high schools in Brat Pack America movies go unnamed) and major scenes take place at the San Dimas Mall (where the historical figures get into all kinds of mischief) and Raging Waters water park, one of San Dimas's biggest attractions in real life (where we learn Napoleon loves the shit out of waterslides). When Socrates (who Bill & Ted call "So-Crates") is giving his presentation to the school, the two translate and tell us the ancient sage "loves San Dimas." There's even an unintentionally funny moment when a jocky classmate presenting his term paper before Bill & Ted runs out of things to say and resorts to yelling, "San Dimas High School football rules!"

It's impossible to forget *Bill & Ted's Excellent Adventure* happens in San Dimas, California. The movie reminds you over and over, yet nearly every moment of it was filmed in Phoenix, Arizona, an hour and a half by plane from San Dimas. Even the famous city landmark Raging Waters gets renamed Waterloo (although that's probably so the Napoleon-having-a-blast-there joke packs more punch), and was mostly shot at the Golfland Sunsplash Water Park at 155 W. Hampton Avenue in the Phoenix suburb of Mesa.

If you were a proud resident of San Dimas at this time and saw *Bill & Ted's Excellent Adventure* featuring "Bill S. Preston, Esquire and Ted Theodore Logan of San Dimas," you'd recognize nothing of your hometown and probably wonder what the hell these two goofballs were talking about. Then you'd see that this is a movie that gets tons of comic mileage out of an *idea* about Southern California teenagers (as dopey, sweet innocents—Jeff Spicoli minus the weed) without committing to the actual place at all. Bill & Ted even have to "cruise history" class in the last weeks of high school, just like Jeff Spicoli had to seven years earlier when, at the end of *Fast Times*, History teacher Mr. Hand dropped by on the evening of the graduation dance to give his worst student a take-home final exam.

Bill & Ted are a more innocent creation than Jeff Spicoli and exist to make a simpler point about friendship, loyalty, and goodness. Of course, they're a little dumb in pretty much the same way, but they aren't misfits or troublemakers. Spicoli might have famously said, "All I need are some tasty waves and a cool buzz and I'm fine" as a life philosophy, and Bill & Ted might have echoed it with their own "Party on, dude!" But when Rufus asks them for their own life philosophy, they first say, "Always be excellent to each other," which is about generosity rather than self-fufillment.

Bill & Ted feel like Jeff Spicoli with the edges rubbed off. You can watch *Bill & Ted's Excellent Adventure* and call them nice kids. Jeff Spicoli seems fun and entertaining, but seems to bring about destruction without meaning to. (He crashes Forest Whitaker's new car, then tells his passenger, "We're lucky I had fast reflexes!"). You also get the sense Heckerling and Crowe had something bigger in mind for Spicoli, a stereotype that also works as satire and social criticism. Bill & Ted are a similar California type (fun-loving, half-baked, a little dim) but defanged, harmless protagonists of a harmless movie. They're a type you want to hug, not like Spicoli, whom you could see hugging after he took a shower but would also never encourage your sister to date.

Fast Times at Ridgemont High, The Sure Thing, and *Bill & Ted's Excellent Adventure* are all comedies horsing around with our preconceived notions of Southern California. They don't stand in opposition to the 1984 Los Angeles Olympic cheerleading of the period—LA as a sunny, unified metropolis—but maintain respectful distance. They are comfortable with conflicting ideas of Los Angeles from different periods in the city's history in a way the 1984 Olympics were not

BRAT PACK AMERICA TALKS TO. . .WRITER/DIRECTOR AMY HECKERLING

MY HECKERLING MAY BE the only filmmaker we can credit with *the* defining teen movie of two separate generations. A graduate of NYU and the American Film Institute, she made her directorial debut with *Fast Times at Ridgemont High* and wrote and directed *Clueless*, her sixth film, in 1995. A number of well-known actors owe their career launches (Sean Penn, Alicia Silverstone) or revivals (John Travolta in *Look Who's Talking*) to her work.

The winner of AFI's Franklin J. Schaffner Alumni Medal and the Crystal Award for Women in Film, we spoke to Heckerling in February of 2016, while she was adapting *Clueless* into a Broadway musical.

Kevin Smokler: Who are your cinematic peers, influences, and disciples?

Amy Heckerling: As far as the ones who were active when I was growing up and I was a student, my big heroes are Woody Allen, Mel Brooks, Martin Scorsese. New York filmmakers. In my own generation, Martin Brest, one of my best buddies and a brilliant filmmaker. Also Harold Ramis, who had the humor and the heart and wanted comedy to say something, too. As far as females, I look at Joan Micklin Silver and Lina Wertmüller.

Filmmakers today? Judd Apatow, Seth Rogan, James Franco, all brilliant.

KS: Judd Apatow would probably call your work an influence of his.

AH: I know him. But his movies are purely his own and are wonderful.

KS: *Clueless* takes place explicitly in Beverly Hills and the Valley. *Fast Times* was shot in the Valley and in Santa Monica, but the story happens in a fictional place called "Ridgemont." What was behind the choice to fictionalize *Fast Times*'s locations while making plain those in *Clueless*?

AH: The characters in *Fast Times* are based on real high school students that Cameron [Crowe] wrote about in his book that was the basis for the movie. At the very least, we had to make the movie its own thing to protect their privacy.

To shoot in LA and not in San Diego, where the high school actually was, that decision was already made when I came on. To shoot on the lot, at the mall nearby, at the school nearby, that meant an executive could stumble out of bed and check on us. Which made sense. It was my first movie and Cameron's first movie. And *Fast Times* was the kind of small-budget film where nobody was being put up in a hotel and everyone drove themselves.

KS: Ridgemont seems like a small town, like when Linda says to Stacy, "We can't even get cable TV in Ridgemont and you want romance," and the LA of *Clueless* feels like a giant, sprawling metropolis, like in the scene where the kids argue about who will drive who home from the party in the Valley…

AH: *Fast Times* may have been based on a smaller town than LA, but not having cable wasn't so unusual in late 1981. Cable would be there very soon. We caught these kids the moment before.

The directions argument in *Clueless* I'm afraid comes straight out of Jane Austen. There's a scene in *Emma* where they argue over who will leave with whom in which carriages. Reading it, you know that, even back then, driving home with someone was really about who gets private time with whom, not just who is going in which direction but who gets to spend time alone with whom. The trick is convincing that person that it was an intelligent solution. It's the same old story, whether you're talking about a carriage or driving or an Uber.

KS: How did you choose to shoot *Fast Times* at the Galleria mall? When you did, it was only a year old and it was before the Frank Zappa song "Valley Girl" made it the mall that represented all others.

AH: I was not, at that time, a mall expert. The theme of the movie was the characters were growing up too fast. They were all working people with jobs even though they were really still children. If they were all in a hot tub and smoking dope, they wouldn't have been as relatable.

I also liked the idea of the action all being in one place, on a single boulevard or consolidated all in the same building under one roof, where kids at different jobs would walk past and run into each other all wearing their uniforms from work. I thought the mall should be rundown, lower-middle-class feeling, matching the downtroddeness of the characters.

The studio didn't like that idea. There was a real push for the kids to be more privileged. But I was coming from New York in the 1970s, when garbage was piled higher than your head and everybody was talking about how this was going to be the first generation of kids doing worse than their parents. I wanted to keep that in mind even though we were filming in LA.

KS: Where did the choice to begin and end the movie at the mall come from?

AH: *Fast Times* opens with a feeling of entering a world with these kids who both work and hang out there. Let's go to this place and meet everyone there. You hear The Go-Gos. There are the fast-food and pizza places, the movie theater, the Hot Dog on a Stick. There are the characters in their element.

The idea came from a movie that I loved called *Mean Streets*. After all the adventures and romance, you get the neighborhood closing down and the lights going off. We've gone on this journey, now we're saying goodbye. There's something deeply satisfying about that.

The studio [Universal] had made *American Graffiti* about ten years before, which ended by telling you what happened to the characters. They wanted to know what happened to everyone, and I thought, do we really need that? We just saw a whole movie showing what happened to them.

We joked that this was "The Universal Ending" because they'd used it brilliantly in one film (*American Graffiti*) and hilariously in another after that (*Animal House*, 1978). So I thought, why not?

KS: None of the endings for the characters are surprising. It makes perfect sense that Brad Hamilton got promoted to manager at the Mini-Mart and Jeff Spicoli hired Van Halen to play at his birthday.

AH: Of course the endings aren't surprising. They aren't grown up yet.

KS: It's staggering the number of actors we know now who got their big break in your movies—Sean Penn, Forest Whitaker, Jennifer Jason Leigh, Alicia Silverstone—when they were very young. What do you look for in casting for a teenage role, when the right actor might be twenty-six or fourteen?

AH: There's usually not a perfect match between the character in my head and the right actor. In the best of all worlds, I find someone who brings something unexpected to the character I hadn't thought of. But ultimately, I'm trying to find the right person for the project, not trying to show the town or the studio how smart I am by whom I chose.

The studio usually has all sorts of suggestions. The right actor may come from there, or it may have been someone you were thinking of but didn't see in the right context right away. So you don't always know if the right person is someone you bump into every day and fall in love with, or did the elders in the community set it up for you?

I'm thrilled that two of them were nominated for Oscars this year—Jennifer Jason Leigh for *The Hateful Eight* and Saoirse Ronan for *Brooklyn*. Saoirse played Michelle Pfeiffer's daughter in *I Could Never Be Your Woman* [which Heckerling wrote and directed in 2007], so I will always think of her as a kid. Meryl Streep in a kid's body.

KS: What are the different sides of you that come out as an artist when writing versus directing?

AH: Two separate people. The writer in you wishes there was a better director; that director is saying, "Who the hell wrote this?"

Fast Times reframed my identity as a director instead of as a writer. I had a script in preproduction before *Fast Times* that didn't happen. Then *Fast Times* came along. After that, you get studios saying what would you like to direct next, not what would you like to write next.

After *European Vacation* (1985), which is a great movie that everyone should rent and fall in love with but was not a great experience for me, I didn't want to work with actors I wasn't crazy about. That shifted my focus back to writing my own scripts and directing my own material.

KS: If the characters from *Fast Times at Ridgemont High* were real people around right now in 2016, what would they be doing?

AH: They were real people from Cameron's book. So I bow to him on whatever the fictional versions of them might be up to know.

KS: Is there a movie left unmade for you?

AH: Oh, I can't say. I know that's a horrible answer. But the evil eye will hear.

CHAPTER 4: BEAT STREETS AND HOUSE PARTIES

The First Hip-Hop Movies

Movies Discussed: *Wild Style, Beat Street, House Party, Krush Groove*

W E'VE BOARDED THE DELOREAN and set course for the eastern edge of Brat Pack America. While we're in transit here, I've a question for you…

Can you name an eighties teen movie that takes place in New York City?

It's harder than it seems. In the 1970s, New York had been *the* setting for movies about wild-eyed young people—*The Panic in Needle Park, Mean Streets, Hair, Saturday Night Fever*, and *The Warriors*. But in the 1980s, our map shows the teen movie heading west to Chicago and Los Angeles and to smaller towns in the Pacific Northwest and mid-South. At the same time, New York movies mostly concerned themselves with adults either working in big business (*Working Girl, Wall Street, Secret of My Success, The Bonfire of the Vanities*), trying to make it in the arts (*Tootsie; A Chorus Line; Bright Lights, Big City*), in mating dances they don't quite understand (*When Harry Met Sally, Something Wild, After Hours*), or saving a city from the Stay-Puft Marshmallow Man (*Ghostbusters*).

At the movie theater, the New York of the 1980s—of Mayor Ed Koch, Wall Street's "Masters of the Universe," the early days of the AIDS crisis, and, Subway Vigilante ,Bernhard Goetz—seemed empty of youth, a kind of *Logan's Run* in reverse. Teen movies would return to New York in the 1990s—*The Basketball Diaries*, *Kids*, and *Cruel Intentions*, to name only a few—but for now, where had all the teenagers and the movies about them gone?

Answer: to street corners in the Bronx, warehouses downtown, and public parks near the East and Hudson Rivers. Carrying two turntables and a mic.

If anything rebalances the map of Brat Pack America by telling the stories of young people in New York during the 1980s, it is the first generation of hip-hop movies. Filmed and then released between 1982 and 1984, this small group of films—*Wild Style*, *Beat Street,* and *Krush Groove*—looked at a nascent arts movement trying to understand its growing power and relevance. Their casts featured real-life rappers and DJs, graffiti writers and breakdancers—manifestations of hip-hop's mythical four elements—all at the top of their game and at the same time struggling with the game getting bigger than them, their friends, and their neighborhoods.

The principal characters in the first hip-hop movies are young people, late teens to early twenties, at the forefront of a young culture about to get very big. As such, they had the same ethical dilemmas as their counterparts at the forefront of vaudeville, country music, jazz, and rock and roll: how to get your parents and friends to accept your passion even if they don't understand it; how not to succumb to easy, sleazy money; which of your friends to trust; and what "making it" really means. Which means if you've seen movies about the pioneers of vaudeville, country, jazz, and rock and roll, you've already got the premise behind these pioneering hip-hop films.

Hip-hop may be the newest of these uniquely American musical cultures, but America was still unwired enough back then (no Internet, cable TV had only 9 percent of total television viewership by 1983) that those in the New York area could believe their movement was the only one of its kind. As a result, all of the early hip-hop films were made, on location and proudly so, in Manhattan and the surrounding boroughs. And since each of these movies tells the story of hip-hop growing up, from a neighborhood art form to a cultural phenomenon, their choices of locations argue for hip-hop's true birthplace, an attempt very early on to set the historical record straight.

This first generation of hip-hop movies were all filmed and released in the first half of 1980s. The hip-hop movie then stayed relatively quiet until 1990, with the release of *House Party*, which effectively transitions the genre out of its first era and into its second. Premiering at Sundance and shot in Los Angeles, *House Party* moved the hip-hop movie to California—the LA-based *Boyz n the Hood*, *Menace II Society*, and *Friday* arrived soon after—at the same time that the national focus on hip-hop shifted from New York to West Coast rappers and producers like Ice Cube, Dr. Dre, and Tupac Shakur. The characters in *House Party* are also young enough to talk about having seen *Krush Groove* and *Beat Street* in movie theaters, indicating a generational passing of time between them and their hip-hop movies of a few years before.

More importantly, *House Party* shows the hip-hop movie changing things up not just by geography but economics: it's the first hip-hop movie to include both working and middle-class kids and characters with differing levels of education and employment. The African-American professional class would have a significant place in the hip-hop movies of the 1990s—see Laurence Fishburne as a neighborhood small businessman in *Boyz n the Hood*, and the documentary *The Show* (1995) about hip-hop's stars learning to be both artists and entrepreneurs—but as we'll see, that inclusion starts with *House Party* and a funny yet powerful conversation about the disadvantages of dating a girl from the projects.

"The Birthplace of"

MUSICAL CULTURES RARELY HAVE a single birthplace. Instead, like scientific discoveries, they bubble up around the same time in different places: Congo Square in New Orleans is the symbolic cradle of jazz, but early jazz players also came from Memphis,

St. Louis, and Chicago. The Rock and Roll Hall of Fame is in Cleveland because Cleveland broadcaster and concert promoter Alan Freed popularized the term "rock and roll." But the songs Freed played on the radio and at the dances he threw for Cleveland teenagers came from performers and record labels based in Memphis, Los Angeles, Chicago, Houston, and New York. The August 1927 recording sessions of the Carter Family happened in Bristol, Tennessee, recognized in 1998 by the US Congress as the Birthplace of Country Music. Atlanta doesn't have such a bill in its pocket, but is still claimed by several historians as the rightful birthplace of country music.

The New York State Office of Parks and Recreation now recognizes an apartment building at 1520 Sedgewick Avenue in the Bronx as the "birthplace of hip-hop." In that building, a Jamaican-American teenager nicknamed Clive Campbell (his friends called him "Kool Herc" thanks to his big muscles which gave him a frame like Hercules) threw a dance party for his younger sister in the community room on August 11, 1973. Herc repeated the break-beat of records to keep his friends and neighbors dancing longer and then talked rhythmically over that beat. The work of West Coast hip-hop scholars like Stanford's Jeff Chang and CSU Long Beach's Oliver Wang show that both the San Francisco Bay Area and Los Angeles had similar grassroots DJ and dance party scenes as far back as 1973.

Few music genres are as consumed by their own beginnings as hip-hop. One listen to Jay-Z's catalog and we know he was born December 4, 1968, and grew up in Marcy Houses public housing in the Bed-Stuy neighborhood of Brooklyn. Listen to the Adele or Coldplay discography and that information doesn't exactly jump out at you. The hilarious 1993 hip-hop mockumentary *Fear of a Black Hat* (think *This Is Spinal Tap* about rap music) jabs at this obsession in its very first scene: The world's dumbest rap group NWH (Niggas With Hats) is being asked by a journalist what neighborhood they come from. None of them can remember, so after looking at each other in disbelief, they yell defensively at the camera, "We don't have to say where we're from!"

Regardless of historical accuracy, a symbolic birthplace gives a musical form a narrative, an opening chapter when telling its story. The first hip-hop movies each had different plots, actors, budgets, and soundtracks. They also had more or less the same goal: to capture what hip-hop was, hint at where it was going, and define, once and for all, where it started and who started it.

John Hughes's teen movies used the north suburbs of Chicago as blank notebooks for you to fill in with your own teenage experiences and dreams. The eighties teen movie in Los Angeles saw the city as a battlefield between the rich and poor. The New York blocks seen in the first generation of hip-hop movies like *Wild Style* and *Beat Street* are statements of hometown pride and clarifying a historical narrative, saying, "Look at this culture we brought into the world. Look at where it came and what can happen to it when the wrong people from outside where we come from try to exploit it."

Wild Style: "The Bible of Hip-Hop"

WILD STYLE IS NOW considered the first hip-hop movie. It was shot for around $75,000 in 1982, released in only a few major cities in 1983, and its fame grew in tandem with the art form it documented. As of this writing, it has an 89 percent fresh rating on Rotten Tomatoes. VH1 Hip-Hop Honors saluted *Wild Style* as a trailblazer in 2007. A sumptuous 2013 DVD release honoring its thirtieth birthday asserted in silicon and cardstock its standing as a classic of music cinema. The rapper Nas has called *Wild Style* "The Bible of Hip-Hop."

Wild Style is the story of a young graffiti artist (Lee Quiñones) who paints under the alias "Zorro," and his girlfriend Lady Pink (Sandra Fabara), also a graffiti artist. Zorro gets profiled in a magazine article on the growing hip-hop arts scene in the South Bronx, which attracts the interest of a downtown art gallery and its well-heeled collectors. He sees this as an opportunity to move his paintings from subway train cars (which get painted over by other graffiti writers and eventually washed away by the transit police) to something more permanent and lasting. But how far will this take him from the neighborhood that nurtured his talent and the culture it helped build in the first place?

Meanwhile, a local promoter named Fade (future *Yo! MTV Raps* host, Fab 5 Freddy) is planning a giant outdoor concert featuring all the major MCs, DJs, and breakdance groups from the neighborhood. Fade asks Zorro to paint a mural for the event, an art piece that commands his time, passion, and awareness of what he and the community are about to bring to a larger world. As if to document that community and this moment in their history, *Wild Style* writer/director Charlie Ahearn supplemented Zorro's story with musical montages of several of the South Bronx's premier hip-hop groups, including Rock Steady Crew and Cold Crush Brothers performing and battling each other for neighborhood supremacy. Future Rock and Roll Hall of Famer Grandmaster Flash has a cameo as (what else?) a DJ demonstrating the scratching and mixing techniques he pioneered in real life.

Originally from the Lower East Side of Manhattan, Lee Quiñones was a well-known graffiti artist when he played Zorro. Sandra Fabara, who played his girlfriend, was also a well-known graffiti artist and Quiñones's actual girlfriend at the time (both are practicing artists today whose work has shown all over the world). Most of the MCs, DJs, and dancers that fill the movie also played versions of themselves. According to a 2013 oral history of *Wild Style*, the performers took Ahearn's script as a suggestion and improvised most of the scenes via quick setups, ad-libbed dialogues, and "one-take filmmaking." Patti Astor, a veteran of the New York experimental film world, who played the reporter that profiles Zorro, was the only cast member with any real acting experience.

Wild Style shot on street corners, empty lots, front steps, and public parks around the South Bronx. Ahearn spent a third of the movie's budget renting an actual MTA train yard for the early scenes, where Zorro, Lady Pink, and friends tag subway cars, so the scene wouldn't have to be recreated somewhere else. Even outside the Bronx, the *Wild Style* crew chose locations that required minimal set decoration and production design, places that could effectively play themselves; Zorro's trip to the downtown apartment of a wealthy art patron was in fact the apartment of a wealthy art patron, playing a wealthy art patron.

Charlie Ahearn wasn't making a documentary, but he wasn't quite making a fiction film either. Watching *Wild Style* now feels like watching an attempt to capture a time and place of an artistic movement by daisy-chaining a loose collection of anecdotes and scenes about it together. It feels like Italian neorealism with a break beat, or music journalism filmed impressionistically like Charles Burnett's legendary debut film *Killer of Sheep* (1978).

"The Bronx Felt Burned"

The story of how *Wild Style* happened came from equal parts improvisation and seeming inevitability. Ahearn had been a kid from Upstate New York who arrived in Manhattan in 1973 with hopes of becoming an artist. He became aware of Quiñones's work a few years later. Quiñones knew Fab 5 Freddy, who had friends and associates in both the downtown Manhattan art world of CBGB and Andy Warhol and in the graffiti art and street DJing and dancing going on in the Bronx. Freddy had seen posters for Ahearn's first film, a martial arts piece called *The Deadly Art of Survival* (1979), and liked its handmade, DIY vibe. When the two ran into each other at an art opening, Freddy said to Ahearn, "Hey, let's make a movie." Ahearn only agreed if the movie could feature Quiñones and his paintings.

Fab 5 Freddy's idea of matchmaking the participants and sensibilities of an uptown Bronx neighborhood culture of black and Latino teenagers and the largely white SoHo and Greenwich Village commercial art establishment of galleries, museums, and professional curators wasn't just another stolen moment from real life that ended up in *Wild Style*. In retrospect, that meeting of minds is also *Wild Style* telling one version of the bigger story of hip-hop itself: born in the Bronx, embraced by Manhattan and its cultural power brokers, and then launched like a rocket out into the rest of the world.

By the time of the *Wild Style* shoot in mid-1982, the fuse on that rocket was already lit. Fab 5 Freddy had appeared the year before in the number-one song "Rapture" by Blondie, friends of his from that downtown scene. Even earlier in 1979, the song "Rapper's Delight" by the Sugarhill Gang had become the first hip-hop song to reach the Billboard Top 40. The Sugarhill Gang wasn't from Sugarhill (a neighborhood in Harlem) but rather Englewood, New Jersey, eight miles northwest and across the Hudson River. They didn't come from any arts community resembling the one depicted in *Wild Style* and were instead assembled from scratch by an enterprising New Jersey producer named Sylvia Robinson. And though "Rapper's Delight" is generally credited with introducing hip-hop to American culture at large (it's been inducted into the Library of Congress's National Sound Registry mostly for this reason), calling it the "first rap song," as many did, is playing a shell game with history. "'Rapper's Delight,'" wrote music journalist and scholar Oliver Wang in *Classic Material: The Hip-Hop Album Guide*, was "a pretty impressive fabrication, lightning in a bottle," but manufactured to take advantage of what a neighborhood and community had created organically. "It's not like the guys involved were the 'real' hip-hop icons of the era, like Grandmaster Flash."

"The people in the Bronx felt burned," Ahearn says in *Wild Style*'s oral history, talking about the success of "Rapper's Delight." "They knew something was up but they didn't know what, and they thought, 'Maybe this guy is it. Maybe we should do this thing with him and maybe it's going to lead to something.' So everybody wanted to be down with it."

Despite his friendship with Freddy and Quiñones, Ahearn was acutely aware of the credibility and trust he'd have to earn in order to film *Wild Style* in the South Bronx. The MCs, DJs, dancers, and graffiti writers of the neighborhood had seen "Rapper's Delight" blow up and be inaccurately named the "first" rap song. The artform they felt they had created had been, literally, sold across the river, and they were angry about it.

Never mind, that hip-hop survived at all *thanks* to "Rapper's Delight," suggested Wang in a July 2015 interview on NPR's *Bullseye*, fabricated as it might have been.

"Hip-Hop was not a recorded culture. It was on its way out in 1979. That record reinvigorated what we know as hip-hop today."

If Ahearn wanted to make a movie about these very early days of hip-hop, this was the climate of confusion and mistrust he was stepping into. The art form's history was up for grabs. *Wild Style* as an attempt to speak of hip-hop's "real" beginnings had everything to do with not only who its founding fathers and mothers were but also where they came from. The South Bronx was hip-hop's Independence Hall, not the only place of the republic's founding, but the one that mattered most, the one that gets put front and center in the first draft of history.

"Hip-Hop's Woodstock"

WILD STYLE ENDS WITH the massive concert Fab 5 Freddy has spent the movie putting together. Ahearn and his team shot the scene in East River Park in the bottom right corner of Manhattan, the same park Quiñones had played in as a neighborhood kid. The East River Amphitheater, which served as the concert's stage, was a neglected, crumbling public space when Ahearn and his team showed up to film. The cast and crew cleaned up and then turned the scene into an actual block party by inviting people from the neighborhood to listen and dance along to the music. The shoot itself had no permits and was therefore completely illegal, but when the police showed up Ahearn played along like everything was registered and legal and thanked them for coming by and checking. The cops nodded and drove off.

At the scene's climax, breakdancers, then rappers, then DJs, and back again take over the stage like waves of an army. The crowd roars in welcome. In the movie's oral history, Patti Astor called it "a hip-hop Woodstock."

Arching over it all is Zorro's mural, two godlike hands emitting a lightning bolt that frames the edge of the concrete half dome of the amphitheater (a visual motif in the movie's animated opening credits). It seems to embrace the performers and lift the crowd. Zorro climbs up the dome, looks out at the sea of his friends, neighbors, and yes, many strangers. Face lit from below, Zorro sees the amazing thing they've all created, the golden present pointing to an unknown future. He mouths the word "Wow."

Roll credits.

The choice of venue was part practical (nobody used it, so nobody would care if *Wild Style* did), part personal (Quiñones grew up nearby), and hugely symbolic—the East River Amphitheater is an hour's ride on the M subway train from the South Bronx. Everyone who performed at Fab 5 Freddy's concert would be leaving home, leaving hip-hop's Garden of Eden and bringing this thing they made out into the world.

The "world" of *Wild Style* doesn't get any bigger than New York, but the story it tells wants it that way. It's 1983, and *Wild Style* knows hip-hop has already escaped the garden. It knows the serpents of commerce and ill-informed outsiders are already here. It knows the world already knows about the culture it has documented. By staging hip-hop's finest moment from its earliest days not in its birthplace but on its launching pad, *Wild Style* can set both the historical record straight and document the moment of innocence before everything changed. Being part fiction, part documentary allows *Wild Style* to say, "This may not be exactly how it happened. But this is how you should remember it."

Wild Style opened in the spring of 1983 at the Embassy Theater at Forty-Seventh and Broadway in Times Square. Ahearn and his team had also chosen this location carefully. The *Wild Style* crew and their friends hung out regularly at the theater, which showed kung fu and grind house movies. But Times Square was also easy to get to via subway and bus from any borough. Early in the film's release, Ahearn later said, this led to "kids from Queens, the Bronx, and Brooklyn lining up around the block" to watch a movie playing only in the dead center of Manhattan.

Times Square at the time was the geographical embodiment of the conflict between fame and heartache, between making it in

New York and losing your soul while trying. Times Square had Broadway and tour buses, but it also had hookers, pimps, and addicts. It had success and struggle at the same intersection. The High School for Performing Arts in *Fame*, one block away from the Embassy Theater, had captured this on screen brilliantly three years before. Now here was *Wild Style*, showing at the world's busiest crossroads and using that location to underline the movie's message, "this is the story of a movement, probably before you knew about it. It's bigger and different now, but once upon a time, we did it our way. We kept it pure and away from how it could have gone wrong. And here we are, at the crossroads of the world, to show you how it first happened."

Beat Street

THE SUMMER AFTER *WILD Style*, *Beat Street* came out, and then *Krush Groove*, both movies filmed and set in New York City, both interested in capturing the early days of hip-hop. *Beat Street* had the backing of a Hollywood studio (Orion Pictures) and a strong pedigree in African-American arts. The film was produced by Harry Belafonte, who saw it as a record of the evolution of black youth culture. Belafonte hired veteran director Stan Lathan, who would go on to direct comedy specials for Dave Chappelle and create the HBO shows *Def Comedy Jam* and *Def Poetry Jam* with Russell Simmons. On *Beat Street*, Lathan worked from a script by pioneering hip-hop journalist Steven Hager.

Structurally, *Beat Street* feels like *Wild Style*, a collection of loosely joined anecdotes with long performance montages, a moving musical finale, and character taking priority over plot. *Krush Groove* had most of those elements, too, but felt linear rather than episodic. *Beat Street* takes its time, giving us the backstories and home lives of its characters, which doesn't happen at all in *Wild Style*. *Krush Groove* feels in an awful hurry, thrown together and scattered, the story of the early days of pioneering hip-hop label Def Jam, but filmed when Def Jam was less than two years old.

Beat Street was a box office success despite the creative team being unhappy with the outcome. "I wanted to get the story told as accurately as possible, and I knew the money was rapidly changing the scene" Hager told Jeff Chang, for the seminal 2005 hip-hop history, *Can't Stop Won't Stop*. But Hager added, "Not a single word of anything I actually wrote made it into that unfortunate film." *Krush Groove* did less well. It recouped its budget, but that was all.

Both *Krush Groove* and *Beat Street* were filmed on location in New York City, yet use the city very differently than *Wild Style*. *Wild Style* wanted to show what happened to hip-hop before the rest of the world found out about it, and used key locations to draw lines between here and there, between then and now. *Beat Street* and *Krush Groove* were also stories of rising young hip-hop artists, but no one is conflicted about "making it." There's already money in the game, some clean, some not so much, but everyone wants it. *Krush Groove* and *Beat Street* replace the question of whether to succeed with how to succeed and with whose help.

Both movies assume that hip-hop has left the garden. It's only a year, maybe eighteen months, after *Wild Style*, but hip-hop culture is now an everyday presence in the lives of teenagers all over New York, not just the South Bronx. Hip-hop now has temples of worship, performance spaces where its best and brightest gather and new talent is discovered. Auditions, demo tapes, decision-makers, and the hopeful are commonplace rather than moments of revelation.

Hip-hop is no longer innocent and golden, but a culture on the move. And though both *Beat Street* and *Krush Groove* also confine their screenplays to New York City, both movies use location to confirm hip-hop already considers all of New York City its own.

"Ya In or Ya Out?" Here

WILD STYLE IS AN outdoor movie. Few scenes happen in homes, schools, businesses, or even the music venues and community centers essential to hip-hop's early days. We know almost nothing about the characters' backgrounds or personal lives. We never meet their parents or see them going to work or to school. Life in *Wild Style* seems to be lived in public, in the streets, in parks and alleys, on subway trains, and for art alone. Other than the finale, its most famous scene happens outdoors, too, a battle between the South Bronx's premiere hip-hop crews on the basketball court of Slattery Playground at 183rd Street and Valentine Avenue, which looks very similar today as then.

Beat Street wanted to capture the same neighborhood arts scene as *Wild Style* ("Street kids in the Bronx and nothing else," associate producer Michael Holman said in a 2014 oral history of the movie), but a few things happened on the way to production. One, the screenplay was rewritten several times to reflect the concerns of both producers and studio. Later drafts included a love story for one of the Bronx boys (Guy Davis) with a midtown Manhattan modern dance choreographer (Rae Dawn Chong). They have an extended first date walk through Central Park, past Tavern on the Green at Sixty-Seventh and Central Park West.

The producers also wanted higher-stakes drama instead of what Hager called "a slice-of-life drama à la Clifford Odets," so one character dies violently and leaves behind a young family. The two Bronx boys—a talented DJ (Guy Davis) and his younger brother (Robert Taylor), a talented breakdancer—live at home with their single mother, who worries about them as they've already lost a brother to street violence.

The characters in *Beat Street* have backstories, which means they also have homes and families and schools and jobs. We see their deep bond to hip-hop culture in that context, decorating a new apartment with graffiti murals, holding an improvised party in a nearby condemned building where a cousin is squatting, practicing a break beat mix in an overcrowded bedroom. Hager may have been after the documentation of a subculture, but *Beat Street* looks like a movie about a subculture that has already found its way into the rhythms and spaces of ordinary life. Early in the movie, while the mother of the two brothers (Mary Alice) tries to serve them breakfast and they won't stop freestyling at the table, she looks at them both and rhymes back: "Eat your eggs. Or I'll break your legs."

Krush Groove also uses indoor locations as an indicator of hip-hop's growing place in the lives of all young people, not just the art form's best and brightest. It's the story of a young record label, a company, a place of employment, so its headquarters are naturally one of the movie's key settings. Krush Groove operates out of the dorm room of one of its founders (the real Def Jam began in the NYU dorm room of cofounder Rick Rubin), where the team packages and ships records, calls radio stations and club bookers, and auditions new talent. But the label's funny money situation sends its other cofounder Russell Walker (Blair Underwood, a brief moment before he joined the cast of *LA Law*, playing Def Jam's actual cofounder Russell Simmons) back to his preacher father to ask for a loan. Russell doesn't get the loan and resorts to borrowing money from a shady neighborhood loan shark (Richard Gant, a few years before he pulled the same fast one on Rocky Balboa in *Rocky V*). In a parallel story, three high school kids who call themselves the Disco Boys (played by real-life hip-hop group The Fat Boys) want more than anything to be signed by Krush Groove. When they are not bringing their classmates to their feet by staging impromptu performances in the hallways of their high school, they are looking for an in—any in—with the label, including getting themselves into a New York City–wide talent contest and (no surprise) winning.

Krush Groove filmed scenes in all of the New York boroughs except Staten Island, in locations as important to the history of hip-hop as the club Disco Fever (more on that in a moment), but also as ordinary as churches, dorm rooms, and high schools. The world of hip-hop isn't enormous here either, but it's big enough to not just be the province of one neighborhood, of only young people, of just blacks and Latinos (Rick Rubin, who plays himself, is a white Jewish fella from the very Jewish Long Island town of Long Beach), or even existing performers with established hip-hop cred (singer and percussionist Sheila E., who played Underwood's love interest, was primarily a veteran of Latin jazz and funk bands). The banality of the locations—offices, churches, schools, fast-food joints—demonstrated that hip-hop was on its way from being underground to being everywhere. That meant unsavory characters were suddenly interested in it, but also that one record label, the one producing *Krush Groove*, a movie about itself, was there to responsibly transition the art form from a Bronx youth subculture to an American pop culture.

It was arguable whether the real Def Jam had done it yet at that point. (They would soon enough—Def Jam signed LL Cool J, Public Enemy, and the Beastie Boys, and Rick Rubin conceived the 1986 Run-D.M.C./Aerosmith crossover "Walk This Way.") It would also be hard to give one company more credit for making hip-hop the sound of young America the way Motown had done a generation before. But all that hadn't happened yet when they made *Krush Groove*. The ordinary backdrops around New York City then solidified a myth still in the telling, that hip-hop was becoming everyone's music and there were stacks of money to be made, but Def Jam was making sure it didn't get too fancy too fast and lose its soul in the process.

"Do You Believe in the Future?"

KRUSH GROOVE, PRODUCED BY and about a record label, had a vested interest in stuffing the film with as many of the label's artists as it could. The Beastie Boys have a cameo as car wash jockeys and a young LL Cool J made his film and music debut as an auditioning/aspiring MC. Run-D.M.C. played (and were for real) the label's signature act.

This also meant that, as they had in *Wild Style,* performances would play a big part in *Krush Groove*. Where those performances happened revealed something as well: that the movie's entrepreneurial main characters not only respected the art form's roots but also represented the next phase of its evolution.

Disco Fever was formally a neighborhood bar in the South Bronx. Opened in 1976 and losing money in its first year, the owners began booking Tuesday nights with DJs like Grandmaser Flash, who they had seen perform in parks around the neighborhood. The event and others like it proved so successful that soon the club featured hip-hop performers every night of the week. Disco Fever received a mention in the Grandmaster Flash song "The Message," and a year later, a 1983 profile in *People* magazine called it "The Rap Capital of the Solar System."

In that article, a young hip-hop businessman and manager named Russell Simmons swore by the venue's power as a tastemaker and showcase for talent. "If a record doesn't go 'round the Fever," Simmons said. "It's fake."

Disco Fever's spot in *Krush Groove* mirrored its role in real life. The movie's stars perform there. The movie's aspiring stars, the Disco Boys, try to weasel their way in. It's where Russell and Rick spot Sheila E., then try and get her to sign with their label.

Disco Fever was nearing its second decade by the time *Def Jam/ Krush Groove* came on the scene. Def Jam was a Manhattan-based label and hip-hop was already headed toward national exposure. Performances in *Beat Street*, released the same year, were filmed at The Roxy, at 515 W. Eighteenth St. in the Chelsea neighborhood of Manhattan, a cavernous airplane hanger of a club compared to Disco Fever's capacity of 350. But Disco Fever's inclusion sent a clear message: *Krush Groove* may be about where hip-hop is going, but it also knows and respects where it came from.

In a weird case of life imitating art, *Krush Groove* proved to be the swan song for Disco Fever. While obtaining filming permits, it was discovered that Disco Fever had been featuring live entertainment for nearly ten years without a New York cabaret license. The local community board had to approve all nearby cabaret licenses and turned Disco Fever's application down. The oversight was enough to get Disco Fever shut down. It never reopened.

A year before, the *Wild Style* crew had, without a permit, taken over a neglected Manhattan park and turned the location into hip-hop cinema's triumphal moment. Just a year later, a hip-hop movie filmed performers in a venue where they'd been appearing for a decade, and it spelled the death of the venue, in part because that venue was beyond successful but not quite legal. One location had been a landmark to hip-hop's humble origins and a testament to its exploding popularity. One little nightclub in the Bronx, in a few short scenes in *Krush Groove*, showed just how far hip-hop had come, then died for it.

The musical and dance climaxes of *Beat Street* happened in The Roxy, a block-long former roller rink. By the time of *Beat Street*'s release in 1984, The Roxy had arrived. Two years before, a British talent manager/nightclub promoter named Ruza "Kool Lady" Blue had begun an all-ages DJ night at the club where hip-hop pioneers Afrika Bambaataa, Jazzy Jay, and Grandmaster Flash were regular performers. The all-ages night's former home had been a reggae club about the size of Disco Fever. When Blue's friend Fab 5 Freddy warned her she might have trouble filling a venue the size of The Roxy, she hung a curtain down the middle of the room and had the DJ play only on one side of it. Soon, though, The Roxy became so popular that the curtain kept getting moved back until it simply functioned as a painting on the wall.

Ruza Blue had come to New York at age twenty-one, drawn by Andy Warhol and New York's downtown punk rock scene. Her first job was working for Malcolm McLaren, the Svengali of the Sex Pistols. Through him, she met Fab 5 Freddy and Afrika Bambaataa and decided hip-hop wasn't some passing kiddie fad from uptown. It needed to be featured downtown, at a place like The Roxy, right in the geographic center of New York nightlife.

"The Roxy was a big mix of fashion people, art people, punks, DJs, Apache Indians, and the Rock Steady Crew breakdancing," Kool Lady Blue said in a 2008 BBC interview. A sixteen-year-old graffiti artist could be standing next to David Bowie. Because of this, Lady Blue called it the anti-Studio 54, but the lines were just as long, the crowd just as deep, the magic still thick in the air. The Roxy was the biggest, loudest, proudest example of the uptown/downtown summit meeting Fab 5 Freddy had organized a few years before. It represented, in the form of an old roller rink packed to the rafters with breakdancers and artists and celebrities, hip-hop's transformation from the subculture of a few into entertainment for all.

Beat Street filmed a number of key scenes at The Roxy, but by far the most important is the movie's finale, a musical wake/tribute to one member of the group of friends who has died violently. The club is filled again, but not with celebrities or even hip-hop's most talented. Mirroring The Roxy's real-life inclusiveness, the cast sits on the floor, like in a community rec room, alongside family and friends from the South Bronx. The stage is maybe two feet higher than the crowd. Hip-hop performers mix and rap alongside a gospel choir and a troop of modern dancers. The scene's final moments are a rhythmic chant of "Do you believe in the future?" with paintings of the deceased friend framing both the stage and the community in attendance.

It looks an awful lot like an indoor version of the *Wild Style* finale, but the feeling isn't the same. This isn't hip-hop discovering itself, no golden light of possibility from below, no wow. It's a culture asking, what do we do next? What will be the future to believe in? A friend has died, and with him the innocence of the beginning of a movement, before anything changed and got bigger, meaner, and more complicated than we once knew.

"What next?" is a question asked both out of grief and cultural context. The moment's power comes in part because we are not only in a cavernous nightclub, but in New York's most popular cavernous nightclub, filled with strobe lights and music and performers only a few scenes before. Here it looks modest and welcoming, like a church social hall: Friends and family sit on the floor. Performers and audience know each other. The lights aren't dark and sexy, but up, so everyone can see.

Can The Roxy, and, by extension, hip-hop itself, be both things—a stage and a community center, a movement that awards talent but also unifies talent and audience, where the boundaries between performer and participant, between family and strangers fall away? It sounds a lot less like a plan than a wish. The use of The Roxy speaks to that wish fulfillment for hip-hop's future, and *Beat Street* as a movie that sees future coming.

"Beat *Beat Street!*"

AROUND THE TIME *BEAT Street* headed into production, the daughter of an Israeli film producer told her father that she had seen a group of kids breakdancing on Venice Beach in Los Angeles. The producer—Menahem Golan, who, with his younger cousin Yoram Globus, owned Cannon Films—saw a potential movie, as he often did. Cannon specialized in making movies fast, cheap, and of questionable taste by the fistful. Some of them you've heard of—*Barfly*, *Over the Top*, *Superman IV*, the sequels to *Death Wish*. Many others you're better off not knowing anything about.

Soon after, Golan learned that *Beat Street* had a June 1984 release date, and saw an advantage in getting his breakdancing movie to theaters first. That meant grabbing talent, script, and crew from wherever it could be found quickest and shooting in Los Angeles where Cannon Films was based, resulting in, as Richard Kraft, a former employee, put it, "Whatever was going to be assembled in enough time to make the release date is what the movie was going to end up being."

"Beat *Beat Street!*" cried Golan to his shotgun cast and crew.

The result was *Breakin'*, which did beat *Beat Street* by a month and landed at movie theaters in May of 1984. *Breakin'* cost just over $1 million and ended up making just over $51 million. It also, for a brief time, focused the cultural conversation on breakdancing (I saw it in the fourth grade and insisted on learning the centipede at recess instead of playing soccer). Breakdancers performed on daytime talk shows, showed up in non hip-hop music videos (see Billy Joel's "Uptown Girl"), and danced for heads of state. Ronald Reagan invited the New York City Breakers to perform at his 1984 Presidential Inauguration Ball.

"I remember seeing *Breakin'* and thinking it was a really horrible film," said Michael Holman, *Beat Street*'s associate producer and manager of the New York City Breakers, in a 2014 oral history of *Beat Street*. "It was one of those low-budget exploitative films that didn't have anything really important to say, made by people who didn't have any vision or idea on how to make a film or what the subject matter was about, and made the talented artists in that film look really stupid."

Nonetheless, the sudden attention helped *Beat Street* at the box office (to the tune of $17 million in revenue) and spun off a world performance tour featuring many of its own talented artists. Plus, the oral history stresses, everyone who mattered knew which movie was the real thing.

"*Beat Street* exceeded and, in a warped sense, substantiated hip-hop on a higher level," said LA Sunshine in the oral history. LA Sunshine, one third of the pioneering hip-hop group the Treacherous Three, was a favorite act of screenwriter Steven Hager and appeared in the movie. "When *Breakin'* came out, cats kind of turned their nose up to it. Then seeing hip-hop in its true essence via *Beat Street*, it was more widely accepted. Like, 'Okay, we get a better gist of what this is about.'"

Breakin' (really just a likeable trying-to-make-it-in-showbiz movie with a few incredible breakdancing scenes) and its sequel, *Breakin' 2: Electric Boogaloo* (really just a complete mess with a few incredible breakdancing scenes), are mostly footnotes to this story. Their producer, Cannon Films, spotted a trend before most of Hollywood had and made three cheap movies (Cannon also produced *Rappin'* starring Mario Van Peebles the following year) to break as much money off of that trend as they could. The main characters in each of Cannon's hip-hop movies are artists with day jobs, young adults in their early to mid-twenties, putting them outside the map lines of Brat Pack America. In addition to popularizing breakdancing and hip-hop culture to a non-urban, non-black-and-Latino America (which, to be fair, was on its way toward happening anyway), the biggest thing we have to thank these movies for is the phrase "Electric Boogaloo," now the all-purpose term for a sequel that never should have happened. The website TV Tropes named their "Oddly Named Sequels" section "Electric Boogaloo." The 2015 documentary on the any-movie-better-than-no-movie history of Cannon (the company went defunct in 1994) goes by *Electric Boogaloo* as well.

The *Breakin'* films took place in Los Angeles and came at what seemed like the end of the first era of hip-hop movies. For the second half of the 1980s, hip-hop stars would play fictional characters in movies riffing on their existing musical personas (The Fat Boys in 1987's *Disorderlies*) or in what amounted to companion pieces to forthcoming albums (Run-D.M.C. in 1988's *Tougher Than Leather*). These movies were evidence of hip-hop as both a power and presence in mainstream entertainment. It seemed hip-hop in movies no longer needed to tell the story of where the culture came from, now that it seemed to be everywhere.

By the end of the 1980s, the hip-hop movie was old enough to go to elementary school, while hip-hop itself was a strapping high schooler in the middle of its second decade. The culture had gone national, with accomplishments that included platinum albums, hit movies, fashion, and linguistic trends and a generation of devoted fans and confused parents, who were telling their kids to "turn that racket down!" just as their parents had over rock and roll a generation before. In the decade to follow, hip-hop would stake out a place for itself in the citadels of American economic and cultural power—the corporate boardroom, the retail showroom, and the Sundance Film Festival.

Sundance was where the hip-hop movie would end its first era and enter its second, where it would use a clever set of locations to pause and admire its accomplishments

House Party

"YOU'RE REMEMBERING *HOUSE PARTY* All Wrong," claims a March 2015 editorial on BET.com to celebrate the movie's twenty-fifth anniversary. Author Matt Barone argues that the musical comedy staring duo Kid 'n Play didn't just nail it at the box office ($26 million, budget one-tenth of that, three sequels to follow) and become a major stop on hip-hop's march from subculture to pop culture. Nor did that success happen solely because *House Party* featured middle-class rather than working-class black kids, a residential rather than urban setting, broad comedy, and rousing musical numbers designed to please any audience rather than just those already in the know. It did all that, wrote Barone, from a premiere at the Sundance Film Festival, where *House Party* won both the Excellence in Cinematography Dramatic and Filmmakers Trophy Dramatic awards. Sundance advertised the movie as a "revealing look at a popular subculture" presumably to appeal to their attendees, who expected revealing looks at subcultures from what would become America's signature independent film festival. Instead, *House Party* creators Reginald and Warrington Hudlin, brothers from Centerville, Illinois, faked right and ran left by making a great piece of mainstream entertainment that also happened to be a slice-of-life story about black teenagers not much younger than themselves. *House Party* felt edgy and different if you didn't know the culture it embodied, and authentic and self-affirming if you did. At the end of the 1980s, it succeeded in showing how thoroughly black teenagers saw hip-hop as their own but also pointed toward an America where young people of all colors felt the same.

Originally a student film that director Reginald Hudlin made while at Harvard, *House Party* stars the rapping duo Kid 'n Play (real names Christopher Reid and Christopher Martin) as high school best friends who want to throw a party and romance girls at Play's house while his parents are away. Nosy neighbors, racist cops, school bullies (played by hip-hop trio/real-life brothers, Full Force) and Kid's overbearing father (the late, great comedian Robin Harris) keep getting in the way. The film takes place over a single day and night. If you picture a hip-hop *Superbad* with Martin Lawrence in the McLovin role, you've pretty much got the idea.

House Party was filmed in Los Angeles, but a very different Los Angeles than glimpsed in *Breakin'* six years before. *Breakin'* showed rapping, DJing, and breakdancing happening in distinct corners of the city—the beaches in Venice and performance spaces like Radiotron in the Westlake neighborhood halfway across town—with a lot of unawareness and indifference in between. (Though, it's never explained where the white characters live or work; they keep referring to where the breakdancing happens as "all the way out in...") *House Party*, filmed primarily in what would now be called the Harvard Heights neighborhood just south of Koreatown, consists of split-level houses with front lawns and porches. Kid's crib at 1585 South Oxford Avenue has a brand-new white paint job with peppermint trim around the windows. Play's house, a pointed-roof Craftsman where the party goes down, has a classy, mid-century, wood door and stone steps leading up to it.

"They wanted it that way," Christopher Reid who played Kid told me over the phone. "Our location and production design people were so good that Kid's house looks just like his dad is out there every weekend with a can of paint touching things up. That's exactly who Robin's character was. Play's house looks like he has two working parents and enough room to throw a party, even though we filmed the party scenes on a sound stage."

Both Kid and Play have their eye on Sharane (A. J. Johnson), a working-class girl who lives in public housing with several siblings and relatives, and Sydney (Tisha Campbell-Martin, who you may recognize as hospital receptionist Damona on the sitcom *Dr. Ken*), a rich kid who lives in what looks like a white Colonial mansion in Beverly Hills, respectively. Sydney sneaks out to go to the party while her parents are attending a black tie dinner that Kid crashes by mistake (the legendary George Clinton is DJing).

"We filmed all over LA," Reid told me. "Kid and Play's houses were near each other but that scene where I'm walking Sharane home from the party, that was in Dogtown, all the way out by the beach. The George Clinton scene? That house was in Altadena. The house party itself was filmed at Culver City Studios."

Reid was quick to give credit to the resourcefulness and artistry of directors Reginald and Warrington Hudlin and their crew. It's well deserved. For a movie with a tiny budget—"Every single thing in *House Party* was done on the cheap," Reid said—where only one lead character has a car, it's completely believable that the teenagers in *House Party* could get everywhere on foot even if the actual locations were forty miles apart from each other.

Most of the characters in *House Party* are the children of middle-class professionals. Their parents work long hours (as Kid's father never gets tired of reminding him) and expect their kids to do well in school and go to college. Kid's only allowed to practice writing lyrics after he gets his homework done. Sharane, the kid from a poorer family, becomes the center of the movie's most honest scene when, in the middle of the party, Kid and Play break down who should pair off with who. Play tells Kid that with no car and a father that can't mind his own business, dating a girl from the projects means too many relatives around her house watching TV and no privacy, when Kid won't have any at his house either. "That'll mess with your dating time. That's mating time," Play says. A girl with professional parents has her own bedroom, a house with a basement rec room, plenty of private space to get busy. "Pull out sofa bed," says Play, "and, boom. In there!"

"I don't remember any conversations about class and economics," Reid said when I asked him about this scene. "Maybe Reggie didn't feel like he had to give us those nuances. We were first-time actors. 'Let me not clutter these guys' heads with this.' But you can tell it was on his mind."

The Hudlins lay the idea of class and money all over *House Party*, even in the movie's central image and title. The word "house" has a double meaning, one lowbrow and thuggish, one sweet and fun. The school bullies want to break into the party and beat Kid up. They joke they'll show up and "house" (a.k.a. disrupt) the party. Then one of them pulls out a can of gasoline and jokes about getting the party "burning up," while the other two dissuade him and say, "Now you've gone too far." "Housing" as a kind of stupid violence is too far, off-limits, low class in the fundamentally safe middle-class world of *House Party*. The word "house" means both a physical spot to throw a party and the vibe surrounding having a good time. The Hudlins even make a joke about the party being so off the hook that the roof of Play's house gets blown off into space.

Jokes aside, houses in *House Party* are equated with economic and cultural achievement. Having a house to throw a party, space for a DJ's equipment, a dance floor, a separate kitchen where your friends can sweet-talk girls, equals having the means to enjoy the innocence of being a teenager.

On the surface, *House Party* borrows from its older siblings, *Wild Style*, *Beat Street*, and *Krush Groove*. It's got real-life rappers and dancers playing kids who live and breathe hip-hop, with extended performance scenes to show off their skills. But *House Party* also takes place a full six years later, well after hip-hop's early halcyon days, and the characters acknowledge it. "Didn't The Sugarhill Gang do that?" says Kid, making fun of Play after his friend uses a hackneyed chant—*The roof! The roof! The roof is on fire!*—to get the party crowd moving. At the end of the night, the friends talk about winding down by watching a little TV. Play has recorded both *Krush Groove* and *Beat Street*, but Bilal the DJ (Martin Lawrence) insists he likes *Breakin'* better.

House Party filming in Los Angeles had two consequences. First, the city's endless supply of single-family homes made it easier and more credible to use houses as both a recurring visual and a theme. (John Singleton, director of *Boyz n the Hood* and a seminal member of the next generation of hip-hop movies, once said, "In LA, even folks in the hood have a front porch.") It also unknowingly reveals the shifting focus of hip-hop itself from New York to California. Many of the best-known hip-hop movies of the 1990s, including *Boyz n the Hood*, *Menace II Society*, and *Friday*, would be filmed and would self-consciously take place in the working-class, African-American neighborhoods of Central and South Los Angeles.

House Party is a great movie, a funny, lively, song-and-dance feast with a good dozen quotable lines you'll repeat for days afterward. By first making it a great time, the Hudlins were able to tuck meaning and thoughtfulness into the pockets of what is otherwise an up-the-middle musical comedy.

It even sounds like they had a great time making it.

"It was a party, a beautiful thing every day," Reid told me. "Everybody got along and people kicked it after work. Play and I were first-time actors, but we were working with performers who'd been at it for decades. The OGs were very gracious; 'Spoon' [veteran comic actor John Witherspoon, who plays the grumpy neighbor living next to the party] has been a friend since then.

Robin Harris and I got tight. When we got our first checks, he said, 'Come with me,' and took me to the bank where he used to be a security guard to cash it."

House Party ushers out the first era of hip-hop movies, both by being about middle-class kids who don't come from the neighborhoods that birthed the art form, and by acknowledging that the characters in this movie are a generation removed from the kids in *Beat Street* and *Wild Style*. Hip-hop in *House Party* is no longer a subcategory of youth culture, but a constant in young people's lives.

Soon after in the 1990s, hip-hop becomes integrated into movies not just about itself, but crime dramas (*Set It Off*), action showpieces (*Trespass*), self-satire (*CB4*, *Fear of a Black Hat*), and horror (*Judgment Night*, *Tales from the Hood*). All these movies used well-known hip-hop artists as actors and had hip-hop soundtracks, but, like *House Party*, are examples of a bigger cinematic category.

Sundance had it all wrong. *House Party* didn't reveal a youth subculture, but rather previewed what became youth culture itself. Hip-hop was now as regular to the teenage experience on film as getting a driver's license and trying to pass math. Hip-hop no longer had a house, a neighborhood, a hotspot, or a setting. It was everywhere.

If the first hip-hop movies wanted to set the historical record straight, our next group of eighties teen movies wanted to point out exactly where in history America went wrong. For the first time in this story, we'll actually be going even further back in time: to the 1950s, meeting up with some teenagers named Marty McFly, Tracy Turnblad, and Ponyboy Curtis.

CHAPTER 5: BACK (AND FORTH) TO THE FUTURE

'80s Teen Movies Set in the '50s

Movies Discussed: *Back to the Future, Peggy Sue Got Married, Stand by Me, Dirty Dancing, Dead Poets Society, Hairspray, The Outsiders*

O F THE NEARLY THREE hundred movies President Ronald Reagan watched during his years in office (1980–1988), few seemed to delight him as much as *Back to the Future*. He saw it in the White House screening room shortly after it came out. When Doc Brown can't believe who's president in 1985, the man who actually *was* president in 1985 laughed so hard that the White House projectionist had to stop the movie and wait for the president to compose himself. The following February, the movie had a cameo in one of the most important speeches of his presidency.

The 1986 State of the Union Address had been pushed back a week (the only time in history this has happened) due to the tragic explosion of the Space Shuttle Challenger on January 28. President Reagan began with a tribute to the Challenger's fallen astronauts and made the theme of his remarks American resilience and ambition, "reaching for the stars." In 2014, *The New Republic* voted it one of the best State of the Union addresses of all time.

About three-quarters of the way through that address, Ronald Reagan said,

"And tonight I want to speak directly to America's younger generation… Never has there been a more exciting time to be alive, a time of rousing wonder and heroic achievement. As they said in the film *Back to the Future*, "Where we're going, we don't need roads.""

Let's think about this for the second. Name-dropping popular culture almost never happens in a State of the Union Address, and Ronald Reagan would be far from the obvious president to do it. He gave the speech two days shy of his seventy-fifth birthday and wasn't exactly what you'd call hip to what "America's younger generation" liked. His favorite movie was *The Sound of Music* (1965), and though he was an above-average cinephile as far as presidents went (Carter watched many more films while in office, Johnson and Kennedy almost none), and did watch primarily contemporary movies while in office, they weren't the ones closest to his heart. He preferred the work of his close friend Jimmy Stewart, as well as selections from his own filmography on special occasions like his birthday.

The context is also not quite right. Reagan wasn't president when the *Back to the Future* movies actually went into the future (*Back to the Future II* came out almost a year after he left office), so using the original *Back to the Future*'s immortal last line as a stand-in for a better tomorrow is, at best, an awkward fit. He did know children and young people would have been watching the Challenger launch (the shuttle contained New Hampshire schoolteacher Christa McAuliffe, the first civilian in space), so perhaps he and his staff felt it necessary to console and remind them of the White House's commitment to their future. But if we're talking politics, President Reagan termed out in two years, his approval rating hovered around 60 percent coming into the State of the Union address, the highest it had been since beginning his second term. He needed a bump in the polls only a little more than he needed a bump on the head.

Given the solemnity of the moment, given all the rhetorical brainpower at his disposal, given his own movie preferences and profile from a far older era of Hollywood, why did Ronald Reagan call upon the closing line of a silly summer blockbuster uttered by a mad scientist to make his point? Was he *that* fond of *Back to the Future*?

He was that fond of the *town* in *Back to the Future*. President Ronald Reagan was that fond of Hill Valley.

"It's Morning in America"

As its 40th president, Ronald Reagan saw a bright future for America as a return to the glory of the past. *Back to the Future*'s image of Hill Valley, 1955 (where teenager Marty McFly goes back to by accident and ends up interfering in his parents' meeting), was exactly what the president wanted to mold the America of the 1980s into and leave it as when he left office. He'd just won his second term by forty-nine states, the largest margin of victory in an election since the Great Depression. His signature television commercial from the campaign (which, in 2012, *Advertising Age* called one of the best political commercials of all time) was colloquially called "Morning in America." It featured scenes of wholesome Americans backlit by sunset, wholesome Americans coming home from work, playing Little League, getting married, and raising American flags up flagpoles. A grandfatherly voice narrates,

It's morning again in America, and under the leadership of President Reagan, our country is prouder and stronger and better. Why would we ever want to return to where we were less than four short years ago?

Morning in America could have been filmed in the Hill Valley of 1955 (no one is sitting at a computer, jabbering to their broker on a cordless phone, or jogging with a Walkman), and that was exactly the point. The success of Ronald Reagan's first term meant America looked like what it had once been, prouder, strong, better, but also smaller, folksier, whiter, and more conservative.

What America had emerged from was the chaos and unrest of the 1960s. Ronald Reagan defined the aspirations and measured the successes of his presidency as getting back America's former glory. As far back as when he had announced his first campaign in 1979, he promised to feed the "hunger for a spiritual revival to feel once again as we felt years ago as a nation."

The Hill Valley of Marty McFly's parents was the embodiment of those "years ago," the uncomplicated small-town wholesomeness Ronald Reagan held so close to his heart. Hill Valley, 1985—where hero Marty McFly lives in a dumpy subdivision, where the town square is littered and forgotten, and where the clock tower hasn't worked in thirty years and looks like hell—was the picture of how America had gone wrong. We needed to rewind that clock tower, thought President Reagan. The Hill Valley where George McFly and Lorraine Bates hung out at the corner soda fountain and fell in love at the Enchantment Under the Sea dance represented America's best days, before what happened between then and now—Vietnam, drugs, rock and roll, feminism, gay liberation, everything Ronald Reagan found upsetting—cast us into darkness.

We know in retrospect that President Reagan's dream of "Morning in America" was, at best, naïve (historian Stephanie Coontz wrote a book about this myth in 1993 titled *The Way We Never Were*), and at worst, a reckless delusion on which to base policy. To be fair, we also know that even though his presidency embodied it, "Morning in America" wasn't Ronald Reagan's idea. As early as the defeat of candidate Barry Goldwater for the presidency in 1964, the Republican Party had zeroed in on a message of restoring America to an imagined former glory. Richard Nixon had deployed it effectively in a 1969 speech by asking a "silent majority" of Americans for their support. Voters who did not wish to join in Vietnam War protests or drop acid in the desert and were pretty sure the sixties was in the process of sending America over a cliff. Versions of restoring the "real" America from whatever tragic wrong turns it had taken (invariably those wrong turns could be laid at the feet of Democrats and what their voters stood for) were a central part of the presidential campaigns of John McCain (2008),

Mitt Romney (2012), Donald Trump (2016), and a lodestar of the formation of the Tea Party.

The eighties teen movie came to life during all this. Brat Pack America is a map drawn in significant part by a sitting Republican president who led with misty-eyed notions about a lost American innocence. Think, then, about many eighties teen movies that take place during that supposed innocence in the 1950s and early Kennedy years—before assassinations or Vietnam or urban race riots, before the 1960s wrecked everything.

"The summer of 1984 was the crest in the wave of Ronald Reagan–era optimism," said critics Aaron Aradillas and Matt Zoller Seitz in a 2009 video essay about the decade's blockbusters. "When America collectively decided to get over Vietnam, the chaos of the 1960s, and inflation/stagnation of the 1970s and feel good about itself again." Many of these blockbusters were set during a time when America felt prosperous, safe, and unchallenged, the late Eisenhower era of poodle skirts, pompadours, and letterman sweaters (*La Bamba*, *The Outsiders*) or the early Kennedy years with just a hint of the sixties in the air (*Dead Poets Society*, *Hairspray*, *Dirty Dancing*).

But the group of eighties teen movies probably the most identified with this past/present split are the ones that happen in both eras (*Back to the Future*, *Stand by Me*, *Peggy Sue Got Married*)—metaphorically speaking, in both Hill Valley, 1955, and Hill Valley, 1985. For these movies, "past" means before the chaos of the sixties, "present" means after the stagnation and malaise of the seventies. But we don't get to see those two wild-haired decades in these movies. Unintentionally, the adventures of Marty McFly, Peggy Sue Bodell, and four junior high school boys who go looking for a dead body censor history by having a "past" and "present," where the two yucky decades in between seem to have never happened.

These "Morning in America" movies give our map of Brat Pack America a fourth dimension. Their sense of place means both physical location and place in time. The setting of *Dirty Dancing* is as much "the summer of 1963, before Kennedy, before The

Beatles"—as Frances "Baby" Houseman (Jennifer Grey) narrates in the opening scene—as it is Kellerman's Resort in Upstate New York. Born of and reacting to the force-fed naïveté of President Reagan's "Morning in America," these eighties teen movies set in the fifties may all in some way be about the lost innocence of an earlier time. But their physical settings—Hill Valley, Kellerman's Resort, Welton Academy, Castle Rock, Oregon—also demonstrate how those same movies don't have much patience for "things were better back then" platitudes and are great films because they complicate our ideas about memory, time, and change.

Back (and Forth) to the Future

BACK TO THE FUTURE, *Peggy Sue Got Married*, and *Stand by Me* are all movies that take place in both the time of MTV and the time of the transistor radio. In *BTTF* and *PSGM*, the main character literally travels between the two eras. I'm going to assume you know how that happens in *Back to the Future*—with a DeLorean, stolen plutonium, the van full of Libyans, and 1.21 gigawatts of electricity. But do you know where the whole idea came from? When cowriter/producer Bob Gale dug up his father's high school yearbook during a visit to his parents over the Christmas holidays and asked himself, "Would my dad and I have been friends had we been in the same high school class?"

In *Peggy Sue Got Married*, a woman in her early forties on the verge of divorcing her husband, who was also her high school boyfriend, attends her twenty-fifth high school reunion, gets crowned Reunion Queen, then faints and wakes up in 1960 as a woman in her early forties who everyone thinks is a high school senior. Directed by Francis Ford Coppola, the movie spends no time explaining how this all happened, since *PSGM* isn't meant to be science fiction but a family drama and acting showcase for the title character (Kathleen Turner got an Oscar nomination for the role).

Why does *Stand by Me* belong to this group? The story of *Stand by Me*—four friends on the verge of junior high go looking for the corpse of a boy their age who went missing from their small Oregon town of Castle Rock—was based on Stephen King's 1982 novella, *The Body*, and takes place over Labor Day weekend in 1959. But the story is told in flashback and opens in the present with the main character, Gordie Lachance, as an adult (Richard Dreyfuss) sitting inside a jeep alone on a country road. A newspaper on his lap contains the headline "Attorney Chris Chambers Fatally Stabbed in Restaurant." The movie ends with adult Gordie telling us that Chris Chambers (River Phoenix), his best friend at age twelve, died in a freak accident, trying to break up a fight between two customers in the restaurant. At movie's end, we see that Gordie, now a writer, has been writing the story of himself and his friends looking for the dead body as he narrates it to us.

As he finishes writing, Gordie's son, about twelve years old, interrupts him, telling him it's time to go. Adult Gordie mumbles that he's coming. His son then mutters to his friend "My dad gets like this when he's writing." The closing shot of *Stand by Me* is adult Gordie chasing his son and friend around the front lawn of the house. The house has a gate, a hedge wall, and a circular driveway (it's actually a mansion at 308 S. San Rafael Avenue in Pasadena, the same spot where Kristen Wiig clocked a giant cookie in *Bridesmaids*). Adult Gordie has either married well or written a few mega-bestsellers.

Watching *Stand by Me*, we get to see Gordie at twelve, a sensitive, wise kid his parents don't appreciate, and Gordie at approximately thirty-eight, a successful professional and parent himself. But we get none of the in-between. Gordie tells us via narration that by high school, he lost track of his other two friends, Vern (Jerry O'Connell) and Teddy (Corey Feldman), who end up leading unremarkable adult lives and never leave Castle Rock. We also learn that Chris, who tells Gordie, "I'm never getting out of this town" where everyone sees him, like his delinquent brother, as "just another lowlife Chambers kid," manages to keep up with Gordie in school, get himself through law school, and become an attorney.

But that's all we know. If Gordie and Chris were twelve in 1959, it means they were both in college during the furor of the 1960s. Maybe they followed the Grateful Dead or campaigned for Eugene McCarthy and maybe they didn't. We can't say. The narrative structure of *Stand by Me* walls off the 1960s and '70s from us by omission.

None of these movies did this for political reasons. The directors of all three are lifelong Democrats whose careers and personal lives made great leaps forward in the 1960s. Furthermore, if you look at the scenes of *Back to the Future*, *Peggy Sue Got Married*, and *Stand by Me* set in the past, change hangs in the air of each one. Hill Valley, Castle Rock, and the Northern California community of *Peggy Sue Got Married* (shot in Petaluma, California, *Back to the Future* director, Robert Zemeckis's, first, but ultimately too expensive, choice for Hill Valley) are each all-American small towns in the middle of becoming something else. And rather than being the sweet hamlets of tradition and permanence idolized in Ronald Reagan's "Morning in America," they all seem excited and optimistic about the future and aren't judged as naïve and foolish for it.

Back to the Future takes place earlier than the other two (1955 vs. 1959 and 1960), but already we can tell big changes are coming to Hill Valley. When Marty first arrives in 1955, he hides the DeLorean time machine behind a giant billboard schilling for Lyon Estates, the housing development under construction, where his family lives in 1985. Marty's mom's family has just bought their first TV (which leads to a great joke when Marty, from the present, tries to explain what a rerun is). The movie theater in downtown Hill Valley boasts "Now with Air Conditioning!" on a banner hung from the marquee.

Hill Valley is a town on the move. It may have reminded Ronald Reagan of a place and time lost to us and worth getting back, but Hill Valley just as easily, and probably more accurately, shows us that everything changes, nothing is forever, and that our actions have consequences—the villain Biff Tannen (Thomas F. Wilson) stealing the time machine in *Back to the Future II* and turning Hill Valley "into a place worse than hell," according to Doc Brown; Doc's own warnings about the disastrous consequences of playing around with the power of time travel; and the trilogy's bleak but necessary conclusion of the DeLorean being destroyed.

You could argue that *Back to the Future* is fundamentally a peak-form time travel comedy, the older brother to *Bill & Ted's Excellent Adventure* (1989), *Groundhog Day* (1993), and *Hot Tub Time Machine* (2010). But if that's what it is, why bother to flesh out Hill Valley, arguably the most memorable fictional small town in movie history, if it's only there to remind us of whether the characters are now in past or present? Do we need to know anything about the setting of *Hot Tub Time Machine* once we've got a hot tub that's also a time machine?

Hill Valley takes *Back to the Future* to another level. The terrible things that do happen in *Back to the Future* present as scars on the face of Hill Valley, the prototypical all-American town Ronald Reagan thought should never change. But Hill Valley gets those scars mostly because characters in *Back to the Future* are reckless, greedy, or drunk with the power a time machine gives them. When Marty takes responsibility for his errors and cleans up his own mess, the 1985 Hill Valley he comes back to looks as sunny and prosperous as it did in 1955, at least in the scruffy neighborhood where his family lives. Downtown Hill Valley's still got litter everywhere and Red, the town bum, is still sleeping on a park bench. But Marty is overjoyed to see all of it. His victory comes as both saving his parents' marriage (and therefore his own existence) and not mucking up the scruffy little town he comes from and loves.

It's thanks to Hill Valley that *Back to The Future* is part science fiction, part teen comedy, and just as much a coming-of-age story about the inevitability of change and our responsibility in the face of it.

Over in Castle Rock, the setting of *Stand by Me*, it's Labor Day weekend, 1959. Buddy Holly, Ritchie Valens, and the Big Bopper have died in a plane crash earlier that February, ending rock and roll's early childhood. Gordie Lachance (Wil Wheaton) and his three friends sing the closing theme from the hit TV show *Have Gun—Will Travel* (*A soldier of fortune. Pal-la-din!*) when starting on their journey to find the body of a missing kid from their town. When they camp for the night, they argue about the Mickey Mouse Club and whether the *$64,000 Question* game show is rigged.

It all feels just like a postcard from 1959, but the radio in the boy's tree house is tuned to a station from Portland, Oregon's biggest city. Rock and roll is in the air. Summer is ending and junior high is starting next week. Castle Rock may be only "one hundred and twenty-one people, but to me it was the whole world," says Gordie in the movie's opening moments. But we already know from the film's prologue that at least two of the main characters grow up and leave. We get the sense that *Stand by Me* opens just as this generation of Castle Rock's children are getting too big for where they grew up. Like the radio in the tree house, a signal from far away—Portland, the 1960s, or just adulthood—beckons.

Peggy Sue (Kathleen Turner) shares her name with the Buddy Holly song, released in 1957 (the movie doesn't make much of the connection for reasons I don't understand). *Peggy Sue Got Married* takes place in 1960, and Holly has already perished the year before. But Peggy Sue Bodell's boyfriend, Charlie, is convinced that the sugary vocal harmonies of his quartet (they all wear letterman sweaters, a costume choice from a musical era even earlier than Buddy Holly) are on their way to becoming rock stars. Peggy Sue is actually a forty-year-old from the future (she even mouths off to her mom by saying, "Maybe I'll run away to Liverpool and discover The Beatles!"), and when she tries to give Charlie the lyrics to The Beatles song "She Loves You," he boneheadedly argues the song would be better with "Ooo, ooo, ooo" as the chorus instead of "Yeah, yeah, yeah."

Charlie soon after tells Peggy Sue he's giving up his singing ambitions so he can marry her and take over his father's appliance store. Peggy Sue knows how this story plays out—in bitter divorce and sadness—but the movie still makes Charlie look not like a naïve kid but a moron. His dreams are small, his ambitions barely there, but neither of those are a crime. *Peggy Sue Got Married* has no pity for Charlie because his plans for the rest of his life depend on life staying exactly the same as the day he graduated high school.

All three of these movies depend on their small-town locations. In the *Back to the Future* series, we need Hill Valley both to measure where Doc and Marty are in the space-time continuum, but also to keep the number of important characters in focus. Make Hill Valley a metropolis, and how does Marty find his parents? How does Biff Tannen bully the entire town of Hill Valley if Hill Valley has a million citizens? In *Stand by Me*, can Gordie, Chris, Teddy, and Vern go looking for a dead kid if they need to cross three interstate highways instead of walking along railroad tracks and through woods? Would they even know where the dead kid was? Won't someone have a hard time believing Charlie's naivete or Peggy Sue's impatience with it, if they are teenagers growing up an hour south down the 101 freeway, in San Francisco instead of Petaluma?

But other than plot logistics, the small-town setting in all of these movies does two things which seem at odds with one another: idolize the past at the expense of the present, then criticize how naïve that is. *Back to the Future*, *Peggy Sue Got Married*, and *Stand by Me* are all movies that equate the past with innocence. Early in *Stand by Me*, Vern says, "This is a really good time." The other friends chime in with, "The most." "A blast." Gordie then narrates that Vern probably meant their adventure, but he could also have meant childhood. "Everything was there and around us," Gordie says. "We knew exactly who we were and where we were going."

By splitting the narrative in two, where the past, the "really good time" Vern mentions, is the innocent fifties and the present is the eighties, *Back to the Future*, *Stand by Me*, and *Peggy Sue Got Married*, it could be argued, show a redacted view of American history where the chaos of the sixties and the aftermath of the seventies are never mentioned, and therefore can be ignored. But look again, and none of these three films pull a "Morning in America" and judge the "really good time" of Eisenhower's America as better.

Hill Valley, 1955, is only better if you ignore the end of *Back to the Future* where, back in 1985, very little has changed in Hill Valley itself, but Marty still says to his girlfriend Jennifer, "Everything is just great." He only feels this because he is home safe, his parents and siblings seem so much happier and fulfilled, and the tired, unkempt Hill Valley of the present is where they all are (it helps that Biff the bully is now waxing his dad's car). Less important than then or now, *Back to the Future* seems to say, is who and where.

Stand by Me, on the other hand, is a painfully sad movie where death hangs over the plot like a shroud. The opening shot is news of Chris Chambers's murder. Gordie's favored older brother Denny died in a Jeep accident four months before their walk to find the body, which explains why his parents ignore and don't understand him. The holy grail of the four friends' quest is the corpse of a boy their age. "The kid wasn't sick," Gordie narrates when they find him. "The kid wasn't sleeping. The kid was dead."

The "good time" Vern mentioned earlier is a momentary break from the pain and grief that haunts nearly every moment of this movie. The true relief, *Stand by Me* argues, is growing up. It looks at Castle Rock as a metaphor for childhood, something you leave behind as soon as you can and, by doing so, are less powerless to bullies, adults who hate kids, and your own parents, who have given up on you. "Maybe going to see a dead kid shouldn't be a party," Gordie says to his friends early on. Few other parts of childhood in Castle Rock seem to be.

By the end of *Peggy Sue Got Married*, Peggy Sue and Charlie agree to begin talking again for the sake of their children and the family they once had together. We realize, a little sadly, that perhaps Peggy Sue Bodell is just as provincial in her outlook and limited ambition as Charlie. The two will try again, as grown-ups and friends, to accept what they've become and not dream about what they were. We have no idea what kind of relationship they will have as adults or whether it will be better or worse. But they will be smarter and wiser than they once were, an argument for now vs. then that *Peggy Sue Got Married* seems fully behind.

All three of Brat Pack America's time-hopping movies use the perceived simplicity of the past as a reminder of the pain of growing up, the difficulty of facing change, but the acceptance of the need to do so. They use their small-town settings as a reminder of what Robert Penn Warren called "the awful responsibility of time" by saying: We remember when Hill Valley, Castle Rock, and Petaluma felt like simple places that held our young, simple lives. We aren't there anymore, and have grown up too much to go back.

"The Time of Your Life" and "Seize the Day"

WHAT DO *DIRTY DANCING* (1987) and *Dead Poets Society* (1989) have in common, besides being great movies that begin with the letter D? Both won Oscars, *Dirty Dancing* for Best Original Song "(I've Had) The Time of My Life," and *Dead Poets Society* for Best Original Screenplay (writer Tom Schulman). Both were modest-budget summer movies and unexpectedly massive hits. And both featured the performance their lead actor would be most identified with after his death—Robin Williams's teacher, John Keating, and Patrick Swayze's dance instructor, Johnny Castle.

Both were also set in the years just before the sixties as we now know it. *Dirty Dancing* not only says as much (its first line is, "It was the summer of 1963"), but also anchors its plot to the transition from one era to another. It's a love story about a privileged teenage girl, Francis "Baby" Houseman (Jennifer Grey), who, while vacationing at a posh Catskills resort with her family, falls for the hotel's lead dance instructor, Johnny Castle (Patrick Swayze). He likes to "dirty dance" to Otis Redding songs with his fellow staff members after a day of teaching senior citizens how to foxtrot. No points for guessing how Baby's father (Jerry Orbach), the personal physician of the resort's owner, who brags that Baby is "going to Mt. Holyoke" to "change the world," feels about their relationship. What follows is a showdown between old values and new, between parental guidance and letting teenagers finding their own way, between daytime foxtrot lessons and nighttime dirty dancing.

Dead Poets Society takes place in 1959. The movie's opening scene is the beginning-of-academic-year convocation exercises at Welton Academy, an elite private school for boys. This year, a new teacher, an alumnus named John Keating (Robin Williams), will be joining the English department. Mr. Keating encourages his students to think for themselves, savor the beauty of literature and poetry, and view learning as preparation for a life well lived instead of for Harvard Business School and a country club membership. No points for guessing that his students, their parents, and the headmaster feel differently about Mr. Keating's teaching philosophy. What follows is a showdown between old values and new, between preparing to be a CEO and preparing to be a fully realized human being, between studying trigonometry on Friday night and reciting Whitman after curfew with the Dead Poets Society.

Both movies use the impending arrival of the 1960s and the values associated with that time to place their main characters on the side of right. No matter how many times you've seen *Dead Poets* or *Dirty Dancing*, it's hard to imagine sympathizing with the stony intolerance of Welton's Headmaster Nolan (the legendary character actor Norman Lloyd, 101 years old and still acting) or the small-minded suspicions of Baby's dad Dr. Jake Houseman (the late, great Jerry Orbach, in a role terribly underwritten and misaligned as the movie's villain). Both men are not only wrong to the teenage protagonists, their students and children, but are on the wrong side of history.

The Dead Poets first meet in a wooded cave in 1959, and Baby propositions Johnny Castle by simply saying, "Dance with me" in 1963. That difference of four years is bigger than it seems, and both movies use their unforgettable settings—Kellerman's Resort and Welton Academy—to show how soon the cultural change symbolized by dirty dancing and dead poets will come. Or if it will come at all.

In *Dirty Dancing*, the 1960s will be appearing any second now, as represented both by the calendar (the summer of 1963 is only a few months before John F. Kennedy is assassinated in Dallas) and the squeaky-clean, bowtie-and-evening-gown entertainment of Kellerman's Catskills resort versus the "dirty dancing" its staff does after hours to the sounds of R&B and Motown. Resort chieftain, Max Kellerman (Jack Weston), laments this very change to his orchestra's conductor right before the movie's climactic final dance scene.

"It's not the changes so much this time," Max Kellerman says after a quick rundown of his hotel's history. "It's that it all seems to be ending. You think kids want to come here with their parents and take foxtrot lessons? Trips to Europe, that's what the kids want. Twenty-two countries in three days. It feels like it's all slipping away."

And it was. The real-life Catskills resorts that inspired *Dirty Dancing* had begun losing business shortly after the summer of 1963 due to the growth of cross-country and international air travel and the ending of discriminatory, no-Jews-allowed practices by the hotel industry. The biggest and most successful of the old Catskills resorts, Grossinger's, was the last to close in 1986. That same year, *Dirty Dancing*, written by Eleanor Bergstein (who, like Baby Houseman, had an older sister, a father who practiced medicine, and spent summers in the Catskill Mountains in the 1950s and '60s) was scheduled to begin principal photography. Except the kind of resort Bergstein had based her screenplay on no longer existed, their Olympic-sized swimming pools, dining rooms, and dance halls left as abandoned ruins. Instead *Dirty Dancing* shot at the Mountain Lake Lodge in Pembroke, Virginia (still in business), and the Lake Lure Inn in Lake Lure, North Carolina (now home to an annual summer Dirty Dancing Festival).

The era *Dirty Dancing* ushers out was so over by the time the movie was made that the crew had to go several states away to recreate it. Anyone who once vacationed at a now-extinct Jewish Catskills resort (as my mother did as a child—she loves *Dirty Dancing*) would also know that a) Kellerman's couldn't have been an actual Catskills Resort, since there weren't any like it still around, and b) the transition into the 1960s that Baby and Johnny represent was a big part of the decline and death of places like Kellerman's that once ruled their summers. "Economic prosperity, the Cultural Revolution, and the anti-war movement reduced the appeal of the area for a new generation of young adults that had other visions of vacation and family life," wrote the *Jewish Daily Forward* of the Catskills resorts in 2013. The split-level stone edifice of the Mountain Lake Lodge that played Kellerman's in the Catskills, but is actually a neighbor of Virginia Tech University and over five hundred miles away from the Catskills, stood for the central theme of *Dirty Dancing*: the death of one age and the beginning of another. In *Dirty Dancing*, we hear that theme echoed in the film's music (the soundtrack containing both contemporary pop and early sixties soul went multi-platinum), feel it in the movie's approach to sex, money, and class, and see it made physical in the stone arches and giant back lawn of the resort we know is an architectural facsimile for something long gone.

Where does *Dead Poets Society* take place? It's tempting to say "somewhere in New England," as just about all the characters have Anglo last names (Keating, Perry, Anderson, Dalton, and Overstreet) and wear plaid sports jackets and repp ties. Plenty of well-known boarding school movies—*Scent of a Woman*, *School Ties*, *The Emperor's Club*—take place in New England. Or maybe because *Dead Poets Society* is about a school with traditions that have stood for one hundred years before Professor Keating showed up to teach there, it feels more right to have the movie happen someplace with a long but inflexible sense of history.

The setting of *Dead Poets* is never mentioned in the movie itself. Principal photography took place at the St. Andrew's School in Middletown, Delaware (about a half hour south of Wilmington), which stood in for Welton Academy. Most of the off-campus scenes were filmed in the nearby village of New Castle, Delaware. The Dead Poets cave where the students hold their secret meanings by moonlight and read poetry is based on the Beaver Valley Cave, about thirty miles to the north on the Pennsylvania border, a historic landmark and the only cave of its kind in the state. But don't bother looking for it: the version of it in the movie is a latex mold. The cave interiors were filmed in a studio.

Like *Dirty Dancing*, *Dead Poets Society* is autobiographical but filmed far away from its source material. Screenwriter Tom Schulman based the story on his student days at the all-boys Montgomery Bell Academy in Nashville, Tennessee, and an inspirational English teacher he had his sophomore year named Sam Pickering. *Dead Poets Society* director Peter Weir chose St. Andrew's, which is coed, after looking at nearly a hundred prep schools in states across America.

In *Dead Poets Society*, Welton Academy has removed itself from the culture of its time. The year is 1959, but none of the boys seem to own a transistor radio, a record player, or listen to early rock and roll. (The closest we get is two of the Dead Poets building their own radio in secret, so maybe such things aren't allowed at Welton.) Roger Ebert gave the movie a negative review in part for using the school's isolation and stodginess as a straw man: *Dead Poets*, he wrote, was a "collection of pious platitudes masquerading as a courageous stand in favor of something." He then dinged the movie for favoring applause and tears over historical accuracy. "The movie is set in 1959, but none of these would-be bohemians have heard of Kerouac, Ginsberg, or indeed of the beatnik movement," which seems less farfetched than Ebert makes it out to be. "There weren't that many of them," wrote essayist Louis Menand, about the beatniks, in a 2015 *New Yorker* article. "The counterculture was small." It wouldn't surprise me if a bunch of prep-school students at an isolated boarding school missed it.

If *Dirty Dancing* happens right in the middle of a cultural shift (summer 1963), Professor Keating arrives to teach at Welton Academy in *Dead Poets Society* at the faint beginning of it (fall 1959). It's six months after the deaths of Buddy Holly and Ritchie Valens and two years after the publication of *On the Road*. Elvis Presley had driven teenage girls wild on the Ed Sullivan Show only three years before. But none of those hints of change have passed under the gothic spires of Welton Academy yet. We don't get the scene where Headmaster Nolan shrugs about time, change, and "it all slipping away" like we do in *Dirty Dancing*. Instead, the movie opens at a hundredth-anniversary celebration of the school and its four pillars, "Tradition, honor, discipline, excellence."

"Tradition" is Headmaster Nolan's favorite. "Tradition, John," he lectures Keating, when the other teachers start to get suspicious of Keating's methods. "Prepare them for college. The rest will take care of itself." At Welton, 1959 probably doesn't look that different from 1929.

But doesn't John Keating's lesson to his pupils—"Carpe diem. Seize the day, boys. Make your lives extraordinary"—sound like the coming of the 1960s? Of the opening up of the young American mind, from which the Weltons of the world can never go back? I remember thinking so when I saw *Dead Poets Society* in high school. In retrospect, I'm not so sure. John Keating is written and played conservatively on purpose. He's a graduate of Welton himself, a dedicated educator whose chief request is that his students take poetry and literature, the same subject evil Headmaster Nolan used to teach, seriously as an intellectual and emotional pursuit rather than a means to an Ivy League admission letter. He wears corduroy pants and sweaters and whistles classical music as he strolls through campus. When the most rebellious student, Charlie Dalton (Gale Hansen), pulls the prank that ultimately leads to Professor Keating's dismissal, he tells Charlie without a smile, "That's a pretty lame stunt you pulled." The movie's unforgettable last scene (desktops: "O Captain! My Captain!") gets most of its power not just because the boys thank their teacher with a small rebellious gesture but because, despite that gesture, he has been fired and can no longer be their teacher.

I wonder what comes immediately after that scene. Do the Dead Poets get expelled for standing on their desks, the way Charlie Dalton already has been? Does Professor Keating go back to London to be with his wife? When the 1960s arrive, do at least some of the Dead Poets end up being bohemians, as Roger Ebert mentioned? We don't get to know.

The "O Captain! My Captain!" final moments of *Dead Poets Society* is, for my money, one of the great last scenes in cinema. But it's really a small gesture, a mini rebellion within the walls of a school firmly committed to another hundred years of "tradition, honor, excellence, discipline," of never evolving nor embracing the present. This isn't Kellerman's Resort in *Dirty Dancing* that sees the future that Baby and Johnny represent and accepts it (Max Kellerman dances right along with the kids in *Dirty Dancing's* final moments). Welton—geographically abstract, architecturally medieval—and its Headmaster actively resist the cultural shift into the next era Professor Keating represents, and in the end, Welton and the headmaster win. It's telling that, in *Dead Poets Society's* second-to-last shot, we see the classroom, Headmaster Nolan yelling, "Sit down!" futilely, and the boys standing on their desks in tribute to their dismissed teacher. But only about half the class has elected to stand. The rest are sitting down, probably more concerned with getting into Harvard.

Tracy Turnblad Saves the World

BY THE END OF the 1980s, writer/director John Waters hadn't made a movie in a long time. *Polyester*, his sixth film, came out in 1981 and had most of the same DNA as his previous five: a cast of friends and favorite weirdos, a made-on-weekends aesthetic, and gross-out humor flung by the handful in the name of satire. Waters and his friends were all movie addicts who liked to make fun of the conventional relationships and sanitized glamour of classical Hollywood. They used their own movies to poke an entire cinematic genre in the eye—*Polyester* was a filthy little homage to 1950s housewife melodrama, 1972's *Pink Flamingos* a knockoff of one of the directors' favorite late sixties exploitation flicks—just to see what would happen.

Beginning with *Mondo Trasho* in 1969, Waters had made a movie about every two to three years. But after *Polyester* in 1981, seven years passed before his next movie, *Hairspray*, came out. *Hairspray* (1988) would be John Waters' first film made with Hollywood money and Hollywood distribution, shown in more theaters than any of his previous work.

Hairspray danced into theaters in February of 1988 but was only a modest box office success. Which is hard to believe now, since, from our park bench here in the present, we know that Waters adapted *Hairspray* into a Broadway musical that won eight Tony awards, and which then got remade as a movie in 2007 featuring John Travolta. As of this writing, the original *Hairspray* has a 97 percent fresh rating on Rotten Tomatoes.

But at the time, *Hairspray* seemed mostly like a perkier, friendlier John Waters movie. It may have been set in 1962 (all of the director's previous work played as though it had been filmed the night before), and starred a then-unknown Ricki Lake instead of the usual rotating group of friends and regular cast members. It may have earned a PG rating, another Waters first, with soft lighting, saturated color palette, and sweet memories of American Bandstand–era dance shows, but it's still a John Waters movie, thanks to a reshuffling of what had made the director's work so unique: a loopy cast (Divine, Waters' leading-lady-in-drag in most of his earlier films, has a killer supporting turn as Ricki Lake's mom), a twisted yet charmed sensibility, and Baltimore, Maryland, as a combination of backdrop, community theater stage, and circus big top.

All John Waters movies blend sincerity, laughter, and scuzz, which makes them, at heart, black comedies. Even in the cotton-candy mid-century universes of *Hairspray* and the movie Waters made next, *Cry Baby* (set in 1954 but released in 1990, and therefore a shade beyond the end date of Brat Pack America), take the innocence of the era Ronald Reagan wished to revive and recast it as parochialism and bigotry. That *Hairspray* did so in the twilight of Ronald Reagan's presidency and plays as both a criticism of said presidency and as a rollicking great time is John Waters' comic genius at work.

To show that comic genius in evolution instead of on repeat, Waters shifts and recasts Baltimore, the setting and muse of his movies. In *Hairspray*, Baltimore isn't just a weird town where weird people do weird things, but is also in on the joke; it's the straight man off of which Waters' sunny memories of growing up there in the early 1960s can both play and also pierce as black comedy.

Tracy Turnblad (Ricki Lake) is a blue-collar Baltimore kid who loves to dance. She wins a spot on the city's premier dance TV show, integrates the segregated program over the objection of station management, goes to jail, and becomes a folk hero for doing so. But before that, she gets a handsome boyfriend, sticks it to his stuck-up ex-girlfriend, and then defeats said mean girl in a local beauty pageant. *Hairspray* doesn't just have the warm retro glow of teenage girls doing the stroll and their boyfriends giving them promise rings. *Hairspray* feels as innocent as twirling in front of a mirror because pretty much nothing bad happens to its heroine. Tracy Turnblad finds her groove and keeps it.

But in the specifics of Tracy's good fortune, John Waters' nasty glee pokes through. Tracy first auditions for the Corny Collins Show (*Corny* Collins? Three minutes in and the movie is already winking at us) over the objections of her mother by saying, "Mother, you're so fifties!" Never mind the mother is clearly a giant drag queen who, in Waters' breakthrough third film, *Pink Flamingos* (1972), had the now-legendary line, "Kill everyone now! Condone first-degree murder! Advocate cannibalism! Eat shit! Filth are my politics! Filth is my life!" Here she's the uptight parent, worried about what the neighbors will think.

When Tracy does get on the show, she gives herself a brand-new hairstyle (announcing "Welcome to the sixties, Mother!") that gets her demoted to Special Ed class at school. (Yes, *the haircut* gets her sent to Special Ed.) Special Ed is filled only with African-American students (ouch), one of whom is the son of "Motormouth Maybelle" (R&B legend Ruth Brown), a record-store owner and the host of the Corny Collins' "Negro Day." Maybelle's son (Clayton Prince) and Tracy's best friend, Penny (Leslie Ann Powers), end up falling in love. In your basic teenage makeout scene, Penny says to her new boyfriend, "I wish I were dark-skinned. Our love wouldn't be so forbidden," to which he adorably replies that's part of what makes it special.

If the scene were any more earnest, these two kids would be reciting the Pledge of Allegiance. Which is why it's a scream. Waters takes the secret kissing scene, perhaps the oldest cliché of teen movies (particularly those with saddle shoes and Buddy Holly on the soundtrack), and has his characters reveal the idiocy of the racism of mid-century America. How? By declaring it makes them hot.

Hairspray takes place in a single working-class, white neighborhood (Patterson Park in East Baltimore, where the Turnblads live) and on North Avenue, the main thoroughfare of 1960s black Baltimore, where Motormouth Maybelle has her record store. When Tracy and Penny visit the store, they rhapsodize, "I've never been to North Avenue before," as if the neighborhood is in another state instead of about two miles away.

I guess that's plausible. I went to college in Baltimore in the early 1990s, and plenty of the city's neighborhoods felt farther away in culture than actual distance. But Waters then has Penny's racist mother follow her to North Avenue and run screaming in terror when a homeless man waves hello to her from across the street. She later hires a psychiatrist to "cure" Penny of her desire to date an African-American boy. If we didn't think this was silly enough, Waters casts himself as the psychiatrist.

In plot twists where explanation adds nothing, Tracy, Penny, and their boyfriends end up in the apartment of a husband and wife tapping on bongos and painting an already painted-over canvas. "You guys are real beatniks," says Tracy's boyfriend, Link (Michael St. Gerard). "Just like New York." Message: Baltimore is a major urban area, but also a small, villagey town, where even kids who go to the same high school may have never visited each other's neighborhoods and the culture of bigger cities hasn't quite arrived yet, a place living in the present and the recent past at the same time. Divine's last scene has Tracy's dad Wilbur (Jerry Stiller) praising his daughter by saying that maybe Tracy "could be some sort of campus leader someday." Divine replies, "Wilbur, the times they are a-changin.'"

The Bob Dylan song of that name didn't exist in 1962. I like to think that joke is Waters reminding us that, here in the present, we can tell *Hairspray* is both about the not-so-innocent parts of a seemingly innocent past and also how, even long ago, we thought we were more evolved than we actually were. "How serious is it to come out for integration in '62?" Waters said in a 1988 interview in *Film Journal*. "Who would say, 'I was really against it in '62? Baltimore was the South, and there was a lot of segregation there. But I'm not coming out as this flaming liberal.'"

Baltimore is a northern industrial city in a state below the Mason-Dixon Line. It's Maryland's biggest city, but surrounded by cities larger than it. Consequently, it can feel contemporary and passé at the same time, its cultural icons present and past shoved up against each other like roommates assigned to the same freshman dorm room. Waters' own movies feel like old Hollywood tropes skewing contemporary manners and mores. The novels of Anne Tyler resemble the work of Jane Austen and George Eliot but are usually set in modern-day north Baltimore where she lives. Over five seasons on HBO, *The Wire* told stories about inner-city Baltimore neighborhoods that resemble the abandoned urban core of the Reagan administration, but also the coming of condos and land developers as the city in the twenty-first century has become an affordable alternative to Washington, DC. The Baltimore Orioles play at Oriole Park at Camden Yards, a stadium built in 1992, on the site of Babe Ruth's birthplace in 1895, in the architectural style of ballparks from baseball's first decades.

Baltimore is a city that lives alongside its recent past. *Hairspray* uses this mashup of then and now for both laughs and sly jabs at the misplaced nostalgic longings of the Reagan Era. In John Waters' fiendish hands, the innocence of the 1950s is a crooked ladder from which to stand and take a cock-eyed but penetrating look at the 1980s.

"Nothing Gold Can Stay"

In March of 1980, a school librarian from Frenso, California, named Jo Ellen Misakian wrote a letter to Francis Ford Coppola, the Oscar-winning director of *The Godfather* and *Apocalypse Now*. She wanted to know if Coppola would turn *The Outsiders*, the first novel by Susan Eloise (S. E.) Hinton and favorite book of her students, into a movie. The tale of a bloody rivalry between rich and working-class gangs of teenage boys in Tulsa, Oklahoma, Hinton had written *The Outsiders* while still a sophomore in high school and based the characters on her friends and classmates. Published in 1967 (shortly before the author's eighteenth birthday), *The Outsiders* has since sold over fourteen million copies, and has been in print for nearly a half century. But when Coppola read the letter, despite have two teenage sons of his own at the time, he had never heard of *The Outsiders*.

Coppola read the book. He and Hinton liked each other and went forward with the project. Released in the spring of 1983, *The Outsiders* did so-so business at the box office but has lived on thanks to how many actors it featured before they became famous—Diane Lane, Rob Lowe, Ralph Macchio, Patrick Swayze, and C. Thomas Howell. Matt Dillon, Tom Cruise, and Emilio Estevez, also in the cast, were either already famous or just about to be. Being in *The Outsiders* didn't hurt their chances for success.

Time is a strange thing in *The Outsiders*, stranger than in any other movie in this chapter. The novel was published in 1967 and, according to Hinton, takes place in 1965. But *The Outsiders* as a fixture of American culture is unmistakably linked to the 1980s. Despite its plot taking place during the Johnson administration, right after the British Invasion and while Elvis Presley was off making movies instead of records, the iconography of *The Outsiders*—slicked hair, denim jackets, Corvette Stingrays, and drive-in movie theaters, feels pure 1950s: James Dean and drag races instead of Vietnam and *Mad Men*. In Coppola's director's commentary for the 2005 reissue of the movie, he also mentions conceiving of *The Outsiders* on film as "*Gone with the Wind* for teenagers," a coming-of-age story told with the sweep of classic Hollywood epics.

The Outsiders takes place over about a week's time and is told in flashback. The bookends of the plot are the main character Ponyboy Curtis (C. Thomas Howell) writing about the events of the plot for a school assignment. Working with Hinton, Coppola chose locations they both decided were true to the memory of when the author wrote of them. Ponyboy's high school was S. E. Hinton's actual high school. The Admiral Twin Drive-in (7355 E. Easton Street on Tulsa's east side), site of an argument teenage S. E. Hinton witnessed between two girls and their boyfriends, has been in business for over fifty years and became the spot in both the book and movie's opening scenes where Ponyboy and his friends Dallas Winston (Matt Dillon) and Johnny Cade (Ralph Macchio) go to the movies and have a run-in with a rival gang.

The short distance between these locations in real life, the novel, and the movie wasn't only in the name of authenticity or good relations between filmmaker and author—by the time of principal photography on *The Outsiders*, Hinton had completed three other young adult novels, all set in Tulsa, which together made up both a timeline and a world. Ponyboy would reappear, two years older, as a minor character in her next book, *That Was Then, This Is Now* (1971). The rivalry between Ponyboy's gang and the rich kids (Socs or Socials) is referenced in her third book, *Rumble Fish* (1975), as events from several years ago that stopped when a few kids got killed. Her fourth book, *Tex* (1978), contains characters from *That Was Then, This Is Now*, as adults instead of teenagers. The locations she recommended to Coppola were part of a literary universe she's built over a decade of writing books, not just places she remembered well from high school.

S. E. Hinton as an artist seems fascinated by time. Her first five books all had teenage protagonists who frequently talk about a lost past rather than worrying about the future. Her characters often reappear in each other's lives after a long time away, leaving them (and us) to wonder what parallel but invisible journey they've been on. The future in a Hinton novel is a place of fear, not because it's unknown but because it might become the present far quicker than any of her characters are ready for. The central metaphors of *The Outsiders*—the sunrise, the sunset, and the Robert Frost poem "Nothing Gold Can Stay"—speak to this idea of time being both inevitable but surprising, scaring you with how fast it seems to move.

I've read and seen *The Outsiders* combined probably thirty times, and never noticed the sunset as metaphor before writing this (I can be slower than a sunset when it comes to these things). It's all over the movie's 2005 reissue (which includes twenty-two extra minutes deleted from the original) and Coppola's director's commentary. The reissue's new opening and closing credit sequences—black and white photos of the two gangs and Tulsa, shot with a golden filter—are literally bathed in sunset. Coppola also speaks in detail about the film's emotional high point, when Ponyboy and Johnny Cade hide out from the law in a mountaintop church after Johnny stabs a Soc kid during a fight, and they watch the sunset together. Coppola photographs the scene in widescreen, making it look like a moment not out of an eighties teen movie but from the playbook of classical Hollywood, something out of *Rebel Without a Cause* or *Giant*. Or *Gone with the Wind*.

Right after the sun goes down, Ponyboy recites the Robert Frost poem "Nothing Gold Can Stay," about the end of innocence, about things changing too fast—perhaps violently so—and how we often notice only after it has happened. It's easy to watch *The Outsiders*, even for the first time, and see this as a moment about nostalgia and longing for the impossible return of something gone. In some corner of his heart, Ronald Reagan based the spirit of presidency on this very impossible dream.

Widen the lens on *The Outsiders* and we have a movie whose key moment looks like a Hollywood classic from the 1930s, taking place in the 1960s using details from the 1950s, filmed for and linked to a generation who came of age in the 1980s, redone in 2005. *The Outsiders* and its overlapping, tangled notions of time complicate the very premise of the "Morning in America" eighties teen movie by lifting the entire idea of "then" being simpler, more innocent and, often, better, into the realm of metaphor. "Then" in *The Outsiders* uses the idea of the past as representative of the fear of not knowing what will come next and never, particularly when we are young, of being truly ready for it.

Which is what *Back to the Future* was saying, despite what President Reagan thought it was saying. There isn't only one past, present, and future, one sunny lost "then" we can only wish for in the grim, ugly now. Instead, *Back to the Future* and Hill Valley, *Dirty Dancing* and Kellerman's Resort, *Hairspray* and pre-Beatles Baltimore, all the eighties teen movies set in movie places before the social unrest of the sixties happens, demonstrate how easy it is to muddy the very idea of then and now. Each of them has characters using the past for both memory and self-delusion, for both moral grounding and myopia. Each of them is set somewhere that complicates the simplistic wish of Ronald Reagan's "Morning in America." Key in the wrong date into the DeLorean, knock down old man Peabody's pine tree, and have everything—past, present, and future—end up differently, and far harder to make sense of than you thought.

CHAPTER 6: THE SWEETEST VICTORY

'80s Sports Movies

Movies Discussed: *All the Right Moves, Vision Quest, Caddyshack, Better Off Dead, Johnny Be Good*

MOST SPORTS MOVIES END in victory, but what that victory means depends on when the movie hit theaters. The 2000s were the decade of the historical sports movie (*Seabiscuit, Cinderella Man, Remember the Titans, Miracle*), but also movies about the relationship between sports and family (*Bend It Like Beckham, Million Dollar Baby, The Blind Side*). For the first group, victory on the field represents a moment of social change. For the second, winning equals an understanding reached between parents and kids. The 1990s sports movie saw athletics as the backdrop of a man's redemption (*Jerry Maguire, He Got Game*), as metaphor for personal or political triumph (*A League of Their Own, Rudy*), or the cost of trying to win at all costs (*Hoop Dreams, Varsity Blues, The Program, Blue Chips*). Here, victories are hard to come by, humbling and less important than what the protagonist learns in the process. Most of these movies end in a quiet moment instead of a loud cheer.

Those downer sports movies of the nineties weren't just inhaling the grimness already in pop culture—grunge, heroin chic, Seattle weather—but reacting to the decade before. The eighties sports movie is largely a celebration of winning, of big games, last-second shots, adoring crowds, and trophies held high. All take different paths to arrive at a big game in their last scenes, but each, from the straightforward (*All the Right Moves*) to the surreal (*Better Off Dead, Caddyshack*) not only ends in victory on the playing field but also uses that victory to tie up all of its plot points. Doubting coaches and best friends, trouble with the boy/girlfriend, bullying opponents who cheat—all of it gets resolved at the final buzzer, which is almost always the last moment of the movie, too. These endings (usually in freeze frame, with the main character's arms raised above their head) remind the audience that nothing before the big game remains unfixed and that everything afterward will be okay.

In order to talk about the eighties sports movie and the stadiums, fields, and towns it puts on the map of Brat Pack America, we must contend with its obsession with winning. The eighties sports movie saw victory as the answer to everything thanks to two self-deceptions: a misreading of the movies that directly inspired them and a big gulp of the decade's hot air about sports.

Pregame: Where the Eighties Teen Sports Movie Came From

In the ninety-year history of the Academy Awards, only three movies about sports have won the Best Picture Oscar: *Rocky* (1977), *Chariots of Fire* (1981), and *Million Dollar Baby* (2004). We'll leave *Million Dollar Baby* alone, as it came along many years after the time of Brat Pack America. The other two are the direct ancestors of the eighties sports movie and its obsession with winning.

In his legendary book about Hollywood, *Adventures in the Screen Trade* (1983), William Goldman (who wrote the screenplays for *All the President's Men, Butch Cassidy and the Sundance Kid*, and *The Princess Bride*) went into some detail about why Rocky beat his own movie for the Best Picture Oscar even though both were well reviewed and did great business. He discusses why despite that *All the Presidents Men* was what Goldman called "A Significant Picture"—about *The Washington Post's* uncovering of the Watergate scandal, which Ronald Reagan himself claimed "cost Gerald Ford the presidency against Jimmy Carter"—*Rocky*, he wrote, "satisfied the most basic Hollywood dream—that dreams do come true."

Given that *Rocky* is now American mythology instead of just a movie, it's easy to forget that it ends with Rocky Balboa (Sylvester Stallone), small-time Philadelphia boxer, losing by decision in his once-in-a-lifetime shot against heavyweight champion Apollo Creed (Carl Weathers). If the "dreams do come true" part of *Rocky* is not about winning but about hard work, hanging in there, and making the most of opportunity when it comes, suppose, then, it's just as easy to forget that the terror of *losing* sulks around *Rocky* and nearly all of its five sequels like a deadbeat relative. Sylvester Stallone (who, in addition to playing Rocky Balboa, wrote and directed most of the *Rocky* films after the first one) included the danger of newlyweds Rocky and Adrian losing their house in *Rocky II*, how wealth and high living zapped Rocky's ring savvy in *Rocky III*, and subplots about sleazy promoters and how retired athletes eke out a living in the franchise's final chapters. No matter how many times Rocky Balboa wins in the ring, the spoils of victory and the security they provide his family are in constant danger.

Rocky came to movie theaters in the years just before the Brat Pack America era, but its sequels pushed well into the 1980s, each a slightly worse copy of the original: early defeat, emotional struggle over early defeat, heart-to-heart with spouse and trainer, training montage, victory in the final fight. The "early defeat" was there to continually reposition Rocky Balboa as an underdog, demonstrating Stallone and his team were smart enough to know that Rocky Balboa's appeal wasn't about superhuman athletic gifts but work ethic, not being the best but coming from modest beginnings and working toward being the best. Though you couldn't imagine as the series went on that Rocky *wouldn't* end up winning, part and parcel of the formula was Rocky's continuously pulling himself back from the edge of almost losing everything.

But say "Rocky Balboa" and no one remembers any of that. More likely, they'll start humming "Eye of the Tiger" with their arms raised above their head. I'm guessing at least a few Academy voters in 1977 pictured themselves in this pose when filling out their ballots. The *Rocky* series, seven films about the high price of winning, have taken their place in our culture as films about winning above all else.

Four years later, in 1981, *Chariots of Fire*, the story of two young British runners who brought victory to themselves and their nation at the 1924 Olympics in Paris, would take the Oscar over *Raiders of the Lost Ark* and *Reds*, both movies about the adventures of uniquely American heroes. Like *Rocky*, *Chariots of Fire* could be called a movie about dreams coming true, but its real gifts are in making victory in sport about dignity and pride, "a celebration of the spirit," wrote Roger Ebert, rather than gold medals and championship belts. And though *Chariots of Fire* often gets lumped in with the surge in conservative patriotism that came with the 1979 election of Prime Minister Margaret Thatcher, the movie's heroes are a Scotsman and a Jew, both proud to be English but who also demand their countrymen evolve their small and bigoted definition of what that means.

The eighties sports movie is the truant younger sibling of *Rocky* and *Chariots of Fire*, imitating their moves, learning the wrong lessons. The success of the two Best Picture winners allowed the eighties sports movies that immediately followed to poach the elements that worked—heroes from modest beginnings, grumpy mentors, supportive wives and girlfriends, training montages set to music culminating in final contests—then perform a moral sleight of hand: arguing that winning is the highest calling—a might-makes-right point of view than can justify anything—while at the same submitting that winners are ordinary people just like you and me who overcame ordinary circumstances on their way of glory.

The eighties sports movie wanted its audiences to know that anyone could win, but that winners were still different and better than everyone else.

Game Day Conditions: The Climate of the Eighties Sports Movie

THE BRAT PACK AMERICA sports movie came about during the only time in American history when a former sportscaster sat in the White House. Long before his career in politics or even as an actor, Ronald Reagan's first jobs out of college were calling baseball games on radio stations throughout the American Midwest. His childhood heroes had been athletes, and he'd been an okay football player at Eureka College in Illinois. (He wore his Eureka uniform when he auditioned for the part of George Gipp, in the 1940 movie *Knute Rockne, All American* (1940), the role that made him famous and gave him the lifelong nickname "The Gipper.") But his real talent lay in amusing his friends by narrating imaginary games using a broomstick as a microphone.

Reagan's first broadcasting gigs coincided with the early days of radio. Details of baseball games far away came into the radio station via telegraph and would sometimes arrive late or not at all. Which meant the young Ronald Reagan had to improvise, to make up narrative and drama where none existed. "The young man's job was to entertain, to reassure, to paint a portrait entirely of his own making," wrote Michael Weinreb in his 2011 book *Bigger Than the Game: Bo, Boz, the Punky QB, and How the '80s Created the Celebrity Athlete*. After becoming a politician, Ronald Reagan would reminisce often about his days as a sportscaster, sometimes telling the truth, often exaggerating or making up stories that fit his romantic memories of the time. Reagan's youthful years in radio, wrote Weinreb, "immersed in the mythology of American sports, were some of the most pleasant of his entire life."

Ronald Reagan's presidency, which pretty much engulfed all of Brat Pack America, lived on in mythology—"Morning in America," a country beaten by the last decade in the process of reclaiming its rightful spot as an example for the world. "With Reagan in office," wrote Weinreb, "all we wanted to do was feel good again. All we wanted to do was *win* again."

Let's make a one-inch lateral move to say that sports and movies are the Apple and Google of mythmaking in America. The eighties sports movie thus had myth in its bloodstream, a particularly American schizoid myth of being what playwright Eric Bogosian called wanting "to be the strongest warrior and the ultimate peacemaker, to have the highest principles but win the popularity contest." The eighties sports movie venerated underdogs scoring once-in-a-lifetime victories during a time that venerated real-life athletics and teams that seemed to win all the time.

The first great American sports story of the Brat Pack America era was one of the great underdog stories in American sports history: the US Olympic Hockey team's defeat of the mighty Russian squad and ultimate winning of the gold medal, the "Miracle on Ice," in February of 1980. But the rest of the decade consisted of the already dominant winning over and over again. The San Francisco 49ers won half of the Super Bowls in the 1980s. The Los Angeles Lakers and Boston Celtics owned the decade in basketball, bringing home eight of ten NBA championships between them. Hockey had the same dual dominance, with the New York Islanders and Wayne Gretzky's Edmonton Oilers winning the Stanley cup eight of ten years. No more than five players in men's tennis and three in women's tennis held the number-one ranking for the entire decade. At the 1984 Summer Olympics held in Ronald Reagan's adopted home of Los Angeles, the United States won eighty-three medals. No other country won more than twenty.

But sports dynasties do not make for good movie drama. The eighties sports movie, then, sees its own time through a cracked mirror: Winning may be the highest goal on the athletic fields of Brat Pack America, but to complete the myth, the heroes of the eighties sports movie must become winners, not start that way. They must come from behind to defeat the best with the goal of becoming the best themselves. The seeming nobility of that struggle obscures exactly how victory comes or what it means. The methods, consequences, or morality of winning would be another concern for another decade. Until then, the eighties sports movie lets you know that winning is noble and complete all on its own.

Home Field Advantage: The Eighties Sports Movie Hometown

WHAT'S IN THE BACKGROUND of those final-shot freeze frames that end most eighties sports movies? Usually, a winning team, a cheering crowd, and an adoring girlfriend. But zoom out farther than that, past the athletic field or the gym, and out into the community. The community of the Brat Pack America sports movie looks ghostlike and quiet, a place well past its prime and slowly collapsing in on itself.

In the 1980s, small and midsized towns in every state lay wounded and bleeding as factories shut down, factory jobs moved overseas, and the American economy began the painful shift from industrial to service-based. Being good at sports had been a way out of small towns for as long as America has had paying sports teams. But that story at this time played right into Ronald's Reagan's romantic notions of American accomplishment and the ennobling fairy tale of victory in sport. Dying industrial towns, therefore, end up on the map of Brat Pack America as the past a young athlete would leave behind on their way to a brighter future.

Two high school sports movies of the 1980s, *All the Right Moves* and *Vision Quest*, are good examples. Each uses its hometown— the fictional Ampipe, Pennsylvania, and the real Spokane, Washington—as a place where you can get stuck or pass through on the way to better things. The drama for both remains the same: winning means overcoming the limiting circumstances of where you were born and where, as a teenager looking to adulthood, you still are.

All the Right Moves (1983), the movie Tom Cruise made between *Risky Business* and *Top Gun*, takes place in a dying Pennsylvania steel town named Ampipe. Cruise plays a seventeen-year-old high school football player named Stef Djordjevic who has dreams of being an engineer. His brother and widowed father both work at the town's biggest employer, American Pipe and Steel, but everyone can see those jobs won't be around much longer. Ampipe has a strong enough football program to attract college scouts and the loyalty of a town that doesn't have a whole lot else to believe in. Stef is a good enough player that a college football scholarship would get him out of Ampipe and into a free college education and the career he wants.

"It's my shot, my way out of here," he tells his family early on. "Djordjevics have been humping steel out of this town for years. About time we had some say about the stuff after it's been made."

Everywhere are chances for Stef's plan to go wrong. His best friend, Brian (Christopher Penn), the team quarterback, is the better player of the two but gets his girlfriend pregnant. Stef and his girlfriend Lisa (Lea Thompson) had planned to go to college together, but she wants to study music and knows no music school goes to dying Pennsylvania steel towns to hand out scholarships. Does Stef want to leave her behind just because no one will pay for her dreams like they will his? Meanwhile, team coach Nickerson (Craig T. Nelson) has been offered a job next season in California. He thinks Stef has a lousy attitude (he does), so why stick his neck out for a good-but-not-great player when he's out of Ampipe and into a better coaching job next fall?

The title *All the Right Moves* is a bitter reminder of these traps. On the one hand, it rings of athletic glory, like the name of an NFL Hall of Famer's autobiography. On the other, it signifies how unforgiving Stef's circumstances are. A teenager totally dependent on sports to go to college in order to not become a professional athlete but an ordinary adult with a professional job is a teenager who cannot afford to mess up in any way. Asking that of a seventeen-year-old seems both unreasonable and unfair.

In the movie's darkest moment, both Stef and the audience confront this. Ampipe has lost a big game. A group of angry locals talk Stef into coming along while they vandalize Coach Nickerson's house. Stef gets caught and blacklisted by the coach. And while the movie's plot depends on Nickerson recognizing his punishment as too severe, it leaves open why the events leading up to it happened at all. What kind of sad, pathetic community vandalizes someone's home over a high school football game? What kind of unfair pressure does it put on a teenager when grown men insist he participate in a crime because of that same high school football game?

At its best, *All the Right Moves* feels like a proto–*Friday Night Lights*, about the hopelessness of dying industrial towns and how their high school athletes shouldn't be held responsible for the happiness of their entire community. Unlike the players in *Friday Night Lights*, Stef is already dreaming of a future somewhere else, off the field and out of Ampipe. Winning is a means to that end, not a goal all its own. Everyone in Ampipe may not have Stef's options, but *All the Right Moves* has its whole cast, not just the athlete hero, feel their community crumbling around them and trapping them in the rubble. It knows this fear under its skin. In this way, it manages to be a little more hopeful than *Friday Light Nights,* which derives much of its power and sadness from how little future the players, or anyone else in town, can imagine beyond high school football.

All the Right Moves was filmed in the autumn of 1983 in Johnstown, Pennsylvania, a steel town about a year into its factories closing down. It would take two decades for the city to refocus its economy on defense contracting, green power, and healthcare.

All the Right Moves punks out in its final moments, substituting Nickerson's change of heart for a touchdown at the buzzer to resolve everything. I don't believe for a moment in the coach's about-face, or that Lisa and Stef's father and brother would suddenly put all their own feelings aside to cheer on Stef and the opportunity to go to college. Since the conclusion seems to arrive in an awful hurry, it almost feels like the movie doesn't believe it either.

But overall, the movie's fake out makes me happy. *All the Right Moves* looks like another eighties sports movie featuring a handsome high school athlete who will work hard, overcome adversity, and win the final games while a pretty girl applauds on the sidelines. Except here, the last shot is not Stef with a trophy hoisted to the heavens, but Stef and Lisa walking out the front gates of American Pipe and Steel. The actual victory of this movie is not sports themselves but the better life sports can give somewhere else, long after your playing days are over.

In his review of *Vision Quest* (1985), Roger Ebert praised the relationship the film's characters have with the movie's location choice of Spokane, Washington.

Spokane, which looks sort of wet and dark in many scenes, and feels like a place that prizes individuality... Instead of silhouetting the Modine character against the city and a lot of humble supporting roles, and turning him into a Rocky *of wrestlers, the movie takes time to place the character in the city and in the lives of the other people.*

The "Modine character" is eighteen-year-old wrestler Louden Swain (Matthew Modine), who opens *Vision Quest* by telling us that "this will be the year I make my mark." He plans to dethrone the state champion wrestler in a weight class below his, which means effectively training twenty-four hours a day to be ready, waking up early to run the Monroe Bridge over the Spokane River, and dropping to do a few push-ups while on break at his job at a downtown hotel. Louden's goal requires him to be constantly moving and obsessed with his own fitness, but Modine plays him as open and curious enough to value the others in his life and learn from them in his moments of standing still. Those others include his boss at the restaurant (J. C. Quinn), his favorite history teacher (Harold Sylvester), and his best friend Kuch, who pretends to be Native American (a post–*Sixteen Candles* Michael Schoeffling). Louden's dad (Ronny Cox, right after playing Lt. Bogomil in *Beverly Hills Cop*) works at an auto body garage in town. His wife left him and Louden for another man.

One night, a young artist named Carla (Linda Fiorentino) on her way to San Francisco brings her car into the garage. Louden's dad invites her to stay with them while her car gets fixed. Yes, she and Louden fall for each other, and Louden's "year to make his mark" (or his "vision quest," in the words of his pretend native friend) becomes as much about losing his virginity as winning a wrestling match. But *Vision Quest* takes its time getting there, and we realize that even though the plot requires the last scene to be on a wrestling mat (with, sigh, a triumphant freeze frame), the best things about it are everything that happens around the requisite plot stops of eighties sports movies. In more ways than one, this is a movie about in-betweens.

Vision Quest's lovers may both be on journeys—Carla's to San Francisco, Louden's to adulthood and the next stage of his life—that intersect in each other's arms. But the idea of being in between applies to pretty much everyone in this movie too: Kuch has an abusive drunk for a father and plots escape. Louden's coach doesn't trust Louden at first to make a new weight class, but knows his attempt will disrupt the team he's been building both now and after Louden has graduated. Louden's boss is an alcoholic in the early stages of recovery but with much time spent at rock bottom. And his dad has lost the family farm, his wife, and has a new stage of life beginning as the empty-nest parent of an adult instead of a teenager.

Maybe they wouldn't put it as dramatically as Louden does. But all the people in his life seem to be in the middle of little vision quests of their own.

Spokane is the place where their separate journeys intersect. The feeling Roger Ebert got that the city "prizes individuality" may be due to the supporting characters largely being photographed alone or in relation to Louden. Or since Louden is still in high school during the day, we mostly see Spokane through his life as a late-night hotel waiter, when the streets are empty. Unlike *All the Right Moves*, Spokane does not feel like a collapsing industrial town, but rather a solid if rather quiet community where, if you're trying to figure out what comes next, people will leave you alone to do it. They're probably in the middle of doing the same.

Vision Quest is adapted from a young adult novel by Spokane native Terry Davis. The town works in the movie version as a place of both passage and grounding, as all of the Spokane residents we meet are on their way to somewhere else and a little unsure about how to begin or where they stand now. But the community feels like a place that gives the characters room for that uncertainty while also drawing them together because of it.

Vision Quest's final freeze frame ends with Louden narrating over an image of himself on the shoulders of his cheering teammates. It's clearly the future, as he talks about his eighteenth year as a time from long ago. He remembers training to win the wrestling match of his life, of meeting the girl of his dreams. And though we feel we are completely in the same wheelhouse as most Brat Pack America sports movies, where victory and individual achievement are the brass ring, Louden shifts course in the speech's final seconds.

"But all I ever settled for is that we're born to live and then to die, and...we got to do it alone, each in his own way. And I guess that's why we got to love those people who deserve it like there's no tomorrow. 'Cause when you get right down to it—there isn't."

Maybe an amiable, curious guy like Louden Swain would have met those people wherever he grew up. But *Vision Quest* gives us Spokane as that place of meeting, where searchers pause in their searching and meet one another, then appreciate the bond we all have of not quite being sure what comes next.

Half Time Show: Eighties Sports Comedies

Two of the most beloved comedies of the 1980s—*Caddyshack* (1980) and *Better Off Dead* (1985)—are also sports movies. At least, they end like sports movies, with our teenage hero winning an athletic contest (golf and skiing, respectively) and in doing so defeating a bully, winning the respect of friends and parents, getting the girl, and resolving all the movie's unanswered questions. But how they get to that finish line involves two distinct kinds of surreal hilarity. *Caddyshack* and *Better Off Dead* use their athletic fields and hometowns as two different ways of achieving it.

Caddyshack is an autobiographical comedy in plot but not location. Comedian Bill Murray and his older brother Brian Doyle-Murray had summer jobs as caddies at the Indian Hills golf course in the North Chicago suburb of Winnetka. (John Hughes territory. A mile north of Indian Hills, at 583 Chestnut Street in Winnetka, was Ferris Bueller's mom's real estate office). Winnetka was an upper-middle-class town, but the Murrays were a working-class Irish family with nine children. Caddies at Indian Hills needed summer employment and were stuck carrying bags for rich kids and their parents, who treated them like servants. The brothers wrote the original screenplay for *Caddyshack*, sensing the comic potential in a standoff between the snobs who are members of a golf club and the staff who work there. One of the movie's taglines became "The Snobs versus the Slobs."

Most of *Caddyshack*'s characters slip around that easy characterization. Protagonist Danny Noonan (Michael O'Keefe, who as an adult was Agent John Redmond on the Showtime series *Homeland*) is a teenager from a big working-class family like the Murrays, who caddies for pocket change and has no particular plan for his future. His father's after him to go to college, so Danny has a vague idea to chase the scholarship offered to caddies by one of the club's snottiest members, a judge named Elihu Smails (pronounced "smells," naturally). Judge Smails (Ted Knight) is furious that Bushwood, the golf club, lets barbarians like Al Czervik (Rodney Dangerfield, in his breakthrough role) onto the links, particularly since Czervik owns the real estate around the club and thinks the eighteenth hole would make a great spot for condominiums. Meanwhile, Danny normally caddies for a rich womanizer named Ty Webb (Chevy Chase) who likes to dispense Zen-inflected advice and doesn't really care who is listening. The Murray brothers (barely) hold down proceedings at either end of Bushwood. Brian Doyle-Murray, as Lou, runs the caddy shack, when he's not busy gambling his employee's tips away. Bill Murray plays the groundskeeper Carl Spackler, who served in Vietnam and plans to use all he learned there to snuff out the golf course's most elusive and industrious gopher.

Scheduled for the fall of 1979, the *Caddyshack* shoot couldn't happen at the actual golf club that inspired it due to the unpredictable nature of Chicago area weather. Also, director Harold Ramis wasn't interested in shooting in Southern California where nosy studio executives could drop by the set with suggestions. Team *Caddyshack* then chose separate country clubs in as far from Hollywood as they could get, the Rolling Hills Country Club near Ft. Lauderdale, which is more often remembered as the site of the movie, and the Boca Raton Hotel and Country Club, about twenty miles north, which seems to play down the association. Rolling Hills had a healthy growth of oak trees around the grounds, so it could pass as a northern suburb of Chicago instead of looking too much like South Florida.

Combined, the two clubs make "Bushwood" appear posh, serene, and verdant, exactly how you'd picture a golf club filled with entitled rich people. In fact, Bushwood is so painfully, exceedingly what you'd expect from a golf club filled with entitled rich people that the oddities of the characters stand out against it like cleat prints on a white carpet. Bill Murray's Carl the Groundskeeper never seems to do any groundskeeping other than plot vengeance against the meddling gopher. But Bushwood seems to not have any other groundskeepers, which tells us that this lunatic Carl is also responsible for Bushwood's perfectly manicured greens and fairways. That Carl lurks semi-invisibly in the corners of the otherwise pristine club, muttering nonsense to gopher and flower beds alike (nearly all of Bill Murray's lines were improvised), adds a hilarious note of menace to what could come off as a broad, forgettable character. Then Bushwood ups the ante on that same joke: the club wouldn't be its beautiful self without this in-house maniac making it that way.

Across the fairway, the millionaires Chase and Dangerfield use Bushwood as something to push against, a staid wading pool of conformity you can urinate in by being boorish (Dangerfield) or just plain weird (Chase) because you know your money is as good as anyone else's. O'Keefe plays Danny with a bemused slack, nonplussed but surrounded by eighteen holes of mounting silliness. Director Ramis rarely photographs him with the typically flattering angels of a lead character, allowing Danny's smug calm to almost fade him into the backdrop. Indeed, Ramis and cinematographer Stevan Larner use few tracking and dolly shots and primarily shoot literal, flat, and unobtrusive. Ramis's direction is painfully ordinary, mimicking the setting, in order for the comedy happening between camera and background to pop out.

Caddyshack also uses the rigidity of golf as comic fodder. Golf is a game of few rules but much tradition and lots of social mores. Which means it's an excellent source of comic exaggeration and mismatching. Why is it so funny when Al Czervik flips on the built-in boom box in his golf bag and yells to anyone near his putting tee, "Let's dance!" Because we know a golf course is a hushed place, so who the hell wires up his golf bag to turn a putting green into a keg party? Why is it so funny that Ty Webb, in tam o' shanter cap and high-water khakis, looking like the very stereotype of a snotty rich golfer, asks his caddy, "Do you do drugs, Danny?" To which Danny replies, "Every day, sir." "Good—then what seems to be the problem?" comes the answer. Because Bushwood seems a hushed, dignified place but if we know anything about the history of golf, we also know it's a game filled with hustlers, con artists, and strange birds like Ty Webb. For years in the 1940s and '50s, golf pro/hustler Sam Snead haunted the Boca Raton Club, where *Caddyshack* filmed many of its scenes. Snead was to golf as Weird Al Yankovic was to pop music: an artist who knew the game so well he devoted his talents to the skilled teasing of it.

Given *Caddyshack*'s choice to both film a long way from its funders and to normalize its surroundings to better highlight the comedy, perhaps it's no surprise that cast and crew used the posh set for their own kind of craziness. An ESPN.com article about the shoot quotes a biography of the film's producer, Jon Peters, saying *Caddyshack* was "an eleven-week party legendary even by Hollywood standards." And in a wonderful case of life imitating art, in the concluding scene, where Danny wins the golf tournament thanks to Carl setting off explosives all over the course to slay the gopher, a pilot at nearby Ft. Lauderdale Airport saw the flames and radioed it in as a downed plane.

I wonder how hard the cast and crew laughed at that. Or, given how crazy and debauched a time they were having already, did it seem par for the course?

Better Off Dead (1985) is the debut film of writer/director Savage Steve Holland. (He would later make *One Crazy Summer* in 1986 and *How I Got into College* in 1989.) Both *Dead* and *Summer* end in sporting competitions, but calling them "sports movies" would be like calling the Wagner's Ring Cycle a bunch of singing in German. Holland's comedic style can best be defined as maximum illogical gestures per minute of screen time.

Better Off Dead claims to take place in a Northern California ski town called Greendale, which I guess means it's somewhere near Lake Tahoe (the name's actually an homage to Greenwich, Connecticut, where Holland grew up). The mountains used for the skiing montages certainly look steep and snowy enough.

The rest of the movie wouldn't pass for Northern California if you painted the Golden Gate Bridge on the film stock. Palm trees, warm nights, lots of teenagers in shorts and sandals, Holland filmed *Better Off Dead* in several towns in the north and northeast San Fernando Valley—Sierra Madre, Monrovia, Glendale, and La Crescenta. The ski scenes were filmed at three separate resorts near Salt Lake City, Utah.

"I wanted Connecticut, I wanted suburbia," Holland told me over the phone. The studio, he said, effectively ordered him to stay put. "You've got three million. Shoot it in Glendale."

Holland and his team weren't being cheap or sloppy trying to pass off this mishmash of Utah and greater Los Angeles as a Northern California ski town. Instead, "Greendale" functions as a scenic representation of Holland's manic sensibility. The entire world of *Better Off Dead* is on a tilt. That Greendale appears to have ski slopes and tanning weather within a short drive of one another in this movie also makes Greendale into a giant road sign saying "Further madness ahead."

"One of the streets we used in Pasadena had mountains in the background, and I figured the audience would assume the snowy mountain where the characters went skiing was right over there," Holland said. "In the end, nobody cared. It may even be funnier that way."

Better Off Dead concerns one Lane Meyer (John Cusack) whose girlfriend, Beth (Amanda Wyss), dumps him for Stalin (yes, Stalin), the class jerk who also happens to be the best skier in their "bodaciously small" ski town. Stalin (Aaron Dozier) has conquered the K-2, Greendale's biggest mountain, and is an asshole about it to Lane. Lane just wants time to grieve the breakup via low-grade suicide attempts (in one, he jumps from a bridge but lands squarely in the back of a garbage truck. The garbage men remark, "Ain't it a shame when someone throws away a perfectly good white boy like that?"). Meanwhile, Lane's father (David Ogden Stiers) wants to send his son's prize possession, a half-repaired Camaro currently rotting on the front lawn, to the junkyard; his mother (Kim Darby) has turned dinner into some combination of big game hunting and performance art (one meal contains a live octopus tentacle in a steaming pot, another a lump of green rubber cement that walks off the plate by itself); and his younger brother Badger (yes, Badger) appears to be constructing a space shuttle in his bedroom.

Across the street, the annoying neighbor kid and his train wreck of a mother have taken in a cute French foreign exchange student named Monique (Diane Franklin), who dreams of visiting Dodger Stadium. Lane's best friend (Curtis Armstrong, the eighties teen movie's go-to best friend) is convinced there's a fortune to be made in selling the snow on the nearby ski slope off as cocaine; and a psychotic paperboy (Demian Slade) terrorizes the neighborhood, demanding his unpaid two dollars plus tip. I haven't even mentioned Lane's part-time job at a burger joint where he's required to wear a pig nose and ears, or the two Asian guys who drag race him to school every morning but speak only in phrases borrowed from Howard Cosell. Or the song performed by a Claymation hamburger.

That *Better Off Dead* ends with a triumphant ski sequence is largely beside the point. The conventions of eighties sports movies exist here to give the anarchic proceedings the barest of boundaries. Holland mostly uses those clichés to keep his singular comedic craziness from exploding outside the screen. He'd do the same in *One Crazy Summer* a year later, and a bit less so in *How I Got into College* in the waning days of Brat Pack America. Both those movies use their locations as *Caddyshack* does: a yardstick of normalcy to measure the lunacy piled high around it. The boardwalk and beaches of *One Crazy Summer* and the school campuses of *How I Got into College* look and feel as you'd expect campuses and boardwalks to, which makes Savage Steve Holland's imagination thrown all over them stand out like red paint. In *Better Off Dead*, Greendale is just one more piece of a completely surreal landscape, like the cliffs behind the melting clocks in Salvador Dalí's "Persistence of Memory."

"Where my movies happen is very key, actually," Holland told me. "You just get someplace stuck in your mind, but nobody seems to care what you've envisioned. As long as you are close and it's funny."

Final Minutes: *Johnny Be Good* and *Texas*

CONSIDER *FRIDAY NIGHT LIGHTS*. Before it became the TV show you begged your doubting friends to watch by promising, "It's not just about high school football!" it was a nonfiction book and movie about a high school football season in the very last years of Brat Pack America. In the autumn of 1988, Philadelphia-based journalist Buzz Bissinger moved his family to Odessa, Texas, to report on the Permian Panthers' quest for a high school state championship, and the lengths their fans and supporters were willing go for their team to win. Those lengths—fudging players' lousy grade point averages, lying to doctors about a star running back's injury, death threats to coaches who dared preside over a losing game—were both desperate and dangerous. Panther fans, reported Bissinger, weren't just loyal and proud but a sad, starved community (Odessa, an oil town, had suffered terribly in a petroleum market crash the year before) who placed all their faith in the winning season of a high school football team because they felt defeated and lost in the rest of their lives.

The *Friday Night Lights* movie adaptation by director Peter Berg (who also brought the story to television) came to theaters in 2004. *Friday Night Lights* the movie has an 81 percent fresh rating on Rotten Tomatoes, and that feels a little stingy. *Friday Night Lights* the TV show has a 100 percent fresh rating on Rotten Tomatoes, and that feels about right.

Now consider *Johnny Be Good*. Released in March of 1988 a few months before the Permian Panthers' season at the center of *Friday Night Lights, Johnny Be Good* is a comedy about the absurd lengths colleges will go to in order to get their hands on a state champion high school quarterback. Anthony Michael Hall played Johnny Walker, the state champion quarterback. Robert Downey Jr. plays Johnny's best friend and doesn't pass for a second as a high school footballer even though the movie thinks he does. Uma Thurman plays Johnny's girlfriend in her big screen debut. The movie's theme song was legendary British heavy metal band Judas Priest covering Chuck Berry's "Johnny B. Goode," a horrible mistake. *Johnny Be Good* has a zero percent fresh rating on Rotten Tomatoes, which feels generous.

And yet...

Johnny Be Good was filmed in Georgetown, Texas, a suburb thirty miles north of Austin, where *Friday Night Lights* the TV show would film two decades later. At first look, everything about *Johnny Be Good* screams Southern California, from its golden-haired cast, over-reliance on convertible cars, and football only being played on sun-dappled fields in the daytime. But no, *Johnny Be Good*, a moronic, two-chuckle comedy about the absurd lengths gone to for a winning football team, plays out on the same visual landscape as *Friday Night Lights,* a cautionary tale about the absurd lengths gone to for a winning football team.

Johnny Be Good is not good. (*How I Got into College* was basically the same movie, done better, the following year.) But without meaning to at all, it signaled the end of the eighties sports movie formula. After 1988, rarely, if ever, would sports movies exalt winning as the only worthwhile goal. Instead, they would largely warn of caring too much about winning or move victory and "big game" finales to secondary status as metaphor or historical detail. After 1988, the winning-solves-everything ethos of the eighties sports movie would seem loud-mouthed, immature, and wrong.

The signal of that transition comes from *Johnny Be Good* feeling like Southern California but actually being Central Texas. The year before, Texas football had been devastated by the same scandals *Johnny Be Good* tried (and failed) to make into comedy. In February of 1987, Southern Methodist University in Dallas received the "death penalty" from the NCAA, terminating the team's entire 1988 season. Investigators had discovered SMU knew of football program boosters effectively bribing active players and high school recruits with money, cars, and illegal drugs. The NCAA has not imposed a death penalty on a college football program before or since.

That fall, the stock market dropped by 502 points, the worst crash since the Great Depression, and with it, the Texas petroleum market went into free fall. Oil-dependent towns like Odessa lost jobs and family businesses. Their high school football teams, already sources of civic pride in a football-crazy state, now also had to represent hope for entire communities that had lost everything else.

None of this sadness is felt in *Johnny Be Good*, as featherweight and thoughtless as a handful of confetti. But if you were a Texan and a football fan at the time, you might not have seen *Johnny Be Good* in the same way. You would recognize that, by accident, this was a comedy about the win-at-all-costs excesses of football set right in the middle of your home state, which at the time was paying a worse price than just about anyone for their win-at-all-costs approach to football.

Overtime: The Consequences of "Winning Solves Everything"

THE EIGHTIES SPORTS MOVIES' obsession with victory reflected the priorities of sports in America at the time. Thanks to the growth of cable television and innovations in advertising and sponsorship, the money in sports grew exponentially in the 1980s. That meant the pressure for players and teams to steal any advantage so they could grow exponentially, too.

In the 1980s, Major League Baseball discovered dozens of players using amphetamines. College football and basketball programs were caught shoveling money at top players and prospects. In 1989, Pete Rose, who had more hits than anyone to ever play baseball, was caught gambling against his own team and suspended from the game for life. "To each sports scandal, whether it involved recruiting, cheating, or drug use," wrote author Haynes Johnson, "public response was the same: a collective yawn and a figurative wink... If ingesting drugs [or] bribing officials helped make one's team win, so be it."

On January 11, 1989, Ronald Reagan, the sportscaster who had become President of the United States, gave his farewell speech from the Oval Office. "We have every right to dream heroic dreams," he told the nation. "Those who say that we are in a time when there are no heroes just don't know where to look." In the decade Ronald Reagan defined, pop culture had already seen the passing of one kind of sports hero in movies defined by victory and triumphant freeze frames. The great sports movies to follow—*Rudy* and *Murderball*, *Hoop Dreams* and *Seabiscuit*, *Love & Basketball* and *Friday Night Lights*—seemed to pick up after that freeze frame, asking what winning meant rather than assuming it meant everything. And the towns that dreamed of and cheered for victory in the sports movies of Brat Pack America would become something more complicated in the sports movies of the 1990s and 2000s, places not carried out of depression on the shoulders of young athletes, but places where we tried to make sure young athletes had somewhere real to go home to after the cheering stopped.

BRAT PACK AMERICA TALKS TO. . .WRITER/DIRECTOR SAVAGE STEVE HOLLAND

I F YOU'VE RECENTLY HEARD someone say, "I want my two dollars!" or "No Whammies!" and you're not sure why, thank the mind of Savage Steve Holland. The writer/director of the eighties teen classics *Better Off Dead* and *One Crazy Summer* trained as an animator at California Institute of the Arts (the birthplace of Pixar), which takes us part of the way to explaining why his movies have both cartoon sequences (*Summer* is narrated by a wavy-lined monster) and characters that feel like cartoons (the lunatic paperboy of *Dead* that won't go away until he gets paid...two dollars). The rest of the way involves making sense of a singing hamburger, a runaway Godzilla costume, and a plot to turn snow into cocaine. Holland's comedic genius comes from stretching the very loose tie between logic and hilarity, which snaps but never breaks.

Savage Steve Holland animated the now-legendary Whammy character of the eighties game show *Press Your Luck* and since the early nineties has been a sought-after children's television director, helming episodes of *Lizzie McGuire*, *Zoey 101*, and *Zeke and Luther*.

I spoke to Savage Steve Holland by phone in the fall of 2015 from his home office in Los Angeles.

Kevin Smokler: What's it like for you as the filmmaker behind *Better Off Dead* and *One Crazy Summer*, which were not successes in their time but are now regarded as comedy classics and an inspiration to a generation of funny people?

Savage Steve Holland: I feel really, really *happy* and relieved that the movies had a second life and are still around after all this time. We recently had a few thirtieth-anniversary events here in Hollywood. The jokes still played to a sold-out audience and I'm very, very proud about that.

Back in the eighties, when it wasn't successful at the box office, I was pretty convinced that I was insane and had no idea what comedy was. After a while, video chains (like Blockbuster) showed up and my movies reappeared on the shelves. I was curious if anyone rented them, and was disappointed when I almost never saw them on the shelves after a while. I figured no one rented them so they never put them out. So I asked, and what I learned was that people would rent them and then keep them, paying the fee for that because they liked them that much.

Then when HBO (I know all this sounds like caveman times to people at this point) came along, they also found an audience for this silliness that never seemed to go away. So bottom line, I feel a little relieved that the movies were as funny as I believed they were to a lot of people. Phew!

KS: How much of *Better Off Dead* and *One Crazy Summer* were autobiographical?

SSH: A lot, but not all. *Better Off Dead* was basically a true story, but exaggerated. In high school, a guy on the ski team was a dick, wouldn't let me join, and tried to bone my girlfriend. I grew up in Greenwich, Connecticut, which is why the town is called "Greendale," and started skiing at twelve or thirteen.

For *Better Off Dead*, I just had idea diarrhea and just barfed everything I could into my stupid script. I didn't have that many ideas for *One Crazy Summer*. I wrote it in about a week because *Better Off Dead* was testing really well on college campuses and Warner Brothers said, "What would you do next?"

One Crazy Summer was based on summertime-of-nightmare trips I took growing up to visit my grandmother on Nantucket.

My grandmother didn't really like kids. It was more like she was saying, "Here come the messy people."

I always looked forward to visiting with the townies and had summer friends. That part was true. But I didn't play basketball (John Cusack's character Hoops McCann got his name from a Steely Dan song) and had never sailed a day in my life. All that stuff with regattas was made up.

KS: How much does "where a movie happens" matter to your kind of storytelling?

SSH: Very key, actually. When you can find a location that's iconic but gorgeous, like that kinda suburbia bitchin' bridge that Lane tries to jump off of in *Better Off Dead*. I could see Lane and his girlfriend having a beer there at night two months before. Before it got used for one of his many suicide attempts. Of course, it's in a lot of other movies, but I had to use it because it was so obvious how it fit into my movie.

Sometimes when it doesn't work out, you think it's going to be fatal, but it never is. For *One Crazy Summer*, I should have had an aerial shot of the ferry boat bringing the gang into Nantucket, which is how I remember visiting as a kid. I regret that a little.

Also, Joanne Greenwald [a character Lane goes on a bad date with in *Better Off Dead*] house is near Dodger Stadium. That wasn't my vision. I had her wealthier than that. We had to keep to a schedule, and since right after we had to shoot the scene at Dodger Stadium and we had so little time to film there, Joanne had to live nearby in Echo Park.

When it comes right down to it, I love lies like that. I love the tricks of movies.

KS: Your movies seem to be really interested in teamwork, gangs of people coming together for a common purpose.

SSH: I was really inspired by *Breaking Away* and how much those guys loved each other. Also, *The Little Rascals*. I think my movies are the teenage version. I also loved *The Karate Kid* and the plot centered on both a big victory but also a set of mismatched people working together.

KS: To that end, you overwhelmingly seem to cast people that look interesting rather than like movie stars.

SSH: That comes from Spielberg. I'm a huge Spielberg fan. Half the cast of *Jaws* looks like it was plucked out of delicatessen.

Take Dan Schneider, who played Ricky the obnoxious across-the-street neighbor in *Better Off Dead*. He was based on my across-the-street neighbor growing up, who was actually from Texas and was kind of hillbilly. But Dan showed up to audition and did this line reading where he spit water out of his nose. I laughed so hard that it didn't matter that Dan playing Ricky meant the character would be much more of a spoiled preppy kid. Dan was right for it because he took Ricky somewhere interesting I hadn't thought of.

KS: Do you have a comedic philosophy?

SSH: I write the beginning joke and the ending joke and try to come up with the middle. If I feel bored for even one second, someone has to get hit in the head. Obviously, my movies are just like a big cartoon. Maybe it's bad that there's no breathing room?

When *Better Off Dead* was longer, people didn't like it. A kid came up to me at a test screening and said, "Better luck next time, dude." How did he know I was the director? So we ended up cutting ten minutes.

KS: What happened in those ten minutes?

SSH: I had Lane's mom being a super clean freak and in a cult. Also, a B story of Lane playing saxophone in the school band while sitting next to a seal who was also in the school band.

KS: I hear you and Bobcat are working on a sequel to *One Crazy Summer*.

SSH: We've been passing notes back and forth, noodling with our script tentatively titled *One Epic Fall* at this point. Bobcat likes to say there were too many unanswered questions from the first movie.

We have a dream to work with Curtis Armstrong and Joel Murray again. Our schedules are very different, so we haven't made mad progress…but the dream lives!

CHAPTER 7: "WE CAN'T REWIND, WE'VE GONE TOO FAR"

'80s Teen Movies and Technology

Movies Discussed: *Weird Science, Real Genius, My Science Project, The Manhattan Project, Gremlins, WarGames*

O N OCTOBER 13, 1983, a business executive named Bob Barnett placed a phone call from behind the wheel of a car. The car was a dark brown Chrysler convertible parked in front of Soldier Field, home of the Chicago Bears football team. The phone Barnett held was the size of his forearm, weighed over two pounds (he called it "the brick"), and had to be installed in the vehicle's trunk by a technician. On the other end of the call was Alexander Graham Bell's grandson, who lived in Berlin.

The call Barnett made was only a few minutes long. It cost the Ameritech Corporation, where Barnett was CEO, a quarter of a million dollars.

That autumn day, Bob Barnett made the first commercial cell phone call. Ameritech would market that cellular phone, which cost nearly $4,000, a $50 monthly surcharge, and calls at forty cents a minute during peak hours, as a toy for the rich and the status conscious, a way to feel important jabbering into a receiver the size of a shoe while driving.

It worked. The technology that 90 percent of Americans now own initially wasn't meant for anyone who didn't start the day in a suit. The first cell phones screamed adult, expensive, complicated, and probably not for you. And yet the product was a hit for Ameritech. On the twenty-fifth anniversary of the stunt, the *Chicago Tribune* still names it "the call that launched a $150 billion-a-year" industry.

Three months later, on January 24, 1984, a California business executive named Steve Jobs unveiled his company's newest product to an auditorium of stockholders and employees. He wore a bowtie and double-breasted suit. The auditorium belonged to the performing arts department at a nearby community college.

The weekend before, Jobs's eight-year-old company, Apple Computer, had told the world, via a mysterious Super Bowl commercial, that "on January 24, Apple Computer will introduce Macintosh. And you'll see why 1984 won't be like *1984*." On January 24, Jobs reran that commercial on video monitors to the audience gathered in the community college auditorium. He then strolled back out on stage holding a small black bag, set the bag on a table, and from it removed a putty-colored box with a pale blue screen, about the size of a twelve-pack of beer standing on its end.

Jobs turned the machine on, inserted a 3.5-inch floppy disk, and with a lead-in from the theme to *Chariots of Fire*, the machine spoke.

"Hello, I am Macintosh. It sure is great to be out of that black bag. Unaccustomed as I am to public speaking, I'd like to share with you a maxim I thought of the first time I met an IBM mainframe: NEVER TRUST A COMPUTER YOU CAN'T LIFT!"

The crowd roared. Macintosh may as well have said, "Never trust anyone over thirty," then handed you a joint. The moment was pure counterculture thumb in the eye of the old way. But what it meant emotionally was that this "personal computer" thing was playful, fun, and human. Jobs had gone back and forth with his engineers and designers to get the Macintosh to resemble a smiling human face.

No one could call this computer "a brick," and you didn't need to be a computer science professor to operate it, nor a Wall Street trader to afford one. You didn't aspire to it. It fit into your life already, like an old friend you hadn't met. It was cool. It thought you were cool, too. The Macintosh was technology for right now and for a bright, new kind of future, for the young and the young spirit in all of us.

The crowd leapt to their feet and applauded the way you do an Oscar Lifetime Achievement winner. The not-yet-thirty-year-old Steve Jobs looked at them and smiled, the way you smile when you're trying not to cry. The ovation continued for five straight minutes.

The Macintosh didn't end up being a commercial success like Ameritech's cell phone did. Nonetheless, at least symbolically, Steve Jobs's introduction of the Macintosh is now seen as the genesis of the personal computer industry.

The symbolic birthdays of the cell phone and personal computer were a scant three months apart. Yet the technology revolutions begun virtually at the same time in the 1980s and that would define so much of the decades to come had in mind two disparate users and visions of how technology fit in their lives.

The Ameritech-Macintosh difference in approach personified the generational and cultural divide of technology—for the few versus the many, for work and power versus games, creativity, and fun—that defined both the 1980s and its teen movies. If we're calling the time of Brat Pack America 1978–1989, look at what technology didn't exist at the beginning of the decade but was normal at the end: cable television, video games, personal computers, portable phones, home video, music devices you walked around with instead of listened to from the living room couch. If the great technological leaps of the 1950s and '60s had been systemic—commercial air travel, the interstate highway—or practical—washing machines, dishwashers, in-home refrigerators—the devices that came of age in the 1980s were personal and designed to deliver entertainment and information. A few of them solved problems, but most were there to show you a good time. That meant the early adopters were usually not commuters or businesspeople or hospitals or homemakers, but teenagers and young people.

The eighties teen movie understood that. But they also understood all this change all at once could be both thrilling and scary. Now that much of what we called "technology" could live in a teenager's bedroom, instead of a corporate office, a university, a lab building with an electrified fence, who was responsible for what it could do? And who paid the price when the technology from the decades before, which had arrived on the jingoism and fear of WWII and the atomic bomb, came face to face with its younger, equally powerful offspring, which was all about having fun? What did it mean when high school students with a computer built from a pile of used electronics could hack into federal nuclear weapons facilities, as six teenagers from Milwaukee actually did a few months before Bob Barnett made his October 1983 phone call from Soldier Field?

The last years of the Cold War combined with powerful technology in the hands of kids led to a mini-boom of eighties teen movies one critic called "high school science fiction." Cautionary cinema about how teenagers could wreak havoc with technology, but also how they could use it to save us from power-hungry military men and inept bureaucrats gave us *WarGames*, *Weird Science*, *The Manhattan Project*, *Back to the Future*, *Flight of the Navigator*, and *Space Camp*. One journalist went so far as to call this new category "1985's genre of the year."

The technological innovations of the 1980s also messed with the boundaries of place and time. This made it possible for a kid in Seattle to screw with a computer at a nuclear facility in Colorado (*WarGames*) and a high school senior in 1980s Tucson to dig up a mysterious power orb buried in the desert by 1950s president Dwight Eisenhower (*My Science Project*). But if we're building a map of eighties teen movies, where do we put eighties teens-and-tech movies, if the technology complicated the idea of place?

The first images teens-and-tech movies bring to mind are not landscapes and landmarks, but computer screens and kids in bedrooms reflected in their glow. Nonetheless, high school science fiction was a quieter but very real part of the map of Brat Pack America in three ways: 1) reminding us that good kids may use technology for mischief but also keep it from falling into evil hands, 2) as a hiding place where bad men can be plotting evil with technology, and 3) as a metaphor for how technology created an uncomfortable blurring of public and private space.

Good Kids, Bad Machines: *Weird Science* and *Real Genius*

TAKE TWO OF THE most beloved movies of this small group: *Weird Science* and *Real Genius*, both released the first week of August in 1985. Both are about groups of nerds who use technological wizardry and resourcefulness to outwit bullies. The bullies want the technology for their own selfish purposes. Our heroes both know how to use technology for fun and to keep it from hurting anyone, which is why the bullies end up neutralized by rogue biker gangs, missiles that grow out of the kitchen floor, and multiple tons of popcorn.

Weird Science, written and directed by John Hughes, stars Anthony Michael Hall and Ilan Mitchell-Smith as best friends and hapless targets of bullies, asshole gym teachers, and a moronic older brother (Bill Paxton in his debut role). One Friday night, the two decide to use a home computer to build the perfect woman. In the middle of this kooky project, lightning strikes and their computer-simulated perfect woman becomes an actual person (supermodel Kelly Le Brock).

Weird Science was a box office hit, John Hughes's second that year after *The Breakfast Club*, but received mixed reviews. It's mostly remembered now as the loveable utility player in his filmography (not as great as *Ferris Bueller* or *Breakfast Club*, but certainly better than *Curly Sue* or *Baby's Day Out*) and an early look at when personal computers started being as common as alarm clocks in teenage bedrooms.

Weird Science takes place in Shermer, Illinois, the same fictional town where nearly all of Hughes's movies happened, and was filmed in the same North Chicago suburbs of Highland Park and Northbrook where Hughes would later shoot *Ferris Bueller's Day Off*. Other than *The Breakfast Club*, *Weird Science* is the only Hughes movie to reference Shermer by name and does so only briefly, in a quick montage of the town during the key lightning storm, where we see a "Welcome to Shermer" sign, inexplicably in green neon. If you look closely, Gary and Wyatt's school is also called "Shermer High."

Real Genius was cowritten by Pat Proft (who would go on to cowrite all three *Naked Gun* movies) and directed by Martha Coolidge, who'd had a hit directing *Valley Girl* two years before. It's the story of Mitch Taylor (Gabe Jarrett), a fifteen-year-old whiz kid granted early admission to Pacific Technical University to research optics and lasers. Mitch ends up rooming with Chris Knight (Val Kilmer, in his second movie), who was a fifteen-year-old whiz kid himself once and is now a graduating senior more interested in partying than partical physics.

Mitch and Chris both work in the lab of Dr. Jerry Hathaway (William Atherton), who seems to be up to something pretty shady. He's got his team of students working on a laser that they don't know will be used by the Department of Defense as a high-powered weapon. Hathaway's also siphoned the money the government's given to the project into renovations on his new house. It's up to Chris, Mitch, and their friends to stop their research from being used to kill people from space and Dr. Hathaway from getting rich off it.

Real Genius was a box office hit, albeit a more modest one than *Weird Science*. Where *Weird Science* gets cited as one of the first movies to show technology as a tool of entertainment in the lives of average teenagers, *Real Genius* has been considered an ahead-of-its-time-look at how gifted, ambitious young people will use technology to wrestle the future away from an establishment that wants to misuse it.

Real Genius and *Weird Science* remain beloved comedies to this day for a whole pile of obvious reasons: great dialogue, memorable characters, and never-say-die performances that never come off as too cool for the silliness of their plots. Both movies also have an essential good nature. You'd have to be pretty cold-hearted not to root for the heroes, boo the villains, and believe for more than a few minutes that things won't all work out for the best. Oddly, both movies anchor their sunny disposition to not just their characters and story, but also to where they happen.

Weird Science was the third of three movies John Hughes wrote and directed that came out within a year of each other. Contractually, Hughes required all his movies to be filmed in the Chicago area. Artistically, the fictional town of Shermer, Illinois, would be the setting for nearly all of Hughes's movies, as well as many of the screenplays, short stories, and novels he would write after he stopped directing movies in 1991.

Shermer, with the same wide lawns, autumn foliage, and basically good kids trying their best as in all Hughes's teen films, reassures us while watching *Weird Science*. The movie throws a lot in the way of our nerd heroes: school jerks, mean gym teachers, and, for reasons best not explained because I wouldn't know how to start, an outlaw biker gang the computer brings to life. But it also doesn't let you think for a second that Gary and Wyatt using a computer to play God will have any real or dangerous consequences. There will be nothing uncomfortable or weird about the outcome of *Weird Science*.

That may be mostly tone. Hughes and his actors calibrate the movie as a broad, sweet comedy. That *Weird Science* happened to arrive in movie theaters at precisely the moment home computers started showing up in suburban households perhaps gives us a look at the wild, unpredictable power these new members of an ordinary family may have. But that look is pretty tame, and Gary and Wyatt are fundamentally well-meaning young men. Their mischief never extends any further than wanting to have a better time in high school and learning that they were okay kids all along. That *Weird Science* happens squarely in Shermer, John Hughes's universe of nice boys and girls, quietly reminds us that, though we might not understand computers quite yet, in the hands of good kids, both they and we are safe.

Real Genius is technically a movie about college students. (I included it here on a technicality; the lead character is a teenager.) It has a bit more sass than *Weird Science*, and while Mitch Taylor may be a sweet innocent the same way Gary and Wyatt are in *Weird Science*, Val Kilmer's Chris Knight as cohero is not. In fact, I'd use the same description for Chris Knight that John Hughes used for Ferris Bueller in his 1999 director's commentary of *Ferris Bueller's Day Off*: "loyal but not virtuous."

In Val Kilmer's hands, Chris Knight is a character/force of nature like Jeff Spicoli in *Fast Times at Ridgemont High* or Long Duk Dong in *Sixteen Candles*. We don't see him evolve or change or learn anything. He simply arrives, fully formed, less character than event. Chris Knight seems to be living in the movie of his own life and passing through *Real Genius* on his way to it.

He's also very Californian, funny but languid, brilliant but too lazy to work at anything other than what he describes as "a long series of attempts to avoid responsibility." Chris Knight always looks halfway between deep thought and deep tanning. His loose-fitting, mismatched ensembles of funny T-shirts (Do you have a knockoff of Chris Knight's "I Love Toxic Waste" shirt? If so, do you know where I can get one?), bedroom slippers with animals on the toes, and site-specific headgear (chef's toque in the dorm kitchen, alien antennae in the lab) all say: 1) dressing silly is fun, 2) I live in a place with 361 annual days of sunshine that makes dressing silly very easy, and 3) I go to school where nobody pays attention when someone wears panda earmuffs indoors.

Many of *Real Genius*'s zanier plot turns were inspired by the real-life zaniness of the Caltech campus during the 1970s, including a student who lived permanently in the university's storm tunnels underground. An alumnus named David Marvit was on set for historical accuracy and has a bit part in the movie. But as legend has it, the university was involved in research for Cold War defense systems similar to those the heroes of *Real Genius* foil, and therefore declined to the let the movie film on the campus that inspired it. Those are unproven claims, but *Real Genius*, the most famous movie ever about Caltech, decided to avoid any trouble and film at the neighboring campuses of Occidental College and Pomona College.

Which still works, because *Real Genius* feels, right down to its fuzzy slippers, like a Southern California movie. I've a hard time picturing Chris Knight, Mitch Taylor, and their gang of pranksters turning a study hall into a swimming pool in a three-hundred-year-old building at Harvard, where doing so might damage priceless artwork in the hallways or the desk where John F. Kennedy sat during Macro Economics. (Harvard has turned down most requests to film on campus since *Love Story* filmed there in 1970 and damaged campus architecture and landscaping. The value of Harvard's real estate and facilities far surpasses whatever revenue or publicity would come from becoming a movie location.) I also can't picture Laszlo (Jon Gries) living in the steam tunnels below Brown University during a Providence, Rhode Island winter. *The Social Network* (2010), about Mark Zuckerberg and the invention of Facebook, was filmed twenty-five years after *Real Genius* not at Harvard, where the actual events took place, but at Johns Hopkins, my alma mater. The redbrick Colonial architecture and marble breezeways, the very East Coast college-ness of Hopkins, makes it seem like a place where a smart kid in a hoodie would spent a below-freezing winter night coding, writing equations on his fogged-over dorm room window, and coming up with Facebook in a blaze of anger because he couldn't get into a campus final club.

Real Genius, which made nerds cool while Mark Zuckerberg was still in diapers, looks at innovation very differently. It gets much of its spirit of zaniness and anarchy via freedom of movement, creating the optimism and unpredictability that anything can happen when a bunch of smart friends find and like each other. Its tone of joy and possibility (plus its many, many musical montages) comes from watching Mitch, Chris, and their pals Jordan and

Lazlo run, hide, scramble, and make mischief around campus. Even the scenes of everyone deep in thought over lab equipment (the 1985 equal of the early Facebookers "jacked-in" coding with headphones in *The Social Network*) are broken up by pranks, silly costumes, and Chris making fun of Mitch for working too hard. For a movie whose plot happens over the course of a school year, you need warm weather and school grounds laid out as if there won't be snow and plowing and everybody pulling out boots and wool hats come November. The gang of nerds we love from this movie needs sunshine and balmy nights to scurry around campus trying to wrest technology from Dr. Hathaway and his kiss-ass, no-fun students. *Real Genius* sets itself up so that its plot needs warm weather for its characters to be themselves.

The adobe-themed architecture, wide archways and porticos, and quads with large but few shade trees underscore the "Pacific" in Pacific Tech. They also line up the likability of the heroes of *Real Genius* with how the movie feels—offhanded, witty, and loose. This isn't an institution that looks hidebound by tradition; rather, a college where "traditions" are the ones the previous class of nerds just like Chris and Mitch created. The scenes in *Real Genius* of turning dorm hallways into ice rinks, lecture halls into swimming pools, and of students screaming across the quad right before finals week were all taken from Caltech campus rituals present at the university the decade before.

If Chris and Mitch's "genius"—glee, iconoclasm, and hard work alongside your pals in service of a greater good—sounds like the world that Mark Zuckerberg now sits atop of, neither of us are the first to make the connection. In 2015, Tor.com, online home of science fiction publisher Tor Books, called *Real Genius* "the geek solidarity film nerd culture deserves."

"Silicon Valley owes a debt of gratitude to *Real Genius*," began an article technology journalist Brian S. Hall wrote the year before. "I honestly do believe that Silicon Valley would be a lesser place— less fun, less daring, less successful, less eager to embrace actual unique personal genius—if not for the movie. Heed and herald the *Real Genius* values: being smart makes you a badass, change the world and have fun doing it. You can beat the system, you can invert the system, and create a world more to your liking."

All the way back in 1997, journalist Virginia Postrel wrote an essay for *Forbes ASAP* about why the Silicon Valley economy took hold in California and not Boston or Philadelphia or Seattle, which all had plenty of technology companies and prestigious universities nearby.

"The California sun," she concluded. "Eventually, all theories wind up there. Silicon Valley's perfect weather means you don't need backup plans, just in case it rains. It means you don't resent spending a beautiful day inside at work, because tomorrow and tomorrow and tomorrow will be just as gorgeous."

"There's nothing more depressing than being in East Cambridge on a rainy, cold, day…it's just generally nasty. It doesn't inspire you," recalls Tom Henry, former CEO of Quote.com and now a Philanthropic Advisor to MIT in Cambridge, in Postrel's article. "That makes a huge difference. No matter how bad your day is, if you look out the window and it's sunny, it's pretty hard to stay down for too long."

The villains of *Real Genius*—mostly Dr. Hathaway and his ass-kisser of a sidekick Kent (Robert Prescott)—are always demanding everyone take them and their work more seriously. They seem ridiculous in part because that's just not the vibe at Pacific Tech. Hard work doesn't mean a dour grind, a rainy cold day, or, as Virginia Postrel wrote, being "eternally hunkered down, hemmed in by clouds, darkness, and narrow streets." It means fun, creativity, a bond with the like-minded over the possibilities of tomorrow. It means not just what Silicon Valley would see as its best qualities years later, but how California has always advertised itself to the rest of the world.

While *Real Genius* maybe could have worked on any college campus, its very Southern California air reminds us whose side we're on and why. Put Mitch Taylor and Chris Knight amid a pine-treed winter at Dartmouth in Hanover, New Hampshire, and they look more like the bums Dr. Hathaway thinks they are. At Pacific Tech, they're model students. The real bums are the ones with the terribly no-fun idea of "genius" that feels like a rainy day in Cambridge.

"Too Many Secrets." Bombs, Science Projects. Gremlins, and Flux Capacitors.

THERE'S ANOTHER GROUP OF teens-and-technology movies that uses its settings not to vouch for the goodness of the characters, as in *Weird Science* and *Real Genius*, but as an indicator of something more sinister that those characters will discover: their hometown may be providing cover for technology meant to do harm. Our teenage heroes may see technology as a fun new frontier. But their parents' generation still sees it as a way to build weapons and kill people.

These cautionary eighties teens-and-tech movies are in two pairs: *The Manhattan Project* (1986) and *My Science Project* (1985), and, more abstractly, *Back to the Future* (1985) and *Gremlins* (1984). All play with this unholy marriage of technology from the age of personal computers and video games and the previous age of the military industrial complex. All carry with them a warning: "technology" may simply be the delivery method of acts of evil and violence. And they could be being plotted in your own neighborhood.

My Science Project and *The Manhattan Project* feel like two versions of the same movie. Both focus on male high school students who discover secret military hardware projects happening in their hometown. In *My Science Project*, it's literally buried in the soil, a mysterious glowing orb President Eisenhower and his Chiefs of Staff interred there in the 1950s. In *The Manhattan Project*, the hero Paul Stevens (Christopher Collet) discovers that his mom's new boyfriend is a scientist at a nearby college and that his lab is manufacturing weapons-grade plutonium.

The hero of *Science Project*, Michael Harlan (John Stockwell), is a latter-day greaser whose only interests seem to be working on cars and passing science class so he can spend more time working on cars. He digs up the glowing orb with a classmate during a night of foraging at the junkyard for car parts and thinks he can pass it off as a science class final project. That is, until his hippie science teacher, played by Dennis Hopper (complete with shoulder-length hair and peace sign medallion), tries to hook up the orb to a power source and ends up getting sucked into some unknown dimension. Michael and his friends then race to get the orb back in the ground before it hooks itself by accident to the town's electrical grid and sucks everyone they know and love into some unknown dimension.

In *Manhattan Project*, Paul, instead of fearing the discovery of plutonium being made nearby, senses opportunity. With that plutonium, spare parts, and some research, he could build his own atomic bomb. He could even use it to win the upcoming science fair in New York City!

Both *Science Project* and *Manhattan Project* were filmed in university towns. *My Science Project* was shot in Tucson, Arizona, a popular filming location for eighties comedies. (*Revenge of the Nerds* used the University of Arizona as its fictional Adams College in 1984. *Can't Buy Me Love*, starring Patrick Dempsey and filmed in Tucson, came out in the summer of 1987.) *The Manhattan Project* filmed in Ithaca, New York. The scientist character, played by John Lithgow, has his plutonium lab at Cornell. A few of the film's other minor characters also work at the university. Paul's mom (Jill Eikenberry) is a local real estate agent with a large "Ithaca is Gorges" poster on the wall of her office.

Colleges and universities in the movies of Brat Pack America are often portrayed as dividing communities in two: townies versus students (the Bloomington of *Breaking Away*), a fading industrial economy versus a brighter future promised by a college education (the Pennsylvania steel town of *All the Right Moves*). Teens-and-tech movies of the 1980s were also by nature worlds divided in two: the new tools of personal computers and home electronics meant for kids versus adults who wish to co-opt them for political and military reasons. Both *The Manhattan Project* and *My Science Project* use the two-sided nature of their university town settings to attack the two-facedness of adults who wish to steal away the technology from the future to fight the wars of the past.

My Science Project takes place in the present day, but dresses up its Tucson settings to feel like the 1950s. Scenes happen in the standard places the kids from *The Outsiders* would hang out—diners, auto body garages, pool halls—while arcades, shopping malls, and video stores are nowhere to be found. Protagonist Michael Harlan wears a grease-stained white T-shirt, engineer's boots, and drives a vintage car. Michael's best friend Vinnie (Fisher Stevens) is a slick-haired, Italian caricature, who mentions about fifty times that he's originally from Brooklyn and looks an awful lot like Sal Mineo in *Rebel Without a Cause*. *My Science Project* then helpfully tosses in a hippie science teacher, who drives an ugly brown VW Minibus, a pointed cultural opposite to Michael and Vinnie's muscle car aesthetic from the decade before.

My Science Project revolves around a terrifying leftover of the 1950s buried under Tucson, then dug up by a teenager in the 1980s. The teenager must destroy it before it destroys his hometown. The metaphor may be dead obvious—the technological sins of the fathers will be dug up by and then visited upon the sons—but Tucson is a place full of sons. Almost every character we meet is a teenager, and parents barely appear at all. Yet the movie's setting looks thirty years removed, with locations and visuals from the time of Buddy Holly in a plot from the time of Kenny Loggins. This duality—of two generations and their different ideas of technology in conflict—reminds us how technology can collapse time, how it can seem to bring us the future and also yet leave us blinded to its consequences.

Fathers and sons are a big theme in *The Manhattan Project*. Our hero doesn't have a dad, and John Lithgow, as scientist and Mom's new boyfriend, ends up looking after Paul. He's even dad-like when Paul does succeed in building a bomb and (big surprise) the military is willing to kill Paul to get it from him. The screenplay posits that Lithgow is naïve and doesn't know his lab is doubling as a munitions factory. In the final showdown, where Lithgow and Paul disable the bomb, Lithgow yells at the FBI sharpshooters assembled that this technology is out there now; you can't hide it from smart kids who want to do smart things with it. If you do, this kind of terrible fate awaits you.

"Too many secrets," Lithgow scolds them, as he and Paul exit the lab into the waiting arms of Paul's mother and girlfriend. "Too many secrets."

Ithaca is a quietly stated presence in *The Manhattan Project,* mostly shown as a town of great natural beauty containing a very important university. We don't get any shots of downtown or a business district or the sense that adults work anywhere but Paul's high school and at Cornell. The lab where Lithgow works has a false corporate name and is on a section of campus fenced off and kept from students and the larger community. It's close and integral enough to Paul's house that he can ride his bike there. That Cornell and the federal government keep the project a secret while *The Manhattan Project* visually demonstrates how much the community revolves around it is seen as a betrayal of trust, emphasizing how tightly woven the lives of universities and their hometowns are, and how easily that trust can be broken.

Midnight Feedings and Flux Capacitors: *Gremlins* and *Back to the Future*

GREMLINS AND BACK TO *the Future* were filmed about a year apart in exactly the same place: the backlot at Universal Studios, ten miles northwest of downtown Los Angeles. The two movies even borrowed backdrops and building fronts from one another. If you look closely, the downtown business district of Kingston Falls, New York (*Gremlins*), looks a lot like the courthouse square of Hill Valley, California (*BTTF*), minus one clock tower and plus a covering of snow.

Both movies take place in idyllic, all-American small towns where sudden disruptive change arrives. Both regard that disruption with suspicion, though much more so in *Gremlins,* structured as a horror movie, than in *Back to the Future,* which looks and feels like a young adult adventure novel come to life.

Both movies were also executive-produced by Steven Spielberg, who was a dozen years into his career as a director and had done quite a few movies about invasions disrupting the quiet regularity of small-town life (See *Jaws, E.T.,* and *Close Encounters of the Third Kind*). In *BTTF* and *Gremlins,* the small towns of Hill Valley and Kingston Falls aren't actively covering for the evils of technology like in *Manhattan Project* and *My Science Project,* but instead stand as warning against using too much technology too fast.

Gremlins concerns a traveling salesman/failed inventor (Hoyt Axton) who brings home an early Christmas present for his teenage son: a small, fuzzy creature than looks like a crossbreeding of a koala bear and a cocker spaniel. The salesman bought the creature (the family decides to name him "Gizmo") from a mysterious old man in "Chinatown" (complete with narrow eyes and a long mustache, a racist caricature *Gremlins* steers right into). The old man warns of the evil that will be unleashed if the creature gets exposed to bright light, comes in contact with water, or is fed after midnight.

Each of these things happens, which causes the creature to multiply into thousands of evil versions of itself. The mutant Gizmos then tear Kingston Falls to pieces. The son (Zach Gallighan) and his girlfriend (Phoebe Cates) ultimately manage to save what's left of their town by blowing up a movie theater filled with the evil Gremlins, then melting their leader, Stripe, via a beam of sunlight. The movie ends on a downer when the old man from Chinatown comes back to Kingston Falls, warns everyone not to mess with powers they don't understand, then puts the original Gizmo back into his box and walks away into the night.

More than once, *Gremlins* has been accused of really being about small-town white America's fear of an imaginary invasion of black teenagers. The movie got called out in *Ceramic Uncles and Celluloid Mammies,* a 1994 book by folklorist Patricia A. Turner, for "reflecting negative African-American stereotypes" even though it has only one African-American cast member (legendary character actor Glynn Turman, a scientist and early victim of the mutant gremlins). A 2014 comedy called *Dear White People* has a funny scene where one character runs down this list of the movie's ethnic clichés: "The Gremlins are loud, talk in slang, are addicted to fried chicken, and freak out when you get their hair wet." *Gremlins* is also number fifty on *Complex Magazine's* 2012 list of the fifty most racist movies of all time.

More accurately, *Gremlins* plays on a 1980s xenophobic fear of American industry being taken over by big money from Asia. The little creature the salesman buys in Chinatown is called a "mogwai," which means "evil spirit" in Cantonese. The name "Gremlins" comes from the teenage hero's next-door neighbor, an out-of-work laborer who complains of foreigners taking all the jobs and their products being infected with evil spirits he calls "gremlins." We're not meant to take the character seriously, but his blabber points to what is supposed to disturb us about *Gremlins*. This movie isn't only about an invasion of nasty little creatures. It's about an invasion of nasty little creatures to this lovely small town that's having a hard go of it already, like so many small, working-class towns in Ronald Reagan's America. Kingston Falls can't call out the National Guard the way Los Angeles could when it was invaded by aliens in *The War of the Worlds* (1953 version, not Tom Cruise's). Kingston Falls is outnumbered and helpless. That the person who let this foreign species in is a failed inventor, a man trying to bring about the future through technology and sucking at it, underlines *Gremlin's* conservative message: even though times are hard, too much change happening too fast is much worse than no change at all.

It's probably stretching to call a little furry creature "technology." But the warning of *Gremlins*, that a kids' toy or a new pet, or whatever we want to call Gizmo, could become a terrifying menace, sounds an awful lot like the dire predictions that come with any new and suddenly everywhere technology. Modern theories such as Google is making us stupid, Facebook is making us lonely, Instagram and Snapchat are making us all narcissists, strike the same tone. Technology, rather than how we use it, should make us afraid.

Differently, *Back to the Future* is one kind of cautionary tale masquerading as another. On the one hand, *Back to the Future* feels like a warning about messing around with technology you don't understand (every fifth line of Doc Brown's is about the dire consequences of doing this). Marty McFly goes back to 1955 in his mad scientist friend Doc Brown's time machine, inadvertently prevents his parents from meeting, and therefore prevents himself from being born. But (important distinction here) Marty goes back in time by accident—the time machine is a DeLorean powered by plutonium that Doc Brown has stolen from Libya. The Libyans come back for it and Marty outruns them in the DeLorean, which then sends him back in time. He ends up back in 1955 because he was running for his life, not because he was messing around with technology he didn't understand.

The "warning" of technology in *Back to the Future* is more like: "Technology points the way to the future. The future is coming. Ignore it at your peril." Here in the present day (the 1985 of the movie), Hill Valley looks like a town that has seen better days. The downtown is grubby, the clock tower needs a restoration, and overgrown thugs like Biff Tannen can be powerful citizens because no one seems to care enough to stop them.

This isn't at all what Hill Valley looks like in 1955, which means something in the past has gone terribly wrong and put the whole town on the slow road to shitsville. Also sometime back then, Doc Brown's family mansion has burned down (the newspaper clippings in the movie's opening scene tell us so), and now Doc has ended up conducting his experiments in a converted garage next to a Burger King. The community of Hill Valley now views Doc Brown as a forgettable lunatic, the town eccentric of a town that only seems to have room for one eccentric (the McFlys get a lot more shit than Doc Brown for just being poor, not strange). But at one time, Doc Brown had a mansion and seemed to be some sort of important man from an important family around Hill Valley. That he's an outcast here in the present demonstrates that Hill Valley is parochial and small-minded, and treats its inventors as quacks and their interest in the future as dangerous. It doesn't look like that point of view has done Hill Valley much good.

In the incredible hands of Christopher Lloyd, Doc Brown isn't played as a wingnut or a martyr, but simply a man out of his time and hiding out in a community that will never understand him. Even in the movie's present (i.e.1985), the character Dr. Emmett Brown feels like he's stepped out of a low-budget science fiction movie from 1955, with his fright wig hair, baggy pants, and ever present-lab coat.

Back to the Future doesn't tell us how seventeen-year-old Marty McFly and middle-aged Doc Brown became friends. It does give us the feeling, though, that, even though Doc would probably keep inventing with or without Marty, their relationship encouraged him to keep going in spite of whatever past setbacks the movie eludes to (i.e. "Brown Mansion Burns Down"). Doc's urge to invent, to see technology bring about tomorrow, seems misunderstood and ignored by conservative, self-destructive Hill Valley, but it's also the glue in the friendship between two of the town's misunderstood residents.

The squeaky cleanness of Hill Valley in 1955 reminds us rather cruelly of how sad it looks in 1985. How the town has ostracized Doc Brown and his inventions reminds us that Hill Valley has not changed with the times and is worse for it. *BTTF*'s actual warning about technology isn't what harm it can do when we invite too much of it into our lives, but what can happen when we ignore it altogether. It's Hill Valley's fear of change that opens the door for Marty to save the day, to be the McFly who does amount to something in the history of Hill Valley, even though Principal Strickland bellows that no McFly ever will.

"The Only Winning Move is Not to Play": *WarGames*

THE ULTIMATE TEENS-AND-TECH MOVIE of the 1980s, the one that epitomized the genre but also used its Seattle setting to bind adolescence, technology, and its consequences together, is

WarGames (1983). Directed by John Badham (who had directed *Saturday Night Fever* and would go on to make *Short Circuit* and *Stakeout* a few years later) and written by Walter Parkes and Lawrence Lasker (who would later write 1992's *Sneakers*, another movie about the scary place technology could bring us to), *WarGames* blazed several trails: as an early look at hacker culture, predicting the domination of video games in pop culture, and as the launch pad for the careers of Matthew Broderick and Ally Sheedy. For our map of Brat Pack America, it also gave an ahead-of-its-time look at Seattle as a technological capitol.

David Lightman (Broderick) is a bright high school kid living in Seattle who spends hours playing video games and messing around on a home computer. In an attempt to grab a copy of a new computer game before its release date, he finds he's accidentally started talking to WOPR (War Operation Plan Response), a Department of Defense computer that plays thousands of "WarGames" in an attempt to predict and respond to scenarios if Soviet missiles were ever launched at the US Forces inside the Defense Department (represented by a twitchy bureaucrat played by Dabney Coleman) have determined that human beings no longer have the courage to release nuclear missiles should the need arise, and that task should be outsourced to a machine. Old-school military general Jack Beringer (Barry Corbin) doesn't "trust this pile of microchips any farther than he could throw it," and says he sleeps better knowing his men are at the switch if the Russians decide to launch.

Back in Seattle, David thinks he's playing an actual video game called "Geothermal Nuclear War" when he begins talking to WOPR. The military thinks someone is trying to start a nuclear war from Seattle and goes looking for him. Once David and his classmate Jennifer (Ally Sheedy) figure out whom (or what) they've been talking to, they realize the only way out of being charged with treason is finding the scientist who designed WOPR, Dr. Stephen Falken (John Wood), whom everybody thinks is dead.

WarGames has exactly one moment that identifies where David and Jennifer live, an across-the-water establishing shot of the Seattle Space Needle at dusk. The rest of the movie was filmed in Southern California. On the director's commentary track of the movie's twenty-fifth anniversary DVD, Badham jokes in a heavy voice that the shot of the Seattle skyline "blew their entire twelve-dollar location budget." Hearing this after watching the same DVD's "How WarGames was made" documentary makes the joke a little darker: *WarGames* had been in development since 1979, had begun filming with a different director, and had fired and then rehired the original screenwriters, as well as bringing in a third writer for a few scenes. It was, to say the least, a difficult movie to get made. Having no budget for location may have been a casualty of all those false starts.

Whatever the real answer is, *WarGames* does not shy away from the idea of its main characters living in Seattle (even though none of the movie is filmed there), and repeats this fact several more times. Watching *WarGames* now, you can see that its claim to Seattle does a few different things. Most obviously, it links fictional David Lightman to the real technological history of the city, in the period between the founding of Microsoft (1975) and Amazon (1994), framing Lightman, perhaps, as a younger brother of Bill Gates and a cool older role model to Jeff Bezos. But if you look at what else was happening in Seattle during the time of *WarGames*, it puts another, grimmer filter on that choice of location.

In July 1983, a month after the premiere of *WarGames*, *Life Magazine* published an article called "Streets of the Lost" about homeless teenagers in Seattle. "Streets of the Lost" would be the source material for *Streetwise*, an Oscar-nominated documentary filmed a year later. In 1988, Mary Ellen Mark, who had photographed the teenagers for the original magazine article, published a companion book, also called *Streetwise*. In the book, Mark indicates that she and magazine writer Cheryl McCall had pitched the original story because at the time the city of Seattle was billing itself as "America's most livable city." Mark's early books of photography had been published a few years before, each concentrating on what she called "people who hadn't had the best breaks in society," patients in an Oregon mental hospital for *Ward 81* (1979) and Indian sex workers for *Falkland Road: Prostitutes of Bombay* (1981). And though McCall made the first line of the article, "Every city has them," her text quickly gets down to the specifics of homeless kids in Seattle: one thousand homeless kids, six thousand reported runaways, a few underfunded facilities to serve them. Mary Ellen Mark, Cheryl McCall, and, later, documentary filmmaker Martin Bell could have documented populations of homeless kids in New York, Los Angeles, or St. Louis. They chose Seattle to demonstrate the stark difference between what Seattle called itself and the desperate population that made the city's claim seem like a lie—what "livable" in Seattle actually meant, and to whom.

In both "Streets of the Lost" and *Streetwise*, the lives of the dozen homeless teenagers profiled meant a horrifying day-to-day existence of eating out of trash cans, turning tricks to get money, avoiding arrest by police and exploitation and abuse by drug dealers and pimps. Many of the kids came to Seattle from elsewhere, because it was the largest metropolis in the region or they knew someone in the city. Ending up homeless in Seattle, McCall wrote, they didn't know where else to go.

None of these kids can go to school—even if they wanted to. They have no permanent address, and schools will not admit them. (One undersized sixteen-year-old, Itty Bitty, hasn't been to school since fourth grade.) Regulations ban those under eighteen from adult shelters, but most of the street kids are too proud to sleep in a room full of alcoholics and bums anyway. Shadow tried it when he turned eighteen this spring. "I'd rather sit in an all-night coffee shop," he says. "The government thinks if it makes it hard enough on the streets, we'll go home. But there's no place to go."

Many of the kids Mark and her team got to know hung out at Pike Place Market, one of the city's most popular tourist attractions, but also ground zero for its homeless teen population. Two of the kids we see in *Streetwise* later ended up dying violently. Memorial plaques to both were laid at Pike Place Market. Pike Place Market is also the location of the very first Starbucks coffee shop and appears in just about every movie set in Seattle.

Mary Ellen Mark and Martin Bell (a married couple as well as artistic collaborators) checked in repeatedly with the kids on successive anniversaries of *Streetwise*. In 2013, they held a successful fundraising drive on Kickstarter to publish another book about one of the kids from *Streetwise* named Tiny. *Tiny: Streetwise Revisited* came out in October of 2015, shortly after Mary Ellen Mark's death that spring.

The Seattle media has done the same checking in, not just because the film is so linked to a specific time in the city's history, but because teenage homelessness in Seattle is a forty-year-old problem that doesn't look to be getting better. Though resources are much more available than in the early 1980s, YouthCare, a Seattle homeless youth services organization, estimates that on any given night in the city, there are seven hundred to a thousand teenagers without a safe place to sleep, roughly equal numbers to the time of *Streetwise*.

David Lightman in *WarGames* is an average Seattle teen from an average middle-class home and lives worlds away from the kids in *Streetwise*. The Lightmans have a basic Colonial house with a small backyard. His parents are odd but happily married. The biggest indulgence in David's life is a room full of home computer equipment and extra quarters for the arcade, where we first meet the character. That he's a teenager in Seattle in the early 1980s, based on what we know about Seattle and its population of homeless teenagers in the early 1980s, introduces the faintest hint of an emotion that will permeate the rest of *WarGames*: deceit. Seattle at that time was a city not being truthful with itself, a city with a huge social problem going unaddressed, promoting its quality of life while looking the other way at the horrible lives kids were living on its streets.

The conflict of *WarGames* is powered by same kind of self-deceit, the willingness to ignore terrible eventualities staring you in the face. All of its characters seem to understand the potential and power of technology; the less noble ones wish to maneuver that power for their own purposes. And they must do this through secrecy, lying, and deceit, especially self-deceit. The DOD fools itself into believing Dr. Stephen Falken is dead so he doesn't get in the way of the computer he invented starting nuclear war. If Falken's computer launches nuclear missiles, terrible consequences can't be ignored. But ignoring those consequences is exactly why a machine has its finger on the big red "launch" button instead of any human character in *WarGames* who could actually consider or take responsibility for them.

The narrative of *WarGames* and the real-life city where *WarGames* took place at this time both worked off a self-serving falsehood. In hindsight, setting the movie there puts this fictional story and the very real place Seattle found itself in 1983 uncomfortably together in the same room. If we know a little about the city's history at the time of *WarGames*, it changes our idea about what to take away from *WarGames*: a respect for technology and innovation, but also a fear of governments and institutions that believe the delusions they create. In both cases, teenagers and their adult allies represent the truth and the need to tell it.

Uncomfortable proximity also describes *WarGames*' most memorable set piece, the "War Room": mission control at NORAD labs where WOPR is stationed, where Dabney Colemen and Barry Corbin square off about what to do when the computer stops listening to them, where David, Jennifer, and Dr. Falken must break in to save the day by re-convincing WOPR that it's actually just playing a game.

As John Badham notes in the director's commentary, the War Room in the movie is about six times bigger than the actual facility that inspired it. Parkes and Lasker visited a missile control center for research and reported it was mostly an empty, undecorated room with a few monitors and offices. *WarGames*' War Room is *Dr. Stranglelove* in the age of the Macintosh and Space Invaders: a dark dome with lit glass catwalks and walls of screens. Its colors are high contrast and exaggerated and workers are scurrying everywhere (Parkes and Lasker also report the control center they based this one on was largely people-free). It's far more boyish fantasy about a military control center than an attempt at realism. Even the actual computer WOPR is based on was little more than a large grey box. Lights and displays had to be added by set dressers to give WOPR, an important supporting character, a little life.

NORAD is about as high security and closed off as it gets, with barbed-wire fences and a bank vault door David, Jennifer, and Dr. Falken must get past. However, the space feels oddly public and ordinary at the same time. There's a key scene where a tour group drops by the facility and the very same monitors that later warn of nuclear meltdown welcome a group of visitors from Birmingham, Alabama. Those monitors also display not only WOPR searching for launch codes to deploy missiles on its own (the movie's climax) but games of tic-tac-toe, how David teaches the computer that some games (like tic-tac-toe and nuclear war) are won by not playing. Earlier, when David is held captive at the facility, he breaks out not via any high-tech knowledge of what goes on there but via a roll of gauze and scissors, supplies he'd have in his own bathroom back home.

Badham and his crew had anywhere from fifty to seventy screens going at once to create the control room set. The smaller ones were simply video monitors outfitted with frames. Since giant computer screens didn't exist yet, the wall displays were actual movie screens with projection cameras running behind them, making this most important set in *WarGames* into literally a giant movie theater. It's a bizarre reminder that this high-security, walled-off space wasn't actually too different from the rooms and buildings where this movie was first seen.

The War Room of *WarGames* is a collision of high security and public access, secrecy and knowing, of what we'd like technology to be for and who will actually get to decide. It's the most important setting in *WarGames*, and not just because the movie's high points happen there. In the very physical materials used to build it, the War Room contains the questions that teenagers, technology, and an explosion of access to it during the 1980s asked, which would show up in eighties teen movies again and again:

Who is technology for? Who gets to decide? And what happens when the answer is quickly becoming "everybody"?

BRAT PACK AMERICA TALKS TO...DIRECTOR MARTHA COOLIDGE

I N THE SPACE OF two years, director Martha Coolidge managed the seemingly impossible cultural feat of making both nerds and valley girls cool. Her second film, *Valley Girl* (1983), launched the career of Nicolas Cage and made the song "I Melt with You" a teen cinema classic. Her fifth movie, *Real Genius*, put Val Kilmer on the map, and is widely considered the forerunner to the smart-people-working-hard-having-fun-together ethos behind start-up incubators and the culture of Silicon Valley.

A graduate of Rhode Island School of Design and NYU, Martha Coolidge's fourteen films have garnered her Independent Spirit, CableACE, and Emmy Award nominations, and the Women in Film Crystal Award. Elected the first female president of the Directors Guild of America in 2002, Coolidge is now a professor of film and media arts at Chapman University.

We spoke in February of 2016 from her office at Chapman. where she was in pre-production for her new film, *Music, War and Love*.

Kevin Smokler: How many times have you been told that "Chris Knight [Val Kilmer's character in *Real Genius*] made it cool to be smart?"

Martha Coolidge: That's exactly what I was after. It was already in the original draft of the script, which was funny, silly, had a lot of good sex jokes but not enough science and not enough plot. I believe a comedy needs just as much risk, jeopardy, and danger as a drama. Doesn't mean you can't just sit and laugh at something, but that doesn't mean I didn't think it could be better.

My proposition was, I'll do *Real Genius* if we make the science smarter. Don't just put a mysterious red box on a table and call it a computer. Let's not treat the science like the audience is stupid. So we hired a leading laser physicist at USC, who later worked on President Reagan's Star Wars program, and had some of the kids who had gone to Caltech at that time on set, too.

To get the dorm set right, we literally photographed the walls of Dabney Hall at Caltech, then invited actual students from Caltech to come write on those walls. I'll say this: the smarter the people, the better the graffiti.

KS: What went into the character of Chris Knight from a director's point of view?

MC: Chris Knight is a fully-formed character because so many people contributed to and understood it. Val did a stealth audition where he was much more of a Loony Tune, but ultimately it starts with the writing. I look for the rhythms in the writing. Chris Knight already had witty, smart dialogue. Val brought to it a self-mocking tone. Then the most inventive costume and props guys said, "I get Chris Knight, I know what he's thinking." That's where the animal slippers came from.

They all become part of Chris Knight, even though there's so much there already. It becomes a snowball.

KS: *Real Genius* has been called a forerunner to the culture of smart people working together on projects they are passionate about we now see in start-up incubators and in Silicon Valley.

MC: I've always been a bit of a science geek and now give time to an organization that aims to improve the depiction of science and who practices science on television. For a bunch of years, I also went to every single Comic-Con because I was working on a script for Blizzard Entertainment [makers of *World of Warcraft*] about a gamer. Those guys are all *Real Genius* fans. The laser guys from Caltech who consulted on the film? They got Nobel Prize–winning friends who became scientists because of *Real Genius*.

KS: There's a theory that part of why Silicon Valley took root in Northern California is the weather: that sunshine inspires creativity, chance meetings, experimentation, and not minding spending eighteen hours inside coding when you know there will be another beautiful day tomorrow. In the same way, *Real Genius* feels like it gets some of its anarchic spirit from being a "California movie."

MC: There's also the "garage myth" of Silicon Valley. I wonder if Apple and Hewlet Packard could have started in garages in places where they have five months of winter? Also, the hippie era. Would Apple have been Apple had Steve Jobs not lived through that time in the San Francisco Bay area?

As far as *Real Genius* goes, the script was based on Caltech even though we didn't shoot it there. Occidental College and Pomona looked enough like Caltech, and it's usually safer to just change the place, because you're not trying to get anyone associated with the real place your movie is about in trouble.

In the 1970s, Caltech students really did make ice rinks in the hallways of their dorms and swimming pools in lecture halls to throw parties for girls from nearby colleges. Could they have done that somewhere else? Maybe. A lot of the legends we heard about what these kids did happened at MIT, too.

KS: You moved to California from New York in 1976.

MC: I came out for Zoetrope [Francis Coppola's company] after I was headhunted by them in New York. This was at a time even when there was no real sign that Hollywood was going to hire women.

One of the movies I worked on for them was a rock and roll love story, where the girl was a poet, the guy was a rock and roller. I did two years' worth of research in the clubs, but when [Coppola] got back from shooting *Apocalypse Now*, my movie got canceled. Later I'd been shooting a movie about the music scene in Toronto. That producer went bankrupt.

Valley Girl was the first "go" picture in Hollywood I'd gotten. It turns out I'd prepped for it with all my club scene research on those other projects.

KS: You've described *Valley Girl* as a "Romeo and Juliet story about a girl from the Valley and a boy from Hollywood," a story about lovers divided by geography and culture instead of family. Was there something brewing in LA at that time that made the Hollywood/Valley division especially pronounced?

MC: I was totally exaggerating the difference, but Los Angeles music culture was and always has been a combination of both. Some kids from the Valley were scared to go to Hollywood at the time because they thought Hollywood meant prostitutes, rough and dirty, but that's why the talent goes there, too. Kids gravitate to the excitement of something more challenging, and those things have to take root where real estate is cheaper.

KS: Tell me about the choice to have the dialogue before Julie and Randy's first kiss in *Valley Girl* unheard under the music.

MC: When you are swept up in romance and love and music, there isn't a word. It wasn't a dream, it was reality, but it was a magical place in-body and out-of-body at the same time. When you are young and these things first happen to you, they are the most powerful experiences you can have. It's why great love stories are written about young people. It gets at something stronger than dialogue.

KS: Why do we not meet Randy's parents?

MC: I feel that Randy is living on his own. As a character, he was scarier and more mysterious that way. They also don't influence the story in particular, though I suppose he could have surprisingly normal parents, too.

KS: Unlike Julie the Valley girls' ex-hippie parents, which I think is one of the best touches in the movie.

MC: I can take credit for that one. Any movie that is specific is better. Even directing a script you didn't write is deeply personal.

KS: Your films are often about class and money. Where does that interest come from for you as an artist?

MC: I came from a middle-class family, but my father died when I was nine. I was very aware of that. Never had any money when we got to the end of the month and ate hot dogs to make it through. It's probably been with me since then.

KS: Your films specifically about young people seem to all be about someone realizing the cage they've put themselves in and then trying to break out of it.

MC: I thank you for saying that. I teach now and am surrounded by college and graduate students. Being smart is cool. Being a little Julie and a little Randy and not being forced to choose is cool. I'll take any part of that my work or I helped make happen.

CHAPTER 8: "NOW THAT YOU'RE DEAD, WHAT ARE YOU GONNA DO WITH THE REST OF YOUR LIFE?"

The Black-Hearted '80s Teen Movies and the End of Brat Pack America

Movies Discussed: *Over the Edge, Taps, Bad Boys, River's Edge, The Legend of Billie Jean, Running on Empty, Heathers*

THE YEAR WAS 1986, and a Los Angeles video store clerk from South Bend, Indiana, was fed up with John Hughes. The Hughes-written *Pretty in Pink* had been a hit that February, the Hughes-written and directed *Ferris Bueller's Day Off* another winner that June. At the cultural height of movies that looked at teenagers with empathy and understanding, this clerk had darker themes in mind. His idea: to write "A Carson McCullers–style" story of a teenage girl who falls in love with the Antichrist.

The clerk had studied screenwriting at McGill University in Montreal, and, as he wrote, his ambitions grew. Originally conceived as a schlock melodrama inspired by adolescent exploitation movies of the sixties and seventies he loved, his finished screenplay numbered 196 pages (over three hours of screen time) with the goal of being "the final word on high school movies." The clerk included every cliché of the genre he could think of—jocks, nerds, dumb principals, gross cafeteria food, and shower scenes—but dunked them in both his own morbid sensibility and the meanness his sister told him adolescent girls inflicted on one another. Most movies about teenagers had clearly defined heroes and villains. In this one, teenagers could be just as awful as clueless parents or fascist gym teachers, the "good kids" as nasty as the bullies who terrorized them.

The movie the clerk wrote ended with the main character's boyfriend blowing up the school and a final scene of a prom in Heaven as the closing credits rolled. He called the movie "Westerburg," the name of the film's high school and in honor of Paul Westerberg, the lead singer of the Minneapolis punk band The Replacements. He set the story in Sherwood, Ohio, choosing Ohio instead of Indiana, where he grew up, he would later say, because it was a state that in presidential elections represented the mood of the entire country. He wanted Stanley Kubrick to direct.

The clerk's name was Daniel Waters. His screenplay found the right collaborators (not Stanley Kubrick, who didn't return his calls) and was released in theaters on March 31, 1989. It ran an hour and forty minutes (at around a hundred pages) and had morphed into the story of a teenage girl whose friends are a group of the three meanest girls in school, all with the same first name. The protagonist's boyfriend was still a psychopath, but a sexy, sly one named Jason Dean. The film took an ax to how teenagers romanticize their peers that commit suicide, but took seriously Jason Dean's pronouncement that "the only place different social groups can genuinely get along is in Heaven" right before he tries to blow up the school with a bomb. This happens after a number of students die under suspicious circumstances.

"Dear diary," the protagonist, Veronica, writes in one scene, "my teen angst bullshit has a body count."

The movie was called *Heathers*. *Heathers* did lousy at the box office (it didn't help that its studio, New World Pictures, was mid-bankruptcy at the time—producer Denise Di Novi paid for the movie's only advertisement in the *LA Times* out of her own pocket), but became a creepy classic thanks to home video. It launched the careers of leads Winona Ryder (who played Veronica Sawyer and still calls *Heathers* the best movie she's ever done), Christian Slater (Jason Dean), director Michael Lehman, producer Denise Di Novi, and Waters himself. In 2012, *Entertainment Weekly* voted *Heathers* number five on a list of the Greatest High School Movies of All Time. In 2014, it became an off-Broadway musical.

Somewhere between bombing in theaters and becoming a cult favorite, *Heathers* closed the door on the era of Brat Pack America. It had blown up (literally) the genre of the eighties teen movie John Hughes had perfected, and in doing so lit the map of Brat Pack America on fire. Movies like *Breaking Away* and *Real Genius* along with filmmakers like Hughes, Amy Heckerling, and Savage Steve Holland had made teenagers into human beings. *Heathers* gave the teenagers in movies that followed it the right to be monsters—unfair, nasty, morally ambiguous, and with no guarantee of a happy ending. Those movies—*Pump up the Volume, Jawbreaker, The Craft, Election, and Mean Girls*—would be built from the ashes of what *Heathers* had burned down.

As for "Sherwood, Ohio," it comes up enough times in *Heathers* to have a spot on the map of Brat Pack America. But its map tack was actually an open flame. The setting of *Heathers* is misdirection, a dupe in plain sight. The name "Sherwood, Ohio" at first seems part of the joke, but the Sherwood we see isn't a place at all. Instead it's a nightmare coming into view that renders the very idea of setting irrelevant.

The sense of place in the eighties teen movie, once so important to a film's meaning and personality, would, going forward, be less important. In a few short years after *Heathers*, the Internet, which complicates the very idea of physical location, would burn up the remainder of Brat Pack America's map.

John Hughes's awareness of and passion for a very specific place enabled him to create a teenage universe that a generation of kids could see as their own. Martha Coolidge, Amy Heckerling, and Penelope Spheeris used certain Los Angeles neighborhoods in teen movies that ended up telling truths about the city it wouldn't face itself. The first generation of hip-hop movies wanted to make sure everyone watching understood that the art form started in New York. The sports movies of the 1980s depended on American small towns in decline as the reason a young athlete would dream of a college scholarship or career in the pros.

It wasn't completely necessary for any of the movies of Brat Pack America to happen in the precise spot they did. One can imagine John Hughes inventing Shermer, Ohio, in suburban Cleveland or Shermer, Minnesota, outside of Minneapolis. Penelope Spheeris could have chosen the Washington, DC or Bay Area punk scene of the early 1980s to inspire a version of *Suburbia*. But for nearly all of the teen movies from the eighties, "where" seems inseparable from "why." Setting and location play a big role in why the movies of Brat Pack America say what they do, why their filmmakers had to say it, and why that still resonates so many years later.

In the decades to come, the places teen movies happened added color, texture, and personality to the stories they told. Undoubtedly *Dazed and Confused, Ten Things I Hate About You, The Princess Diaries,* and *The Perks of Being a Wallflower* are more interesting movies thanks to Austin, Seattle, San Francisco, and Pittsburgh. But none of them need Austin, Seattle, San Francisco, and Pittsburgh to achieve their meaning or purpose. None of them need their settings to be themselves.

Somewhere after *Heathers,* or maybe predicted by it, teen movie places become nice extras instead must-haves, interior decoration instead of architecture.

Did *Heathers* have to kill the John Hughes teen movie so *Scream, Cruel Intentions,* and *The Virgin Suicides* could live? It's a tempting thought, but plays into a lingering fairy tale we keep telling about the eighties, that the decade split neatly into opposites: America vs. Russia, City vs. Suburb, Just Say No vs. Cocaine, Material Excess vs. Moral Austerity, Mainstream vs. Alternative. It's easy then to see *Heathers* as the teen movie equivalent of Kurt Cobain, slaying what author Susannah Gora called the "sunny, redemptive spirit" the mainstream John Hughes pictures represented so the grittier honesty of the underground *Heathers* embodied could rise up and win.

But that wouldn't be quite right. The black-hearted genius of *Heathers* wasn't a spontaneous revolution but a long time coming. A good few years before John Hughes's optimistic, thoughtful interpretation of teenagers, a batch of movies from Brat Pack America saw teenagers as, well, brats. As early as 1979, four years before Hughes's first produced screenplay, both smaller indie films and bigger, commercial teen movies showed growing up in post–Vietnam America as growing up in a world that didn't want you.

When Veronica's mom in *Heathers* tells her daughter, "Excuse me, Little Miss Voice of a Generation. But it seems to me that when teenagers complain about being treated like human beings is when they are being treated like human beings," she's actually speaking to what's inside the dark heart of this whole family of eighties teen movies—*Over the Edge* (1980), *Bad Boys* (1983), *The Legend of Billie Jean* (1984), and *River's Edge* (1986)—that led up to *Heathers*: the Kafkaesque nightmare of being a teenager in America. But whose fault is that, these movies, ask? America's, or its teenagers'?

Over the Edge: Troubled Youth, Parental Negligence, and Real Estate Development

THE STORY OF THE darker, more brutal neighborhoods of Brat Pack America begins in a place that doesn't seem dark or brutal at all: Larchmont, New York, eighteen miles northeast of midtown Manhattan. Larchmont in popular culture has long been code for "white, upper class, and suburban." One of Gordon Gekko's executive buddies in *Wall Street* (1987) has just bought a house in Larchmont. The 2007 Pulitzer Prize–winning play *Rabbit Hole* is about an upper-middle-class family in Larchmont whose considerable resources are helpless to aid them in grieving their dead son. Joan Rivers grew up in the area, and her early stand-up persona of a well-bred young woman who says filthy things without realizing they are filthy depended on her being the well-bred daughter of a Larchmont doctor.

In 1978, at a Larchmont middle school, a teenager got the break of his life by embodying the contradictions of a town like Larchmont. The second of six children in a close-knit Irish-Catholic family, the kid's father made a good living as a stockbroker and sent his children to a wealthy, highly regarded school. That year, a talent scout named Jane Bernstein came around on behalf of her friend Jonathan Kaplan. Kaplan had been hired to direct a movie called *Over the Edge* about a group of teenagers making mischief in a lifeless planned community called New Granada, Colorado.

The high school, hearing "casting agent" and "teenagers," offered up, as Kaplan would report on *Over the Edge*'s director's commentary, "whomever had starred that year in *Bye Bye Birdie*." Kaplan and Bernstein said no thank you. Given what *Over the Edge* was about, Kaplan said, "We were more interested in the kids cutting class and smoking out in the parking lot."

The stockbroker's son was one of those kids. Bernstein first spotted him ditching class trying hard to "play the tough guy. Maybe Rocky Balboa. Or the Fonz from *Happy Days*," she reported in a 2009 oral history of the movie. When asked to audition, he didn't believe the filmmakers were serious and showed up copping the same attitude. "She don't do shit!" he bellowed to Kaplan and Bernstein when they asked him what his mother, a homemaker, did for a living. When they asked about his father, the tough guy put-on began to unravel. "He's a stockbrocker," the kid said, knowing this made him a teenager who didn't have it nearly as hard as his pose would make it seem. "He was as middle class as they came," said Bernstein.

The teenager's name was Matthew Raymond Dillon. The contrast between whom he pretended to be and whom he actually was matched up perfectly with the movie Kaplan and his team had in mind. *Over the Edge* was based on the true story of a rash of crimes perpetrated in the early 1970s by the teenagers of Foster City, California, a planned community twenty miles south of San Francisco. Nearly a quarter of Foster City's residents at the time were under twenty-five, and the developers who'd built the town on an engineered landfill just a few years before hadn't thought of this. Bored, stuck, feeling unwanted and harassed by police, the kids of Foster City did precisely what you'd expect a bunch of teenagers to do in those circumstances. Foster City soon had among the highest rates of teen vandalism, petty crime, and arrests in the state of California. As the *San Francisco Examiner* reported in the November 11, 1973, article that brought the story to the *Over the Edge* screenwriters' attention:

> Mousepacks. Gangs of youngsters, some as young as nine, on a rampage through a suburban town. One on a bike pours gasoline from a gallon can and sets it afire. Lead pipe bombs explode in park restrooms. Spray paint and obscenities smear a shopping center wall. Two homes are set ablaze. Antennas by the hundreds are snapped off parked cars in a single night.

The situation came to a head when a group of local teens interrupted a town meeting, demanding better treatment from adults and law enforcement. Facing off in one room, with anger and misunderstanding burning between them, stood the two sides of Matt Dillon the *Over the Edge* team had witnessed in Larchmont: how teenagers saw themselves, and their community's ideas of what a "good" teenager needed and wanted.

Matt Dillon received a supporting role in *Over the Edge*, the beginning of an acting career that continues, four-dozen films and an Academy Award nomination later, to this day. Dillon's character Ritchie seems the oldest of *Over the Edge*'s five principal teenage friends, the group's de facto leader, and visibly the poorest of the bunch. Ritchie lives with his mother and younger brother in what looks like a Bronx housing project set down on a tabletop of grass in Colorado. (Foster City became New Granada, Colorado, as California labor laws would have made it cost prohibitive to film in Foster City with a cast made up almost entirely of minors.) The rest of the kids live in houses that look designed by the architecture firm Mr. Brady worked for in *The Brady Bunch*. Several are on unfinished blocks, where the end of the street means frames of unfinished houses, then nothing beyond but grass, trees, and mountains. In a place like New Granada, where nothing seems to be happening, turn the corner and you can end up at nothing pretty quickly.

"Nothing in town was older than the kids were," said *Over the Edge*'s coscreenwriter Charlie Haas on the movie's director's commentary. "There wasn't anything to look back at or forward to. It existed outside history. It contributed to the idea that the place was disposable."

Most of the kids in *Over the Edge* hang out at the rec room, a converted Quonset hut with a pool table and board games. The action, what little there is of it, consists of the occasional joint or stolen bottle of booze, breaking into houses under construction, shooting BB guns off the freeway overpass, and getting into it with the town's thickheaded police officer (Harry Northup, coming off work in Martin Scorsese's first six films). A terrible misunderstanding with a stolen real gun leads to one kid getting killed by the cops. Around that same time, a group of developers from Texas visit New Granada and are turned off by what they perceive as kids running wild. It doesn't help that the cops have closed the rec room that day, presumably so the out-of-town money don't get the idea that New Granada has a bunch of teenagers running wild, or any teenagers in town at all.

"Seems you all were in such a hopped-up hurry to get away from the city, you turned your kids into exactly what you were trying to get away from," the developer declares, right before saying "no thanks" to investing in New Granada and sprinting in a taxi back to the airport. As in real life, *Over the Edge* comes to a head at a town meeting to discuss what has been referred to as "the juvenile problem." Different from real life, this town meeting ends with a full-scale rebellion by the kids of New Granada and pretty lousy consequences for everybody.

Orion Pictures, *Over the Edge*'s studio, feared the movie's conclusion would lead to the same kind of violence in and around movie theaters. Movies about youth gangs were in fashion at the time (*The Wanderers* and *Boulevard Nights* had both been released in 1979, the same year as *Over the Edge*) and scattered incidences of violence had plagued early screenings of *The Warriors* (also

1979). But *The Warriors* took place in an ailing New York City with a murder rate the highest it had been since 1965, and nearly four times that of today. Roving gangs of young men at war with each other weren't just the movie's plot, but a reasonable proxy of how New Yorkers felt about what had happened to their city. What scared Orion about *Over the Edge* wasn't just the possibility of violence, but the possibility of violence in the "good neighborhoods" of kids who lived in places like New Granada.

"The real problem with the film was that it dealt with suburban white kids who cause a bit of violence—never against people, mind you, but against objects," said *Over the Edge*'s producer George Litto in the *Vice* oral history. "If these kids had been urban and black, I think it would have scared Orion less."

"They just dropped it. It wasn't shown anywhere," added Tim Hunter, *Over the Edge*'s coscreenwriter. They were afraid of copycat violence. It was hugely disappointing."

Orion's cowardice was a business decision, a gutless, maddening, and probably racist business decision, but fundamentally about keeping bad publicity away and not much more. But the danger the studio perceived also pointed to a larger cultural fear permeating teenage movies in the early days of Brat Pack America. Right before Orion panicked and yanked *Over the Edge* from theaters, they tried marketing the film as a horror movie instead of a movie about teen rebellion. *Over the Edge*'s first posters showed an artist's rendering of the five principal characters with pale faces and wide demonic eyes, far more *Children of the Corn* than *Rebel Without a Cause*. The poster's tagline, "Watch Out for Children." The idea: to play on the adult fear of teenagers running wild. If it can happen in a nice community like New Granada, it can happen where you live, too!

The nightmare of a country gone to hell with reckless teenagers as symptom or cause showed up in enough eighties teen movies to not be dismissed as coincidence or studios piggybacking on each other's hits. And the visual connection Orion made on the *Over the Edge* poster to horror movies was not an accident. The decade before *Over the Edge* featured classic horror movies like

The Exorcist (1973), *The Omen* (1975), *Carrie* (1976), and *The Shining* (1980), each about demonically possessed children, each striking at the very real fear of post-1960s flower children now growing up, settling down, and starting families. It's not a stretch to imagine that, come the 1980s, the Regan MacNeils, Damiens, and Danny Torrances of the 1970s horror movies were now teenagers. Which makes the darker nihilistic teen movies of Brat Pack America feel somewhat like updates of the prevailing kind of horror movie of the 1970s. The earlier films spoke to a fear of an evil manifest in the form of your own child. The parent of a teenager might later watch a movie like *Over the Edge* and fear what happens when your own child is now a teenager, old enough to escape your control, armed with violent contempt for the nice community where you tried to raise them.

Watch *Over the Edge* now and you can see how completely this fear misses the point. As of this writing, it has an 89 percent fresh rating on Rotten Tomatoes. *The New York Times'* Vincent Canby complimented *Over the Edge* for making the unconventional choice that its "villains are not simply preoccupied parents but architects and urban planners. Just as boring and alienating to us as it does to the unfortunate children who live there." A 2006 review in *Time Out* called it "one of the best movies to date about the generation gap." Although the parents and teachers are never reduced to uncaring stereotypes, their blind, status-oriented decisions and actions provide adequate fuel for the justly frustrated kids." Were I old enough to have seen *Over the Edge* as an adult in 1979, I'd have concluded that the "teen crime problem" in New Granada would have been easily fixed not by law enforcement but the rec center having longer hours and a few weekend bus trips to Denver.

Depending on who you are, *Over the Edge* can be a movie about parental fear ("We tried to do what we thought was best for our kids, and look what happened!") or the terrible naïveté at the root of that fear ("Move kids to the middle of nowhere with nothing to do, and what exactly do you expect to happen?"). At first it's harder to believe that teenagers today would turn to crime out of ennui (at the very least, they'd have cell phones and video games and five hundred channels of TV). But *Alpha Dog* (2007) and *The Bling Ring* (2013) are also movies based on true stories of bored teenagers turning to violence. And each of those came about well after the invention of Facebook.

The filmmakers are clearly on the side of the kids. But the enemy on the other side isn't the parents or the cops, but New Granada, the bricks-and-mortar representation of their parents' misplaced intentions. There are no evil grown-ups in *Over the Edge*, just pathetically clueless ones. The teenagers don't rob or assault, but steal and commit vandalism, acts of aggression against a place rather than the people who brought them there.

Kaplan opens the movie with a billboard stuck in parched earth with a scattered knot of houses in the distance. "Welcome to New Granada: Tomorrow's City…Today" the sign says. A crawl of text then appears which essentially mocks the sign.

> This story is based on true incidents occurring during the seventies in a planned suburban community of condominiums and townhomes, where city planners ignored the fact that a quarter of the population was fifteen years old or younger.

Midway through the film, right before one of the most famous moments (four of the kids break into a half-finished house and dance with a loaded gun while Cheap Trick's teen rebellion classic "Surrender" plays on a boom box), the kids walk past a sign for the unfinished street at the edge of town. "Strawberry Fields Forever" the sign says. Kaplan and his team have added graffiti that has crossed out "Forever" and replaced it with the word "Never."

Over the Edge was filmed in the Denver suburb of Aurora, Colorado. Though not a new planned community (Aurora was incorporated in 1927), it looked and felt enough like a place trying and failing to build community from nothing. It's just a coincidence, but a terribly sad one, that if you drive twenty miles due south from Aurora on Interstate 25, you arrive in the South Denver suburb of Littleton, practically at the front door of Columbine High School.

After its initial abandonment by the studio, *Over the Edge* might have been forgotten if not for a bizarre combination of people who rescued it. In 1981, Joseph Papp, creator of Shakespeare in the Park, screened *Over the Edge* as part of a series of overlooked cinema at his Public Theater in Downtown Manhattan. The movie received strong reviews, but more importantly came to the attention of New York celebrities like Al Pacino and their influential friends. The film next found a long life in the growing markets of home video and HBO, both technologies that suited the young, bored, resentful, and up late at night.

But the final push *Over the Edge* needed, to go beyond being what Roger Ebert called "a funeral service held at the graveside of the suburban dream" that only a funeral's worth of teenagers saw, came thanks to one fan from the depressed logging town of Aberdeen, Washington.

"*Over the Edge* is a story of troubled youth, vandalism, dysfunctional families, parental negligence, and most importantly, real estate development," he would write in his journals, relating to growing up in a place that offers you nothing. *Over the Edge*, he's on record as saying, "pretty much defined my entire personality." Years later, when the fan was in his twenties and it came time for his band to make their first video for a song he had written about his anger at the apathy of his own generation, he took the riot at the climactic end of his favorite movie as inspiration. The video (of a riot in a school gynasmium) and the song are now seen, along with *Heathers*, as one of the key cultural moments when the 1980s ended and the 1990s began.

The song was called "Smells Like Teen Spirit." The musician was Kurt Cobain.

The rogues' gallery of movies that would follow *Over the Edge* asked many of the same questions: Was this alternative history of eigthies teen cinema on the side of the teens, or a warning about the trouble they would make? Did it blame their actions on them or the time in America they were growing up in?

The settings of five of these movies served as character witnesses on both sides of the debate. In *Taps* (1981), *Bad Boys*

(1983), *The Legend of Billie Jean* (1985), *River's Edge* (1986), and *Running on Empty* (1988), the teenage protagonist's relationship to their surroundings grapples with the question of blame and responsibility by showing teenagers both confined and on the run.

Worth Defending: The Confinement of *Taps* and *Bad Boys*

TAPS ARRIVED IN MOVIE theaters on Christmas Day, 1981, right around the time *Over the Edge* was getting a second chance at the Public Theater in New York. Like *Over the Edge*, *Taps* is a story of confinement, of young people trapped somewhere, and how they react to it. Both movies were criticized for selling out their strengths—the naturalness of the performances and an understated filmmaking style that gave those performances room—for ridiculous final scenes of guns and explosions. I suppose given the title—"Taps" is the bugle piece played at military funerals, when we ruminate on the consequences of guns and explosions—the ending of *Taps* might have been something even its detractors saw coming.

Be that as it may, realism, unlike in *Over the Edge*, doesn't seem to be the goal of *Taps*. The plot centers on Bunker Hill Military Academy, a 141-year-old school that has just been sold to developers ready to turn it into condominiums. The school is run by career officer Brigadier General Harlan Bache (George C. Scott). On graduation day, General Bache informs his student soldiers of the closing and the single-year extension the board of directors has given them to come up with a way to keep Bunker Hill in business. But before the school's highest-ranking student, Cadet Major Brian Moreland (Timothy Hutton, in his first movie after winning an Oscar for *Ordinary People* in 1980), and his friends, the moral but conflicted Cadet Captain Alex Dwyer (Sean Penn in his film debut) and the shoot-first-ask-questions-later Cadet Captain David Shawn (Tom Cruise, in his first starring role), can get there, a freak accident occurs at the school's end-of-year dance. A group of townies (pickup trucks, dirty T-shirts, beer cans, and all) show up at the school gates to harass the cadets and their dates. A fight breaks out and a townie is killed by a misfired round from the ceremonial pistol on General Bache's uniform. The general is arrested.

The board votes to seize control of Bunker Hill immediately. Before they can, the cadets seize control of the school using weapons stockpiled for training drills in what they call "a military-style operation." Their goal: keep Bunker Hill Military Academy open and let them fulfill their dream of becoming soldiers.

"*Taps*, I suppose, means to be the terrible last word on the military mind run amok, and on the sort of thinking that led the United States into Vietnam not long ago," wrote the *New York Times'* Vincent Canby, who didn't like the movie very much. In reading several reviews from the time, the critical consensus seemed to regard *Taps* as a warning about how easily young people can be influenced by a charismatic adult pedaling terms like "honor," "service," and "valor." But within the history of American military schools, *Taps* can also be viewed as a Hollywood dramatization of a very real turning point. After the Vietnam War, military education found itself out of fashion. Nearly 450 institutions in the United States either closed or became regular boarding schools. The Vietnam War is barely mentioned in *Taps*, but the movie contains the same conflict many movies of the 1980s—*Coming Home, Platoon, Born on the Fourth of July*—had regarding Vietnam's legacy: does our old way of viewing American military might and service as a heroic act hold any truth for who we are now?

Taps tells a conflicted but unresolved story about that question. It's a pretty scary thought that what are effectively a group of sixteen- and seventeen-year-olds might seize control of their school with deadly weapons when they don't get what they want. That's probably what the detractors of *Taps* latched onto. But we can't ignore the sentiment of Brian Moreland telling his comrades "other kids are vandalizing their school, we want ours to stay open. Now if we behave like soldiers and not a bunch of kids in a riot, we can win this."

The townie kids who provoked the initial conflict are painted as thugs. In a choice echoing the conservative turn of the early Reagan era, the protagonists in *Taps* get in trouble for wanting to stay in school, enter the armed forces, and for believing in things like "honor" and "country." The real bad kids are the ones giving them a hard time over it.

Taps has essentially one location, the Valley Forge Military Academy in Wayne, Pennsylvania, twenty minutes northwest of Philadelphia. It stood in for Bunker Hill and put cast members through the same forty-five-day orientation as incoming cadets. The filmmakers had already approached nearly a dozen military academies, several of which turned them down on political grounds. Neither Culver Military Academy in Indiana nor the Hargrave Military Academy in Virginia liked how *Taps* ended or showed students going rogue. The Fishburne Military School was in contention for a time but did not have a front gate the screenplay required, where police cars, local authorities, and ultimately a tank could roll through when negotiations between the kids and the outside world break down.

In an ironic twist, the eventual "Bunker Hill" didn't have an adequate front gate either, and the set piece crucial to so much of *Taps* had to be built for the shoot and dismantled afterward. The front gate is where the townies harass the cadets the evening of the dance that sets the plot in motion. It's also the no-man's-land between the cadets barricaded inside the school and the authorities gathered outside. Symbolically, it's the door that lets the outside world in, what the students fear will happen to their school, but what ultimately has to (the cadets demands are to speak to the board about keeping the school open, not to be handed the keys) if they are to save it.

Taps is a movie of outsides and insides folding back upon themselves. These teenagers have willingly sequestered themselves inside Bunker Hill, away from the outside world. Now they must physically barricade themselves inside to keep the school running, close the school in order to keep it open.

Are these kids misguided? Or are they young men who merely want to finish the education they've started and the national service that comes afterward, even if the world has no place for their kind of education anymore? The self-confinement of the cadets can be seen as either, or both, or neither. Open, closed, or permeable, just like the front gate.

If Sean Penn played the disciplined moral center of his first movie *Taps*, he'd covered the entire spectrum of teenage males and their relationship to authority by his third movie, *Bad Boys* (1983). Penn plays Mick O'Brien, an Irish-American hoodlum from Chicago. Mick O'Brien has little past, no plans for the future, and a bleak, unending present of petty crimes and showdowns with criminal rivals. Had they gone to high school together, Mick O'Brien would have mugged Alex Dwyer, Sean's Penn's *Taps* character, in the cafeteria. Between *Taps* and *Bad Boys*, Sean Penn played loveable burnout Jeff Spicoli in *Fast Times at Ridgemont High*. If Alex Dwyer thrived on structure and Mick O'Brien lived to bust through it, Jeff Spicoli was too lazy to pay it much mind.

Bad Boys's Mick O'Brien worries about nothing but getting caught. When his girlfriend JC (Ally Sheedy) says kids like him get killed all the time and she worries about him, he shrugs. "That's the way it goes." Soon after, an attempt to steal a rival named Paco's (Esai Morales, essentially playing a teenage version of his character from *La Bamba*) drug money ends in the rival's younger brother getting killed. Mick has a long rap sheet and ends up getting shipped off to a juvenile detention center. The rest of the movie will take place there, as Mick gets into it with the youth prison's resident badass (Clancy Brown, a decade before playing the prison guard version of this character in *The Shawshank Redemption*) and attempts escape to visit JC on the outside. His rival Paco knows the best way to mess with Mick while Mick is locked up is through his girlfriend. Paco rapes JC and she reports it. Paco then gets sent to the same detention center where Mick is incarcerated, and we know that *Bad Boys* will inevitably end with a showdown between Mick and Paco.

The tagline on the *Bad Boys* poster is, "There's only one person left who believes Mick O'Brien can make it…Mick O'Brien. Life has pushed him into a corner. And he's coming out fighting." Which strikes me as trying to cash in on Sean Penn's rising star power at the time. The movie doesn't spend much time on how hard Mick O'Brien has it (save one early scene of his ditzy mother and her oily boyfriend in the bathtub) or motivations for his criminal behavior. Mick, Paco, and the other teenagers in this movie are mean, single-minded, and without mercy or motivation. *Bad Boys* works better by focusing on actions, rather than backstory, on characters living through hardship as the only reality they know. They don't ask why, and neither does the movie.

The youth detention center becomes the main set piece about thirty minutes into the movie, the consequence of what happens earlier. Until Mick arrives at the detention center, *Bad Boys* happens on the streets of Chicago's Pilsen and Bridgeport neighborhoods on the city's South Side. In case we didn't recognize it, the opening shot is of tall skyscrapers on the banks of the Chicago River with an elevated train rolling by. The word "Chicago" is then shown, redundantly, center screen.

We know from several other teen movies set in Chicago during the 1980s that the city played two extremes: a town of tourist attractions, where Ferris Bueller could spend a day off, or the northern neighborhoods where nice white kids like Rob Lowe and Demi Moore in *About Last Night* could have first jobs and apartments; but also dangerous, crime-filled, and run by thuggish stereotypes (i.e. people of color and working-class young white men). Nice kids like Tom Cruise's Joel Goodson in *Risky Business* (released four months after *Bad Boys*) might have a night of mischief in Chicago, but they ran back to the suburbs as soon as they could. Kids already in trouble like Mick and Paco, called Chicago itself home.

Bad Boys seems eager to remind us that, due to where they came from, Mick and Paco never really stood a chance to be anything other than bad boys. The film's opening credits are a montage of photos of young boys from the cradle to perhaps the tenth grade. The music is sad and regretful. Since the movie is called *Bad Boys*, we know these kids didn't turn out so great. The opening credits seem to be setting us up for either shock or horror over what has happened to these kids, or sadness at how far gone they must already be.

Bad Boys works brilliantly as a gritty crime drama, since its greatest pleasures are visceral and kinetic—charismatic performances, a knife-edge of a plot, darkly sensual set pieces, and a mood of corrosive fury. Though the final showdown between Mick and Paco is predictable and probably not needed, it's the capper on the best parts of the movie, the ninety minutes spent on how the characters survive being locked up together in a prison for kids young enough to still be in high school. This majority portion of the film doesn't ask too many questions about how or why the teenagers in the movie got this way, but instead focuses on how they try to survive it. But by offering no background or explanation for the character's nihilism, then frontloading itself with unnecessary attention to where the first thirty minutes of the movie happens, *Bad Boys* offers a half-baked attempt to explain a pathology the rest of the movie wisely avoids trying to explain.

Bad Boys and *Taps* are both movies that look at teenagers in confinement, then ask whether they deserve that confinement or are being unfairly punished by it. The three other important movies in our look at the dark corners of Brat Pack America ask similar questions but spread themselves over larger ground. *River's Edge*, *The Legend of Billie Jean*, and *Running on Empty* are all movies about teenagers not confined, but on the run.

"What the Hell Happened to These Kids?"

BESIDES *OVER THE EDGE*, 1986's *River's Edge* is the only movie in this group based on real-life events. Tim Hunter cowrote the former and directed the latter. *Over the Edge* is about kids trapped by geography and the naïve intentions of their parents. *River's Edge* is about kids running from a horror of their own making.

On November 3, 1981, fourteen-year-old Marcy Renee Conrad was raped and murdered by a classmate at Milpitas High School in Milpitas, California, sixteen-year-old Anthony Jacques Broussard. Broussard left Conrad's body on a hillside in nearby San Jose, California, then bragged to friends about the crime. When they didn't believe him, he told them where they could see the body. Nearly a dozen students went to view Marcy Renee Conrad's body over the next few days but said nothing to the authorities.

Eventually, a worker at a nearby factory discovered the body of Marcy Renee Conrad. The crime made national news as a terrifying example of the apathy and coldness of teenagers. "I've never seen a group of people act so callous about death in my fifteen years of police work," Santa Clara County Sheriff Gary Meeker told the Associated Press. "What the hell happened to these kids?"

River's Edge's screenwriter Neal Jimenez took the events surrounding Marcy Renee Conrad's murder as a jumping off point. Jimenez made the group of friends/accomplices much smaller (about a half dozen, the same size as the group of friends in *Over the Edge*), changed the murderer from a jockish black kid to a lumberjacky white kid, and the setting from near Silicon Valley to an unnamed town. *River's Edge* was filmed primarily in Sacramento, 110 miles northeast of where the events that inspired it took place.

A modest film from a small studio, *River's Edge* won both Best Picture and Best Screenplay at the 1987 Independent Spirit Awards, which had begun just a few years before. Its cast had a number of actors early in their long careers—Keanu Reeves, Crispin Glover (about a million miles from George McFly in *Back to the Future*), Ione Skye, and Dennis Hopper at the beginning of a mid-career comeback after *Hoosiers*. Hopper played Feck, a local pot dealer with a thing for life-sized dolls.

River's Edge has very little action. The kids hang out, get high, talk of "blowing this place and going where nobody knows us." (They suggest Portland, only one state away, but I guess anywhere else seems far away when you feel stuck.) Distracted parents pass through. Younger siblings are frightened that the group of friends are growing up and leaving them behind. Once the murder enters the story, everyone is in a holding pattern, wrecked over what to do. To run would arouse suspicion, to tell an adult means ratting on a friend who is capable of killing someone. The group argues over what to do but seem to know they've gotten themselves in a situation that will resolve badly no matter what. They need to remove themselves from association with a terrible act of violence without appearing to go anywhere or do anything.

The filmmakers shot *River's Edge* on windless, cloudy days in Sacramento with a flat literalness that bears a passing resemblance to Walker Evans photographs. Locations are deliberately vague and removed from context. There's no sense of where the friends live in relation to one other, how far their houses are from school, which road leads to Feck's house, where they score pot. The camera rarely moves; the lighting is diffuse and grim. The kids, even when their feet shuffle and their bodies twitch with anxiety, seem pasted against the background like dead insects pinned to Styrofoam.

River's Edge is one of the most hopeless of all eighties teen movies. Unlike the media coverage of the true story it's based on, the movie doesn't dwell on the cold hearts of teenagers who wouldn't report a heinous crime. Instead, it shows everyone— scared teenagers, ineffective parents, younger siblings who bully each other—as prisoners of the awful deeds of one. No argument that the killer is a bad kid. The others? Can we say we, at age sixteen, would do something different in this situation? If so, we can understand the fear associated with their inaction too. Does that mean *River's Edge* is a portrait of a morally bankrupt place or time in history? The haunted stillness of the movie—plain backgrounds, frozen camera, lighting resembling the sky before a storm—gives us two points of view, both of which are awful. Either these kids are trapped by their own moral failings, or the world they inhabit rewards inaction and lack of empathy.

The only thing that moves and changes in *The River's Edge* is the river. It's also the place where this whole terrible mess started.

Legends and Legacies

THERE'S A FINAL PAIRING of Brat Pack America movies about teenagers on the run, one of which sees escape as empowering, the other as an unfairness passed on from parents to children. Overall, *The Legend of Billie Jean* (1985) and *Running on Empty* (1988) are miles apart. *Billie Jean* was a poorly reviewed chase-and-pursuit action movie that bombed at the box office and time has mostly remembered for giving us the Pat Benatar song "Invincible." *Running on Empty* has an 85 percent fresh rating on Rotten Tomatoes (versus *Billie Jean*'s 44 percent), and both *Empty*'s lead actor, River Phoenix, and screenwriter, Naomi Foner, received Oscar nominations. *Billie Jean* is hard to find on DVD and is widely considered a cinematic misstep, a suped-up music video trying to cash in on the rising popularity of MTV. History has seen *Running on Empty* as an important look at the legacy of the 1960s and, arguably, the last great movie on director Sidney Lumet's resume, which had included *12 Angry Men, Serpico, Dog Day Afternoon,* and *Network.*

And yet both movies concern teenagers who must flee authorities after being wrongly accused. Both also use geography, the arena of the chase, to demonstrate how we as a society have unfairly forced these kids to run.

The Billie Jean of *Legend* is Billie Jean Davy (Helen Slater), a kid growing up in a Corpus Christi trailer park with her younger brother, Bix (Christian Slater in his film debut; no relation to Helen Slater). Bix gets into an argument with a local rich jerk named Hubie Pyatt (Barry Tubb), who ends up beating him up and trashing Bix's motor scooter. Billie Jean heads down to the souvenir shop Hubie's family owns to demand the $608 needed to fix the bike. Hubie's dad (Richard Bradford) not only doesn't give her the money but also makes a pass at her. In the struggle, a gun goes off and hits Mr. Pyatt in the shoulder. Billie Jean and her brother, who were ignored by the police when the initial crime happened, take off with two friends (Martha Gehman and Yeardley

Smith, right before becoming the voice of Lisa Simpson) with the law at their heels.

At one stop, Billie Jean cuts her hair and videotapes herself saying she and her brother have done nothing wrong, all she wants is $608 to fix the bike, and an apology.

"You think you can do anything you want and then lie about it and we just have to take it, because what are we? Just a bunch of kids," she yells into the camera. "Well, not this time. From now on we're doin' this our way. No lyin', no cheatin', fair is fair!"

The ensuing media coverage turns Billie Jean into a generational symbol of the raw deal adults give teenagers. "I got a teenager myself, and no one's gotta tell me what this younger generation's about," says Mr. Pyatt to a TV reporter, after first putting out a bounty on Billie Jean. Later he tries to profit by slapping her image on T-shirts and bumper stickers and selling them to the same teenagers he despises. When the lead investigator, Lt. Ringwald (Peter Coyote), questions Bradford's motivations, he holds up a bundle of letters. "Average citizen is sick and tired of kids running wild," he says. "I got letters from parents, educators, businessmen. All of them is voting age."

"What do you think of this Billie Jean character?" a different TV reporter asks a teenage girl on the street.

"She's a rebel," the teenager answers. "I think they're picking on her because she's a girl and I think that's disgusting."

In the world of this movie, being singled out for being poor, female, and a teenager are all versions of the same thing, an injustice adults in power perpetrate against you because they make the rules.

The Legend of Billie Jean was filmed on location in and around Corpus Christi, Texas, in the early autumn of 1984. As we'll see also in *Running on Empty*, the specific city or town is neither here nor there to the plot. But team *Billie Jean* makes a noticeable choice in setting early on in the plot that changes the movie's message by its end.

More than a few of the places Billie Jean and her brother and friends stop to refuel are places associated with childhood—

swimming pools, toy stores, shopping malls, an abandoned amusement park named Candyland. But while the entire movie is shot on location using existing buildings and structures, Candyland is a constructed set. The scene at Candyland makes no difference to the movie's plot. And yet the filmmakers took the time to create a series of stunning, melancholy shots of rusting amusement park rides against the setting sun, ruins the size of dinosaurs with Billie Jean and friends in miniature at their feet.

I'm guessing writer/director Matthew Robbins and his team wanted *The Legend of Billie Jean* to be seen as not only a cry of outrage but also the murder of childhood. In becoming a symbol of justice, Billie Jean (as well as Bix and their friends) can no longer be children or even teenagers. They get singled out for being young, then must surrender their youth just to be treated like human beings.

"Billie Jean is the best. Fair is fair!" says one caller to a local radio station, which has raised the $608 in order to broadcast the public spectacle of Billie Jean showing up to claim it. A mass of teenagers has shown up to give their support to one of their own. Of course the Pyatts will be there selling merchandise, and have erected a giant papier-mâché statue of Billie Jean behind their souvenir tent. The eventual showdown with Mr. Pyatt ends not in glory but with Billie Jean walking away. Her supporters are unified but demoralized and walk away too, refugees instead of an army. Her reign as a hero is done. "Things don't always work out the way you want," says Helen Slater on the DVD's commentary. "Even when you are right."

It's here that *The Legend of Billie Jean* seems less a glamorous portrait of teenage rebellion than a far more conservative argument for modesty and restraint. Billie Jean wins, but at the price of her childhood and the entire life she once knew. She's backed into a corner and becomes a hero only so she and her brother can be treated fairly. She then sees how easily heroism is corrupted.

Locations of a lost and abandoned childhood are all over Billie Jean's quest for justice. They rub the sexy edges off her legend by showing just what you give up to be a legend. Especially if all you wanted was your money back and an apology.

The Legend of Billie Jean is a movie set relentlessly in the present. The movie offers very little space to guess what happened before the story begins, and not much room to speculate on what becomes of Billie Jean and her brother Bix after its end. True to its premise and name, *The Legend of Billie Jean* happens in a headlong dash and then is over.

Running on Empty is a film where 90 percent of the story has happened before the movie starts.

In 1971, Arthur and Annie Pope (Christine Lahti and Judd Hirsch) were part of a group of Vietnam War protestors that set off an explosive in a laboratory producing napalm. The bomb paralyzed a janitor not scheduled to work that night. At the time, the Popes had a two-year-old son named Danny. When *Running on Empty* begins, Danny (River Phoenix) is a teenager and has a ten-year-old brother named Harry (Jonas Abry). The FBI has been hunting the family for over a decade. In the movie's opening scenes, the family is living in Florida City, Florida, under an assumed name. When Danny senses federal agents watching him play a pickup game of softball, the Popes split town and start over somewhere else, under different names and identities. You get the sense they've done this many times before.

With the help of friends in the political underground, the Popes relocate to a New Jersey suburb not far from Manhattan. They leave the family dog behind, cut and bleach their hair, and adopt fake names from the obituary pages of the local newspaper. "It's terrific not recognizing yourself in the mirror," Danny says to his mom after they arrive in New Jersey. "It's wonderful to have a new name every six months." With running being all he's ever known, Danny seems ready to have his own life, one not ruled by a crime his parents committed when he was in nursery school.

The Popes settle into a new life in New Jersey, where the music teacher (Ed Crowley) at Danny's high school notices his talent as a pianist. He invites Danny to perform at a recital at his home, where Danny meets and falls for his daughter, Lorna (Martha Plimpton).

The teacher thinks Danny could win a scholarship to Juilliard. But applying means finding a full set of school records (which are scattered across several states under as many names) and, more importantly, leaving his family behind. If Danny goes to college, he will never be able to see his parents again. Even if he lives a normal life, the FBI will still be watching. Trying to reconnect with his family would mean putting them in danger of arrest.

Running on Empty is a movie about the sins of the 1960s being visited upon the children of the 1980s. But when framed as a movie about running, about a teenager having to escape from a crime he didn't commit, it's as much a movie about the long and painful reach of unintended consequences. The political reasons for the Popes' actions have long ceased to matter. Now the only way the father Arthur Pope (Judd Hirsch) can imagine them all staying a family is by staying together in hiding. Annie Pope (Christine Lahti) knows this isn't fair to their sons, who are innocent but serving the same sentence as their parents. No matter how well intentioned running and hiding might have been for their family then, the consequences of staying together now outweigh it. And so Annie Pope makes a decision.

In the movie's most important scene, Annie meets her estranged father (Steven Hill, just before becoming District Attorney Adam Schiff on *Law & Order*) at a fancy Manhattan restaurant. It's the middle of the day and he's wearing a suit. We learn early in their conversation that he has come from work and lives in New York City, where Annie grew up. She asks him to take care of Danny while he attends Juilliard. Annie's father agrees, but first they talk about how much he misses her, how her decision to go into hiding meant Annie's parents not only lost contact with their daughter but their grandchildren, too. In that moment, Annie realizes the extent of the pain her decision has caused and reveals, without saying so, that perhaps she wanted their running to end, even before Danny had the opportunity to go to Juilliard. Her family has ended up this time, probably not by accident, within striking distance of Annie's childhood home. Annie also tells her father that when their younger son becomes an adult, she will turn herself in.

"I worry when you go to the city. That's where they get everyone," Arthur tells Annie right before she leaves to see her dad. Arthur is from near "the city," too, a Bronx-born Jewish kid, "a red-diaper baby son of Bolsheviks." He and Annie still have Danny's younger brother Harry to think about, so they cannot stop running quite yet. But Danny will have to leave them for now and begin his life as Danny Pope, as himself.

For a movie about hiding, pursuit, and escape, *Running on Empty* begins after most of the running is done. My sense is that the feeling of arrival, of landing when no place before has felt permanent, echoes what we are supposed to feel about this family and the heartbreaking choice they must make. *Running on Empty* is about that choice leading only to the acceptance of consequences they could not have predicted from decisions made long ago. The only specific place in this movie is the last one they will be at together, a town in New Jersey, near the largest city in America, which once meant home.

"Sherwood, Ohio"

THERE'S A FUNNY MOMENT on the commentary track of *Heathers'* Twentieth Anniversary Edition DVD where director Michael Lehman jokes about the movie's "lone palm tree." Said palm tree appears after about forty minutes in the upper left-hand corner of the frame when jock bullies Ram and Kurt (Patrick Labyorteaux and Lance Fenton) are chasing two nerds across the front lawn of a church. *Heathers* ostensibly takes place in Sherwood, Ohio, and I don't need to tell you there ain't no palm trees in Ohio. So right after mentioning this palm tree (producer Denise Di Novi and screenwriter Daniel Waters, also on the commentary track, are still laughing), Lehman dryly adds, "Not one foot of this film was shot in Ohio."

All three then explain why: *Heathers* had a tiny budget, a four-week shooting schedule, and a distributor on the verge of bankruptcy. It didn't matter that Waters had made the setting "Sherwood, Ohio" on purpose, or that the movie contains a great joke about the town's homophobia. ("This is Ohio," Christian Slater's character says. "If you're not holding a brewski, you might as well be wearing a dress.") In the name of financial solvency, not one foot of the movie could be shot any further than driving distance from where everybody lived in Los Angeles. The church, if you're wondering, is at 1100 Avenue 64, in southwest Pasadena.

Does it matter that *Heathers* is explicit about taking place in Ohio even though in wasn't filmed there? In this case, yes. Because the name and the idea of "Sherwood, Ohio" gets right to the heart of what *Heathers* is and isn't.

On the one hand, I, along with many others, have made the mistake of thinking that "Sherwood, Ohio" was a satiric kiss-off to "Shermer, Illinois," the teen universe John Hughes invented. In a 2014 *Entertainment Weekly* oral history of the movie, Daniel Waters says:

> The teen films of the time, the John Hughes films, were fun. But there's a whole other wing of the high school they weren't going into—the dark, Stephen King wing that nobody wanted to look at. And I think *Heathers* was refreshing. It was the first time a lot of people lost their dark humor virginity.

Daniel Waters had seen *Heathers* as an anti–John Hughes movie from the very start. But he never meant Sherwood, Ohio, as an anti-Hughes joke.

"There were a tsunami of reasons why I named it Sherwood," Waters told me over the phone. "I grew up on Sherwood Street, which makes my porn name 'Booclay Sherwood.' I wanted it to sound like a combination of 'Winesberg, Ohio' and 'Sherwood Anderson' so a critic who felt guilty about liking a teen film could latch onto that literary reference. And I liked the idea of it sounding like Sherwood Forest and Veronica and Jason robbing from the rich and stealing from the poor, high school style. That Sherwood sounds like Shermer? That fact is only gravy."

John Hughes knew the north suburbs of Chicago intimately. He used that knowledge to use to make the imaginary community of Shermer generic enough for most any teenager to relate to it as their town. Daniel Waters also created Sherwood, Ohio, based on where he grew up, but everyone on team *Heathers* knew they couldn't make their movie there and instead had to find stand-in locations around Los Angeles. Director Michael Lehman and cinematographer Francis Kenny then did something fiendish with this fake Sherwood, Ohio—something that brought *Heathers* out of the relatable and into the surreal.

The look of Sherwood is fifties melodrama meets eighties mall photo studio, saturated yet blurred, ripe yet stagey and airless. Director Michael Lehman was a big fan of director Douglas Sirk, whose most famous movies—*All That Heaven Allows, Written on the Wind, Imitation of Life*—were stylish 1950s melodramas with female protagonists who looked like women's magazine advertisements come to life. Critics in Sirk's time hated his work, but filmmakers as different from each other as John Waters, Quentin Tarantino, and Pedro Almodóvar all cite Sirk as an influence. Film scholars since the 1970s have also praised Sirk's crisp, colorful otherworldliness as a method of exploring issues of gender and power in the Eisenhower era.

The team behind *Heathers* played with this same tension, having the audience see their own darker tendencies on screen by having the movie unfold somewhere they *might* recognize, then twisting and distorting it. The settings in *Heathers* (minus perhaps the funerals and croquet games) are all capital clichés of other high school movies—cafeterias, gymnasiums, convenience stores, illicit parties, and the woods behind school where mischief happens. But none of these places have any relationship to each other; there are almost no scenes of characters driving or walking from one place to the next. The movie cuts and we're somewhere else. The backgrounds of scenes are often hazy or obscured by bright light so characters enter the frame like ghosts. The central set piece, Westerburg High, is taken from footage in four different high schools throughout the Los Angeles area, which are stitched together through simple cuts instead of continuous tracking or dolly shots. The score, a creepy, minimalist series of metallic phrases by composer David Newman, seems to crawl up the wall like a tarantula.

The result: while the plot of *Heathers* hangs together beautifully, the look is a series of disparate moments, like pieces of a dream or stages of a fugue.

Watching *Heathers* now, for perhaps the eighty-fifth time, I'm still struck by how much I feel and relate to the characters even though I'm watching them move through a world that seems barely connected to reality. We feel for Veronica and JD and Betty Finn and Martha Dunnstock even if we barely notice the movie's violent and disturbing moments sneaking up on us. But the "where" it all happens is meant to look familiar the way a scary corner of your imagination might, not real life. Sherwood, Ohio—which sounds like a place one could visit, maybe a rival town to Shermer, Illinois, in high school sports—isn't meant to be anywhere real. Sherwood, Ohio, severs the connection between how eighties teen movies make us feel and the connection between those feelings and where eighties teen movies happen.

Heathers feels like the logical end of the eighties teen movie era. It came in the last year of the decade and predicted the cynical turn pop culture would take—grunge, heroin chic, Quentin Tarantino—in the decade to follow. Its conception as a satire of a John Hughes movie meant "the John Hughes movie" was now a genre with its own rules and clichés which could be satirized, the first sign a cultural movement's time has passed. That *Heathers* called attention to its setting as a joke, naming it and then contorting how it looks so its name no longer mattered, made locations abstract instead of actual, captivating but not essential to teen movies. It put "Sherwood, Ohio" on the map of Brat Pack America then torched the map behind it.

BRAT PACK AMERICA TALKS TO. . .WRITER DANIEL WATERS

I N HIS EARLY TWENTIES, screenwriter Daniel Waters was working at a Los Angeles video store when he decided to expand a short film he'd written in college into the story of a high schooler who falls in love with psychopath. The result: *Heathers* is now considered one of the funniest, darkest, and best teen movies of all time. Waters won an Edgar Award in 1990 for his screenplay the same year *Heathers* took home the Independent Spirit Award for Best First Feature.

Daniel Waters went on to write the screenplays for *Hudson Hawk* (1991), *The Adventures of Ford Fairlane* (1990) and cowrite *Batman Returns* (1992) and *Demolition Man* (1993). He's directed the films *Happy Campers* (2001) and *Sex and Death 101* (2007) and collaborated with his younger brother, director Mark Waters, on the movie *Vampire Academy* (2014).

I spoke to Daniel Waters over the phone in October of 2015.

Kevin Smokler: Where in the project did you decide this was "an anti–John Hughes"?

Daniel Waters: That was part of the mission statement, the desire to do a different kind of teen film. It was murder one and not manslaughter. I was trying to kill and resurrect it. It was me looking back on what it was to be a teenager as well as elevate the high school film with a heightened reality, a grand operatic style I could have some fun with. It was almost out of annoyance more than anything. I couldn't find the kind of teen film I wanted to see, so I wrote it myself.

My intentions were highfalutin. I was jealous of Shakespeare. Where was the Stanley Kubrick of the teen film?

You know that line in *The Breakfast Club*, "When you grow up, your heart dies." My response was, "Your heart dies when you are twelve." That "Excuse me, Little Miss Voice of a Generation" speech in *Heathers* is probably a response to John Hughes, who always found a way to blame the adults for everything.

But really, none of it came from a hatred of what Hughes was doing. John Hughes and I were on the same team. We both wanted to make better teen movies. Negligible and generic are the enemies. Neither of these words describes John Hughes.

KS: Where were you in life when you started writing *Heathers*?

DW: I was working at Video House in Silverlake. It's now a computer repair store. It gave me a lot of time to do a lot of thinking. Completely naïvely, I wrote *Heathers* and did everything wrong. But they say if you can get one person other than yourself to like it…

Most of the people who I was living with worked in some capacity with [*Heathers* director] Michael Lehman's student film. Lehman's calling, giving me notes, and I'm like, "Who's this fucking guy?" Me, Michael, and Denise [Di Novi, *Heathers*' producer] ended up having the same agent.

I'd take meetings where people would say, "We love the script, but this will never get made. Would you like to write a teen film about a wacky genie who becomes a lunch lady?" So now, when I talk at schools, I say, "Don't sell out until you are asked to."

KS: How much of *Heathers* comes from "Troubled Waters," your high school newspaper column?

DW: "Troubled Waters" was my blog long before the term was in the stratosphere. Me being adorable and strained about pop culture.

In high school, I was 82 percent nerd but friends with all the cliques, and the vaguest of vague celebrities because I was the guy who had his own column. I would say scabrous things and maybe get in trouble for it. Also, my sister was part of the popular crowd and told me a lot about it.

But really, *Heathers* started as a short script at I wrote at McGill [University] about three girls named Heather, and the main character gets burned at the stake at the end.

KS: How do you write best?

DW: Scribbles, notes, and index cards. When I sit down to write, it's already done. I am much more a collector of acorns. My idea of a good day is another writer's idea of writer's block.

I can spend all day obsessing over names, because they can't just be one thing. That's why "Veronica Sawyer" (Winona Ryder's character in *Heathers*) is both "Veronica" from the Archie and Veronica comics and also like Tom Sawyer. Her old best friend is named "Betty Finn," same reasons.

KS: "Is there anything in *Heathers* that you wish had been changed or left out?

DW: That scene where Veronica and Jason are running around in the forest after the jocks are killed. It goes on forever and feels naked and endless at that point in the screenplay. Same with the endless boiler room fight at the end of the movie.

Also, one line people love that I never understood was when Veronica says, "Lick it up, baby" to Heather #1. During the musical, everyone cheers. I said to myself, Jeez, that one made it into the lexicon?

KS: Where do you see *Heathers* in the history of eighties teen movies and teen movies in general?

DW: It behooves my ego to clutch onto the "last word of the eighties teen movie" label it's gotten. But the bad thing *Heathers* created was an upping of the ante that teenagers in movies have to be more clever than other teenagers. Certainly, in a TV show like *Dawson's Creek*, everyone was a little too erudite.

I sometimes get a sense that everything has become a teen film. Even if it's lawyers and doctors, everyone has to have a snarky repartee and the relationships have to be pitched as though this is a teen film dressed up as an adult film. The glibness in *Heathers*, they took the ball and ran with it. It can give a movie a feeling of unearned superiority.

KS: Your younger brother, Mark Waters, directed *Mean Girls*, clearly a younger sibling of *Heathers*…

DW: *Mean Girls* is a hilarious movie and doesn't fade a bit when you see it again. The way the Eskimos have fifty words for snow, I have fifty words for teen films. So we joke that I'm Joy Division, he's New Order. Sure, they're similar, but they're also different.

My brother will say, "I'm brilliant and he's smart," and you need that combination in life. I can have amazing flights of fancy and he's the brother that holds the map. My brother didn't see *Star Wars* growing up, because why would you be inside watching a movie when you could be outside playing basketball?

Maybe it's the difference between haute couture and ready-to-wear. I tell him, "If you're the one making the money, at least it will go toward our mother's Christmas presents."

KS: Is there anything you wish had made it into *Heathers* that didn't make it?

DW: You'd think since my first draft was over two hundred pages that there would be a lot of stuff I miss, but there really isn't. I had a grander conception of the exploitative song "Teenage Suicide (Don't Do It)" by Big Fun that runs throughout the film, including an awesomely awful video with two Wham!-like pop stars pulling suicidal kids out of ovens and such. It was a whole other layer of satire…but a little too expensive.

KS: What's the strangest thing somebody's told you/you've heard about *Heathers*?

DW: I've been told "*Heathers* saved my life." I thought I was showing high school as a brutal place, that I wasn't going to coddle you like John Hughes, I'm going to wipe the smile off of everybody's faces. But I was surprised how cathartic it was for people. They've had a bad day, they put on *Heathers* and Veronica's bad day makes them feel better.

Fans under thirty or under forty like the happy ending. Veronica coming out alive is badass and cool.

I wrote a bunch of other endings. The one that almost ended up in the movie was JD succeeds in blowing up the school and the last scene is a prom in Heaven. The one I liked the best, Martha stabs Veronica at the end and says, "Fuck you, Heather." Veronica says, "My name's not Heather, my name's not Heather," as she lies bleeding.

KS: Did you ever meet John Hughes?

DW: Twice. The first was during the shoot of *The Adventures of Ford Fairlane* [1990 film written by Waters]. We got put together in a sweaty kitchen during the shooting of a sexy sorority house scene. I could tell he was not a *Heathers* fan. But he was very polite, a very nice guy.

The second time we ran into each other at Tower Records, when it was still around on Sunset. Turns out we had the same musical tastes.

CHAPTER 9: AFTER THE MOVIES CAME TO TOWN

Cities and Towns Changed by the '80s Teen Movies Shot There

Movies Discussed: *Breaking Away, Footloose, The Goonies, Stand by Me, Mystic Pizza, The Lost Boys*

L OOK BACK AT THE movies of Brat Pack America and it's easy to think you are seeing a lost world of video arcades and video stores, of cavernous shopping malls and seedy urban downtowns. Few, if any, of these places exist anymore. It would be even easier, then, to think the eighties teen movies and the places they happened are exercises in nostalgia, fun but ultimately sad trips to a land and time that is gone and never coming back. That we have been looking at a map now reduced to ashes. That we are now sitting in a flying DeLorean with no place left to land.

It's what I thought I'd feel when I started this road trip. I was wrong.

In Bloomington, Indiana, the Little 500 bicycle race immortalized in the very first eighties teen movie, *Breaking Away*, continues, bigger than ever, to this day. Held on the third weekend of April, "Little Five" takes over the Indiana University campus and parts of Bloomington in what *Grantland* called "five days of nonstop partying...a sprint down the home stretch with commencement right around the corner." The AXS TV network (owned by IU alumnus Marc Cuban) has telecast the race since 2002. Barack Obama dropped by while campaigning for president in 2008. Teams now train all year long for the race and recruit potential riders as soon as the academic year begins. And somewhere in Bloomington, amid this "Super Bowl of cycling," the movie that brought the event to the world's attention gets screened every year for the community and a new class of students and fans.

This is a long way from when *Breaking Away* re-staged the race for its climactic final scenes in the summer of 1978. Back then, the film's crew couldn't find enough local extras and had to keep shifting the ones that showed up around the stadium so it looked filled to capacity onscreen.

"A lot of students weren't in town because of vacation," Kevin Richey, who at the time worked in the IU Student Union catering department that fed the actors and crew, told me in an email. "And at the time, no one knew this movie was going to be such a big deal."

The race is now sixty-five years old, the first running held in 1951 and modeled after the Indianapolis 500. *Breaking Away*, released in July of 1979, now sits just past the midpoint of its history. The "Cutters" team at the movie's center, made up of working-class Bloomington kids trying to figure out life after high school and stick it to the snotty fraternity-backed teams in the race, is fiction; Little Five only allows fully registered IU students to compete.

And yet, since 1984, a team called "Cutters", which wears the same white jerseys with black lettering from *Breaking Away*, has won the race twelve times, with five straight victories from 2007–2012.

The "Cutters" team just means "best riders not in a frat," Brian Janosch, who covered the race for the IU student newspaper from 2003–2007, told me. In the spirit of the movie that inspired their name, the "Cutters" formed in the mid-eighties as a group of riders who "broke away" from the old Delta Chi fraternity chapter.

"You can walk right downtown this very minute and buy yourself a Cutters T-shirt," said Miah Michaelsen, assistant director of economic development for the arts for the city of Bloomington. "*Breaking Away* is in the community's DNA… There's a short list of things people think about when they think about Bloomington… [sexuality researcher] Alfred Kinsey, [songwriter] Hoagy Carmichael, IU basketball coach Bobby Knight, [violinist] Joshua Bell. *Breaking Away* is at the top of that list."

Bloomington's brand-new downtown transit center, a muscular L-shaped building with big windows and narrow roofs, has a cycling mural on its western wall called "Breakaway." For years, the city's Convention and Visitors Bureau's slogan was "Break away to Bloomington." Indiana University Press has an imprint called "Break Away Books." The University's hospital cafeteria is called "The Breakaway Café."

"Obviously the movie gets talked about more on the anniversary years," Ms. Michaelsen told me. "We just had the thirty-fifth, and things will probably be a little quieter until the fortieth…but not too much time goes by in Bloomington without some mention of *Breaking Away*."

Breaking Away came out in 1979, and would later influence eighties teen movie directors like John Hughes and Savage Steve Holland. The link it creates between growing up, sports, and escaping a hometown that promises very little future would show up later in Brat Pack America movies like *All the Right Moves* and *Vision Quest*.

But despite how big the bike race it put on the map has become, people I spoke to around Bloomington seem to love *Breaking Away* as much for how thoroughly it understands both growing up ("One of my high school gang was exactly like Moocher, and everyone knew a Mike," Jim Schroeder, a Bloomington pharmacist who has lead *Breaking Away* bicycle tours, wrote me) and the personality of Bloomington, rather than just the town's biggest amateur sporting event.

"Opening the movie in that stone quarry meant whoever wrote it knew Bloomington," Janosch told me. In *Breaking Away*'s now-legendary first scene, the four friends chew on high school being over and what comes next before having a run-in with some IU students who've come to swim in *their* stone quarry. "The scene is just the four friends talking, and it doesn't need to be in a quarry," said Janosch. "But IU students still go swimming in that quarry as a rite of passage. Every IU student who sees the movie knows that spot. It's famous in Bloomington."

The university and the city may be several thousand people larger than in the days of *Breaking Away*, the limestone industry long gone. (Rooftop Quarry, as seen in the movie, still exists, but is privately owned and forbids swimming. Students come anyway.) The movie nonetheless maintains its hold on Bloomington in part because no other movie has been filmed in town since, and in part because, even as a moment in the community's history from long ago, *Breaking Away* illustrates a conflict still playing out there today.

Given that *Breaking Away*—a box office hit, an Oscar winner, an inarguable classic—cannot be separated from the town where it took place, it surprised me that no other movie I can think of had Bloomington as its setting. Why had *Breaking Away* not created a pile of filmed-in-Bloomington movies, the same way *Slacker* (1991) did for Austin or Gus Van Sant's early movies did for Portland?

"The state of Indiana has not been particularly welcoming to Hollywood," Michaelsen told me. "Slow to the table would be a generous description." Even as I write this, the state is having a bit of a cultural moment (*Parks and Recreation*, about a city government in the fictional southern Indiana town of Pawnee, ended a seven-season run in February 2015, right as *Unbreakable Kimmy Schmidt*, about a Hoosier who escapes a cult and moves to New York City, debuted and became a hit Netflix series). The filmmakers behind classic Indiana sports movies *Rudy* (1993) and *Hoosiers* (1986) are now also based in Bloomington. Even so, Michaelsen told me, the town that cannot be separated from *Breaking Away* has no interest in canonizing it or making room for its successor.

"There's a certain Midwestern attitude that we're just not going to brag on ourselves," said Michaelsen. "That if we gotta put up a *Breaking Away* museum for you, then you just don't get it." Never mind, she said, that it's also not easy for film crews to get themselves there. Bloomington is forty miles off an interstate highway in south-central Indiana, and its nearest major cities—Indianapolis, Louisville, and Chicago—are one, two, and four hours away, respectively.

But *Breaking Away* isn't just *the* Bloomington movie because it has no competition. It's "become shorthand for a kind of mythic innocent past...a haze of *aww shucks, wasn't that great?*" said Michaelsen. But what past exactly isn't clear. Bloomington in the late seventies? Bloomington when it still had a factory rather than an academic economy? Even within *Breaking Away*, Bloomington is a town not frozen in memory, but in transition from a community of manual laborers to one of college students and university employees.

The Bloomington residents I spoke to are all over the map about the nature of that transition. But none question that the divide existed when *Breaking Away* came to town, and still does now.

"There wasn't any integration between the two," said Jim Schroeder of the student/local/working-class/college kid divide the movie portrays. "Retail businesses in town at the time would cater to one or the other."

"[The divide] made for a good story but didn't really exist," Kevin Richey told me in an email. A lot of "town people worked at IU... The university did and still drives this town."

"There's at least as much of a student versus student divide as a student versus local divide," Brian Janosch said, offering a third opinion. "Students from Bloomington and Indiana, even from other parts of the Midwest, felt very separate from kids from one of the coasts."

Janosch and everyone else I spoke to also reminded me that Bloomington still has a significant born-and-bred local population whose relationship with the town exists independent of the university. Which makes it very different from college towns like Cambridge, Massachusetts; Berkeley, California; or Charlottesville, Virginia, where the cost of living has effectively priced out working-class natives who don't have jobs on campus.

"You can live a perfectly happy life in Bloomington, not come downtown, and have nothing to do with the university,"

Michaelsen said. "West of N-37, the university doesn't exist," Jim Schroeder agreed. "Leave city limits and it gets rural pretty quick. Five miles out and you might as well be in Mississippi."

Differences, real or imagined, tend to snap into focus when people are afraid. In the last fifteen years, two different female IU students have disappeared and were later found murdered. The suspects in both cases were men from the rural communities outside of Bloomington.

On June 3, 2011, Lauren Spierer, a twenty-year-old IU Student from Greenburgh, New York, vanished after a Friday night out and has not been seen since. That same year, twenty-nine-year-old Crystal Grubb, a divorced mother of two and a Bloomington local with a history of meth addiction, was found strangled to death in a cornfield outside of town. Grubb had vanished the year before after going on a hike with friends. Both cases remain unsolved, but Spierer's made national news. Crystal Grubb's death, to put it charitably, did not.

"The Lauren Spierer case generated a real *Breaking Away*–like attitude," said Jim Schroeder, of the civic feud between locals and students at Bloomington's heart. Perhaps the even darker side of that is what happened when Crystal Grubb went missing: difference turning coldly into lack of empathy and concern.

In her 2014 book, *Ghettoside: A True Story of Murder in America*, author Jill Leovy submits that homicide is overwhelmingly a crime of proximity, violence between people who know each other or whose lives are economically and culturally intertwined. Even in large cities, rates of murder are disproportionally higher in neighborhoods that effectively function like small towns (usually poor neighborhoods with high population density and neighbors who know each other) or where groups of strangers are suddenly thrust together (in neighborhoods experiencing gentrification or population spikes). There's an argument to be made that these recent student killings and abductions in Bloomington may be a result of its disparate populations seeing more of each other up close than ever before.

But that is changing. Just as Bloomington's economy is refocusing on biotech (the city's second-largest job sector, according to the Bloomington Economic Development Corporation) and entrepreneurship (IU's Kelley School of Business has the nationally ranked Johnson Center for Entrepreneurship and Innovation), the town's main highway, N-37, is in the midst of being upgraded to Interstate 69 and will be completed in 2017. At that point, Bloomington will be connected via interstate highway to Indianapolis, Chicago, and, more so, the rest of America. What will happened then to the self-contained yet divided town seen in *Breaking Away*—"preppies" versus "cutters," but now just as much students from other states versus Indiana natives and locals—when a lot more of America and the world can come riding in?

In Lehi, Utah, a half-hour south of Salt Lake City, the Lehi Roller Mills has been family-owned and producing flour continuously since 1906. Situated at the corner of E Street and Main Street, Lehi Roller Mills gets its best reviews for their pancake and pastry mix, which they ship all over the world. Via their online store, you can also purchase a "Footloose Basket" for $39.99 that contains three baking flour mixtures, a bag of milk chocolate popcorn, and a *Footloose* DVD. Open the popcorn and pop in the DVD, and you'll see one of the few locations from *Footloose* (1984) still standing, which also happens to be the mill that just sent you the popcorn and the DVD. Lehi Roller Mills was where Kevin Bacon's character, Ren McCormack, had a part-time job and where, in the movie's climax, he would throw a senior prom for the small conservative town that had previously outlawed public dancing.

"I had no idea what kind of impact it would have," Sherman Robinson, the mill's third-generation owner, said of *Footloose* to the Deseret News in 2004. "We got calls from all over the world after the movie came out. We still have people come up and ask if they can take a picture on the front porch."

The mill's front porch appears in a pair of *Footloose*'s minor scenes. In the first, Ren McCormack stacks a few heavy bags of flour into a pile as his boss Andy (Timothy Scott) offers up his facility for a high school prom. The town Ren has moved to, Bomont, Illinois (actually Payson, Utah, a half-hour south of Lehi along Interstate 15), has outlawed public dancing for teenagers, but the mill lies across the Bomont city line. Ren, having convinced his chief opposition, Reverend Shaw Moore (John Lithgow), that a prom will not bring about any spiritual corruption, gets his classmates to convert the mill into a dance floor with twinkling lights, glitter ball, and balloons. In the movie's final scenes, Reverend Moore and his wife (Dianne Wiest) park their car across the road from the mill, which sits in an empty field. The Moores reminisce about being young themselves and falling in love as they gaze at the mill, converted into a senior prom, glowing warmly in the darkness.

The Lehi Roller Mills is one of the few locations from *Footloose* still standing. The warehouse where Kevin Bacon did his now-legendary angry dance (restaged brilliantly with the backstage crew of *Late Night with Jimmy Fallon* for the film's thirtieth birthday in 2014) closed in 2001. The Atchafalaya Nightclub in Provo, a.k.a. the county and western bar outside of town where Ren and friends sneak out earlier in the movie to go dancing, was torn down in 2010 to make way for the Utah Valley Convention Center. The hamburger stand where Reverend Moore's daughter Ariel (Lori Singer) defies the city's dance ban by turning up her boyfriend's boom box belonged to a now-extinct local chain called Hi-Spot. It's now a flower shop.

The Lehi Roller Mills continues on as the remaining landmark of *Footloose*, even if its surroundings are now completely different. Were Reverend and Mrs. Moore to look in on a senior prom happening at the mill today, they'd be sitting not on a country road but in a McDonald's parking lot. Over the mill's shoulder now, instead of an empty field, would be the warming glow of a Jiffy Lube.

Physically, there aren't enough locations left from *Footloose* to have a Footloose Day in Utah the same way, as we'll see in a moment, Astoria and Brownsville, Oregon, have Goonies Day and Stand by Me Day. But even if there were, a *Footloose* celebration would be less a pilgrimage than multi-stop road trip, which makes Lehi Roller Mills both the most significant piece of *Footloose* left standing and the one spot of a half dozen around America that could lay claim to representing the movie that launched Kevin Bacon's career, the song "Holding Out for a Hero," a Broadway musical, a 2011 remake, and the world's most famous angry warehouse dance.

Footloose may be the only movie in the story of Brat Pack America that has its own inset on the map.

That story begins in the small town of Elmore City, Oklahoma, population around seven hundred, an hour south of Oklahoma City. A livestock and ranching community, Elmore City hadn't allowed public dancing since the town's founding in 1861. It still had no bars, no movie theater, and one liquor store when, in 1980, the junior and senior class at Elmore City High School petitioned the school board to hold a prom. By a vote of three to two, the board said yes, and the prom with the theme "Stairway to Heaven" went off without a hitch in the school cafeteria. When the senior class of Elmore High School graduated that spring, they took the town's hundred-plus-year-old ban on public dancing with them.

The Elmore High School prom made national news and caught the attention of Dean Pitchford, who had just written the lyrics for the songs in the movie *Fame*. Pitchford took himself to Elmore City, interviewed residents and students, and wrote the screenplay that became *Footloose*.

In *Footloose*, Elmore City got its name changed to Bomont. For reasons I haven't been able to track down, even though the movie was filmed in Utah with mountains visible in several scenes, *Footloose* places Bomont in downstate Illinois, with Ren a Chicago kid from the big city a few hours north.

Jump to 2008, and Paramount, the studio that produced the original *Footloose*, decides to fast track a remake starring Zac Efron, hot off the *High School Musical* trilogy. The project lost its first director, choreographer Kenny Ortega, and Efron in 2009. Eventual director Craig Brewer (*Hustle and Flow*) came on soon after to punch up the screenplay. When given the directing job, the Memphis-based Brewer wanted to shoot in his home state, but the Georgia Film Music and Digital Entertainment Office came in with better tax breaks and easier location scouting through local tourism directors. Brewer then shot *Footloose* (2011) in the fall of 2010 in Acworth, Covington, Senoia, Franklin, and Atlanta, Georgia.

In the remake, Ren (Kenny Wormald) became a kid from Boston instead of Chicago (Wormald is originally from suburban Boston, but that's the only reason I've found for the switch), and Bomont, Illinois, became Bomont, Georgia. But in a backward-looking twist, when *Footloose* (2011) opened on October 14, 2011, it sold the most opening weekend tickets in the Salt Lake City market, where the first *Footloose* had been filmed nearly thirty years before.

To visit every place the story of *Footloose* has happened would require going to five states and a dozen cities and towns. The Lehi Roller Mills may be the place basking longest in the afterglow of the movie because it's still here. But take in the whole of *Footloose*—origin story, remakes, and all—and the mill becomes the brightest star in a constellation, not a moon against a dark sky.

In the spring of 2010, Elmore City High School marked the thirtieth anniversary of their historic prom by recreating the dance and inviting the class of 1980 back. Leonard Coffee and his high school girlfriend Mary Ann Temple-Lee, who lead the effort for the 1980 prom and served as the inspiration for Ren and Ariel in *Footloose*, were the grand marshalls of the town parade and guests of honor at the dance.

The 1980 prom had been called "Stairway to Heaven," with a slow dance to the Led Zeppelin anthem as the event's centerpiece. But it wasn't the highlight this time. The 2010 Elmore City High School prom remake opened with the Kenny Loggins tune "Footloose," the theme of the movie about what had happened in that cafeteria and in that town thirty years before.

In Astoria, Oregon, June 7 is now, by mayoral decree, Goonies Day. In the early summer of 2010, Mayor Willis L. Van Dusen made the announcement at a twenty-fifth anniversary celebration of *The Goonies* (1985), the beloved movie of a group of teenagers trying to save their neighborhood, called the Goondocks, from developers by hunting down an old pirate treasure, which shot for three weeks in Astoria in November of 1984.

"Whereas our beloved and world-famous movie *The Goonies* was directed by Richard Donner and produced by Steven Spielberg and filmed in Astoria in 1985..." the mayor, clad in a black tuxedo, began. "Whereas *The Goonies* has been entertaining millions worldwide for twenty-five years... And whereas *The Goonies,* through its story and style, is firmly a part of Astoria and its two-hundred-year history and an exciting part of our culture..." He then declared the day the movie opened in theaters back in 1985 a citywide holiday for the imagined home of "The Goondocks."

A few days later, Mayor Van Dusen cut the ribbon on the Oregon Film Museum at 732 Duane Street in Downtown Astoria. The museum celebrated the state's history in cinema and the movies—*Animal House, One Flew Over the Cuckoo's Nest, Mr. Holland's Opus,* and *Free Willy*—filmed there. The building once served as the Clatsop County Jail, and also starred in the opening jailbreak scene of *The Goonies.* The museum's largest permanent exhibition is simply called "Goonies Gallery."

"Yes, Lewis and Clark wintered here. Yes, we are the oldest American settlement west of the Rockies," laughed Regina Willkie, marketing manager for the Astoria Warrenton Area Chamber of Commerce and big boss of Goonies Day celebrations. "We're even home to the first movie filmed in Oregon that had a plot: *The Fisherman's Bride* in 1909. People visit Astoria for those reasons, too. But people love *The Goonies* and feel this need to see where it happened."

Before 2005, the year of *The Goonies'* twentieth birthday, Willkie told me that a few tourists each season would shyly inquire at the town's visitor center where they could find the jail or Mikey and Brand's house from the movie's opening moments. They'd even make their friends do it because they were embarrassed. Now, said Willkie, "they just march right in and ask."

The first ever Goonies Day was held the first weekend of June, 2005, right around the beginning of the town's regular tourist season, after a group of fans who came to know each other on

TheGoonies.org decided to have their first in-person meeting in Astoria and got in touch with the Chamber. Willkie and her team pulled the event together, which included a visit from Jeff B. Cohen, who played Chunk but now practices entertainment law and was in the midst of a college speaking tour called "Growing Up Goonie." Sean Astin, who played Mikey, happened to be in Portland on business and was a last-minute addition. Planned were bus tours and autograph sessions, but given only six months lead time, the organizers kept their expectations in check, crossed their figures, and hoped.

Nearly five thousand fans showed up. Since then, Astoria has put on a larger *Goonies* celebration at five-year intervals (an estimated fifteen thousand fans showed up in both 2010 and 2015), and offers self-guided tours and smaller events on the years in between. Visitors, Willkie told me, have come from all fifty states, every Canadian province, and nearly twenty foreign countries.

Originally a port city with a manufacturing base in timber and fish canning, Astoria also has mountains, seascapes, and historic significance that have made it a popular tourist destination since the 1980s and a Hollywood stand-in for a kind of beautiful yet hearty small town. In addition to *The Goonies, Kindergarten Cop* (1990), *Short Circuit* (1986), *Free Willy* (1993), and portions of Sean Penn's *Into the Wild* (2007) were filmed there. Astoria seems to be a go-to location for movies about normal people living unglamorous yet honest lives until, one day, something wondrous happens.

But there hasn't been cause for a *Kindergarten Cop* weekend or an *Into the Wild* day. Not yet, anyway.

"Compared to *The Goonies*, there isn't as much interest in the other films that were made here in Astoria," said Willkie. "We did have a small group of *Short Circuit* fans come to Astoria for a meet up a few years ago. We've talked about a celebration of all our Astoria films and could expand on Goonies Day."

"Astoria is the eighth Goonie," Jeff B. Cohen told a packed room at Goonies Day 2015. He's been to each of the five-year celebrations since 2005.

And yet, you can't ignore that *The Goonies* makes almost no mention of Astoria, and only about twenty minutes of the movie's plot actually take place there, the rest in underground caves, which were sets built on Warner Brothers soundstages in Burbank. Even the reason why the town was chosen as the home of the Goonies has been lost to time. ("No one remembers exactly why," Derek Hoffman, Vice President of *Goonies* director, Richard Donner's, company, told me. "But no one remembers when it wasn't, either.") Within the movie itself, Astoria gets referenced in a newspaper headline, when the kids read of the criminal gang named the Fratellis escaping from prison, and a sign in front of the Astoria Historical Society where Mikey and Brand's father works. At the end of the movie, Mikey and Brand's dad (Keith Walker) has the famous line about his kids "being home safe. That makes me the richest man in Astoria." That's about it.

The setting of *The Goonies* is nowhere near as obvious as other Brat Pack America movies like *Breaking Away*, which contains a speech from the mayor of Bloomington on what a great town Bloomington is, or *Mystic Pizza*, whose setting of Mystic, Connecticut, is right there in the title.

On the other hand, the setting of *The Goonies* isn't hidden behind a fictional name and state like in *Footloose*, which was filmed in Payson, Utah, but named Bomont, Illinois. Instead, Astoria in *The Goonies* lies somewhere between obvious and obscured, a detail that emerges from watching the movie repeatedly and nerding out over its finer points. Knowing Astoria as the location of the Goondocks then becomes a kind of merit badge of fandom. And since the town lies in the northwest corner of Oregon, across the Columbia River from Washington State, two hours' drive from the nearest airport in Portland, to go to Goonies Day and see where twenty minutes of a 114-minute movie happened earns the double fan cred of not just knowing where the Goondocks are in real life but the willingness to schlep there, too.

Erin Hensley, an accountant for an interior design firm in Los Angeles, has made the schlep three times. She first saw *The Goonies* on video at age twelve, and estimated to me that she'd watched the movie more than five hundred times by the time she attended Goonies Day in 2010.

"As the kid, I remember feeling like the movie really had everything—comedy, adventure, all the sections of the video store represented," she told me. "As an adult, *The Goonies* makes me feel like anything's possible. However unfeasible the way the Goonies saved the day, the movie tells you you're never too small to right wrongs, to stand up for what you believe in."

Hensley has a tattoo she got in Astoria at Goonies Day of the phrase "Never say die." I told Regina Willkie about this. She sounded delighted, but not the least bit surprised.

"We've had long discussions about why but never quite put our finger on it," she said, referring to the acts of devotion—dressing as the characters, marriage proposals during the celebration, tattoos—Goonies fans show by coming to Astoria, and why *The Goonies*, more than other films shot there, inspires them. The core audience, those aged ten to fourteen when the movie came out, Willkie said, had the benefit of *The Goonies* coming along in the early years of home video, meaning its memory had less chance of fading since it could be rewatched at birthday parties, sleepovers, and on rainy weekend afternoons. But even bigger than that is a theme we see over and over again on the map of Brat Pack America: visiting a movie place allows a fan not only to recreate their favorite parts of their favorite movie (for a photo, video, Facebook post, or just a story to tell later) but also to bring the *theme* of that movie to life. Coming to Astoria to see the locations of a movie about a treasure hunt *feels* like a treasure hunt. It's way easier to photograph yourself doing that than, say, befriending a whale like in *Free Willy*, or bringing a robot to life like in *Short Circuit*.

"Fans feel like this is a story that could actually happen. Many tell me about 'playing *Goonies*' when they were kids," said Willkie. Erin Hensley did this with her twin brother. The hit sitcom *The Goldbergs*, about a suburban Philadelphia family in the 1980s, anchored an episode to "playing *Goonies*" in March of 2014.

On the first night of the 2015 celebration, I met three childhood best friends from Winston-Salem, North Carolina. When they "played Goonies," they called themselves "the Boonies," since they lived way outside the center of town.

"Being here in Astoria is almost like playing *Goonies* in real life," Hensley told me when we met up at Goonies Weekend 2015. "The kids in the Goonies were a little rough around the edges, working class like real kids. The gadgets Data (Ke Huy Quan) built were all from stuff around the house!"

"I grew up a poor kid. Getting kicked out of your house was no joke," said Joshua Watts from Queen Creek, Arizona, whom I had coffee with on day three. His wife Jessica organizes a group trip of ten *Goonies* fans to share a house in Astoria and volunteer for Goonies Day every year.

"We're all Goonies here in Astoria," said Jessica. "But really, our time here isn't real until we visit the house."

"When I see the house and it's still there," Joshua said. "It's like I know the Goonies won."

The house they mean sits on a small hill in a cul-de-sac at the end of a dirt road on the northeast side of Astoria. The peaked roofs, white paint job, and wraparound porch are the same as in the film. The window trim is now black, not red. The fence that Chunk had to stand outside of until he did the "truffle shuffle" has been replaced by an arbor and flowerbeds.

In the movie, the house belongs to brothers Mikey and Brand (Sean Astin and Josh Brolin), where they and their friends find the treasure map in the attic that begins the adventure. It's also the physical representation, in wood, peaked roofs, and a wraparound porch, of "the Goondocks," the neighborhood in danger of being obliterated by a golf course, and, symbolically, the reason for their treasure hunt.

Fundamentally, as Willkie and several fans reminded me, *The Goonies* is a movie about loyalty and community, about not just saving a house but the very idea of home. That's the easiest explanation for why the house is far and away the most visited site from *The Goonies*, the place the entire movie is about saving.

But the Goonies House is also someone's actual home, not a movie set or a landmark preserved by the city. Sandi Preston, who lived in San Diego when *The Goonies* came out, bought the property in 2001. She and her children had loved the movie and Astoria reminded them of Eastport, Maine, near where Ms. Preston would visit her grandmother growing up. The Prestons were living in another part of Astoria when the house, which hadn't been lived in for some time, went up for sale.

"There was a lot of wood rot, many leaks, and it was just generally rundown and in poor condition," Sandi Preston wrote me in an email. "Raccoons came up through the rotted floor in back… I'd get wet walking up the stairs to the bedroom."

Back then, before Facebook or smartphones, only a few adventurous fans could find the location on an Astoria hillside—usually with some help from the visitor center or a local in the know. After the first Goonies Day celebration in 2005, the number of fans visiting the location grew beyond anything anyone would have guessed, Ms. Preston and Willkie included. And now those visitors can document their visit and share it with friends and strangers online. While the Chamber of Commerce and visitor center continues to advise *Goonies* pilgrims that the house is a private residence, not a public attraction, Ms. Preston has watched visitation go from maybe two hundred in a day after the first reunion, which she told me was "manageable," to 1,200 a day coming to do the truffle shuffle in her driveway.

"Most of the fans are kind, lovely people," Ms. Preston told the *Pittsburgh Post-Gazette*. One had a son who had died and *The Goonies* was his favorite movie. Ms. Preston let his mother scatter his ashes in the house's garden. Others have gotten engaged in front of the house then brought their children to see it years later. Ms. Preston loves those stories, too.

"At one time, I didn't lock my doors during the daytime," Ms. Preston wrote me. "In the early years, prior to the house being finished, I invited many in and allowed them to take pieces of wallpaper that was actually in the movie."

But lately too many haven't shown much respect for the spiritual home of the Goondocks. The sign at the base of the hill reading "Private Drive. Goonies on Foot Welcomed" keeps getting stolen. Fans loiter in the middle of the street and refuse to move when the neighbors drive up. Some visit Ms. Preston's house in the middle of the night. Others threaten her and her family when she asks them to leave or not use her lawn and flowerbeds as a public toilet.

"People have kicked my dogs, they leave their dogs' feces for me to pick up, throw their trash and cigarette butts for me to dispose of," she wrote. "They flip us off, shout obscenities, on and on. I haven't been able to garden or even sit on the porch and read without constant interruptions and noise."

Now the Goonies House has become a nightmare for Ms. Preston and a nuisance for the entire neighborhood.

"I've seen the impact of what's torn my community apart," Roger Warren, a neighbor, told *The Daily Astorian* six weeks after the thirtieth anniversary celebration.

"I think it's a cute movie, too," said Jodie Dittman, who lives at the other end of Thirty-Eighth Street. "But there's a real lack of respect. Some of us actually have to live here."

Having visited the Goonies House during the thirtieth anniversary celebration, I can vouch that the city, the Astoria Warrenton Chamber of Commerce, the neighborhood, and the homeowner have made a good faith effort at working together to allow fans to see it, and for Ms. Preston and her family not to have to live like zoo animals. The Chamber hired a flag crew during the celebration to direct traffic away from parking on the street. Residents have special permits so they can get in and out of the neighborhood without having to run over Goonies walking in the middle of the road. Fans coming down from the house shoo fans going up the hill to not stand in traffic or climb on the neighbors' porches and front steps. An enterprising kid on the street was running a refreshment stand. I can also vouch that her "Goondocks Lemonade" was delicious.

But I'd only been standing in front of the Goonies House for about twenty minutes on a beautiful summer afternoon when I saw the ugly face of fandom. Most of the fans that talked with me were parents with kids, who shared a few laughs about *The*

Goonies, took a picture, and left. An obnoxious few climbed on Ms. Preston's porch, attempted to open her windows or pry rocks up from the walkway. Three men in their early thirties set up expensive camera equipment on the front porch, lenses pointed inside the house.

I hope someone shooed them away. I probably should have yelled at them. But in that moment, the behavior of my fellow Goonies fans made me feel sick. I left as quickly as I could.

By mid-August 2015, two months after Goonies Day, Sandi Preston had enough. Writing on the 30th Anniversary Facebook Page, she said, "The [caliber] of people/generations is changing, and not for the better... We choose to have some privacy. It's been unrestricted for fourteen years and we are worn out."

Shortly after, Sean Astin posted the following on his own Facebook page.

> On behalf of all Goonies, I tell you that today, our home is under siege again. This time it's not real estate developers but fans of the film, most gracious, some obnoxious, who are threatening the peace of this sanctuary. To all who would journey to see her, 'the Goonies House' needs rescuing. She needs room to breathe from adoring fans and tactless and insensitive trespassers. It's ugly and unfair to take advantage of the goodwill of the private owners. The current owner of the Goonies House is entitled to respect and common courtesy. So, it's my childhood home, sort of, and I'm telling everyone to BACK OFF!!!

Now head up Duane Street on your way up the hill and you'll pass a sign reading, "Access Closed to Goonies House," rope, and "Private Property. No Trespassing. Absolutely No One!" warnings hung from trees around the cul-de-sac. The windows and front porch of the property have been draped in blue tarp, as if being fumigated for roaches.

"I've been deprived of the sunlight that I so enjoy, but even with that, it's better than having hundreds of rude and inconsiderate people on this postage stamp of property that is this hill, hurling trash and insults," Sandi Preston wrote me. "At least I've reclaimed some of my power."

The saga of the Goonies House is not over. Some fans have suggested the city buy it and turn it into a tourist attraction. Most understand that Ms. Preston has been far nicer about thousands of fans gawking at her home than she had to be, and respect her decision. A few think buying a house that's an icon of so many of their childhoods and then getting angry when they want to come see it is Ms. Preston being unreasonable.

I think their idea that being fans of a movie entitles them to invade another fan's privacy is unreasonable.

The Chamber of Commerce, in the short term, has encouraged visitors to look at the Goonies House from the Astoria Riverwalk on the north side of the hill, and asked the conductors on the Astoria River Trolley to discourage tourists from visiting. Meanwhile, come next June, it's Goonies Day again, and then what?

"It's a really difficult problem, and I think that it's going to take some time to cure," Astoria City Councilor Russ Warr told a city council meeting that summer. "But the city and the chamber together are working very hard to try to figure out what to do with it." At the same time, Councilor Warr admitted there's only so much they can do. The house is private property. The street it sits on is a public thoroughfare, and "we can't stop people from using a public thoroughfare."

As of this writing, Ms. Preston and her neighbors have petitioned for a portion of the street to be made a private road, but they need approval from the city attorney's office for this to happen. The Chamber of Commerce has also removed the name "Goonies House" from Google Maps and create a viewing area where fans can see the residence but not walk right up to it.

On my first night in Astoria, I met a musician named Manuel and his girlfriend Irene, who'd come to Astoria from Madrid. They'd chosen this weekend for their first trip to the US as a kind of "freak honeymoon."

"Being in Astoria is a lucid dream, something from our childhood that binds us as a couple," he told me. "We would have given anything to be here."

The love for *The Goonies* and the town that holds its memories that Manuel, Irene, and everyone I met at Goonies Weekend have is both intense and gentle. To the one, they were horrified at what had become of Sandi Preston's privacy and peace of mind. They offered support to her, to Regina Willkie and her team in the form of money, time, and effort to reach a fair and equitable solution. I can only hope that once a solution exists, there is still a Goonies Weekend that represents not just how devoted fans are, but also how good the devoted can be to the extended family and the spiritual home of *The Goonies*, too.

About three hours south of Astoria, in Brownsville, Oregon, a group of dedicated community volunteers has, since 2007, put on a celebration of *Stand by Me*, which was filmed there in the summer of 1985. Linda McCormick, who had moved to town only a few years before, had begun volunteering with the Chamber of Commerce, and her colleagues noticed fans were coming to the small town of about 1,600 to see how much it still looked like the fictional "Castle Rock, Oregon" in 1959, where *Stand by Me* took place. Many wanted to visit the tree where the four main characters had their tree house. Others wanted to pick a penny up at the same street corner where the character Vern (Jerry O'Connell) finds a penny in the film's closing scenes.

Then a call came. The Austin-based Alamo Drafthouse movie theater chain wanted to do a screening of *Stand by Me* in Brownsville the following summer. The Alamo was on its third season of showing movies in the places where they happened and didn't do anything halfway. A screening of *Repo Man* (1984) happened next to the Sixth Avenue Bridge in Los Angeles and gave away a replica of the movie's famous vintage Chevy Malibu. A screening of *The Warriors* (1979) in New York included a scavenger hunt, where volunteers dressed in gang colors chased the participants around town. So when the Alamo brought *Stand by Me* to Brownsville, the event included a sock hop, a classic car cruise-in complete with the actual Studebaker from the movie, and a blueberry pie eating contest. Because why screw around?

"The audience can immerse themselves in the aesthetic of the movie," said Zack Carlson, who worked in programming for the Alamo back then. "When you're in that place, fiction gains power and memory gains power."

Linda McCormick and her colleagues were the Alamo's on-the-scene partners. Two other volunteers at the Chamber of Commerce had already been helping out with *Stand by Me*–related tourism and, as Ms. McCormick told me over the phone, "I was there to help them." Then a local newspaper ran an article about the *Stand by Me* screening and mislabeled McCormick the event's chairman. So she took on the job mistakenly assigned to her by the media.

"That's what happens when you volunteer in a small town," laughed McCormick, in better spirits than I would be about it.

From 2007–2011, McCormick and a group of volunteers picked a weekend in the summer to celebrate *Stand by Me*. But after four years, her team was getting burned out. Unlike Goonies Day in Astoria, Stand by Me Day had been volunteer-based from the start, not run by a city agency. With a population one-fifth the size of Astoria, Brownsville/Castle Rock's celebration has always been scrappier and a bit more homemade than their counterpart to the north.

"I ask them a lot for ideas," said McCormick. "They've already done what we're trying to do, but bigger."

The organizers' choice of July 23 as the day of the official celebration (for logistical, not symbolic, reasons—*Stand by Me*'s actual release date was August 8) gave them a standing date to set up partnerships with many of the same local businesses who complained thirty years ago that the movie crews hurt revenue by shutting down the streets downtown. Now, says McCormick, "they embrace the whole thing."

Loyalists of *Stand by Me* have come to the celebration from as far as New Zealand, Germany, Italy, and Spain. Japan sends more fans than any foreign country, who seem, said McCormick, to be fascinated by America in the 1950s. An enterprising native speaker has created a small business of picking up Japanese visitors at the airport and driving them around to *Stand by Me* locations in Eugene, Cottage Grove, and Veneta, Oregon, before depositing them in Brownsville for the celebration.

By far the most-visited site from the movie, McCormick reports, is the tree that contained the four boys' tree house, where they first get the idea to go looking for a dead body. "It's in someone's backyard now, but he's pretty nice about having people visit and take pictures," McCormack said. The dirt path where we see Chris Chambers (River Phoenix) for the last time also stands on private property. The house where Vern hides a jar of pennies under the front porch gets frequent regular visits from fans asking if they can bury something under the porch, too. So many people wanted pictures of themselves picking up pennies at the intersection where Vern finds one at the end of the movie that someone finally embedded a 1959 penny in the crosswalk at that very spot.

"It's jumping into a painting or your favorite book. Kind of like Mary Poppins," Dominic Pace, a character actor from Los Angeles who has visited over 250 movie locations but made a special point of coming to Brownsville to celebrate his ten-year wedding anniversary, wrote me in an email. "You need to have a bit of an imagination, but if you do, the feeling is quite amazing."

"Brownsville is such a picturesque, adorable, one-stoplight town. Practically nothing had changed since the filming," Kerri Avenengo, a veterinary technician from Portland, wrote me. "Walking across the bridge into town, I remember getting goosebumps thinking, 'River Phoenix walked across this very bridge… It's really sad thinking of how Chris loses his life, and of course how River lost his life at such a young age.'"

Many of the fan rituals that happen at *Stand by Me* Day we've seen elsewhere. People arrive wearing costumes, show off tattoos inspired by the movie (Kerri Avenengo has a large piece of the movie's four main characters walking alongside the Royal River across her back), take pictures and videos of themselves at the movie's key locations. McCormick told me about an eleven-year-old girl from Missouri (born five years after the movie came out) who got fake glasses right before the event so she could look like Corey Feldman's bespectacled character Teddy Duchamp. Another young woman from Japan wanted a picture of herself leaning out the window of Gordie's (Wil Wheaton's) house at 352 Fisher Street, just as Gordie does in the opening moments of the film. McCormick called the homeowner and he volunteered to put a stepstool next to his kitchen sink at the window so the young fan could photographically insert herself into her favorite scene from her favorite movie.

The love for *Stand by Me* is enormous. Yet for the time being, *Stand by Me* Day remains small and hands-on enough for McCormick and her volunteers to perform these acts of kindness themselves. It's unclear whether the event will grow or whether its current staff could support it growing by much.

Stand by Me is also a very different movie than *The Goonies,* even though both take place in small Oregon towns and have Corey Feldman as a mouthy sidekick. *The Goonies* is ultimately a happy-ending story of friendship and loyalty ("Goonies never say die!"). *Stand by Me* is also story of friendship and loyalty, but living inside a sad meditation on how growing up means losing people we love. It begins and ends with death, and in the middle the four friends search for the dead body of a kid their own age. Unlike *The Goonies,* which derives much of its fan love from the idea that the story *could* happen, *Stand by Me* is told from the point of view of an adult man in flashback, a story that has happened long ago.

Stand by Me's most quoted line may be Vern's claim that his favorite food is "cherry-flavored Pez. No question." After the movie had been a box office hit, the Pez line got a place of honor on a version of the movie's poster. But *Stand by Me*'s "Goonies never say die!"—the piece of dialogue that captures the film's soul—is the heartbreaker Gordie writes down in the last scene.

"I never had any friends later on like the ones I had when I was twelve. Jesus, does anyone?"

If visiting the site of one's favorite movie resembles, as Domonic Pace put it, "jumping into a painting or into one's favorite book," it matters how doing that makes us feel. And *Stand by Me* is a movie of great beauty and warmth, but also a painful story of death and loss.

"The characters of *The Goonies* and *Stand by Me* were, in a way, my own friends. I had always put myself in the mischievous adventures of both films," Avenengo, who used to live in Astoria and been to the celebrations for both movies, told me in an email. But *The Goonies* holds a special place in her heart, she wrote, thanks to its "sense of abandonment and adventure." *Stand by Me* she feels equally close to, but as a "coming-of-age lesson" that "makes me feel some deeply sad pitted feeling every time I watch it."

Stand by Me fans are just as loyal as *The Goonies'*. McCormick told me about one fan she met that owned a railroad tie from the bridge where the four boys are almost run down by a train (she didn't ask how he got it). Another came all the way to a *Stand by Me* Day from Australia, and confided to her that what he really wanted most in the world was a picture of himself under a streetlight from his favorite scene in the movie. "I've waited a long time to touch this lamppost," he told her, then fell dead silent in the summer heat on a street corner thousands of miles from home.

"The reality of being in charge of this took a little while to understand," said McCormick. "But I love helping people. The most empowering thing for me is to make someone's day… It's a gift that I get to give, and their smiles give it right back."

But the smaller size and quieter timbre of its celebration demonstrates that Stand by Me Day isn't so much a showcase of fandom (in both its beauty and ugliness) but a modest tribute to the hard work and hospitality of the citizens of "Castle Rock" and the gratitude of those who benefit from it.

That may also better suit the quieter movie *Stand by Me* is. As Gordie reminds his friends when they set off to find the missing corpse of boy their own age…

"Maybe going to find a dead kid shouldn't be a party."

On February 25, 2015, a fan from New Zealand posted a video of himself in Brownsville during the previous year's celebration called "*Stand by Me*: Lost and Found." In it, he sits in front of the *Stand by Me* tree wearing a green T-shirt with the words "Gordie, Chris, Teddy, and Vern" printed on it. He then tells us that there were three objects lost in the movie—Gordie's Yankee hat, Vern's comb, and Vern's jar of pennies. In tribute to the movie he loves, he leaves a jar of pennies and a comb under the tree that contained their tree house all those years ago. The song playing while this happens is John Waite's 1984 ballad "Missing You."

IN MYSTIC, CONNECTICUT, THE last few years have not been good ones for the Mystic Pizza restaurant at the corner of Main and Bank Streets. In the fall of 2014, the US Department of Labor ordered owner John Zelepos to pay $105,000 in back pay to employees after three of them filed complaints. DOL investigators had discovered that Zelepos had, between 2012–2014, paid 110 of his workers less than minimum wage and failed to compensate them for overtime. In April of 2015, Zelepos also plead guilty to income tax evasion after prosecutors demonstrated that, between 2006–2010, he diverted over a half million dollars he owed the government into his own bank account and those of family members. In August of 2015, John Zelepos, the second-generation owner of arguably America's most famous pizza parlor, was sentenced to a year in prison.

The irony here lies pretty thick. The Mystic Pizza restaurant owes its success and fame to the movie *Mystic Pizza* (1988), a coming-of-age story about three waitresses (Lili Taylor, Annabeth Gish, and, in her breakout role, Julia Roberts) who work at a pizza parlor in the seaside town of Mystic in southeast Connecticut. Two are sisters and all three are from working-class Portuguese-American families, looking across the counter and out the door into adulthood. Their no-nonsense boss Leona (Conchata Ferrell, long before her twelve-season run as Berta the housekeeper on *Two and a Half Men*) takes no shit and tells them to move their tails when customers are waiting. But in the end she gives

Kat (Annabeth Gish) money for college and offers to leave the restaurant to Jojo (Lili Taylor). "We're not going to have children," Leona tells the three. "You girls. You're my kids."

Let's think about that. *Mystic Pizza* ends with the owner of the pizza joint assuring a financial future for her employees. The real-life Mystic Pizza restaurant the movie made famous (and presumably rich) just admitted in court to cheating their employees out of theirs.

To understand what happened to the real-life Mystic Pizza restaurant means digging and trying to understand the phrase "tourist trap." The "trap" in "tourist trap" gets reserved for businesses and institutions that exploit romantic notions of a place for their own gain, stealing a sensation or a memory, then marketing a cut-rate version of it to a visitor who doesn't know any better.

Does the M&M store in Times Square sell an overpriced candy dispenser by piggybacking on the idea of New York as the capitol of world entertainment and fun? Does Fisherman's Wharf in San Francisco get to mint money from second-rate bowls of clam chowder based on the moldy idea of the city as a working fishing port? They do, and that's also why we call them tourist traps. Parisians might not drop by the Eiffel Tower every weekend, but the Eiffel Tower is thought of as a tourist trap far less than, say, Faneuil Hall in Boston. Faneuil Hall wants you to open your wallet while in a phony dream of stepping back into Revolutionary War times. The Eiffel Tower is just sitting there, being the Eiffel Tower. It's a place tourists go, sure. But it's not being dishonest, not promising a trip back to the 1889 World's Fair for which it was built. The Eiffel Tower is a place that tourists visit, but not a "tourist trap."

Is the Mystic Pizza parlor just sitting there being itself, growing when it had to in order to meet demand, but still serving up, as Leona said defiantly in the movie, "The real thing right here. The mystic pizza!" Or did the real-life Mystic Pizza get a lucky break almost thirty years ago and has been milking it since? Is it a place that tourists visit or a tourist trap? Have they been stewards of their fame, generated by nostalgia for the movie that shares their name, or have they choked on it?

Are they an Eiffel Tower or an M&M store?

The issue might be (I'm sorry) a matter of taste. *Mystic Pizza*'s primary subplot hinges upon Leona's unwillingness to share her secret sauce formula with Jojo, who has dreams of taking over the restaurant when her boss retires, and a visitation by an imperious food critic (Louis Turenne) who loves trashing local dining establishments. It's not the most important or memorable part of *Mystic Pizza*, but the movie still devotes plenty of time to how good Mystic Pizza tastes. It's fair to ask, do visitors eat at the Mystic Pizza restaurant from all over the world just to sit in a mock-up of one of their favorite movies? Or do they hope some of Leona's magic got baked into their slices, too?

Mystic Pizza was called "Ted's Pizza" when Stefanos Zelepos bought the business in 1973 and changed the name. His son John started working there at age ten. One of their customers was a screenwriter named Amy Holden Jones, who had grown up vacationing in Mystic with her family. Jones used the pizza parlor as an anchor for her story, which began filming in Mystic and a few surrounding towns on Columbus Day, 1987.

"I didn't know they were the girls in the movie," John Zelepos told the Associated Press in 2000. The three lead actresses, none of whom were movie stars yet, ate dinner at his restaurant during filming. Zelepos had to tell them no when they came into the restaurant, ordered drinks, and couldn't produce ID.

Director Donald Petrie used the exteriors of the restaurant during principal photography, but Mystic Pizza's interior was too small for the movie's crew, and to shoot there meant closing the business for six months. Zelepos couldn't afford to do this, so the pizza parlor, with the plants in porcelain urns and the red-and-white-checkered floors we know so well, was a studio set built in the nearby town of Stonington.

Mystic Pizza came to movie theaters October 21, 1988, and was a modest hit. But soon after, the restaurant's owners noticed "the weekends started getting busier and busier." During the summer months, visitors came from all over the country and waited in lines out the door.

"I couldn't keep anything with our name on it on the tables anymore," John Zelepos told the Associated Press. "Salt and pepper packets. They disappeared… Beer glasses with our name on them. They disappeared."

The Zeleposes saw an opportunity, and remodeled the interior of their restaurant to resemble the pizza parlor in the movie. In a meta-move, photos of the movie about a pizza parlor adorn the walls of the actual pizza parlor that inspired the movie, which now looks like a set from the movie it once inspired.

The original restaurant expanded in 1996, opened a second location in North Stonington in 1998, and by 2008 had licensed a line of frozen Mystic Pizzas. The "Little Slice of Heaven" T-shirts seen in the movie are sold as souvenirs, along with copies of the movie on DVD. The movie plays on repeat on the restaurant's televisions.

"I can almost make a living on merchandise alone, without any food," Zelepos told the Associated Press. The secret sauce, the movie's chief subplot, Zelepos reported, isn't a secret at all. "It's just basic ingredients—garlics, salt, stuff like that."

Is the pizza any good? As of this writing, Yelp reviews average three and a half out of five stars, with the positives split pretty evenly between loving the food (the mozzarella sticks and onion rings score particularly high), the restaurant being family friendly, and, as one put it, "It's all about being there and hoping Julia Roberts serves you pizza." The negative reviews focus on the pizza not delivering on the hype created by the movies. It's also clear that, by a wide margin, the reviewers are not Mystic residents but visiting from out of town.

Some of that makes sense. Mystic has always been a tourist destination, with a world-famous aquarium and seaport and an economy dependent on summer visitors. Fishing and lobster boats are the business of nearby Stonington, but the movie fudges that detail and locates them around the corner from Mystic Pizza. Kat and Daisy's mother, as well as Jojo's fiancé Bill, all work on the docks. In real life, though, Mystic's economy has always been geared toward visitors, not local industry.

"Mystic has always been a picture-postcard New England town, a Stars Hollow by the Sea," said Melissa Chipman, a Louisville-based journalist who moved to Mystic at age thirteen, the same year the movie came out. "I think it's hard to say if *Mystic Pizza* had much to do with how chic Mystic has become, but the movie put us on the map. There are two Mystic exits on I-95 between Boston and NYC. I'm sure there has been many a driver who has seen those signs and decided to pull off the highway because of the movie." But, as Chipman clarified when we spoke on the phone, the film made the Mystic Pizza restaurant "a landmark, but not a beloved local institution."

"I think the movie did a great job capturing the Mystic of my youth. I was definitely a Kat," said Chipman, "a supernerd from a lower-middle-class family. I always worked service jobs all throughout high school. Not to mention that my family is Portuguese." In the movie, Kat gets a part-time babysitting job for the young daughter of an architect who's in the middle of remodeling a house. In real life, the house belonged to the grandparents of Chipman's ninth-grade boyfriend.

But Chipman separates that praise from the restaurant at the movie's center. "My go-to pizza places were and still are Avanti's (about a mile east of Mystic) and Angie's (about five blocks away)."

"It's kind of an ironic thing to say, but Mystic Pizza the restaurant seems out of place in Mystic itself," said resident Nat Bulkley, an internal consultant for the pharmaceutical industry (and, full disclosure, my childhood babysitter), who moved there with his family in 2008. "The attractions of Mystic are of an old seaport town and an aquarium that shows the wonder of the ocean, something permanent and enduring. A restaurant commemorating its own role in a movie from a few decades ago," Bulkley said, "doesn't really jive."

"It's always cool to see a film of a place you know," Bulkley continued. He saw (and enjoyed) *Mystic Pizza* for the first time shortly after moving to town. "And Mystic isn't that big. You can't miss the restaurant." But in his seven years of living there, Bulkley hasn't gone himself yet, or taken his wife and young son.

"It feels like the Hard Rock Café, standing in for something rather than being the real deal. If you feel nostalgic for the movie, you might feel different than me. I know that's what they are catering to. Whereas if you live here..." He trails off as if to say, "I think you understand." And I do. I live in San Francisco and don't feel the need to eat at any restaurant with the words "cable car" in the name.

Bulkley and I grew up in Ann Arbor, Michigan, the birthplace of Domino's Pizza. That meant pizza at every birthday party, potluck, or ice cream social you attended, and it's pretty much impossible to be from Ann Arbor and not acquire a taste for the stuff. I swear by Escape from New York Pizza on Haight Street in San Francisco. Nathan Bulkley has lived in the Northeast, and sampled pizza from all over. In Connecticut, he alone endorses Pizzetta's Pizzeria, also in Mystic (Pizzetta refurnished an old fire truck and uses it to make and sell its pies at public events) and Pepe's Pizza, an hour to the west in New Haven.

"There's four to five really good pizza places in any of the counties in the state," he tells me. "Nobody around here talks about needing to go into Mystic Pizza."

What happened to the restaurant made famous by a movie? Was there too much fame, leading to too much money that the Zeleposes couldn't resist? Zelepos, now in prison, has refused comment (my emails and phone messages to the restaurant were not returned). But I do wonder if he took in the real messages of the movie that changed his life—loyalty, friendship, hard work, and honesty. I don't think he's dreaming when, on their website, his business calls itself "the most famous pizza house in America." But the picture of him on that website isn't in front of a pizza oven or over a vat of sauce, but next to a glass case of merchandise. His story and that of the real-life Mystic Pizza leaves me asking, would Leona or her girls want their original Mystic Pizza to have become famous this way?

The Santa Cruz Beach Boardwalk in Santa Cruz, California, a forty-minute drive from Silicon Valley and an hour and a half down the coast from San Francisco, is the state's oldest surviving amusement park. Operating continuously since 1907, the park is California Historical Landmark #983. Its most famous roller coaster, the Giant Dipper, has been named a National Historic Landmark.

As one of defining locations of the area, dozens of commercials and television shows have been filmed on the Boardwalk. In movies, it's been featured in the counterculture classic *Harold and Maude* (1971), the Dirty Harry thriller *Sudden Impact* (1983), the schlock horror favorite *Killer Klowns from Outer Space* (1988), and the surfing biopic *Chasing Mavericks* (2012).

Since 2010, the Santa Cruz Beach Boardwalk has shown movies every summer Friday on a giant outdoor screen hung over the beach. Hundreds show up with blankets and folding chairs to take in a movie with sand under their feet and a star-filled sky overhead.

Every year, the same movie has opened the Santa Cruz Beach Boardwalk's summer film season. And it's not *Harold and Maude* or *Dirty Harry* or biographies of surfing legends or a horror movie about Killer Klowns. Instead, it's an eighties teen tale about a family who moves to Santa Cruz, only to find it crawling with teenage vampires.

Every year, *The Lost Boys* (1987), filmed on the Boardwalk in the late spring of 1986, opens the Boardwalk's summer movie season. *Will it always?* I asked Marq Lipton, VP of marketing for the park, when I visited his office the day of the summer 2014 season. "Ask me tomorrow," he told me. Karley Pope, director of promotions, waves her hand and smiles. "Yes, for the foreseeable future."

I went to the screening that evening and couldn't find a seat. Kids, teenagers, parents, and grandparents covered every inch of beach and all the staircases leading down from the Boardwalk to the sand. On the screen about seventy feet high was a movie from the time of Brat Pack America, playing at its exact point on the map of Brat Pack America. The crowd filled in where, twenty-nine years before, a gang of vampires went racing down the surf on motorcycles.

Considered a box office disappointment when it came out in August of 1987, *The Lost Boys* now ranks as both a cult classic and *the* Santa Cruz movie. It's great, silly fun, not much more, but so are plenty of teen movies from the 1980s that didn't outlive the decade. *The Lost Boys* survives thanks to vampires, which seem to come back into vogue about once a decade, the career renaissance of one of its lead actors, Kiefer Sutherland (who now cannot be separated from Jack Bauer, his character on the TV series *24*), and its unbreakable bond to an amusement park you can still visit.

Many of the places on our map of Brat Pack America you can't visit. They've been torn down, built over, or look nothing like they did in the movies from this time. The Santa Cruz Beach Boardwalk looks very much the same as it did in *The Lost Boys*. Any fan can make a snarling vampire face or make motorcycle noises bumping down the concrete steps (I did both of these things). Around thirty-five Yelp reviews of the Boardwalk mention *The Lost Boys* nearly three decades after the fact.

It seems part of this flop from 1987's hold on the present is that you can still visit its most recognizable setting and interact with it much as the characters in the movie did.

The Lost Boys filmed on the Santa Cruz Beach Boardwalk in May of 1986, a moment in time between two changes that altered Santa Cruz forever. Historically a conservative beach community, the University of California at Santa Cruz opened in 1965, bringing a flood of young people and progressive politics to town. A flood of young people usually comes with a few creeps that prey on young people. Two serial killers, unknown to one another, terrorized Santa Cruz from 1971–1973, one specifically preying on college students.

When District Attorney Peter Chang offhandedly called the town "Murderville, USA," a reporter picked it up and sent it to wire service as "Santa Cruz: Murder Capital of the World." The fictional town Santa Carla in *The Lost Boys* also calls itself "the Murder Capital of the World." But by then, Santa Cruz had shaken that reputation. Known primarily in the sixties and seventies as a bit of wild hippie surfing town, due to the growth of the Silicon Valley economy and Santa Cruz's reasonable commute distance (thirty miles south on Highway 17), the 1980s saw an influx of money and well-paid workers from companies like Apple and Silicon Graphics. *The Lost Boys* in 1987 used a nickname for Santa Cruz outgrown at least a decade before.

"We were always a commuter town," Elijah Mowbray, a civil engineer with the City of Santa Cruz who grew up in town, wrote me in an email. "But with what would become one of the largest economies in the world just over the hill? That will drive things."

That economic tractor beam of Silicon Valley had already begun to pull on Santa Cruz when *The Lost Boys* came to town. Three years later, in 1989, the Loma Prieta earthquake, with its epicenter in the Santa Cruz Mountains, struck on October 17 at 5:04 p.m. Nearly seventy people died, nearly four thousand injured throughout the region. Much of downtown Santa Cruz lay in piles of rubble. The 6.9 quake destroyed the beach bandstand seen at the beginning of *The Lost Boys* and damaged the exterior wall of the Boardwalk's indoor pool, the Plunge, which, fortunately, was in the middle of being removed from the park altogether. As a result, watching *The Lost Boys* now we see not just a moment before everything changed in Santa Cruz (the city's entire downtown had to be rebuilt after the earthquake), but in the physical body of the Boardwalk how little has changed. That the Boardwalk in *The Lost Boys* still looks a lot like it did reminds us that a Santa Cruz icon and the movie's iconic location just a few years later narrowly escaped disaster.

The Lost Boys opens on a nighttime tracking shot across the Pacific Ocean (a favorite of director Joel Schumacher's; he'd use it again to open *Flatliners* in 1990) landing on the Boardwalk, roller coasters and ride glowing with gaudy sensuality in the darkness. We see David (Kiefer Sutherland) and his four friends dressed like a Duran Duran motorcycle gang, watching the historic carousel go around. A security guard tells them to beat it. "Okay, boys," David says. One scene later, the Boardwalk's lights go dark, the security guard walks to his car in the Boardwalk's now empty parking lot, then vanishes.

Lights up on the next day as the credits roll over a montage of "Santa Carla" (the city of Santa Cruz didn't want to be associated with a movie about teenage vampires and did not allow use of their name). The music playing is a cover of "People Are Strange" by The Doors. Strange people seem to occupy every corner, if you consider kids with piercings and tattoos strange (I'm not even sure they were in 1987, but anyway). There are several close-ups of missing children posters. Schumacher mentions in the movie's DVD commentary that the posters were not props but real, and his crew simply filmed them as they were. We then zoom in on the Anderson family, a mother (Dianne Weist) and two teenage brothers, Michael and Sam (Jason Patric and Corey Haim), who are moving to town to live with their grandfather (Barnard Hughes).

"Grandpa, is it true that Santa Carla is the murder capital of the world?" they ask him after seeing a pronouncement to that effect spray-painted on the back of a billboard.

"Well now, let me put it this way," he says. "If all the corpses buried around here were to stand up all at once, we'd have one hell of a population problem."

The city of Santa Cruz received the nickname "murder capital of the world" in the early 1970s. Although some film critics have made a connection between that time in Santa Cruz history and *The Lost Boys* borrowing the phrase a decade later, by all accounts there isn't one to be made.

"We hung out downtown without parents, went to the beach without parents, rode our bikes at night, no problem," wrote Elijah Mowbray, who at age fifteen was an extra in the movie. The idea that Santa Cruz at that time was as scary and dangerous as *The Lost Boys* says Santa Carla is, Mowbray told me, was a fiction of moviemaking.

"*The Lost Boys* is a scary movie with a wink and a nod," said Christina Glynn of the Santa Cruz County Film Commission, when I spoke to her over the phone. "The Boardwalk, which has entertained generations, and the thousands of people who come see the movie there every summer are a reminder that it's all in good fun."

Joel Schumacher also mentions in his DVD commentary that he knew Santa Cruz was the perfect location for his version of a vampire movie the moment he saw the lights of the Santa Cruz Beach Boardwalk throbbing against the night sky and the fog rolling off the cliffs that surround it.

"I knew this is exactly where I'd want to hang out if I were a teenage vampire at this time… But the city wanted the Boardwalk to attract children and families."

What I hear Schumacher saying, by not quite saying it, is that the Boardwalk works so well for *The Lost Boys* because we associate amusement parks both with childhood and childhood fears. Which made it perfect for the needs of his movie, and perfectly objectionable to the City of Santa Cruz. I understand where the city was coming from, but, cutting right to it, does anyone film anything in Santa Cruz *without* using the Boardwalk? That sounds like shooting a movie in Seattle and leaving out the Space Needle.

There's also another way to look at *The Lost Boys* and fear. If we accept that horror movies are usually a reflection of what scares us at any at any one time in history, what scared us in the summer of 1987? Nuclear war? Russians? AIDS? Let's also throw in the memory of the 1960s, which we talked about in Chapter 5.

So many eighties teen movies took place during the Eisenhower era as a way of erasing the memory of the Kennedy and Johnson eras. Is it possible that Santa Carla, one-time murder capital of the world, seaside hamlet where the town anthem seems to be "People Are Strange," is a freaks' paradise turned rotten, a hangover from the 1960s, where a nest of vampires can hide in plain sight at the town's amusement park because no one other than a suspicious grandfather notices or cares anymore? Is the haunting of Santa Carla's family entertainment centerpiece *The Lost Boys* making smart use of a location associated with families and children, or does the movie also derive fright by showing a family entertainment destination overrun by freaks and bloodsuckers?

Either way, the very fact we remember *The Lost Boys* all these years later seems inseparable from its time spent on the Santa Cruz Beach Boardwalk. The Santa Cruz Beach Boardwalk, 109 years old this year and still thriving, and *The Lost Boys* combine for the best use of an amusement park in the teen movies of the 1980s, and the most prominent "point of interest" marker on the map of Brat Pack America. The Boardwalk may give *The Lost Boys* its iconic look just by being a legendary amusement park, but it also shades and deepens both the movie's plot and its moment in the city's history. The Boardwalk's staying power and how little it has changed makes *The Lost Boys* seem less like a time capsule and more like a movie that comes from both the past and the near present.

That staying power has spilled over to other *Lost Boys* locations, too: The Atlantis Fantasyworld comic book shop, in Santa Cruz since 1974, acted as the store where Corey Haim finds out Santa Carla is infested with vampires. A copy of the comic book *Vampires Everywhere*, used as a visual aid in the scene, now hangs on the wall of the store.

Atlantis Fantasyworld (1020 Cedar Street at Union Street, downtown) had all of about five minutes of screen time in *The Lost Boys* and has changed addresses three times since then (the original location, blocks south on Pacific Avenue, perished in the 1989 Loma Prieta earthquake). But owner Joe Ferrara told me when I visited the store last summer that "no more than two days goes by without someone coming in, asking about the movie or us taking that comic down so someone from Belgium can get their picture taken with it."

"The guy on Monday was actually from Italy," Nate, the inventory manager, interjected.

The Santa Cruz Beach Boardwalk's willingness to honor a movie filmed there nearly three decades ago by effectively opening its high season with it demonstrates not only this collapsing of past and present but that *The Lost Boys* has passed from being frightening into an afterlife of nostalgic fun. Maybe I'm wrong, but it seems hard to be scared by a movie when you can turn your head, look away from it, and see the exact place it was made. Isn't that the same as pulling back the curtain on the Wizard of Oz?

For the foreseeable future, then, at the beginning of every summer, a fan can simply walk onto the Boardwalk, settle into the sand, and fear not the dark but feel charmed to share it with vampires.

The DeLorean has picked us up on the beach in Santa Cruz and dropped us off back here in the twenty-first century. I've got an important question for you…

CHAPTER 10: "WHERE WE'RE GOING, WE DON'T NEED ROADS"

The Brat Pack America of Today

H AS OUR TRIP REALLY been all about nostalgia? Have the last few hundred pages, visiting movies from long ago as well as the landmarks they created, been just an excuse to sigh ceaselessly into the past? Are your Shermer, Illinois; *Lost Boys* Boardwalks; and *Stand by Me* Day celebrations just memory triggers and collectibles from long ago, not much different than a Goonies lunch box or a Mr. Miyagi bobblehead?

I sure hope not. Nostalgia is not a harmless instinct, and the sentence beginning with "Remember when..." often has bitterness right behind it. Because when someone answers, "Oh yeah," to "remember when," it's a quick move from there to how times were more innocent/simpler/better back then, followed by another sigh, knowing those times are gone, and—lacking a plutonium-powered DeLorean—will never come back. By sighing and saying, "Remember when" too many times, one can fall into the trap of believing the present holds nothing sacred, the past nothing profane.

Our friends and heroes from the movies of Brat Pack America understood this as a lie. "Whether you avoid the future or not, it happens," Duckie tells Andie in *Pretty in Pink,* a few months before their prom, graduation, and the beginning of adulthood. "When you get old, your heart dies," Allison tells the other four members of *The Breakfast Club,* which earns its triumphal ending because, it part, we believe the five new friends are going to try not to let this death of the heart happen to them. "Don't you realize?" Mikey says to his fellow *Goonies,* "the next time you see sky, it'll be over another town. The next time you take a test, it'll be in some other school." The very future of the Goondocks depends not on memory or nostalgia but on right now. Because as we all know, "Down here it's our time."

Mikey and his friends do find the treasure and save the Goondocks, but the adventure still ends. Josh Brolin, who made his movie debut at age seventeen playing Mikey's older brother Brand, is now forty-seven, has two ex-wives, and an Oscar nomination to his credit. Mikey (Sean Astin) has three daughters, the oldest of whom just enrolled at Harvard, and a role in a Best Picture winner himself, albeit as a Hobbit. His youngest daughter was twenty years away from being born when he told his friends, "Down here it's our time," and to not ruin it by riding up Troy's bucket. At a recent thirtieth anniversary screening for *The Breakfast Club,* fifty-five-year-old Judd Nelson took one look at his character John Bender and said, "I'm that kid's dad now."

Being real with ourselves, how do we then *not* look at teen movies of the 1980s as artifacts from long ago? Ralph Macchio is now the same age (fifty-three) as Pat Morita was when he played Mr. Miyagi. Pat Morita is gone. So is John Hughes, River Phoenix, Kim Walker (Heather #1 in *Heathers*), Paul Gleason (Principal Vernon in *The Breakfast Club*), Ray Walston and Vincent Schiavelli (Mr. Hand and Mr. Vargas from *Ridgemont High*), and three of the four grandparents from *Sixteen Candles.* A subdivision now sits on top of where Mr. Miyagi's house used to be. The across-the-county-line empty warehouse where the prom in *Footloose* happened now abuts a giant strip mall.

Is the map of Brat Pack America no different than One-Eyed Willie's treasure map, a dusty attic document we've cleaned up for this adventure, only to watch it sail away back into memory while the Goonies wave goodbye from the beach? Are we fooling ourselves to think these places matter beyond memory triggers from movies we love?

Maybe so (sigh). I wouldn't have invited you on this trip back to the 1980s had I not grown up then and fallen so in love with these movies. We're all disproportionately mad for the era of our adolescence, when every emotion is heightened and we didn't yet understand that the world isn't as boundless as it feels. When that realization comes, many years later, it's human nature to look over your shoulder and idealize what once was. "Then" might never be empirically better than "now," but the image of "then" feels better. Time has scrubbed "then" of tedium, difficulty, and pain.

On its worst days, nostalgia strikes me as fear of change disguised as sensitivity. The word "nostalgia" is of Greek and German origin and means "severe homesickness." Which makes me ask: "If nostalgia by definition is supposed to hurt, why do that to yourself voluntarily?" Instead, on its good days, nostalgia should look more like its relatives—memory and ritual. To remember and relive something isn't being afraid of moving forward but charting the progress of moving forward. So if you watch *The Gremlins* every year on Christmas Eve, it serves the same purpose as another candle on your birthday cake—a waypoint from which you can see how much time has passed and how you've changed. *The Gremlins* and the cake with candles are just mile markers on the long and hopefully rich journey of life.

"We live in a box of space and time. Movies are windows in its walls," began Roger Ebert in his 2003 book *The Great Movies*. "The audience for a brief time is somewhere else, sometime else, concerned with lives that are not its own. Of all the arts, movies are the most powerful aid to empathy."

That relationship works in reverse, too. In our favorite movies, we also see ourselves, our own strengths and shortcomings, our dreams and failures, reminders of who we are and who we could be. The longing to be in the exact spot where a favorite movie happened comes from that place, the deep pool of emotion that envelops a pilgrimage, a homecoming or a renewal of vows, to be in communion with a moment that changed your life, whether or not you were present when that moment first happened.

But visiting Gettysburg or Sun Studios or the site of your first kiss collapses time. You in the present stand in the exact spot where something miraculous happened in the past. Visiting the location of a favorite movie collapses both time and reality. You are not standing where a cast of actors and crew of technicians went to work one day, but within a moment of a story. For a moment in the present, you are both witness to that story's history and part of its narrative. For a moment, at least in your heart, that story is real.

The eighties was not a subtle decade, and even its best teen movies—filled with wood-paneled station wagons, rotary dial phones, casual sexism, and crimes of side ponytails and hairspray—cannot hide from when they came. Plenty from the 1980s—rotary dial phones, side ponytails, casual sexism—are best left behind. One can miss them but probably shouldn't. Our culture has learned how to do better and moved on.

Places are different. For a house or office building or public park, newer doesn't always mean better. Function isn't dictated by fashion. Calling Amazon an improvement on the bookstore or Spotify a twenty-first-century record store may depend on your goal, efficiency versus experience, catalog versus curation. But just because the efficiency and deep catalogs of an Amazon or a Spotify seem to win more often than charm or personality here in 2016, doesn't mean their analog ancestors from an earlier time have gone extinct.

Instead, several kinds of places we associate with the culture and climate of the 1980s, the kinds of places that dot our map of Brat Pack America, have found surprising usefulness here in the twenty-first century. Nostalgia is undoubtedly one of the reasons why. A teenager in the 1980s is now in their mid-to-late forties, with money to spend on souvenirs of their youth. But maybe some of it is function, too. The old argument that a vinyl record sounds better than an .mp3 just makes us misty-eyed for when vinyl was all there was. A third answer, maybe what software engineers and designers call user experience: it's a different thing to play video games at an arcade than on your iPhone. And until you can order beers, pal around with your friends, and flirt with a stranger all at once on an iPhone...

In the simplest terms and most convenient definitions...

LET'S START WITH THE obvious big winners. Some films are so popular and influential that they never went away. A small all-star team of eighties teen movies were giant hits in their day, never lost their popularity, and beat a quick path from box-office smash to classic without breaking stride—*Back to the Future*, *The Breakfast Club*, *Ferris Bueller's Day Off*, *The Karate Kid*, *Stand by Me*, *Dirty Dancing*, and *The Goonies*. *Ferris Bueller's Day Off* was selected for the Library of Congress's National Film Registry in 2014. Brat Pack America cohorts *Fast Times at Ridgemont High*, *Back to the Future*, and *Stand and Deliver* were already there. The National Film Registry was established by a series of federal laws in 1988 "to ensure the survival, conservation, and increased public availability of America's film heritage... They reflect who we are as a people and as a nation." In the eyes of the Library of Congress, *Back to the Future* is as important to America's cultural heritage as *Citizen Kane* and *The Wizard of Oz*.

These winners soar above the 1980s and whatever memories we have of that time. If you love the movies of Brat Pack America and love to knit, help yourself to pink hand-dyed yarn named after Molly Ringwald. You can get *Breakfast Club* and *Lost Boys* T-shirts at Hot Topic. There's a championship intramural volleyball team at my gym named the Truffle Shuffles. No one on that team was alive when Chunk did the truffle shuffle for the other *Goonies*.

The recent blizzard of contemporary remakes of eighties movies—*Karate Kid*, *Footloose*, and the all-female *Ghostbusters*, to name a few—have something do to with the nostalgic yearnings of executives who were teenagers in the 1980s and now hold positions of power in Hollywood. But none of these remakes would happen if they couldn't bring in big profits outside their own demographic rather than because of it. New versions of *Ghostbusters*, *Mad Max*, and an upcoming *Goonies* sequel speak less to the buying power of the generation that first saw them (that buying power is real, but not gigantic; Generation X is quite a bit smaller than the Baby Boomers and the Millennials) than their status as enduring entertainment brands, no matter to what decade they belong. The spigot of money they turned on in the 1980s has never been turned off.

Places linked to these movies ride on their long coattails. The *Back to the Future* set was part of the Universal Studios tour for decades after the movie came out. The "Goonies House" in Astoria became city's second-most visited tourist location after the movie's twentieth anniversary celebration in 2005. A resort hotel in middle-of-nowhere North Carolina wouldn't get visitors from around the world to its annual Dirty Dancing Festival if *Dirty Dancing* wasn't filmed there, didn't clean up at the box office, and wasn't a favorite movie of an entire generation of women, and now their daughters.

Success for these gigantic eighties teen movies came fast and never diminished, which is why they no longer feel of one decade, but for all time. One can be wistful for the first time you saw *Ferris Bueller's Day Off* or the era it captures on film, but not through some act of "rediscovering" it. *Ferris Bueller's Day Off* can't be rediscovered because it never went anywhere. It's been popular since the day it was born.

Movies of this magnitude remind us that some pop artifacts aren't artifacts at all, but monuments, seemingly built to endure forever. But they don't tell the entire story of eighties culture in the twenty-first century any more than winners are the only ones writing history.

"An Amalgam of Many Earlier Times"

"IN REALITY, WE LIVE in the past. That is, the world that surrounds us is not new," said filmmaker Thom Anderson in his 2003 documentary *Los Angeles Plays Itself*. "The things in it, our houses, the places we work, even our clothes aren't created anew every day. So any particular period is an amalgam of many earlier times."

Anderson said this over a decade ago, but could have just as easily been talking now. Every day we pile pop culture from different eras on top of itself, in our iTunes playlists and Netflix queues, when we reread a book when it gets remade into a movie, when we recommend movies and television and video games to someone younger than us and someone older returns the favor. How easy it is to do this in 2016 depends on boundaries of time and access being so low they may as well not exist. How does one reconfigure clips of Doc Brown and Marty McFly (from 1985) as a *Brokeback Mountain* (from 2005) parody without affordable video editing software, blazingly fast download speeds, and YouTube to host it? (It's called "Brokeback to the Future." 6.6 million views and counting.) To sit on your couch and leap effortlessly from television to song, to videos, to photos and video games and back again, from now, from a year ago, from a hundred years ago, can't happen with the old-fashioned idea that contemporary pop culture gets consumed in the present and everything else is "old" and reserved for a nostalgic rainy day.

This was the standard question I asked customers when I worked at video stores in my twenties. "Would you like a new release or something old?" That question is now as irrelevant as, well, video stores. The ease of access has rendered "now" and "then" distinctions essentially meaningless.

Or at least temporary. How fast does a piece of pop culture go from new to passé, to forgotten, to kitsch, to nostalgia, to rebooted? How then can a movie stay "in the past" if we keep finding new contexts for it in the present?

Social media only increases those contexts by a hundredfold. Organizers of both Goonies Day and *Stand by Me* Day celebrations told me that at least half their attendees were too young to have seen the movie being celebrated in the theater. But all wanted photos of themselves (that could then be shared on social media platforms) in the real places brought to life by those movies they loved, even though the movies came from a time before they were born. "They see the richness in the storytelling of having an experience, rather than buying one expensive item," remarked a 2012 *Forbes* article on consumer patterns of the Millennial generation (those born between 1982 and 2003). Paradoxically taking a picture of yourself in a place brought to life by your favorite movie is an act you have to be physically present for in order to then humble brag about it digitally.

And yet three decades have passed between the time of Brat Pack America and when social media made currency out of "being there," and very little in the built environment stays the same for that long. How kind will time be to pilgrims of these movies in five, ten, or twenty years? The movies will be here, but the places may not. Arcades, record stores, and movie theaters, as common in the eighties teen movies as high schools and house parties, all suffered terribly as it became just as easy in the 1980s to consume video games, music, and movies at home. Homeowners move away, business owners retire, people die. Film, by definition, captures something with light, celluloid, and photo chemicals that will never be the same again.

Arcades like where Jeff Spicoli mooched quarters, record stores like where Duckie serenaded Andie with "Try a Little Tenderness," the malls, video stores, and movie theaters once identified as the zenith of youth culture, died a long time ago. Or so a grumpy person over forty will tell you. You might stumble over one in a college town or a tourist trap and ask yourself, "Is it still here because people over forty are nostalgic for it and can't let it go? Does it have any real reason here in the twenty-first century?"

It would appear it does.

Brat Pack America Today

I. The Alamo

Do a Web search on "best movie theaters in America" and you'll discover that the Alamo Drafthouse based in Austin, Texas, makes every list. Founded by the husband-and-wife team of Tim and Karrie League, the chain now includes twenty-two theaters in eight states. A San Francisco location opened at the end of 2015, a fifteen-minute bus ride from my house. Since I went to graduate school in Austin in the late 1990s and practically failed out my first year because I spent four or five nights a week at the original Alamo, I commemorated my first trip to the Alamo Drafthouse San Francisco by weeping tears of joy.

The original Alamo in downtown Austin set the model for not only the other Drafthouses but part of the future of the entire movie theater industry. At the original Alamo, you bought your ticket, sat in a chair with a lunch counter in front of it, and could order snacks, appetizers, full meals, and booze from a server dressed all in black while watching the movie. And if you're worried this is distracting, trust me, it isn't. The Alamo is not only ruthless about no talking or using a cell phone during the movie (i.e. doing it more than once means getting expelled from the auditorium), but also doesn't allow unaccompanied minors or kids under six (unless it's a designated "Baby Day") or late arrivals. Get there after the lights go down and you're out of luck.

You'll get a version of this nowadays at iPic, Sundance Cinemas, and other national theater chains. The large chains saw that overpriced sodas and popcorn, which had paid their bills for nearly a century, were losing money, and customers had better movie experiences watching on large-screen TVs in their own living room. Now an iPic theater will sell you a leather reclining seat and a server to take your nachos order. But it was a long time coming. The original Alamo had been hiring chefs, designing menus, and serving heaps of spaghetti during the company's annual Spaghetti Western festival while its larger national competitors were still trying to squeeze revenue out of a five-dollar cup of Coke Zero.

"There aren't that many businesses that are based on a Willy Wonka–like obsession with fun," Zack Carlson, the Alamo's colead programmer from 2006–2013, told me over the phone. "The Alamo model from that time was a completely childish obsession with sharing our love for movies. We were all like five-year-olds."

The early Alamo team had all grown up during the 1980s and treasured going to movie theaters, watching them on late-night television, haunting video stores, then having friends over to eat greasy food and keep the VCR humming until dawn. A movie theater that showed both classics and schlocky up-all-night horror and gangster movies, where you could get your hamburgers and pizza delivered to your seat, seemed a perfect blend of all their different kinds of cinematic obsessions. Not coincidentally, it was also exactly the programming model of the original Alamo theaters.

In 2005, they took the concept on the road. Tim League had the idea for what came to be known as the Rolling Roadshow, a summer of great movies shown in the places they happened—*North by Northwest* in the same cornfield where a biplane almost took down Cary Grant, *Bullitt* in the streets of San Francisco, and *Goonies* on the beach where One-Eyed Willie sets sail. And though the Alamo team considered any movie they could get ahold of fair game for a Roadshow screening, the staff had mostly grown up in the 1980s and disproportionately hosted live screenings from that time.

The Roadshow proved tremendous fun, but hardly profitable. ("You can't monetize hundreds of people showing up on a beach," Carlson told me. "How do you to sell them tickets?") Nonetheless, the Alamo continued doing road shows each summer for several years and one-off events as the company grew. Early Roadshow screenings of *The Goonies* in Astoria and *Stand by Me* in Brownsville lead to the creation of annual celebrations of the movies in both communities. The Alamo screened *The Lost Boys* on the Santa Cruz Beach Boardwalk in 2010. *The Lost Boys* now opens the Boardwalk's summer movie series every year.

"There are probably two kinds of movie people, those who would say 'Watch [*2001: A Space Odyssey*] on the moon? Sign me up,' and those who would say, 'It's just a movie, a good movie, but why does it matter where you see it?'" said Carlson. You may be only a footnote to the story of that movie when you see it "on location," he continued, but do hundreds of people show up to watch a thirty-year-old movie like *The Lost Boys* that flopped at the box office because being a footnote feels like a waste of time?

To anyone in the exhibition business, where you see movies matters. The Alamo, way before its bigger, richer competitors, ended up being the prime example of *how* you see a movie mattering, too. It combines the best of era movie palaces in the 1920s and '30s (that theaters were special, unique places) with the localism of the repertory movie houses from the 1960s and '70s (that the theater understands the tastes and interests of its community and programs accordingly; "It's each theater's team's opportunity to excel or screw up," League said in a "Talks at Google" session in 2015. "So it's a reflection of the community's personality and not mine.") with the benefit of movie-watching from early days of home video (fun takeout food at your seat.)

In my last cross-country move, I lost the picture I'd drawn of Sloth at a special *Goonies* screening at the original Alamo back in 1999. It happened on a Saturday morning, where you got in free if you showed up in pajamas. You also got a free bowl of Froot Loops with your ticket, and each seat had crayons and a character from the movie to color in. I think there was even a coloring contest that I didn't enter because I wanted to take my Sloth picture home.

The Alamo San Francisco screened *Star Wars: The Force Awakens* as its first movie. I would have voted for *Bullitt*, with the film print being driven at top speed over the hills of the city. I've still spent many a Saturday there in the few months it's been open, watching movies like we did in the basements and family rooms of the early days of Brat Pack America—at odd hours, with food that gave you indigestion, classic and schlock seen one after the other. It was movie-watching from the past that ended up looking like the future.

II. "Barcades"

In the early 2000s, five college friends from Syracuse University wanted to quit their day jobs and open a bar. They loved American craft beer and arcade games from the 1980s, which they had all grown up playing. One of the friends, Paul Kermizian, had already been an arcade game collector before he and his buddies had the idea for a place to put them.

The location they chose was on a not-great stretch of Union Avenue in Brooklyn near the Brooklyn-Queens Expressway, in the neighborhood where the five all lived. The bar they had envisioned opened in 2004 with the name Barcade.

"We were lucky to open in Williamsburg during the upswing of irony and hipsters," laughed Kermizian when I spoke to him over the phone. "Some of those customers played our games for the retro cool or for their goofiness. Older customers of ours remembered the games well. Some just liked the beer."

Barcade now has six locations in Brooklyn, Jersey City, Manhattan, and New Haven. It had a cameo in *Sex and the City* and a designation from *Esquire* as one of America's best bars in 2008. In 2011, the *Wall Street Journal* cited arcade bars as saving the video arcade from oblivion.

The concept has been repeated in cities all over America—San Francisco; Lexington, Kentucky; Portland, Oregon; Las Vegas; Denver; and Cedar Rapids, Iowa. At the same time, standalone arcades, filled with vintage games from the 1980s where you pay by the hour or for a flat fee, have popped up in cities like Red Bank, New Jersey; San Jose, California; Minneapolis; and in downtown Pasadena. The standalones that don't serve alcohol usually have parents (who grew up going to arcades) and children (who have played video games at home their whole lives) as their core customers. And though there's some debate over who invented the concept, Kermizian and his friends registered "Barcade" as a legal trademark and have sent out nearly one hundred cease-and-desist orders defending it.

Each of Kermizian and friends' Barcades has around forty machines with a mix determined by type of game (maze games like Pac-Man, driving games like Out Run) and era (first-generation video games like Dig-Dug from the 1980s, fighting and combat games like Street Fighter from the 1990s). A Barcade where the clientele skews younger will skew toward Mortal Kombat machines instead of Defender.

Kermizian told me that although Barcade's "sweet spot" is people his age (thirty-nine) who remember playing the games as teenagers, they comprise only about 25 percent of his customers.

"Craft beer brings in an older crowd," Kermizian said. That customer prefers to drop in after work instead of on Friday and Saturday nights. "We also get a ton of twenty-first birthdays. Even people who were too young to play those games the first time around probably have played them on their iPhones." It helps, he said, that vintage video games keep popping up in movies like *Wreck-It Ralph* (2012) and *Pixels* (2015), a summer action movie release where aliens interpret arcade characters like Donkey Kong as a declaration of war.

The arcade, once thought doomed thanks to home video game systems, rising rents, and an inflexible business model (acquiring games is very expensive; if they don't pay out, getting rid of them is, too) has returned. Only in the twenty-first century, it comes paired with Buffalo wings and IPAs on tap. The staple "third place" of Brat Pack America, a hangout in practically every teen movie of that time, has been reimagined as tavern recreation for adults, darts and pool tables but with pixels.

"A lot of people appreciate having another stimulus at a bar besides drinking as much as they can," Scott James, a co-owner of the EightyTwo arcade bar in downtown Los Angeles, told *Bloomberg Business* in 2015. The games provide entertainment beyond getting plowed. The beer lets you feel like an adult and a kid at the same time.

The business challenges are game repair (most vintage games don't have replaceable parts) and vibe. An arcade has historically been a dark, crowded room. The energy and the noise of the games concentrates, resulting in the sensation, ironically, that everyone playing is actually playing games together instead of alone. One arcade bar flopped in Minneapolis because the space was, according to *Bloomberg Businessweek*, "giant and empty and devoid of energy." You might want to play games at a place like that if you grew up going to birthday parties at Dave and Buster's, but would you want to drink with your friends at an establishment described as "giant and empty and devoid of energy"?

"Everything has a shelf life," Kermizian told me, pointing to the biggest business challenge of all. "Right now, the concept translates to younger people, but one day it may not. At which point we would probably lose interest and sell the company."

Until then, insert coin, open taps, and game on.

III. Record Store Day

MOLLY RINGWALD IN *PRETTY in Pink* worked at a record store called Trax. In *Fast Times at Ridgemont High*, Mike Damone tries to teach Mark Ratner how to talk to girls on first dates in front of a mall record store (he uses a cardboard cutout of Blondie's Debbie Harry as a prop). The kids in *Hairspray* visit a black-owned record store because their friend Seaweed, the owner's son, has told them his mom hosts the best dance party in town there. He's right.

The American record store had been around for decades by the 1980s, and belongs less to the era than arcades or shopping malls or video rental outlets. But record stores were in the middle of an upswing in the 1980s, thanks to the switch from vinyl and cassette tapes to compact discs and the rise of MTV and Top 40 radio. ("Radio plays 'em, record stores sell 'em, Billboard ranks 'em, AT 40 counts 'em down," Casey Kasem used to say on his American Top 40 broadcasts.) National chains like Musicland (owner of Sam Goody and Suncoast) benefited from the era's boom in shopping mall construction and expanded rapidly. Tower Records hadn't quite gone national but was on its way.

The movies of Brat Pack America catch the record store in transition, from records and tapes to CDs, from eccentric local business to standardized mall retailer. It's a clubhouse where teenagers hang out and flirt with each other, but it's also a workplace not much different than Burger King or the Gap.

The great record store movies would come in later decades, films about threatened small businesses (*Empire Records*), zones of budding romance (*Before Sunrise, 500 Days of Summer*), and symbols of stunted male emotional development (*High Fidelity*). But in the 1980s, record stores were just becoming common enough to be the backdrop of the kind of average teenage existence captured in the movies of Brat Pack America. Andie Walsh in *Pretty in Pink* might seem hipper than Stacy Hamilton in *Fast Times*, but Trax Records and Perry's Pizza serve the same role in both their lives.

We all know what happened next—mass consolidation, followed by Napster, then iTunes, then streaming services. Tower Records went bankrupt in 2006. The Musicland chain now only exists as FYE retail outlets that do as much business in DVDs and video games as they do in music. Between 2000 and 2010, four thousand independent record stores in the US went out of business. Music retail in America now consists of big box stores like Best Buy and Target, as well as Amazon, iTunes, and, as of 2012, sixteen hundred remaining independent record stores.

A meeting of these independent record stores in 2007 resulted in the idea for Record Store Day. One member asked why his fellow merchants didn't have something like Free Comic Book Day, an annual promotional event celebrating independent comic book shops and comic book culture that had been around since 2001.

The resulting first Record Store Day, where record labels offered special releases only sold at independent shops and bands met their fans at designated shops, happened on April 19, 2008. The event not only coincided with an uptick in sales of vinyl for the first time in a generation but, in retrospect, has also been given credit for accelerating vinyl's comeback.

According to Billboard, Record Store Day 2015 sales were the highest in the event's history, with over a half million units sold, nearly four hundred unique releases (the first RSD had ten), and stores in countries all over the world participating.

Who bought all that vinyl? Overwhelmingly, people under thirty.

"I really think there's a whole generation of people fascinated with a mechanical age that they totally missed out on," Marc Weinstein, cofounder of Amoeba Music in California, told *The*

Guardian in 2015. Amoeba can often have lines of two hours or more on RSD. I've waited in them.

"When things were made with quality and people used to sit around and listen to a record that's curated the way the artist intended—it's a whole different experience," said Weinstein. "A CD never quite afforded you that feeling. It never had the romance of an LP."

"They didn't grow up with a record player or physical content at all," Rob Sheeley, owner of Mill City Sound in Hopkins, Minnesota, told the local CBS affiliate. "As a matter of fact, they didn't grow up with CDs!"

"I feel like a lot of the appreciation of music is lost because of how easily it is shared (digitally) now," Dan Ketterer, a nineteen-year-old college student who queued up in the early morning hours of Record Store Day 2015, told *The Poughkeepsie Journal.* "I think having a physical copy is pretty cool."

He isn't alone. According to the Record Industry Association of America, thirteen million vinyl records were sold in 2014, nine million in the first half of 2015. Half of those record buyers are under twenty-five.

Record Store Day is now big enough to change the fortunes of an entire store's sales year. It won't bring the music industry back to its pre-.mp3 bonanza of the late 1990s. But I don't see that as the point. Record Store Day demonstrates that the pop culture places of long ago can have multiple lives and different meanings across time and generations.

It's too easy to rewatch our favorite movies from Brat Pack America and bemoan the seeming death of bookstores and arcades and record shops. Record Store Day demonstrates that's far from the whole story, and not even the truth. People too young to remember record stores now care about them too much to see them go away.

"Roads? Where We're Going…"

I BEGAN THIS TRIP with you by telling my own story of trying to find Hill Valley, California, the fictional town in *Back to the Future*. My heart broke when I discovered it wasn't real. It then glued itself back together when someone told me I could visit the next best thing, the historic Gamble Mansion in Pasadena that stood in for Doc Brown's house. If Hill Valley wasn't real, I could enter the movie around it by visiting the places in *Back to the Future* that were.

My story of finding Hill Valley, and, by extension, understanding something called Brat Pack America, has a happy ending. Enough of the places from our favorite eighties movies still exist just to not make them seem lost to time forever. If they are gone, they have an afterlife in the efforts of the people who have visited, taken pictures, and cataloged what has happened to the spot where great movie moments happened.

A big reason for this is the moment we are living in and our distance from the 1980s themselves. Through an accident of history, the 1980s were a time in America where suddenly there was both a burst of new places for teenagers to be teenagers and personal technologies never seen before, which teenagers embraced first. That collided with the careers of filmmakers like John Hughes and Amy Heckerling, Penelope Spheeris, Martha Coolidge, and Savage Steve Holland, who all cared about telling the stories of those teenagers, even though most of them were a decade or more past their teens when they did. And it all happened during a political time, a "morning in America" where America started to feel good about itself again. And optimism, no matter how naïve or misguided, is always associated with youth and the promise of the future it represents.

From those specific circumstances, in addition to all the wonderful things we can already say about *The Breakfast Club, Valley Girl, Better Off Dead,* and *Some Kind of Wonderful,* we can add that no set of movies from another time in history has ever seen the landscape of the American teenager in quite the same way, with quite this much affection, understanding, and love for what it meant to be growing up in America at that time. I'm not sure any decade ever will again.

The eighties teen movie is far from perfect, and has all the same flaws of the era it came from. That makes it both a lot of great and not so admirable things. "Forgettable" isn't one of them.

The movies of Brat Pack America will exist long after most of the places we saw in them do, and, I'd like to think, until long after we are gone. I remember the 1980s being the age of "out of print" and "hard to find" and "no longer available" and don't have an ounce of romance about any of those. I am no supporter of piracy but, on balance, the more anyone can see the movies I've written about here without hassle, the better.

Maybe it's wrong to say I've been "looking" for a Brat Pack America these few hundred pages, because it was always there, waiting. Ferris Bueller and Sloane Peterson's romance probably didn't make it past the first year of college, but Ferris, Sloane, and Cameron are probably still best friends to this day. The same goes for Andie and Duckie from *Pretty in Pink*. Maybe the kids from *Suburbia* started a nonprofit program like My Friend's Place, a respected (and real-life) homeless youth service in Hollywood for kids who were like them once. Maybe we owe some significant part of our twenty-first-century technical lives to the brilliance of David Lightman and Jennifer Mack from *WarGames* or the Mitch Taylors and Chris Knights of *Real Genius*. The Silicon Valley giants of today seem to think so.

Of course, this is all my imagination running away with itself. But most movies don't even encourage that. They're instead forgettable noisemakers that amuse us for an afternoon and are forgotten. We've wanted, for thirty years, to know what the real ending of *Pretty in Pink* was, or what happened to the Goonies— enough to beg for a sequel—or whether Shermer, Illinois, exists, because these movies have lived on in the hearts of their fans, in the careers of the artists that made them, in the younger filmmakers they inspired, and in the eyes of children and grandchildren who will continue to see them for the first time. The places these movies made real, themselves made of soil, brick, and steel, remind us of that permanence.

In late October of 2015, my father and I happened to be in New York City at the same time and heard about a special thirtieth-anniversary screening of *Back to the Future* at Radio City Music Hall. The thirtieth anniversary wasn't celebrated the day the movie came out (it hit theaters in July of 1985), but thirty years to the day when Marty went back in time (October 26, 1985). What better time to see *Back to the Future* with your dad?

Coscreenwriter Bob Gale was on hand, along with special guests Christopher Lloyd (Doc Brown) and James Tolkan (Principal Strickland). A live orchestra accompanied the movie under the direction of Alan Silvestri, who composed the film's score. I told my dad to expect audience members in Doc Brown fright wigs and Marty McFly orange vests. We counted eleven before lights went down.

At intermission, my father stands up and remarks, "We are in the future. This movie is now the past." The next day, I email him a few articles that talk about this. "All of *Back to the Future* is now safely in the past," wrote critic Matt Zoller Seitz. In one of those articles, since, he argued October 26, 2015, was the farthest forward in time the series went. "It doesn't seem to matter," my dad emailed me back. "*Back to the Future* now feels like a movie that could have been made when I was growing up. It belongs to forever now, for all time."

Nothing is forever. A decade is only special based on your relationship to it. I've always loved the culture of the 1980s because that time encompassed my safe and happy childhood. For my parents, who had three children, careers in flux, and were younger in the 1980s than I am now, the decade raced by in a blur of survival and obligations. They now remember every movie, book, TV show, art exhibit, and play they attended, in semi-retirement. I understand why.

But here we are in the future, and Marty McFly, Ferris Bueller, Baby Houseman, and Veronica Sawyer come from a time and place long ago. Yet they seem to have held on, seem to still mean the world to generations, especially those too young to have met them as teenagers. We can be nostalgic for the first time we met them, the era and time in America they represent. But it's impossible to mourn something that never died. The greatness of these movies isn't what they were, but what they are and continue to be.

Who knew a place called Brat Pack America might outlive us all?

88 MILES PER HOUR. LIFT OFF...

Thank you to my talented and loyal agent Amy Rennert for her wisdom and for believing.

Thank you to the team at Rare Bird Books: Tyson Cornell, Julia Callahan, Alice Marsh-Elmer, Winona Leon, and their gang of interns who turn crazy ideas into beautiful books. They are the magicians of our culture. Stay gold. All of you.

The Mayors and Townspeople of Brat Pack America—Regina Wilkie, Linda McCormick, Melissa Chipman, Nat Bulkley, Sandy Bitman, Monica Bartyzel, Justin Sondak, Bill and Amanda Fessler, Andrew Huff, Cinnamon Cooper, Scott Smith, and Erin Shea Smith—thank you for your hospitality, guidance, and shelter from the rain.

This book would not be itself without the artists of moviemaking who gave so generously of their time and thoughts. Thank you Amy Heckerling, Savage Steve Holland, Daniel Waters, Billy Higgins, Christopher Reid, Gedde Watanabe, Martha Coolidge, and Jeff Cohen for speaking with me.

James Hughes has been the guiding spirit for so much of what you've read here. Thank you my friend. Lunch on me for the next many years.

Portions of and ideas for this book appeared in Salon, Buzzfeed, Vulture, NPR.org *and* Book Riot. *Erin Keane, Isaac Fitzgerald, John Sellers, Linda Holmes, Rebecca Schinsky, Michele Filgate, Wendy McClure, and Amanda Nelson are the editors, advocates, and brothers and sisters in arms all writers hope for.*

Writers without comrades are movies without popcorn. Without friends like Holly Payne, Clive Thompson, Susan Orlean, Roman Mars, Justine Musk, A. J. Jacobs, Mike Gluck, David Dylan Thomas, Adam Mansbach, Bob Kolker, Jeff Rider, and Baratunde Thurston, I lead a tasteless, sad professional life.

To Jason Diamond and Hadley Freeman: I love our special society of Dead Poets.

My own band of Goonies—Carlos and Lisa Herrera, Manuel Cuesta, Irene Bayon Pinto, Heather Leigh Miles, Kim Hawkins Raker, Kelly Burke Caldwell, Udi Ben Lou Lou, Jimmy Grosse, Vanessa Soares Pagan: it is always your time.

To the good people of Philz Coffee on Castro Street in San Francisco, thank you (again) for the space to dream, warmth, and bottomless iced coffee.

My parents, brothers, sister-in-law, and nephews. Thank you for making me proud of where I come from.

And to my wife Cariwyl Hebert, who listened, believed, stood by, stood strong, and watched a lot of movies she didn't have to. At the end of the day, our little theater is my light in the dark.

. . .TOUCH DOWN.

SELECTED BIBLIOGRAPHY

INTRODUCTION:

ABC News. "GMA's On Location Vacation: Visit the Top Spots Seen in Sleepless in Seattle." ABCNews.com, Sept. 7, 2015. http://abcnews.go.com/Entertainment/gmas -location-vacation-visit-top-spots-sleepless-seattle/story?id=33521683

Blum, David. "Hollywood's Brat Pack." *New York Magazine* (June 10, 1985). http://nymag. com/movies/features/49902/

Hyden, Steven. "REO Speedwagon's *Hi Infidelity.*" *A.V. Club* (Aug. 23, 2011). http://www. avclub.com/article/reo-speedwagons-ihi-infidelityi-60780

Short, Doug. "Trends in the Teenage Workforce." *Advisor Perspectives* (Aug. 10, 2015). http://www.advisorperspectives .com/dshort/updates/Teenage-Workforce

Tropiano, Stephen. *Rebels and Chicks: A History of the Hollywood Teen Movie.* New York: Back Stage Books, 2006.

CHAPTER 1:

A.V. Club Staff. "Eugene: The Cafeteria from Animal House." *A.V. Club* (June 27, 2011). http://www.avclub.com/video/eugene-the -cafeteria-from-ianimal-housei-57334

Biskind, Peter. *Easy Riders, Raging Bulls: How the Sex, Drugs and Rock n' Roll Generation Saved Hollywood.* New York: Simon & Schuster, 1998.

Ebert, Roger. "John Hughes: When You're 16, You're More Serious Than You Ever Will Be Again." RogerEbert.com (April 29, 1984).

Fame. "Director's Commentary." DVD. Directed by Alan Parker (1980). Warner Brothers, 2009.

Flanagan, Caitlin. "The Dark Power of Fraternities." *The Atlantic* (March 2014). http://www.theatlantic.com/magazine /archive/2014/03/the-dark-power-of-fraternities/357580/

Grease. "Director's Commentary." DVD. Directed by Randal Kleiser (1978). Paramount, 2006.

HBO. *A Good Job: Stories of the FDNY*. Documentary. Directed by Liz Garbus. HBO Documentary Films, 2014.

Miller, Mark Crispin. ed. *Seeing Through Movies*. New York: Pantheon, 1990.

Miller, Scott. *Sex, Drugs, Rock & Roll, and Musicals*. Boston, MA: Northeastern University Press, 2011.

National Geographic. "Lift Off." *The '80s: The Decade That Made Us*. Television. National Geographic Channel: April 14, 2013.

Rabin, Nathan. "Los Angeles: Griffith Observatory, Home of *Rebel Without a Cause* and *Terminator*." *A.V. Club* (June 25, 2012). http://www.avclub.com/video/los-angeles-griffith-observatory -home-of-irebel-wi-81692

Scott, A. O. "The John Hughes Touch." *New York Times* (Aug. 7, 2009). http://www.nytimes.com/2009/08/08/movies/08appraisal .html

Simmons, Matty. *Fat, Drunk and Stupid: The Inside Story of the Making of Animal House*. New York: St. Martin's Press, 2012.

Springsteen, Bruce. "Jackson Browne: Rock 'n Roll Hall of Fame Induction Speech." Rock and Roll Hall of Fame, Cleveland, Ohio (Oct. 22, 2010). https://www.youtube.com/watch?v =8YFyC6pnz-k

The Warriors, Ultimate Director's Cut. DVD. Directed by Walter Hill (1979). Paramount, 2005.

CHAPTER 2:

Diamond, Jason. "I Grew Up in a John Hughes Movie." *BuzzFeed* (Aug. 24, 2014). http://www.buzzfeed.com/imjasondiamond/i -grew-up-in-a-john-hughes-movie#.jomKZpR4k

NPR. "Director John Hughes was 'Philosopher of Puberty." Web. Narrated by Neda Ulaby. NPR Morning Edition (Aug. 7, 2009).

Dogma. Directed by Kevin Smith. Lion's Gate, 2009. Accessed via YouTube. https://www.youtube.com/watch?v=89Ou-iK2_kQ

Ebert, Roger. "John Hughes: When You're 16, You're More Serious Than You Ever Will Be Again." RogerEbert.com (April 29, 1984).

Ebert, Roger. *Life Itself: A Memoir*. New York: Grand Central Publishing, 2012.

Ferlinghetti, Lawrence. *A Coney Island of the Mind*. New York: New Directions Publishing, 1968.

Ferris Bueller's Day Off, Bueller...Bueller...Edition. DVD. Directed by John Hughes (1986). Paramount, 2011.

Gora, Susannah. *You Couldn't Ignore Me If You Tried: The Brat Pack, John Hughes and Their Impact on a Generation*. New York: Three Rivers Press, 2010.

Honeycutt, Kirk. *John Hughes: A Life in Film*. New York: Race Point Publishing, 2015.

Hughes, James. "Home Alone: John Hughes's son on Chicago Without Ebert." *Slate* (April 8, 2013). http://www.slate.com /articles/arts/culturebox/2013/04/roger_ebert_john_hughes_son_remembers_another_chicago_legend.html

Kamp, David. "Sweet Bard of Youth." *Vanity Fair* (Feb. 10, 2010). http://www.vanityfair. com/news/2010/03/john-hughes-201003

McLellan, Dennis. "John Hughes dies at 59; Writer/Director of '80s Teen Films." *Los Angeles Times* (Aug. 7, 2009).

"Movies Filmed in Chicago by Year." Chicago Film Office. Accessed March 14, 2016. http://www.cityofchicago.org/city/en/depts/dca /supp_info/chicago_film_office6.html

O'Rourke, P. J. "Don't You Forget About Me: The John Hughes I Knew." *The Daily Beast* (March 22, 2015). http://www. thedailybeast.com/articles/2015/03/22/how-john-hughes-made -conservatism-funny.html

Rankin, William. "Cartography and the Reality of Boundaries." *Perspecta* 42 (Spring 2010): 42–45.

Ringwald, Molly. "John Hughes Oscar Tribute." Dolby Theater, Hollywood, CA. Posted March 10, 2010. https://www.youtube .com /watch?v=DvmVYNr0lk0

Schmidlin, Charlie. "Listen: John Hughes' Out of Print Commentary for 'Ferris Bueller's Day Off.'" *Indiewire* (Nov. 27, 2012). http://blogs.indiewire.com/theplaylist/listen-john-hughes-out-of-print-commentary-for-ferris-buellers-day-off-20121127

Smith, Kevin. "Introduction to Breakfast Club 25th Anniversary Screening at Lincoln Center." Lincoln Center, New York City, NY (Oct. 7, 2010). https://www.youtube. com/watch?v=q _RGvxLgcvo

M. Smith, Sean. "Teen Days That Shook the World: An Oral History of *The Breakfast Club*." *Premiere* (Dec. 1999).

Stein, Ben. "John Hughes, RIP." *The American Spectator* (Aug. 7, 2009). http://spectator. org/articles/41113/john-hughes-rip

CHAPTER 3:

Balko, Radley. *Rise of the Warrior Cop: The Militarization of America's Police Forces*. New York: Public Affairs, 2013.

Chaney, Jen. *As If! The Oral History of* Clueless *as Told by Amy Heckerling, the Cast and the Crew*. New York: Touchstone, 2015.

"Christopher Commission Findings: Excessive Force." *LA Times*, (July 10, 1991). Accessed March 9, 2016. http://articles.latimes .com/1991-07-10/news/mn-1973_1_police-commission

Cowan, Jared. "How a Movie Shot in the San Fernando Valley Made Us All *The Karate Kid*." *LA Weekly* (June 17, 2014). http://www.laweekly.com/arts/how-a-movie-shot-in-the-san -fernando-valley-made-us-all-the-karate-kid-4790700

Domanick, Joe. *To Protect and To Serve: The LAPD's Century of War in the City of Dreams*. New York: Pocket Books, 1994.

Ebert, Roger. "Repo Man." RogerEbert.com. Jan. 1, 1984. http://www.rogerebert.com/ reviews/repo-man-1984

Fast Times at Ridgemont High. "Director's Commentary." DVD. Directed by Amy Heckerling (1982). Universal Studios, 2004.

Gates, Daryl. *Chief: My Life in the LAPD*. New York: Bantam, 1992.

Hsu, Hua. "The Branding of the Olympics." *Grantland* (Feb. 1, 2014). http://grantland. com/features/1984-olympics-los-angeles -branding/

The Karate Kid. "Director's Commentary." DVD. Directed by John G. Avildsen (1984). Sony Pictures Home Entertainment, 2005.

Leibowitz, Ed. "How L.A. Stuck the 1984 Olympics." *Los Angeles Magazine* (July 16, 2014). http://www.lamag.com/the80s/how-la-stuck-the-1984-olympics/

Marshall, Colin. "The City in Cinema: Repo Man." Online video clip. https://vimeo.com/ channels/thecityincinema/105946303

Martino, Alison. "Finding the Beat with the GoGos." *Los Angeles Magazine* (June 19, 2014). http://www.lamag.com/the80s /finding-the-beat-with-the-go-gos/

Morrow, Lance. "Feeling Proud Again: Olympic Organizer Peter Ueberroth." *TIME* (Jan. 7, 1985).

Rabin, Nathan. "Penelope Spheeris." *A.V. Club* (March 10, 1999). http://www.avclub.com/ article/penelope-spheeris-13584

Rabin, Nathan. "Alex Cox." *A.V. Club* (Sept. 20, 2000). http://www.avclub .com/article/ alex-cox-13678

Reilly, Phoebe. "Underground with Punk Icon Penelope Spheeris." *Los Angeles Magazine* (July 16, 2014). http://www.lamag.com /the80s/underground-with-punk-icon-penelope-spheeris/

Roderick, Kevin. *The San Fernando Valley: America's Suburb.* Los Angeles: Los Angeles Times Books, 2001.

Smith, Kevin. "Kevin Smith's SMoviola Presents 'Valley Girl.'" Film Society at Lincoln Center, New York, NY. June 11, 2011. https://www.youtube.com/ watch?v=FgrwnTGE2vg

Spitz, Marc and Brendan Mullen. *We Got the Neutron Bomb: The Untold Story of L.A. Punk.* New York: Three Rivers Press, 2001.

Starr, Kevin. *Coast of Dreams: California on the Edge 1990–2003.* New York: Vintage, 2006.

Suburbia. "Director's Commentary." DVD. Directed by Penelope Spheeris (1984). Shout Factory, 2010.

The Sure Thing. "Director's Commentary." DVD. Directed by Rob Reiner (1985). MGM, 2006.

Valley Girl. "Director's Commentary." DVD. Directed by Martha Coolidge (1983). MGM, 2006.

Walker, Alissa. "How L.A.'s 1984 Summer Olympics Became the Most Successful Games Ever." *Gizmodo* (Feb. 6, 2014). http://gizmodo.com/how-l-a-s-1984-summer-olympics-became -the-most-success-1516228102

Weinreb, Michael. "The American Ideal." ESPN.com (July 8, 2009). http://espn.go.com/ espn/page2/story?page=weinreb/090708

Zappa, Moon Unit. "Valley Girl." Music video. Accessed March 12, 2016. https://www. youtube.com/watch?v=Qb21lsCQ3EM

Zirin, Dave. "Want to Understand the 1992 LA Riots? Start with the 1984 LA Olympics." *The Nation* (April 30, 2012). http://www.thenation.com/article/want-understand-1992-la-riots -start-1984-la-olympics/

CHAPTER 4:

Adler, Bill. "The South Bronx Was Getting a Bad Rap Until a Club Called Disco Fever Came Along." *People* (May 16, 1983). http://www.people.com/people/archive/article/0,,20084997,00 .html

Barone, Matt. "Commentary: You're Remembering House Party all Wrong." BET.com (March 9, 2015). http://www.bet.com /news/celebrities/2015/03/09/commentary-you-re-remembering-house-party-all-wrong.html

Chamberlin, Chris. "The Birthplace of Country Music Museum—Not in Nashville." *Nashville Scene* (Aug. 6, 2014). http://www .nashvillescene.com/countrylife/archives/2014/08/06/the-birthplace-of-country-music-museum-not-in-nashville

Chang, Jeff. *Can't Stop Won't Stop: A History of the Hip-Hop Generation*. New York: St. Martin's Press, 2005.

Charnas, Dan. *The Big Payback: The History of the Business of Hip-Hop*. New York: New American Library, 2010.

Electric Boogaloo: The Wild Untold Story of Cannon Films. Directed by Mark Hartley. Warner Brothers, 2015.

Fear of a Black Hat. DVD. Directed by Rusty Cundieff. Sony Pictures Home Entertainment, 1994.

"First Person: Kool Lady Blue." *BBC World News America* (Nov. 17, 2008). Online video. http://news.bbc.co.uk/2/hi/programmes /world_news_america/7734647.stm

Gale, Alex. "The Oral History of *Wild Style*." *Complex* (Oct. 11, 2013). http://www.complex.com/pop-culture/2013/10/oral-history-wild -style

Hart, Ron. "*Beat Street*: The Making of a Hip-Hop Classic." *Wondering Sound* (Aug. 15, 2014). http://www.wonderingsound .com/feature/beat-street-movie-oral-history/

The Museum of Broadcast Communications History of Television (Cable penetration statistic). http://www.museum.tv/eotv /unitedstatesc.htm

Wang, Oliver. Interview with Jesse Thorn, *Bullseye* (July 28, 2015). Podcast audio. http://www.maximumfun.org/tags/legions-boom

Wang, Oliver Ed. *Classic Material: The Hip-Hop Album Guide*. Toronto: ECW Press, 2003.

CHAPTER 5:

Aradillas, Aaron and Matt Zoller Seitz. "The Evolution of the Modern Blockbuster: Part 1." *The L Magazine* (Aug. 24, 2009). http://www.thelmagazine.com/2009/08/the-evolution-of-the -modern-blockbuster/

Back to the Future. "The Making of Back to the Future." Supplemental material. DVD. Directed by Robert Zemeckis (1985). Universal Studios, 2011.

Borger, Julian. "The Best Perk in the White House." *The Guardian UK* (June 3, 2004). http://www.theguardian.com/film/2004/jun/04/1

Coontz, Stephanie. *The Way We Never Were: American Families and the Nostalgia Trap*. New York: Basic Books, 1993. Reprint.

Cormier, Ryan. "25 *Dead Poets Society* in Delaware Facts." *The News Journal* (April 4, 2014). Accessed March 18, 2016. http://www.delawareonline.com/story/pulpculture/2014/04/03 /dead-poets-society-delaware-anniversary/7252149/

Ebert, Roger. "Dead Poets Society." RogerEbert.com. June 9, 1989. http://www.rogerebert.com/reviews/dead-poets-society-1989

"Films President and Mrs. Reagan Viewed." Ronald Reagan Presidential Library and Museum. Accessed March 18, 2016. https://reaganlibrary.archives.gov/archives/reference /filmsviewed.html

Gaines, Caseen. *We Don't Need Roads: The Making of the Back to the Future Trilogy*. New York: Plume, 2015.

Hinton, S. E. "Inside *The Outsiders*," *Interview on 'Think'*. KERA 90.1 FM, Dallas (April 24, 2014). Radio. http://www.kera .org/2014/04/24/turning-greaser/

Jones, Abigail, "Rediscovering Beauty Amid Ruins of Once-Glorious Catskills." *Jewish Daily Forward* (Sept. 22, 2013). http://forward .com/culture/183901/rediscovering-beauty-amid-ruins-of-once-glorious-c/

Kinstler, Linda and Kevin Mahnken. "The Best State of the Union Addresses, Ever." *The New Republic* (Jan. 26, 2014). https://newrepublic.com/article/116314/best-state-union -addresses-history

Kolomitz, N. "Hairspray." *The Film Journal* (Feb/March 1988).

Lazendorfer, Joy. "15 facts About *Dead Poets Society*." *Mental Floss* (Feb, 3, 2016). http://mentalfloss.com/article/59232/15-facts -about-dead-poets-society.

Menand, Louis. "Out of Bethlehem: The Radicalization of Joan Didion." *The New Yorker* (Aug. 24, 2015).

"Morning in America." Ronald Reagan 1984 Presidential Campaign Commercial. Online video clip. Uploaded April 4, 2011. Accessed March 18, 2016. https://www.youtube.com /watch?v=NUKAkm8A9nM

Newport, Frank, Jeffrey M. Jones, and Lydia Saad. "Ronald Reagan from the People's Perspective: A Gallup Poll Review." Gallup.com (June 7, 2004). http://www.gallup.com/poll /11887/ronald-reagan-from-peoples-perspective-gallup-poll-review.aspx

The Outsiders: The Complete Novel. "Director's Commentary." DVD. Directed by Francis Ford Coppola (1983). Warner Home Entertainment, 2005.

Reagan, Ronald. "Address Before a Joint Session of Congress on the State of the Union." Washington, DC (Feb. 4, 1986). http://www .presidency.ucsb.edu/ws/?pid=36646

Ritchie Valens Offical Site FAQs. Accessed March 18, 2006. http://www.ritchievalens.com/faqs.html

Roderick, Kevin. "Ritchie Valens, Garage Band Success, was 17." *LA Observed* (Feb 3, 2011). http://www.laobserved.com /archive/2011/02/ritchie_valens_singer_was.php

Snyder, Pete. "Forget the Super Bowl: Which Political Ad Was the All-Time MVP?" *Advertising Age* (Feb. 7, 2012). http://adage.com /article/campaign-trail/political-ad-ailes-trippi-murphy-snyder-pick/232576/

Studio 360: American Icons: The Outsiders. May 4, 2012. Podcast audio. http://www.wnyc.org/story/205279-american-icons -outsiders/

Troy, Gil. *Morning in America: How Ronald Reagan Invented the 1980s*. Princeton, NJ: Princeton University Press, 2005.

CHAPTER 6:

Bissinger, H. G. *Friday Night Lights: A Town, a Team and a Dream*. Boston, MA: Da Capo Press, 2000.

Bogosian, Eric. *Sex, Drugs, Rock & Roll*. New York: Harper Collins, 1990.

"Pony Excess." 30 for 30. ESPN. November 9, 2010.

Ebert, Roger. "Chariots of Fire." RogerEbert.com. Jan. 1, 1981. http://www.rogerebert. com/reviews/chariots-of-fire-1981

Ebert, Roger. "Vision Quest." RogerEbert.com. Feb. 15, 1985. http://www .rogerebert.com/ reviews/vision-quest-1985

Goldman, William. *Adventures in the Screen Trade: A Personal View of Hollywood and Screenwriting*. New York: Warner Books, 1983.

Hutchinson, Sean. "15 Things You Might Not Know About Caddyshack." Mental Floss. com. http://mentalfloss.com/article /56693/15-things-you-might-not-know-about-caddyshack

Meyers, Kate. "Cult Classic an Homage to Doug Kenney." ESPN.com (April 16, 2004). http://espn.go.com/golf/news/story ?id=1784074

Ronald Reagan's Farewell Address. The White House, Washington, DC. January 11, 1989. http://www.presidency.ucsb.edu/ws /?pid=29650

Weinreb, Michael. *Bigger Than the Game: How Bo, Boz, the Punky QB, and How the '80s Created the Modern Athlete*. New York: Gotham Books, 2011.

CHAPTER 7:

Berger, Knute. "Seattle's Notorious Donut Shop: Runaway Haven or Sweet-Tinged Trap?" Crosscut.com (March 19, 2014). http://crosscut.com/2014/03/seattle-donut-shop-runaways-part -one-knute-berger/

Dear White People. DVD. Directed by Justin Simien. Lionsgate, 2014.

Hall, Brian S. "Silicon Valley owes a debt of Gratitude to the Movie *Real Genius*. We All Do." Tech.pinions (Feb. 17, 2014). https://techpinions.com/brian_s_hall_real_ genius/27445

Isaacson, Walter. *Steve Jobs: A Biography*. New York: Simon & Schuster, 2011.

Mark, Mary Ellen. *Streetwise*. Redding, PA: Aperature Press, 1992. Reprint.

"The Marketing Genius of Steve Jobs—Part One." *Under the Influence* (Feb. 18, 2012). CBC. Narrated by Terry O'Reilly. Podcast audio. http://www.cbc.ca/radio/ undertheinfluence/the -marketing-genius-of-steve-jobs-part-one-1.2801867

McCall, Cheryl. "Streets of the Lost." *Life Magazine* (July 1983). Accessed February 23, 2016. http://www.maryellenmark.com /text/magazines/life/905W-000-021.html

Ong, Josh. "Call History: Witness the First Commercial Cell Phone Call Made in 1983." *The Next Web* (April 17, 2012). http://thenextweb.com/shareables/2013/04/17/call-history -witness-the-first-commercial-cellular-phone-call-being-made -in-1983/#gref

Perin-Asher, Emily. "30 Years Later, *Real Genius* is Still the Geek Solidarity Film That Nerd Culture Deserves." Tor.com (May 21, 2015). http://www.tor.com/2015/05/21/30-years-later-real -genius-is-still-the-geek-solidarity-film-that-nerd-culture -deserves/

Postrel, Virginia. "Resilience v. Anticipation," *Forbes ASAP* (Aug. 24, 1997). Accessed March 1, 2016. https://vpostrel.com/articles /resilience-vs-anticipation

Reardon, Marguerite. "Cell Phone Industry Celebrates its 25th Birthday." CNET (Oct. 13, 2008). http://www.cnet.com/news/cell-phone-industry-celebrates-its-25th-birthday/

Samuels, Alana. "25 Years Later, Cell Phones Less About the Calls." *Chicago Tribune* (Nov. 3, 2008). http://articles .chicagotribune.com/2008-11-03/news/0811020099_1_cell -roger-entner-verizon-wireless

Streetwise. Directed by Martin Bell. Angelika Films, 1984. Online video. https://www.youtube.com/watch?v=jtwv9h5CSKE

Thomas, Sarah. "*Social Network* Taps Other Campuses for Harvard Role." *Boston Globe* (Sept. 24, 2010). http://www.boston.com /yourtown/news/cambridge/2010/09/harvard_at_the_movies _schools.html

Turner, Patricia A. *Ceramic Uncles and Celluloid Mammies*. New York: Anchor Books, 1994.

WarGames. "Director's Commentary" and "Loading *WarGames*" supplemental content. DVD. Directed by John Badham (1983). MGM, 2008.

Winslow, Timothy. "I Hacked into a Nuclear Facility in the '80s. You're Welcome." CNN.com (March 11, 2015). http://www.cnn.com /2015/03/11/tech/computer-hacker-essay-414s/

YouthCare. "Our Approach." Accessed March 16, 2016. http://www .youthcare.org/our-approach.

CHAPTER 8:

Bowie, John Ross. *Heathers*. Berkeley, CA: Soft Skull Press, 2011.

Canby, Vincent. "Scott as General in *Taps*." *New York Times* (Dec. 9, 1981). http://www.nytimes.com/movie/review?res =9800E4DC103BF93AA35751C1A967948260

Canby, Vincent. "Film: Kaplan's *Over the Edge* Ennui to Rebellion." *New York Times* (Dec. 15, 1981). http://www.nytimes.com/1981/12/15 /movies/film-kaplan-s-over-the-edge-ennui-to-rebellion.html

Cobain, Kurt. *Journals*. New York: Riverhead Books, 2002.

Ebert, Roger. "Over the Edge." RogerEbert.com. Aug 26, 1979. http://www.rogerebert.com/reviews/over-the-edge-1980

Heathers 20th High School Reunion Edition. "Director's Commentary." DVD. Directed by Michael Lehman (1989). Anchor Bay Entertainment, 2008.

History of the International Association of Amusement Parks and Attractions (IAAPA). Accessed March 12, 2016. http://www .iaapa.org/about-iaapa/history-facts/iaapa-history

Faraci, Devin. "The Pyschos Who Turned Surf City into Murder City." *Birth.Movies.Death* (July 28, 2013). http://birthmoviesdeath.com/2013/07/28/the-psychos-who-turned-surf-city-into-murder-city

King, Ritchie. "217 Years of Homicide in New York City." *QZ.com* (Dec. 31, 2013). http://qz.com/162289/217-years-of-homicide -in-new-york/

Koon, Bruce. "Mousepacks: Kids on a Crime Spree." *San Francisco Examiner* (Nov. 11, 1973).

The Legend of Billie Jean. "Commentary." Performed by Helen Slater and Yeardley Smith (1985). Sony Pictures Entertainment, 2011.

The Lost Boys. "Director's Commentary." DVD. Directed Joel Schumacher (1987). Warner Brothers, 2008.

Markovitz, Adam. "*Heathers*: An Oral History." *Entertainment Weekly* (April 4, 2014). http://www.ew.com/article/2014/04/04/heathers -oral-history

Marshall, Penny. Interview with Kevin Smith, *SMovieMakers* (Aug. 14, 2014). Podcast audio. https://itunes.apple.com/us /podcast/smoviemakers-7-penny-marshall/id409706073?i =126455365&mt=2

Over the Edge. "Director's Commentary." DVD. Directed by Tim Hunter (1979). Warner Home Entertainment, 2011.

"Over the Edge." *Time Out.* Accessed March 16, 2016. http://www .timeout.com/london/film/over-the-edge

Sacks, Mike. "*Over the Edge.* An Oral History." *Vice* (Sept 1, 2009). https://www.vice.com/read/over-the-edge-134-v16n9

"Teen-ager Brags of Killing Girlfriend." *The Spokesman-Review* (Nov. 25, 1981). Access March 14, 2016.

Yamanaka, Sharon. "Serial Murders in Santa Cruz County." Accessed March 1, 2016. http://www.santacruzpl.org/history /articles/116/

CHAPTER 9:

Bengel, Erik. "The 'Goonies House' Goes Off Limits." *The Daily Astorian* (Aug. 18, 2015). http://www.dailyastorian.com/Local _News/20150818/the-goonies-house-goes-off-limits

Bloomington Economic Development Corporation Local Data. Accessed March 10, 2016. http://comparebloomington.us/local -data/

Demaret, Ken. "You Got Trouble in Elmore City: That's Spelled with a 't,' Which Rhymes with 'd,' and That Stands for Dancing."

People (May 19, 1980). http://www.people.com/people /archive/article/0,,20076503,00.html

Finke, Nikki. "Hollywood Worries About Weak Box Office: *Real Steel* #1 After *Footloose* Stumbles; *The Thing* #3; *The Big Year* Comics Bomb."*Deadline Hollywood* (Oct 15, 2011). http:// deadline.com/2011/10/hollywood-worries-about-weak-box-office-footloose-reboot-1-real-steel-2-the-thing-3-big-comedy-stars-bomb-in-the-big-year-183334/

Hyde, Jesse. "Flour Mill Grows Up After *Footloose*." *Deseret Morning News* (Sept. 23, 2004). http://www.deseretnews.com/article /595092957/Flour-mill-grows-up-after-Footloose.html?pg=all

John Center for Entrepreneurship & Innovation Rankings. Accessed March 10, 2016. http://kelley.iu.edu/JCEI/AboutUs/Rankings /page1131.html

Majchrowicz, Michael. "Beyond the Posters: How Demographics Factored in Spierer, Grubb Cases." *Indiana Daily Student* (Nov. 10, 2011). http://www.idsnews.com/ news/story.aspx?id=84052

McDonnell, Brandy and Sheila Stogsdill. "Elmore City Recreates Prom that Inspired *Footloose* Film." *The Oklahoman* (April 16, 2010). http://newsok.com/article/3454315

Owen, Rob. "In Astoria, Oregon, Visit the 'Goonies' House and More." Pittsburgh Post-Gazette (April 26, 2015). http://www.post -gazette.com/life/travel/2015/04/26/In-Astoria-Oregon-visit-the -Goonies-house-and-more/stories/201504260039

Robinson, Kenton. "After 20 years, Mystic Pizza Still Draws Visitors to Connecticut." USA Today (Nov 5, 2008). http://usatoday30 .usatoday.com/travel/destinations/2008-11-05-mystic-pizza_N.htm

Scott, Christopher. "Mayor of Astoria Declares June 7th 'Goonies Day.'" *Examiner.com* June 5, 2010. http://www.examiner.com /article/mayor-of-astoria-declares-june-7th-goonies-day

Seely, Mike. "Remembering the Cutters and Tasting the Rainbow at the Little 500 Cycle Race." *Grantland* (April 29, 2014). http://grantland.com/the-triangle/little-500-cycling-race -bloomington-breaking-away/

Smith, McKinley. "Good, Bad, Goonies." *The Daily Astorian* (July 21, 2015). http://www.dailyastorian.com/Local_News/20150721 /good-bad-goonies

"Stand by Me Day: Lost & Found." YouTube. Uploaded Feb. 25, 2015. Accessed March 10, 2016. https://www.youtube.com /watch?v=n6lv9u6UWZM&feature=youtu.be

Vejnoska, Jill. "Tennessee Didn't Get to Dance in *Footloose* Remake." *The Atlanta Journal-Constitution* (Oct. 10, 2011). http://www.deseretnews.com/article/700186758/ Tennessee -didnt-get-to-dance-in-Footloose-remake.html?pg=all

Weizel, Richard. "Owners of Connecticut's 'Mystic Pizza' fined over unpaid wages." *Reuters* (Sept. 26, 2014). http://www.reuters .com/article/us-usa-connecticut-mystic-pizza-idUSKCN0HL1UH20140926

Wood, Robert W. "Mystic Pizza Owner Gets Jail For Tax and IRS Cash Report Crimes." Forbes.com (Aug. 25, 2015). http://www .forbes.com/sites/robertwood/2015/08/25/ mystic-pizza-owner -gets-jail-for-tax-and-irs-cash-report-crimes/#72ee6d577ff7

CHAPTER 10:

Christman, Ed. "Record Store Day Sets Twelve-Year Sales High for Indies, 'Certainly One for the Books.'" *Billboard* (April 23, 2015). http://www.billboard.com/articles/ news/6539051/record-store -day-sets-records-twelve-year-sales-high-indies

Esquire's Best Bars in America 2008. Accessed Feb. 14, 2016. http://www.esquire.com/ food-drink/bars/a4474/best-bars-list -0608/

Faw, Larissa. "Meet The Millennial 1%: Young, Rich, and Redefining Luxury." *Forbes* (Oct. 2, 2012). http://www.forbes.com/sites /larissafaw/2012/10/02/meet-the-millennial-1-young-rich-and -redefining-luxury/#14daed158caa

Ferro, John. "Record Store Day Brings Rekindled Love of Vinyl." *The Poughkeepsie Journal* (April 18, 2015). http://www .poughkeepsiejournal.com/story/news/local/2015/04/18/record -store-day-millennials-vinyl/25988383/

Hayes, Brit. "Alamo Drafthouse New Movie Policy: Arrive Late and You Won't Get In." *Screen Crush* (Nov. 6, 2012). http:// screencrush.com/alamo-drafthouse-arrive-late/

Jane, Laura. "For Amusement Only: The Life and Death of the American Arcade." *The Verge* (Jan. 16, 2013). http://www .theverge.com/2013/1/16/3740422/the-life-and-death-of-the -american-arcade-for-amusement-only

League, Tim. "Alamo Drafthouse: Them's the Rules." CNN.com (June 10, 2011). http://www.cnn.com/2011/SHOWBIZ/Movies/06/10 /alamo.drafthouse.league/

League, Tim. Talks at Google. Google Campus, Mountain View, CA. Aug. 19, 2015. https://www.youtube.com/watch?v=thexz7pvIyU

Linares, Edgar. "Get Ready To Celebrate 'National Record Store Day.'" WCCO CBS Minnesota (April 17, 2015). http:// minnesota.cbslocal.com/2015/04/17/get-ready-to-celebrate -national-record-store-day/

Meek, Andy. "California's Amoeba Records Turns 25: 'We're Like an Art Museum.'" *The Guardian UK* (April 3, 2015). http://www .theguardian.com/music/2015/apr/03/amoeba-music-record -store-marc-weinstein

Seitz, Matt Zoller. "*Back to the Future* Is Now All Back and No Future." RogerEbert.com. Oct. 21, 2015. http://www.rogerebert .com/mzs/back-to-the-future-is-now-all-back-and-no-future

Stone, Brad. "The Arcade Is Back, Now With Beer." *Bloomberg Businessweek* (April 1, 2015). http://www.bloomberg.com/news /articles/2015-04-01/arcade-bars-vintage-games-craft-beer -gen-xers-ka-ching

Weiss, Jennifer. "Building a Retro Nightlife Empire." *Inc.* (Aug. 2011). http://www.inc.com/articles/201108/building-a-retro-nightlife -empire.html

Weiss, Jennifer "For Arcades, Survival Hinges on Alcohol." *Wall Street Journal* (April 22, 2011). http://blogs.wsj.com/metropolis/2011/04/22 /for-arcades-survival-now-hinges-on-alcohol/

Author photo by Julie Michelle

KEVIN SMOKLER is the author of the essay collection *Practical Classics: 50 Reasons to Reread 50 Books you Haven't Touched Since High School* (Prometheus Books, 2013) which the *Atlantic Wire* called "truly enjoyable" and the editor of *Bookmark Now: Writing in Unreaderly Times*, a *San Francisco Chronicle* Notable Book of 2005. His writing on pop culture has appeared in the *LA Times, Salon, BuzzFeed, Vulture*, the *San Francisco Chronicle* and on NPR. In 2013, he was Book Riot's first ever Writer-in-Residence.

He can be found on twitter at @weegee. He lives in San Francisco with his wife, cat and most of MTV's first year on vinyl.